The Geography of Border Landscapes

A Study Group on the World Political Map was established by the International Geographical Union in August 1984. Its brief was to 'search, on the widest possible front, for a fuller understanding of the political problems of territory, the oceans and human resources'.

In August 1988 the Study Group was replaced by a Commission on the World Political Map. The Commission is chaired by Professor David B. Knight of the Department of Geography, Carleton University, Ottawa, Canada K1S 5B6.

Since its establishment, the Group/Commission has held a series of conferences and has produced several books containing some of the papers presented. To date, the following have been produced by Routledge in connection with the Commission:

Political Geography: Recent Advances and Future Directions
Edited by Peter Taylor and John House

Maritime Boundaries and Ocean Resources
Edited by Gerald Blake

Nationalism, Self-Determination and Political Geography
Edited by R. J. Johnston, David B. Knight and Eleonore Kofman

Developments in Electoral Geography
Edited by R. J. Johnston, F. M. Shelley and P. J. Taylor

The Geography of Border Landscapes

Edited by Dennis Rumley
and Julian V. Minghi

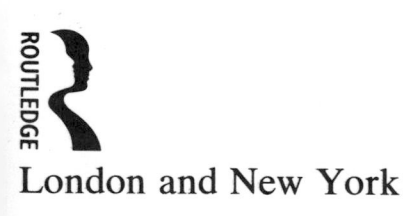
ROUTLEDGE

London and New York

First published 1991
by Routledge
11 New Fetter Lane, London EC4P 4EE

Simultaneously published in the USA and Canada
by Routledge
a division of Routledge, Chapman and Hall, Inc.
29 West 35th Street, New York, NY 1001

Filmset in Linotron Times by
J&L Composition Ltd, Filey, North Yorkshire
Printed and bound in Great Britain by
Biddles Ltd, Guildford and King's Lynn

British Library Cataloguing in Publication Data
The Geography of Border Landscapes.
  1. Political geography
  I. Rumley, Dennis 1947–   II. Minghi, Julian V. 1933–
  320.12

  ISBN 0–415–04825–7

Library of Congress Cataloging in Publication Data
The Geography of Border Landscapes/Edited by Dennis Rumley and
  Julian V. Minghi
    p. cm.
  Includes bibliographical references and index.
  ISBN 0–415–04825–7
  1. Boundaries I. Rumley, Dennis, 1947–   II. Minghi, Julian
  V. (Julian Vincent), 1933–
  JC323.G46   1991
  320.1'2—dc20   90–42325
                                                        CIP

To Alison, Christopher, Hilary, Lee and Monica

Contents

Plates

Figures

Tables

Contributors

Ulrich Ante	Institute of Geography, University of Wurzburg, Germany.
Stanley D. Brunn	Department of Geography, University of Kentucky, Lexington, USA.
Milan Bufon	Slovene Research Institute, Trieste, Italy.
John E. Chappell Jr	San Luis Obispo, California, USA.
James Drummond	Department of Geography, University of Bophuthatswana, South Africa.
Alasdair Drysdale	Department of Geography, University of New Hampshire, Durham, USA.
Werner A. Gallusser	Institute of Geography, University of Basle, Switzerland.
Vladimir Klemencic	Department of Geography, Edvarda Kardelja University, Ljubljana, Yugoslavia.
Walter Leimgruber	Institute of Geography, University of Fribourg, Switzerland.
Andrew H. Manson	Department of History, University of Bophuthatswana, South Africa.
Ronald J. May	Department of Political and Social Change, The Australian National University, Canberra, Australia.
Shinsuke Minamide	Faculty of Letters, Otemon Gakuin University, Ibaraki City, Japan.
Julian V. Minghi	Department of Geography, University of South Carolina, Columbia, USA.

George Ohshima	Department of Intercultural Studies, Tezukayama Gakuin University, Osaka-Sayama-shi, Japan.
Dennis Rumley	Department of Geography, University of Western Australia, Nedlands, Australia.
Mohammed Ismail Siddiqi	Department of Geography, University of Karachi, Pakistan.

Preface

This book arose out of the final meeting of the Study Group on the World Political Map held as part of the 26th International Geographical Union Congress in Perth, Western Australia, in August 1988. The Perth Conference on the theme of 'Border Landscapes' took place prior to the main IGU Congress in Sydney at which the Group obtained Commission status, and the book is therefore the first to be published on behalf of the new Commission.

Needless to say, we are grateful to many people for their assistance and encouragement in bringing this book to fruition. First, we are indebted to all of the contributors who cheerfully corresponded over a fairly lengthy period. Second, we would like to thank all of those who helped to make the Perth Conference a success. Most, but not all of the present authors participated in the Perth meetings. However, not all Perth participants are represented in this volume and we would therefore like to acknowledge the valuable contribution made at the Conference by Sandy Crosbie, Harm De Blij, Jim Forrest, Verena Meier, Hiroshi Tanabe, Martyn Webb and Faye Whitfield. The following individuals and organisations also helped in various other ways to make the Perth Conference a success and deserve our sincere thanks – Chris Berry, Ian Cowie, Patric de Villiers, Viv Forbes, Joseph Gentilli, Harry Grainger, Lindsay Hunter, Charles Johnston, Barrie Melotte, Don Newman, Bob Pearce, MLA, Brian Shaw, Les Smith, Geoff Ward and Oren Yiftachel; Nedlands College of Advanced Education; WA State Planning Commission; Town and Country Building Society; University of WA; Transperth (including one unforgettable bus driver!); Fremantle City Planning Department; WA Football League; Kingswood College; Bond Brewing; Houghton's Wines and Ansett Airlines. Hilary Bailey and Chris Dickinson (Perth) gave cheerful secretarial help under pressure and Guy Foster (Perth) and Jerry Ulrey (Columbia) provided timely

cartographic assistance. The Davis family (UK) and LSE Geography Department helped in the latter stages. Finally, we would like to sincerely thank the members of the IGU Commission on the World Political Map, especially its Chair, David Knight, for continued support and encouragement.

Dennis Rumley and Julian V. Minghi

Foreword

David B. Knight
Department of Geography, Carleton University, Ottawa, Canada

The cultural landscape – the physical environment as moulded and modified by intentional and unintentional human actions – has long been the focus of study by geographers. A rich literature exists which explores many facets of cultural landscapes, in terms of their contemporary patterns as well as the historical processes involved in their development. One old theme which still demands exploration is the impact on landscape of political decision-making and actions which may reflect ideological commitments. This volume is about border landscapes, with emphasis on the varying impact that political decision-making and ideological differences can have on the environment at border locations, for example.

Political boundaries represent the areal limit of the political organisation of territory. For states, they thus form the areal limit of the state, even as there are also usually many intra-state boundaries for the many sub-divisions of territory within the state. Boundaries may be permeable or impermeable, or may be permeable at one point in time and impermeable at another, or may be permeable for some functions and impermeable for other functions. Where political territories and systems meet – or have met in the past – there may be demonstrable effects on the people's patterns of movement and on the landscapes around them. How these boundaries are used and perceived may in turn have additional impacts on the landscape. Boundaries may be long-lasting or they may be open to considerable change, as states have vied for control over contested areas, or as new structures have been imposed or accepted, including, possibly, their functional dismantlement. Boundaries may be the source of friction between competing political entities or they may serve as peaceful reminders of contrasting but accepted differences. Boundaries may reflect the areal extent of ethnic and national identities or they may cut across such identities.

Political boundaries, in short, are locations (sometimes as lines, sometimes as zones) that may separate or may link, but most often accomplish both functions at one and the same time. The International Geographical Union Commission on the World Political Map has as one of its goals the need to better understand political boundaries. This volume of essays by political-geography experts from many countries provides important insights specifically into border landscapes and so serves to further our understanding of aspects of cultural landscapes.

Abbreviations

ABM	Australian Board of Missions
ANC	African National Congress
BNPP	Barisan Nasional Pembasan Pattani
BP	Bechuana Protectorate
BRN	National Revolution Front (Thailand)
BSAC	British South Africa Company
DAIA	Department of Aboriginals' and Islanders' Advancement
DICC	Dauan Island Coordinating Council
DNA	Department of Native Affairs
EC	European Community
5MP	Fifth Malaysian Plan
FMS	Federated Malay States
FS	Italian State Railways
GDR	German Democratic Republic
IASER	Institute of Applied Social and Economic Research
IGU	International Geographical Union
IIB	Island Industrial Board (Queensland)
KGO	Karafuto Government Office
LMS	London Missionary Society
maf	Million acre-feet
MAP	Medical Aid Post
MCA	Malaysian Chinese Association
MIC	Malaysian Indian Congress
NEP	New Economic Policy
NWPP	North West Frontier Province
OAS	Organisation of American States
OAU	Organisation for African Unity
OPM	Free Papua Movement
PAN	National Action Party (Mexico)
PAS	Islamic Party of Malaysia

PRI	Institutional Revolutionary Party (Mexico)
PULO	Pattani United Liberation Organisation
RTV	Refugee Tentage Village
SNCF	French Railways
UFW	United Farm Workers
UMNO	United Malays National Organisation
UNDP	United Nations Development Programme
ZAR	Zuid Afrikaansche Republiek

Introduction: The border landscape concept

Many human geographers have used or do use landscape concepts from time to time in their teaching and research. Needless to say, there is a good deal of debate about the landscape concept (for example, see James and Martin, 1981). Among other things, there is controversy over what might be actually included in a definition of landscape (Mikesell, 1968). These controversies aside, most human geographers would have some notion of what they understand by the term landscape. In the case of the 'border landscape' concept, however, there has been relatively little conceptual debate, and, indeed, many human geographers have only a vague and hazy notion of what the concept might entail. This is clearly a problem, not only for geographers, but especially for other social scientists. What statements there are in the geographical literature, in general, are fraught with conceptual vaguary and inconsistency. Furthermore (and perhaps more importantly) one searches geographical dictionaries in vain for some precise and helpful conceptual statement. This clearly implies that the concept has had little, if any, impact upon the discipline. Little wonder, therefore, that it has essentially been ignored by other social scientists.

The primary purpose of the present volume is to initiate a proper debate over the nature of the border landscape concept and how it might be used. It is therefore to be regarded as a first step towards conceptual clarification and definition and, to that end, represents the views and perspectives of a wide range of geographical and non-geographical traditions. The editors wish to argue that only by 'opening up' the concept in this way can it be effectively liberated from the conceptual closet to which it has been confined, and hence be put to some creative use by helping us to understand better the political organisation of space.

PAST CONCEPTUAL SCOPE

Political boundaries have long been of interest as objects of study to political geographers (for example, Ratzel, 1897: chapters 17–19; Minghi, 1963). Furthermore, this line of research has traditionally tended to be more concerned with the international scale than any other (for example, Prescott, 1987). The reasons for this are not hard to find. In particular, international political boundaries provide the most obvious manifestation of the linkage between geography and politics since they are palpable spatial manifestations of political control displayed in some way in the landscape and also, of course, on maps (although interpretations of precise boundary locations might differ between contiguous states). In addition, as a *de jure* expression of the spatial 'limits' of state power, the location of international political boundaries has been subject to changes in that power with resultant conflict between and within states. The study of the evolution of primarily land-based international political boundaries has thus tended to preoccupy political-geographical inquiry in this area (Prescott, 1965).

The specific definition of border areas as opposed to boundaries as the objects of analysis remains unclear in much of the literature, although the focus on disputed areas in conjunction with national boundaries provides concrete examples of an areal or regional milieu as opposed to a linear one (Minghi, 1963: 414–16). In similar manner, studies that are organised around the phenomenon of a change in boundary location tend to take a before-and-after approach in examining the impact of the change on the area actually undergoing the change of sovereignty as well as on the adjoining areas immediately adjacent to the relict and the new boundary, thereby defining a differentiated borderland (Minghi, 1963: 416–19).

In his influential work of over fifty years ago, Derwent Whittlesey examined the impress of central authority in moulding the landscape and found that borderlands are apt to 'be strewn with features intended by central authority to maintain security' (Whittlesey, 1935: 87). Two years later, Stephen Jones (1937) actually used the term 'borderlands' in the title of an article on a section of the Canada–United States boundary along the forty-ninth parallel. He found the cultural dissimilarities existing in this 'borderland zone' to be in large part not intrinsic to but rather engendered by the presence of the boundary. He suggested the explanation for these dissimilarities fell into three classes as a result of (1) local causes, (2) national contrasts,

or (3) different immigration policies, with the borderland providing a venue for all three.

More recently, John Augelli observed that 'borderlands ... tend historically to be zones of cultural overlap and political instability where the national identity and loyalties of the people often become blurred' (Augelli, 1980: 19). He found this to be particularly so on the island of Hispaniola along the borderland between Haiti and the Dominican Republic for the 150 years between the establishment of the boundary and the rise to power in 1936 of the Dominican dictator, Trujillo. In the late 1930s, Trujillo initiated a 'nationalisation' policy in the Dominican segment of the borderland by which a largely 'Haitian' landscape was to be converted to a Dominican one. Indeed, in a 1960 visit to the borderland, Augelli found this policy to be a success and 'abundantly apparent to the geographer attuned to landscape' (Augelli, 1980: 33).

John House has suggested an operational model for the study of frontiers based on transaction flow analysis and on the core–periphery concept (House, 1981). He went on to apply it to the analysis of the Mexico–United States borderland and specifically to the conceptual definition of the frontier zone or borderland in terms of some measurable or perceived distance–decay effect from the boundary line (House, 1981: 296; House, 1982).

From the viewpoint of geographical research on international border landscapes, Prescott has recently reiterated four main research concerns which have to date preoccupied political geographers (Prescott, 1987). These areas of research are concerned with (1) the political boundary as an element of the cultural landscape; (2) the effect of the boundary upon the landscape and on economic activity; (3) any impact the boundary might have on the attitudes of border inhabitants; and (4) the effect of the boundary upon state policy (Prescott, 1987: 159–74).

There are clearly a number of difficulties with the way in which these four concerns have been addressed in the political geography literature, some of which are alluded to in passing by Prescott, but which may go some way to explain why traditional border landscape research has not attracted any significant attention from other non-geographical scholars. One of the principal limitations of previous research is that it has tended to be overly descriptive and classificatory, preferring to pursue a conceptually narrow approach which was primarily concerned with physical artifacts (for example, boundary markers).

A second difficulty is the descriptive/unique case syndrome evident

in much traditional regional geography. There has been a lack of real concern with the development of border landscape theory, the implicit assumption of uniqueness and even a general disinterest in theoretical and conceptual questions. Coupled with these problems has been a lack of concern with explanation and a consideration of process.

As has been pointed out, one of the assumptions of this approach to landscape is that geographical areas are identifiable by mapping visible cultural elements produced by unitary cultural groups. More recently, however, cultural geographers have become more concerned with the symbolic qualities of landscape emphasising the social (and political) meanings attributed to them. Such an approach leads away from descriptive morphologies and towards interpretations and explanations (Cosgrove and Jackson, 1987: 96).

A further difficulty in previous border landscape research has been the problem of 'separating out' cause and effect. On the one hand, this problem touches on the question of the 'limits' of state law and jurisdiction being expressed differentially across a political boundary in terms of, for example, land use. On the other hand, it raises the issue of whether the boundary actually *caused* that land use difference. The resultant conundrum can involve the effect of a boundary being inferred from a model which assumes that it is not even there! In any event, it would be a mistake to necessarily assume an unchanging effect along the full length of a political boundary.

In addition to overcoming these problems of traditional approaches, there is a need in border landscape studies to move away from a fixation with visible function toward a consideration of border landscapes as the product of a set of cultural, economic and political interactions and processes occurring in space (House, 1982). In addition, there is scope for comparative analysis of intra-state differences in conflict and power which become manifest in the border region in addition to a concern with conflict or cooperation between contiguous states. More emphasis needs to be placed on a comparative approach which sees the border landscape and its problems from the viewpoint of the contiguous states and their inhabitants. Finally, too little concern has been given to conceptual developments in the other social sciences which might have some relevance to an understanding of border landscapes.

One such development is Rokkan's attempt to construct a general model of political development in advanced industrial societies which emphasises comparative analysis, nation-building, the relationships between economic and cultural cleavages and the opposition between

centre and periphery (Torsvik, 1981). Taking the centre–periphery opposition as a starting point, political geographers may well find that Rokkan's framework has considerable potential for the comparative analysis and understanding of intra-state differences in conflict and power which become manifest in the border region.

To date, the centre–periphery model has been used as a framework of analysis in various ways and at different scales. For example, for some the model functions as a symbol of the systematic structuring of space implying an opposition between a dominant centre and a subordinate periphery. Central 'dominance' may well be most marked in traditional societies (Gottmann, 1980). The model has been used to characterise at least two often related types of 'dominance' – social-ethnic and economic-political. From a social-ethnic perspective, control is seen to be exercised by dominant groups over national minorities (Rokkan and Urwin, 1983). If modernisation is unsuccessful, then there is likely to be an increase in ethnic conflict.

An economic-political view of centre–periphery relationships assumes an economically dominant centre to which there is a continuing net flow of resources from a weaker periphery. Thus, at the international scale, the structure of Western capitalism comprises a centre or 'core' of the world economy consisting of the economically and technologically advanced states of North America, Japan and Western Europe (Wallerstein, 1979). At the national scale, the centre generally contains the national capital and thus is also the centre of political power.

Apart from describing spatial aspects of the distribution of economic and political power, the centre–periphery model is suggestive of the likely political behaviour of those located in either centre or periphery which in turn can potentially lend some insight into the causes of political conflict. At the international scale, for example, there appears to be a tendency towards authoritarian regimes especially in post-colonial peripheral states (Rumley, 1985). In such cases, mass political participation is minimised. At the national scale, some regions are more integrated than others into the channels of political communication and thus it is to be expected that those located near the centre will participate more than those closer to the periphery.

In summary, following Rokkan·the concept of peripherality can be broken down into at least four basic dimensions: cultural, economic, political and geographical. The cultural dimension is concerned with conflicts between elite and minority ethnic groups. The economic dimension is concerned with conflicts which arise out of economic exploitation and an uneven distribution of wealth. The political

dimension is concerned with conflicts which arise out of variations in political participation and political power. The geographical dimension is related to distance and perception of strategic territorial advantage as well as with local regional conflicts. The latter may well arise as a result of the geographical coincidence of any one or more of the other dimensions.

Clearly, the potential for border landscape conflict is greatest where the four dimensions coincide. It is likely, especially in the developing world, that inhabitants of border regions tend to enjoy the least political power of any group in the state and they participate less. In addition, within the state they are likely to be regarded as culturally and/or economically peripheral. Per capita incomes, for example, are likely to be lower and state allocations of economic resources per capita are likely to be significantly lower in the periphery, save for grants designed to alleviate or deal with 'special circumstances'. Peripheral inhabitants tend to be more culturally independent and more conservative than those in central locations and are therefore less willing to change and to adapt to a national culture and a national set of norms. Strong national pressure to fully adopt national norms, however, may well force peripheral inhabitants into radical political action.

PRESENT CONCEPTUAL CONCERNS

In Chapter 1, Julian Minghi suggests the need to refocus research on the character of the border landscape. He asserts that most of the literature to date is based on research done on boundaries involved in conflict situations in which war and its aftermath, hostile relations between neighbours, and often shifts in the actual location of political boundaries dominate the human geography of the borderland. He examines closely the evolution of the border region of the Alpes Maritimes between France and Italy since the Second World War and finds that the conclusions of studies completed in the first decade or so of this period are dominated by a 'conflict syndrome'. Research in the last decade, however, presents an entirely different picture of the border landscape, now under the dominance of close and harmonious relations between the two states. Minghi discovers, however, that elements of conflict remain, some national in nature, but most are actual products of the friendly relations between Italy and France which have frequently generated conflict of a new kind, pitting local interests either side of the boundary together against the policies of international cooperation. This realignment of interests, Minghi

finds, is a necessary product of the shift from warlike to peaceful relations between the two neighbours, and he goes on to speculate on the impact that a proposed agreement to cooperate in economic development between Jordan and Israel might have on the borderland of the Rift Valley between the Dead Sea and the Gulf of Aqaba.

Werner Gallusser, in Chapter 2, summarises a significant body of research on political boundaries which has been carried out at the University of Basle over the past fifteen years. The major focus of this programme of research has been on the differential impacts of political boundaries on the cultural landscape both within states and between contiguous states in the 'Regio'. Research on the Aargau–Baselland area indicates that since the boundary changed its status from 'national' to 'internal', there has been a diminution of differentiation in the cultural landscape on either side of the earlier boundary. In part, this process of diminution has been associated with economic considerations. In the Swiss Jura, on the other hand, it has been shown that the agricultural landscape is differentiated along linguistic lines. The type of agricultural produce and the goals and economic aspirations of the region's farmers are closely related to language differences. Research along the French–Swiss boundary also illustrates the association between nationality and landscape. Agricultural landscape and agricultural practice, income levels and urbanisation processes are all shown to be differentiated by national affiliation. Given the economic interdependence of 'Regio', some interesting findings are presented on the behavioural patterns of and attitudes towards cross-boundary commuters. Overall, it is suggested that current political-economic and urbanisation processes are likely to lead to a reduction in landscape differentiation in the future.

In Chapter 3, Walter Leimgruber asserts that boundaries as human creations are an expression of territoriality, reflecting people's basic need to live in a bounded space. From this point of view, borders separate, reflecting centripetal forces within territories. However, since territories interface at boundaries, they are also points or lines of contact, favouring centrifugal tendencies, and, hence, in the border zone both forces operate side by side, visible in a variety of installations on and movements across the boundary. In addition, they are landscape evidence of different attitudes towards and evaluations of the land by the people on either side. Leimgruber concludes that landscapes are thus a mirror of a person's perception of regions located at the periphery of a territory.

Specifically, he studies these aspects by referring to a land use survey undertaken in the Swiss–Italian border area in 1981. The

marked differences in land use reflect political, economic and social processes, in part dating back to the nineteenth century, and in part being of more recent origin. Although the region under study forms part of the Milan urban agglomeration, the political boundary he finds exercises a strong differentiating influence. Leimgruber makes the case that border landscapes should not remain exclusively a field of political-geographical study, but could find their place in the wider context of cultural geography.

In Chapter 4, Ulrich Ante selects a region in the former Federal Republic of Germany of Upper Franconia in northern Bavaria along the borderland with the former German Democratic Republic for detailed analysis. He examines the evolution of a border landscape in a region which possessed an hermetically sealed boundary for over forty years. The temporal factor becomes critical as he observes this borderland at the interface of contrasting world ideologies passing through a series of periods, each defined in terms of changing conditions external to the region.

The region was located within the 'Zonenrandgebeit', a 40-kilometre-wide strip defined by the Federal Republic as eligible for special subsidies for economic development to maintain 'equivalent living conditions' with the rest of the country. This policy met with limited success and new European Community regulations on regional subsidies presented a threat to the region's viability. The relocation of public facilities in an economy with increasing emphasis on the service sector remained the most promising policy for this region. Ante studies the decision to relocate the Bavarian Administration College in the borderland in 1982, and its consequences. Of particular importance is the analysis of survey data relating to attitudes of the College's employees and the applicant group for positions on the staff about relocating in the Upper Franconia region. Results indicated that the trouble in filling staff positions at the College lay in the very negative attitudes of potential applicants to this border region, and Ante is led to conclude that this perception derived primarily from its peripheral location.

Vladimir Klemencic and Milan Bufon collaborate in Chapter 5 to discuss the unique set of historical circumstances which have contrived to create a 'special type' of border landscape along the Italian–Yugoslav boundary. Over the last century, this international boundary has been subject to a great many demarcation changes primarily induced by extra-regional forces. Klemencic and Bufon evaluate the relevance of the different bases which were used in each of the boundary change proposals, especially the principles of ethnicity,

'natural boundaries' and functional coherence. Boundary changes initiated before the First World War tended to divide ethnic groups and resulted in economic disruption. After the Second World War, boundary changes exhibited an inconsistency between functional and ethnic considerations. One of the important outcomes in both cases was that there was significant cross-boundary migration of Slovenians and Italians for economic and political reasons. However, especially since the 1950s, the character of the Italian–Yugoslav border landscape has changed from one of conflict to one of increasing cooperation via a series of economic, political and cultural agreements. As a result, cross-border economic transactions have markedly increased, although there is considerable variation along the boundary in terms of their current intensity and direction.

Shinsuke Minamide, in a very detailed, descriptive Chapter 6, discusses the role played by the Karafuto Government Office (KGO) in settling the southern part of Sakhalin Island following its transfer from Russia to Japan in the early years of this century. Clearly, the KGO did not face an untouched, yet relatively hostile, natural environment, since the Russians had undertaken their own settlement programme during the latter half of the nineteenth century. The resultant border landscape effect was that many pre-existing sites were chosen for Japanese settlement, other locations were abandoned, and in some cases, the Japanese established new planned settlements. Minamide develops a basic classification scheme for the three main settlement types which emerged as a result of this process. The initial preference of the KGO was to adopt in Sakhalin a dispersed village plan following the township settlement system which had been successfully applied to neighbouring Hokkaido. However, Minamide points out that the three settlement types which resulted principally derive from Slavic culture and indicate their successful adaptation to the Sakhalin environment.

In Chapter 7, Dennis Rumley argues that the process of border landscape evolution, especially in the developing world, can be enhanced through a consideration of the various dimensions of peripherality and their association with government policies of contiguous states. Rumley suggests that these characteristics will be present irrespective of the political-geographical structure of the respective states. He emphasises the ways in which peripherality is associated with social, economic and political conflict along the Thai–Malaysian international boundary. Examples are discussed of conflicts over the physical delimitation of the boundary, the geographical concentration of political opposition, Chinese resettlement and

economic development policies. Rumley argues, however, that the conflicts inherent in border landscapes cannot be completely understood without reference to the local historical, social, economic and political context.

In Chapter 8, Ronald May, one of two non-geographers represented in this volume, examines a number of problems inherent along the Indonesia–Papua New Guinea border landscape in the context of asymmetrical relations between the two neighbouring states. May's discussion centres on the causes of these problems, the administrative arrangements created to deal with them and their overall impact on Indonesian–PNG relations. Although the border itself is seemingly not a problem *per se*, it has been a source of tension arising out of the activities associated with 'border crossers', the *Organisasi Papua Merdeka* (OPM or Free Papua Movement), the military, and border development. Border crossings are not only a result of traditional village interactions, but also consist of Irianese nationalists seeking asylum, villagers seeking temporary refuge and OPM guerrillas. The nationalist movement associated with the latter has been in existence since the early 1960s and has continued to be one of the more important sources of border tension. This has been reinforced by its partial association with border violations by the Indonesian military. In general, border development policies, seen by many as a solution to border problems, have been unsuccessfully applied by both states.

In Chapter 9, George Ohshima reinterprets data collected as part of a long-standing research interest in the Torres Strait to demonstrate the various ways in which the international political boundary between Australia and Papua New Guinea in the Strait has affected the social and economic life of island people. From a cultural-geographical perspective, Ohshima compares two islands in the Torres Strait – Dauan in Australia and Parama in Papua New Guinea – each of which has been subject to differential government policies and differential missionary impacts. The Europeanisation and Christianisation of Dauan has had a fundamental impact upon the local landscape and upon social and economic life. The inhabitants of Dauan thus tend to live in European-style houses compared with the more traditional styles in Parama. In addition, clan spatial segregation is still maintained in Parama but is largely absent in Dauan. These differences are clearly symbolised by the ways in which the two groups of islanders make use of flags. In Dauan, integration is symbolised by the use of an island flag, compared with the more traditional house flag of Parama residents.

Mohammed Ismail Siddiqi, in Chapter 10, analyses the impact of

inter- and intra-regional conflicts upon the Pakistan borderland with Afghanistan. He describes the complexity of tribal relations of a number of 'transborder peoples' and their relationship with the local environment in Pakistan. Siddiqi argues that these relationships, along with the security situation in Pakistan in general, have been jeopardised as a direct consequence of Soviet intervention in neighbouring Afghanistan. In particular, the enormous influx of Afghan refugees into Pakistan, especially since the late 1970s, has severely strained the resources of the borderland environment. For example, often refugee camps are located in previously uninhabited barren lands formerly unable to support the local border population. For the future, problems of resettlement and rehabilitation necessitate sensitively designed regional development programmes, taking due consideration of local tribal sentiment.

In Chapter 11, Alasdair Drysdale discusses the evolution of political boundaries in the Gulf of Aqaba region and explains why the border landscapes of the four riparian states differ so greatly. One of the primary reasons why the Gulf exhibits a complex pattern of border landscapes derives from its differing importance to each riparian state. These differences, in turn, are due mainly to the broader political-geographical environment.

Overall, the Gulf is relatively unimportant to the Saudi Arabian state and its section of coastline (150 out of 385 kilometres) is almost completely undeveloped since the political-geographical core of the state is located far to the south. Egypt, on the other hand, having the largest section (200 kilometres), ascribes considerable strategic importance to the Gulf arising out of its historical conflict with Israel. Furthermore, since the Israeli withdrawal from the Sinai, Egypt has developed some of the economic potential of the region. Israel's relatively short section (10 kilometres) is also considered to be relatively important, especially for trade access through Eilat to East and South Africa, Asia and Australasia, even though 80 per cent of total trade goes via the Mediterranean. Jordan, in contrast, is most reliant on the Gulf of Aqaba since it is its only coastline and this is clearly expressed in the landscape. Jordan's section (25 kilometres) is by far the most developed, for example, and it is the sector with the greatest potential for continued growth.

James Drummond and the historian Andrew Manson collaborate in Chapter 12 to examine the problems arising from superimposed colonial boundaries in southern Africa. Specifically, they focus on a particular section of the Botswana–Bophuthatswana borderland in an attempt to measure the contemporary geopolitical significance of the

region in reference to the location of the boundary and the evolution of the human geography of the borderland between Botswana, independent since 1966, and Bophuthatswana, declared an 'independent ethnic homeland' by South Africa in 1977. The boundary had been first demarcated by the British in 1897 and had served as a veterinary cordon as a result of severe regulations against diseased cattle moving south into what became the Union of South Africa in 1910. Botswana's independence served to change the borderland considerably and encouraged the decline of Mafeking when a new capital outside of the borderland region was adopted. A decade later, Bophuthatswana's 'independence' – part of South Africa's apartheid policy – gave rise to a new set of circumstances in the borderland. Botswana's policy of non-recognition of this new political entity as neighbour rendered negotiation of a boundary water rights dispute impossible and was to the detriment of Botswana. Also, Bophuthatswana, as a transit state to ports in South Africa for Botswana, applied pressure for control of cross-boundary interchange in trade and human movement. These attempts at winning recognition from 'front line states' for an apartheid-created entity have been successfully resisted, but have nevertheless had a disruptive impact on the borderland, including the potential for direct armed conflict with Bophuthatswana Defence Force bases, including South African forces located within 15 kilometres of the Botswana border. The colonial origin, the differential evolution of the two segments of the borderland, including the chronology of independence, and the broader context of conflict between independent African states and South Africa's apartheid regime, all combine to give this borderland a very distinctive character and an uncertain future.

In Chapter 13, John Chappell Jr focuses his study on the delta region of the Colorado River, the borderland defined by the US–Mexican boundary. Not surprisingly, Chappell finds stark contrasts at this interface between the developed and the Third World, with the US as the upstream state and Mexico as the downstream. He traces the agricultural development of this desert region over the past century in which the availability of useful water has been crucial, and the downstream handicap of Mexico critical. In recent years, the amenity factor has served to attract a large retirement population and high-tech industries on the US side, which in turn have attracted a sharp growth of migrants from other parts of Mexico on the Mexican side. Chappell concludes that the 'cultural averaging' which takes place within countries – the tendency for the standard of living and related cultural features to be averaged out spatially and

homogenised – goes a long way to explain the contrasts in this borderland, without reference to local conditions. He also detects, however, that a type of cultural convergence may be occurring in the borderland as habits are influenced by the dominating heat and aridity of the region. A major contrast remains, however, in the land tenure pattern; on the Mexican side redistribution of land into *ejidos* and *colonias* 30–50 years ago contrasts with the US side in which corporate ownership dominates. This has tended to be associated with an increase in democratisation in Mexico and a swing to right wing politics in the US segment of the borderland, which Chappell suggests could be called borderland cultural reversal. These findings, based on the application of environmental causation theory, may well be open to challenge but they do demonstrate yet another potentially fruitful methodology for the analysis of border landscapes.

Stanley Brunn, in Chapter 14, studies the nature of the United Nations peacekeeping forces (awarded the 1988 Nobel Peace Prize) and identifies the distinctive features of peacekeeping landscapes along borders of conflict, including a new concept – peacekeeping cartography. Brunn reviews the over forty years of United Nations peace missions and operations and finds that the contributions to support them have come on both a regional and international basis. Distinctive features of a peacekeeping borderland are the strategic location of the UN military presence in a buffer zone to prevent hostilities by monitoring all potentially hostile movements while at the same time clearly marking all installations, vehicles and troops for clear recognition as UN forces – the opposite of camouflage and concealment. The presence of a UN peacekeeping force adds a whole new dimension to the landscape of a border in conflict and Brunn suggests more systematic study of this feature could contribute to our understanding of the process of borderland conflict resolution.

REFERENCES

Augelli, J. P. (1980) 'Nationalization of Dominican borderlands', *Geographical Review*, Vol. 70, pp. 19–35.
Cosgrove, D. and Jackson P. (1987) 'New directions in cultural geography', *Area*, Vol. 19, pp. 95–101.
Gottmann, J. (1980) *Centre and Periphery* (London: Sage).
House, J. W. (1981) 'Frontier studies: An applied approach', in A. D. Burnett and P. J. Taylor (eds) *Political Studies from Spatial Perspectives* (New York: Wiley), pp. 291–312.
House, J. W. (1982) *Frontier on the Rio Grande: A Political Geography of Development and Social Deprivation* (Oxford: Clarendon Press).

14 *Introduction*

James, P. E. and Martin, G. J. (1981) *All Possible Worlds* (New York: Wiley).

Jones, S. B. (1937) 'The Cordilleran Section of the Canadian–United States borderland', *Geographical Journal*, Vol. 89, pp. 439–50.

Mikesell, M. (1968) 'Landscape', *International Encyclopedia of Social Science*, Vol. 8, pp. 575–80.

Minghi, J. V. (1963) 'Boundary studies in political geography', *Annals, Association of American Geographers*, Vol. 53, pp. 407–28.

Prescott, J. R. V. (1965) *The Geography of Frontiers and Boundaries* (London: Hutchinson).

Prescott, J. R. V. (1987) *Political Frontiers and Boundaries* (London: Allen and Unwin).

Ratzel, F. (1897) *Politische Geographie* (Munich: Oldenbourg).

Rokkan, S. and Urwin, D. W. (1983) *Economy, Identity, Territory* (London: Sage).

Rumley, D. (1985) 'The geography of political participation', *Australian Geographer*, Vol. 12, pp. 279–86.

Torsvik, P. (ed.) (1981) *Mobilisation, Centre–Periphery Structures and Nation-Building* (Bergen : Universitetsforlaget).

Wallerstein, I. (1979) *The Capitalist World Economy* (Cambridge).

Whittlesey, D. (1935) 'The impress of effective central authority upon the landscape', *Annals*, Association of American Geographers, Vol. 25, pp. 85–97.

1 From conflict to harmony in border landscapes

Julian V. Minghi

'Good fences only make good neighbors
When they are not made out of sabres.'

Kenneth Boulding, 1989

INTRODUCTION

Political geographers share a compelling interest in borders and borderlands that is, in one way, the reverse of the regional model. We focus on the edges, not the cores of regions. We can observe landscapes at local scales but also must be aware of their international significance. Our methodology must incorporate the ability to study comparatively two or more borders, yet at the same time to analyse a borderland in its temporal setting. We need to consider boundaries in the traditional political-geographical mode, as lines marking the edge of national space and also as interfaces separating national units. The additional dimension that follows from the above viewpoint is essential for understanding the concept of a 'borderland' – the boundary creates its own distinctive region, making an element of division also the vehicle for regional definition. This paradox is at the core of the borderland concept. Boundary dwelling characteristics, unique to either side of the line, become dominant moulders of the cultural landscape within the shadow thrown by the boundary, and yet these characteristics disappear as one moves away from the borderland in either direction into the territorial domain of the states divided. Geographers have found some distinct advantages in applying this concept of borderland. It provides a basis for a legitimate and useful regional focus that could otherwise be over-looked – a small, local-scale dimension within an international context – and at the same time, the concept creates a type of miniature but very readable barometer of the changes in the relations between the states divided when studied in a temporal setting. Hence, the analysis of the cultural landscape of the border becomes the dominant focus of study.

I find John House's (1981) operational model for frontier studies

Figure 1.1   Borderland transaction flow model

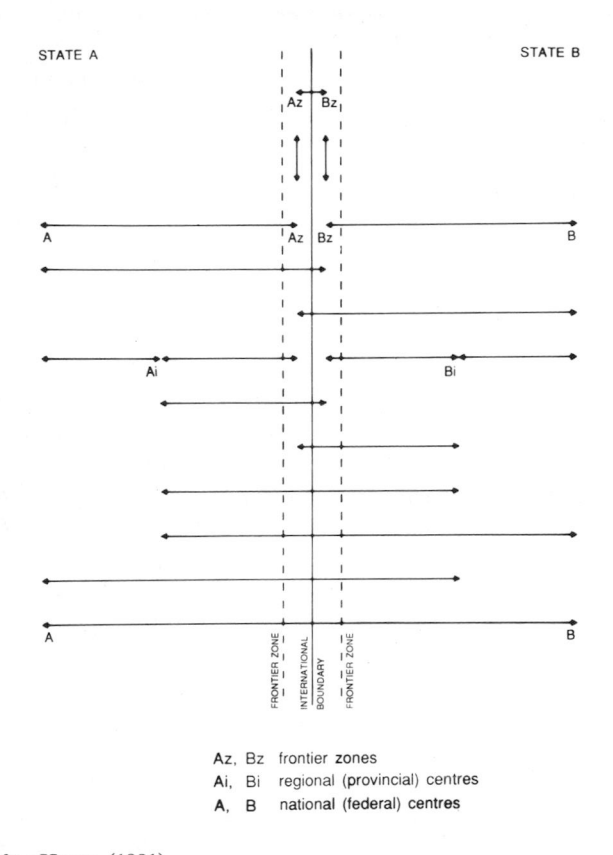

STATE A

STATE B

Az, Bz   frontier zones
Ai, Bi   regional (provincial) centres
A, B   national (federal) centres

Source: after House (1981)

most helpful in defining the basic thesis of the present chapter – the study of border landscapes can fruitfully benefit by shifting the analytical focus from conflict to harmony (Figure 1.1). House aggregates borderland transaction flows which are integrated progressively in terms of space and time. The locally generated Az–Bz 'borderland' transactions are virtually non-existent along a boundary under the stress of confrontation and the threat of conflict. With the dominance of national interests and actions in whatever transboundary transactions (A–B) that take place, transactions of the Az–Bz variety are usually discouraged and often illegal. Hence, with a borderland that evolves from an extreme conflict situation, such as the chaos of open war and its consequences of instability, toward a

more harmonious status, one would expect to see a marked change in the nature of A–B transactions *and* a sharp rise, indeed often a dominance, of the local Az–Bz transactions. The present chapter will focus on the conflict-versus-cooperation aspects in the time dimension and in the spatial context, with special emphasis on the changing nature of A–B transactions and the rise in importance of Az–Bz transactions in the shift from conflict to harmony.

BORDERLAND STUDIES

The analysis of border landscapes in political geography has generally been directly related to the study of boundaries. The vast majority of these studies has traditionally carried an emphasis on stress and conflict, viewing the boundary as an interface between two or more discrete national territories and subject to problems directly reflecting the relations between the nation-states it divides. Consequently, the ebb and flow of boundary studies have tended to be associated with periods of territorial conflict and hostility.

In a review of boundary studies a generation ago (Minghi, 1963), it was clear that most of the boundary literature had been written during the two World Wars or in their aftermath. Many sought the causes of friction between nations and the means of avoiding it. In particular, the redrawing of boundaries based on a variety of considerations in the post-War periods attracted much research interest, whereas boundaries as political-geographic phenomena had attracted little interest in normal times. Hence most studies fell into categories such as shift in location, delimitation and demarcation, and disputed areas. Recently, Prescott (1987) confirms this finding but also points out that a boundary is a line of physical contact between states and hence affords opportunities for both discord *and* cooperation. Indeed, while discussing border landscapes, he talks about the 'temptation for scholars to concentrate on the dramatic' at the expense of the routine, with the dramatic tending to be conflict and the routine more normal, peaceful situations (Prescott, 1987: 160).

We find, therefore, a heavy concentration of conflict-related studies written at a time in which the collapse of regimes, states and entire empires, the creation of new states, and shifts in the location of national frontiers by occupation, conquest or treaty, all provide grist for the study mill of boundary problems and of the human geography of the borderlands to which these problems are linked. This political geography sub-field of research endeavour has consequently taken on

a cyclical nature, with periods of intense, almost feverish research activity often funded by national interests, alternating with times of little or no attention when more normal, peaceful conditions prevail between fixed neighbours.

FROM CONFLICT TO HARMONY

I would like to argue for a new focus on boundary studies which will encourage research on the more 'normal' situation in boundary landscapes. This in turn will place boundary studies more in tune with recent trends in political geography which has seen a rise in the concern for making a more positive contribution to the study of peace. Specifically, I would like to see a shift from the context of war to the prospects for peace in the analysis of border landscapes, and indeed, I claim that such a shift is already under way. I make this claim based on the results of three decades of research in a variety of borderlands. I would further make the case that not only should boundary studies focus more on normal and harmonious contexts, but that such a focus on the changing nature of the human geography of borderlands tends to yield findings that can shed light on the subtle workings of the political process at all levels between and within states. Our increased understanding of such workings in the context of a borderland may well have a direct impact on our ability to understand political geographical processes within one state or the other, and should be applicable to an understanding of the geography of borderlands in other regions. This aspect of applied geography is particularly important as a potential contribution to understanding the processes of conflict resolution and peace.

Two regional examples – one actual and the other potential – will be used to make these points. The first is the Alpes Maritimes borderland of France and Italy viewed over three decades. The other, which is discussed more briefly, is the Israel–Jordan borderland in the Rift Valley between the Dead Sea and the Red Sea.

THE ALPES MARITIMES

My close observation of this borderland for over thirty years, starting in 1956 as an undergraduate field research assistant to John House, leads me to conclude that this shift from the context of war to the prospects for peace – from conflict to harmony – is very clearly reflected in the evolution of the border landscape. In the context of the aftermath of the Second World War in which France and Italy

had been bitter enemies, and, in particular, following a major shift involving 410 square kilometres in the location of the boundary in favour of France in 1947, the most meaningful research questions about the borderland in the mid-1950s concerned the impact of the boundary change, so thoroughly asked and answered by House in his frequently reproduced study of this classic borderland (House, 1959). A decade after the 1947 peace treaty, borderland life was dominated by six major sets of factors.

1 Severe out-migration, especially of the Italian population. Within six months of the peace treaty, residents of the exchanged area were to become automatically French citizens. During the previous decade, a large number of Italians had migrated into the area for jobs in the expanding public sector, such as the state railways or in construction and provision of military facilities. Following Italy's defeat and the territorial gains by France, there was little incentive to retain this mainly urban element of the population.

2 The separation of constituent parts of the ecological whole of alpine communities adjoining the new boundary, with high pastures separated from arable land on alluvial fans in the valleys and village settlements separated from communal forest land. Indeed, the actual village site of Olivetta-San Michele was left in Italy but many of its high summer pastures and virtually all of its forest land were now in France. Possible compromises were discussed to minimise this type of disruption of the cultural landscape and, at one point, a Swiss arbitrator was appointed. The bitterness of the War and the resultant territorial growth of France in the borderland allowed for no compromise at the national level and these severe local problems were allowed to fester.

3 The flooding of entire valleys by a France with far greater needs than Italy for hydroelectric power in the adjacent region of the booming Côte d'Azur. In the first two decades after the War, the Electricité de France (EDF), France's national power generating and distribution agency, pushed the hydroelectric generating capacity in the alpine regions to the limit, and nowhere more than in this newly acquired high alpine region so close to the power hungry Côte d'Azur, France's fastest growing region. In a sense, the local landscape was remade to meet broader regional needs. Headwater diversions, tunnelling, and other hydrologic engineering techniques raised the area's electricity generating capacity several fold over the previous Italian level but only at the expense of accelerating the rate of decline of the rural economy, with the

flooding of arable valley land as well as access routes to pastures. In addition, the temporary but large male and predominantly Algerian labour construction crews brought in to build the new dams tended to seriously disrupt the social life of these small alpine communities.

4 The conscription of males to fight in French colonial wars in North Africa and Indochina. One of the blessings of the War for Italy, was the loss of all colonial territories. France, on the other hand, struggled for over a decade to hold on to its many colonial holdings in South-east Asia, North Africa and elsewhere. This in turn, led to a major colonial war in Indochina and later in Algeria. The male population of military age in the French segment of the borderland found themselves conscripted to fight in these wars, a bitter irony for those in the exchanged territory who had optimistically voted in a plebescite to choose a more victorious and more prosperous French state over an Italy that had brought them fascism and war.

5 The continuing dominance of security preoccupations moulding the landscape with a heavy concentration of French alpine troops. Italy had built up a large military presence in the borderland prior to the invasion of France in 1940 and hence France took particular pains to ensure a significant military occupation of the borderland in the years after the war.

6 The continued dereliction of the Roya Valley railway, the major artery linking the region to the Po Valley and the Mediterranean Coast. Running under the Col de Tende and down the Roya Valley, this railway was completed in 1929 and destroyed during the War (Figure 1.2). The middle section of this line was now in French territory and France, although agreeing in the peace treaty to cooperate with Italy in rebuilding the railway, showed no interest in improving Italian access to the borderland or in raising the competitive status of Italy's Mediterranean port of Ventimiglia over the nearby French port of Nice.

Given the above factors dominating in the region for well into the second decade after the War, any study of the border landscape made during this period was without doubt one of the results of conflict and hostility. Over a generation later, the same borderland offers an entirely different set of research questions. Times have changed. The bitterness and recriminations of the 1950s are gone and with it the psychology of occupation and military pressure by France to offset the previous Italian era. France and Italy are close, founder members of the European Community. The complex of social, political and

Figure 1.2 The Roya Valley railway

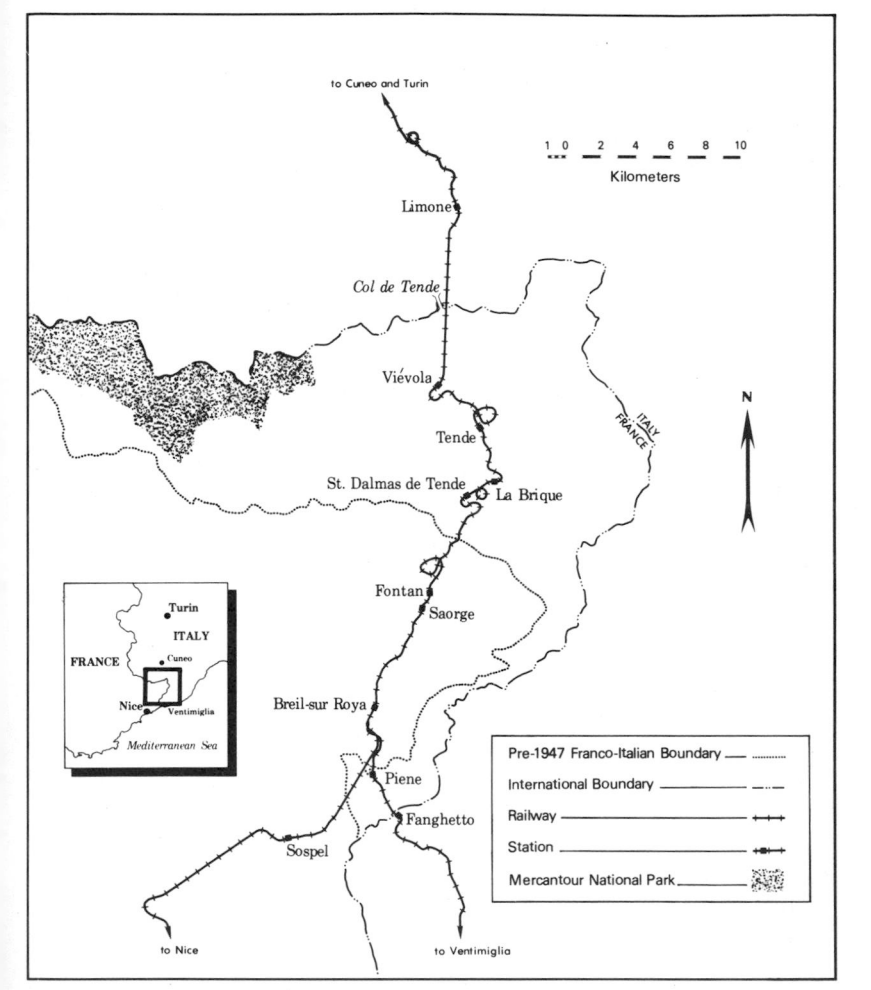

economic relationships generated by this partnership have had a fundamental impact on improving the status of the borderland (Minghi, 1981, 1984). The high alpine segment of the area ceded to France in 1947 is now the Mercantour National Park directly linked by design to a tract of similar high mountain terrain across the border also declared a national park in Italy. The railway is now rebuilt and links the borderland with the North Italian Plain and the Italian city of Ventimiglia as well as to Nice in France. The central point in the

line, the junction at Breil, still remained pock-marked with shells and in a derelict state into the early 1970s, thirty years after the War, whereas at its reopening in 1979, the beautifully redesigned station won the French architectural prize of the year. Similarly, the station at Tende, which remained derelict and served as a boys' camp for thirty years, is now also refurbished for the reopened line. And all over the borderland one can find landscape evidence of the reconstructed line. Scenes of war destruction and abandonment from a generation ago are now replaced by the evidence of peace and cooperation behind the decision to rebuild. The reopened line is advertised widely as a symbol of international cooperation with posters in major French and Italian cities showing the distinctive diesel units – red French and green Italian – side by side in the alpine setting of the borderland. The borderland region is virtually demilitarised and its century-old role as a stage for military occupation and confrontation between France and Italy is over. Forts and battlements remain as fading relics in the border landscape, reduced to the role of historical curiosities. Local inhabitants can move freely across the border and adjustments were finally made in the 1960s to overcome some of the disruptions of ecological balances between settlements and their operating space. While outmigration remains a factor in the borderland's demography, it is more on a par with other alpine regions. Indeed, some settlements in the borderland have expanded their tourist facilities in anticipation of successful exploitation of their borderland character as highly symbolic convention sites for the many Franco-Italian agencies and interest groups spawned by the success of the European Community.

Has all conflict disappeared in this new peaceful borderland? Certainly not. Some is still 'national' in origin. The issue of electrification of the reopened railway line remains. The Italian State Railways (FS) want to integrate it with their own system so that direct freight trains with efficient electric traction can run between Italy's north-west industrial core and its Ligurian ports. French Railways (SNCF) have no interest in electrification as their spur to Nice is inferior, with steep grades and low capacity. Hence, as the line is now in France, SNCF is in control and has blocked installation of the Italian system. Instead, both SNCF and FS diesel passenger units run a joint service, with all units using Italian crews except on the Nice–Breil spur. This has raised a new issue, internal to France, with the French railway workers' union protesting the loss of jobs and pointing out the higher accident rate of the FS. Furthermore, the SNCF has introduced a highly profitable 'ski train' daily round-trip

Plate 1.1 First World War memorial plaque on the wall of a church in Libre in the Alpes Maritimes

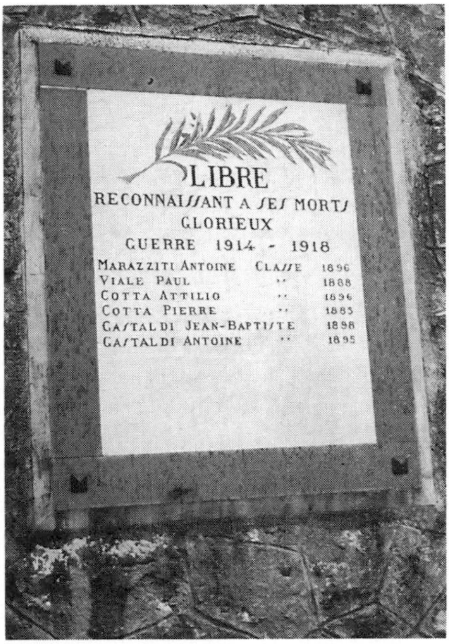

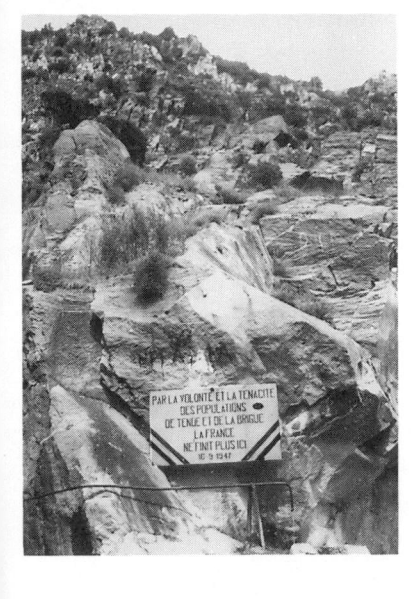

Plate 1.2 Sign on the Roya Valley road in the Alpes Maritimes at at point where the relict pre-1947 boundary between Italy and France crossed the valley

run in winter to link Nice with the Italian ski resort of Limone, now on the border. This action has led to a serious loss in business for the more expensive and less accessible French resorts south of the boundary, thus creating another internal conflict.

The leadership elites of local communities served by the reopened line in both the French and Italian borderland have made united and vigorous requests that train schedules be rearranged to benefit commuter travel of local inhabitants to jobs on the Italian and French Riviera, but without success as the FS and SNCF seem satisfied in operating this expensive line as a symbolic regional link between Piemonte and the Riviera. It is no coincidence that the line reopened just in time for the celebration of the bicentennial of the completion of the 'Route Royale' between Turin and Nice, linking the two major cities of the old transalpine kingdom of Savoy in 1780.

Another issue cutting across the boundary and drawing together the local borderland community was generated by the joint French and Italian decision to create the two adjoining alpine national parks in the early 1980s. The change of status of such large tracts of high mountain terrain was seen as a threat to the traditional hunting activity of local montagnards as well as putting a permanent halt to any further winter sports development. The preservation of pristine high alpine environments for future generations of French and Italian citizens is viewed as in direct conflict with the future economic well-being of the local communities. Evidences of this local-versus-national conflict can be seen directly reflected in the landscape; there is a neatly printed statement on the railway viaduct above the town of Tende, in which Tendasques vent their anger at the hated ecologists who, they feel, have abused the rights of citizens by nationalising their native land.

The most persistent elements in the cultural landscape of the borderland that continue to reflect the conflict of the past are, not surprisingly, related to the dead. In the graveyard in Tende, head-stones in a family plot were all in Italian until 1947 and since – by law – are all in French. And an original memorial plaque on the wall of the church in Libre commemorating the dead of the First World War – when Italy and France were allies – was replaced with a French language version in the early period of national fervour and intolerance after the 1947 boundary change (Plate 1.1). First names have been made French and even the starting date of the War has been changed – from 1915 for Italy to 1914 for France! Even so, one can still find a surviving First World War monument to the Italian Fallen in the centre of Tende in a good state of repair and clearly still the

Plate 1.3 Sign at the entrance to La Brigue near Tende in the Alpes Maritimes

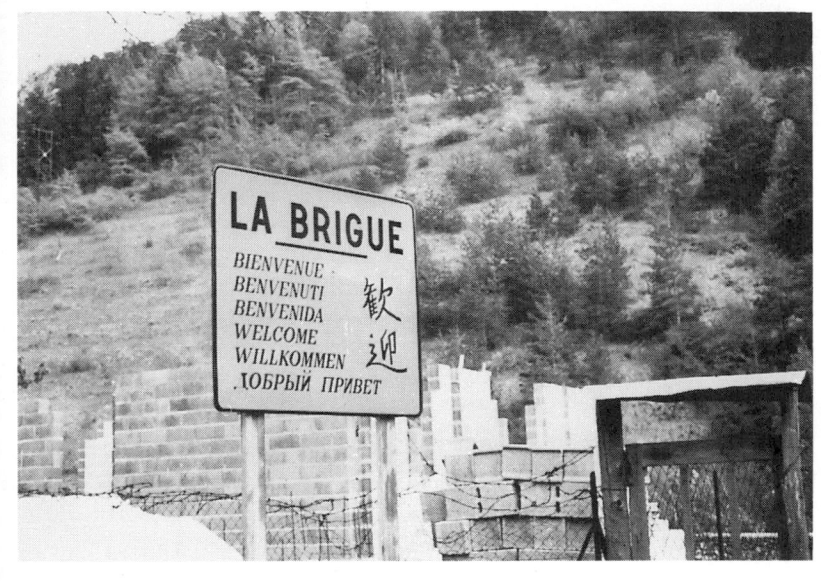

object of tender loving care. Wilbur Zelinsky (1988) has studied the 'welcoming sign' in American culture, divining that its distinguishing mark is found in the commodity it purveys – the image of the particular locality. One can see in two signs in virtually the same location in the Alpes Maritimes very different messages (Plates 1.2 and 1.3). The first, taken in 1966, is still full of aggression generated by the two-decade-old boundary shift in favour of France – 'As a result of the wishes of the local population France no longer finishes here' – marking the relict boundary, lest anyone forget. The second, twenty years later, has replaced the former with the positive ring of multilingual welcome, purveying the town of La Brigue as a site of friendly international cooperation. Both signs are borderland-conscious and portray images of the locality at different points in time. Perhaps more succinctly than anything else, they epitomise the shift from conflict to harmony along this borderland.

THE ISRAEL–JORDAN BORDERLAND IN THE RIFT VALLEY

Two scholars at Ben Gurion University of the Negev (one a geographer, Yehuda Gradus) have recently made a proposal for a

Figure 1.3 The Israel–Jordan borderland in the Rift Valley

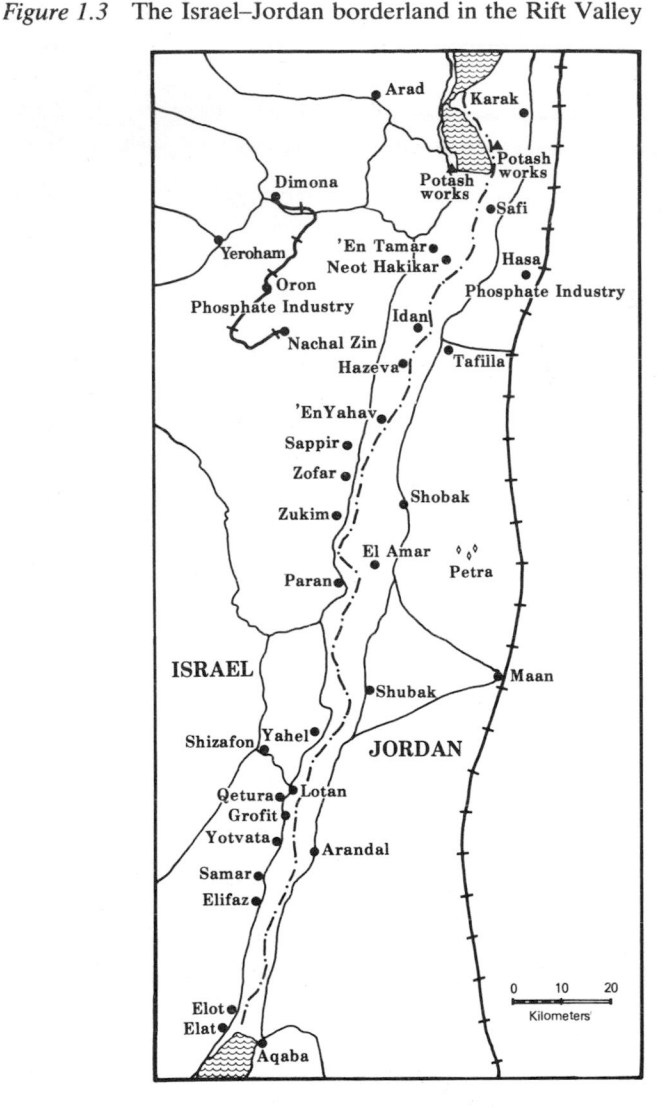

peace initiative between Israel and Jordan in the Rift Valley based on a series of projects for joint resource development between the Dead Sea and the Red Sea (Gradus and Leibowitz, 1988). They propose a programme of research and development with an emphasis on harmony and cooperation replacing the official state of war and confrontation between Israel and Jordan that has lasted for over forty

years. This borderland region along a 160 kilometre span of the Rift Valley is dominated by aridity, intense heat and its location on a north–south access route between the Dead Sea in the north and the Gulf of Aqaba and the Red Sea to the south (Figure 1.3). Currently, in a period characterised by the relative absence of military conflict, both Israel and Jordan have developed independently their mineral resources with what could be considered wasteful duplication, each side of the border being almost a mirror image of the other – a duplicate borderland of potash plants, phosphate industries, north–south routeways, settlements, and so on. The potential benefits in a shift from conflict to harmony are tantalising: Israel sharing the Jordanian rail system; underused Eilat port facilities in Israel relieving the congestion of Aqaba; a jointly built and run Eilat–Aqaba airport which would be of great symbolic as well as economic value; the growth of international tourism with an open border that would combine the attractions on both sides and possibly even with Egypt now that the Taba dispute has been settled; joint endeavours in processing plants and transport facilities in order to exploit the vast phosphate deposits in both countries at the south end of the Dead Sea; and the combination of Israeli expertise in arid region agronomy and geohydrology with Jordanian land in supporting a thriving agriculture for winter crop export to Europe. It is a bold initiative in the best of causes – a conscious attempt at applied geography, to create harmony from conflict in a borderland.

Yet at the same time, at the opposite end of the country, Israel extends conflict into Lebanon by the 'security zone', established in 1985 following the Israeli withdrawal of troops that had invaded Lebanon in 1982. This 10-kilometre strip, 80 kilometres long, has been more properly labelled an 'insecurity zone' (Weiss and Eknes, 1988). Recent events show that Israeli settlements on or near the border are actually less secure, and today lives of Lebanese in villages in the borderland are constantly at risk. UNIFIL's presence offers some hope for peace but this borderland has actually moved further from harmony toward greater conflict. Clearly, despite the peace treaty with Egypt and the subsequent withdrawal from the Sinai, Israel and her neighbours have far to go in creating harmony from conflict along their borderlands. At best, they are at the earliest stages in this process, and there seems, alas, little hope in the near future of anything approaching the creation of the European Community of the late 1950s encompassing the Middle East region within which neighbours can work their borderlands through this process from conflict to harmony. The couplet quoted from Kenneth

Boulding's 'War and Peace' poem at the start of the chapter serves to remind us of this hard truth about fences and sabres and is especially apt as the poem was written in the context of a political geography seminar on the theme of 'Peace, War and Geography' in Israel in early 1989.

CONCLUSION

In an era of international peace and cooperation, the issues of significance in a borderland are no longer drawn on national lines, but more on local and regional interests *across* the boundary. The creation of cross-boundary agencies to favour policies of local benefit along borderlands undergoing similar trends is clear evidence of this crucial reorientation of issues. For example, in the Alpes Maritimes, there is 'Alp-Azur', and in the Basle urban region of three nations (Switzerland, France and Germany) there is the 'Regio Basiliensis'. The evidence supports this finding in the Alpes Maritimes, which is typical of many Western European borderlands, and we are probably on the verge of seeing similar changes along borderlands between Eastern and Western Europe, most dramatically demonstrated in the spring of 1989 when Hungarian authorities made tearing down the boundary fence with Austria a community project for its borderland settlements. The authorities are subsequently allowing the sale for private profit of suitably mounted pieces of the barbed wire fence for Austrians and Hungarians wishing to retain on their walls a symbolic reminder of the period of conflict as they enjoy the greater harmony of the borderland. Indeed, during his visit to Hungary in July 1989, George Bush was presented with a gift of this item as evidence of the improving relations of Hungary with the West.

The Mont Blanc tunnel, opened in the late 1960s, also serves as an impressive symbol in the border landscape of Franco-Italian accord. A church steeple still protrudes above the ice of Resia lake in the Italian South Tyrol near the Austrian border and perpetuates the strong negative feelings of the South Tyrolese against the Italianisation policy of the Fascist era, which flooded villages in the name of progress in creating hydroelectric power systems. Yet the contemporary landscape symbols on both sides of the Italian–Austrian border at the Brenner Pass now emphasise cooperation by the improvement of communications. The Swiss city of Basle solved its problem of finding suitable space for an airport by an agreement with France by which the facility has been built on French soil, is shared with the French city of Mulhouse, and is served from Switzerland by a

closed access highway from Basle. Even the new 1947 boundary between Italy and Yugoslavia – very much the result of war – is now reflecting in its landscape a shift to more peaceful circumstances. The realigned roads to maintain Italian access between Trieste and Gorizia remain, but the spectacle of an impenetrable border fence between the city of Gorizia, left in Italy, and its station on its east side ceded to Yugoslavia, is somehow softened and even ridiculed by the rusting and ignored sign on the Italian side warning violators of the dire consequences of photographing such a spectacle.

In Western European – and many other – borderlands, conflict has not been removed, but the borderland as a region of national confrontation, security dominance and potential war no longer exists. The issues are those of local and regional control in which national borderlands, hitherto denied that right in a straitjacket of national space separated by the boundary, team together in their own self-interest across the border to protect themselves from policies which, in a spirit of international cooperation, can work to the detriment of the borderland community. Such is the irony of peace. In borderlands, it allows for normalcy and it is this process that takes us from war to peace and hence from conflict to harmony at the national level; this could become the major thrust of borderland study.

REFERENCES

Boulding, K. (1989) 'Verses inspired by the Conference on Peace, War and Geography in Haifa, Israel, January 1989', *Newsletter*, Commission on the World Political Map, International Geographical Union, 3–4 March.

Gradus, Y. and Leibowitz, S. (1988) *The Israel-Jordan Rift Valley Initiative: A Proposal* (Beer Sheva: Ben Gurion University).

House, J. (1959) 'The Franco-Italian Boundary in the Alpes Maritimes', *Transactions*, Institute of British Geographers, No. 26, pp. 107–31.

—— (1981) 'Frontier studies: an applied approach' in A. D. Burnett and P. J. Taylor (eds) *Political Studies from Spatial Perspectives: Anglo-American Essays on Political Geography* (New York: Wiley), pp. 291–312.

Minghi, J. V. (1963) 'Boundary studies in political geography', *Annals*, Association of American Geographers, Vol. 53, pp. 407–28.

—— (1981) 'The Franco-Italian Borderland: Sovereignty change and contemporary developments in the Alpes Maritimes', *Regio Basiliensis*, Vol. 22, pp. 232–46.

—— (1984) 'Railways and borderlands: The rebirth of the Franco-Italian Line through the Alpes Maritimes', *Tijdschrift voor Economische en Sociale Geografie*, Vol. 75, pp. 322–8.

Newman, D. (1987) 'Military and civilian presence as alternative methods of

effective territorial control.' Paper read to Conference on Large Spaces and Small Spaces, Paris, November.

Prescott, J. R. V. (1987) *Political Frontiers and Boundaries* (London: Allen and Unwin).

Weiss, T. G. and Eknes, A. (1988) 'Israel's "Insecurity Zone" in South Lebanon', *Christian Science Monitor*, 2 June, 14.

Zelinsky, W. (1988) 'Where every town is above average: Welcoming signs along America's highways', *Landscape*, pp. 1–10.

2 Geographical investigations in boundary areas of the Basle region ('Regio')

Werner A. Gallusser

INTRODUCTION

At the international symposium on 'Boundaries and the Cultural Landscape' which took place in Basle in 1981 (see *Regio Basiliensis*, Vol. 22), and which in some respects could be viewed as a forerunner to the Perth Conference, we discussed some basic research questions on the theme of a 'Geography of boundaries'. Thereafter, our understanding of this problem area has been enriched as it has been developed and cultivated at Basle in recent years. The main purpose of this chapter is to summarise briefly the results of geographical boundary research undertaken since 1974 at Basle University Geography Department, mostly as MA and PhD theses. Research on boundary effects is an important part of the Basle human geography research programme, which perhaps is no surprise given the boundary situation of our University (Plate 2.1).

As was previously discussed in 1981, it is one of the tasks of political geography to assist in the explanation of the functioning of political boundaries as a necessary means of human spatial organisation, and to live with them in a more conscious way. The following have been key questions in our programme of boundary research:

1 An analysis of their spatial delimitation – for example, by a systematic evaluation of the regional variations in quality of life on both sides of the boundary line.
2 Explanations of differentiated and differentiating impacts of boundaries on the cultural landscape (and its various elements).
3 A growing consciousness of the contingency of political boundaries and therefore the possibility of crossing and change. In practice, this would mean support for cross-boundary developments.

Most of our research has been based on the second question, that is, on the impact of political boundaries on the 'lived space'

Plate 2.1   The boundary situation of the University of Basle

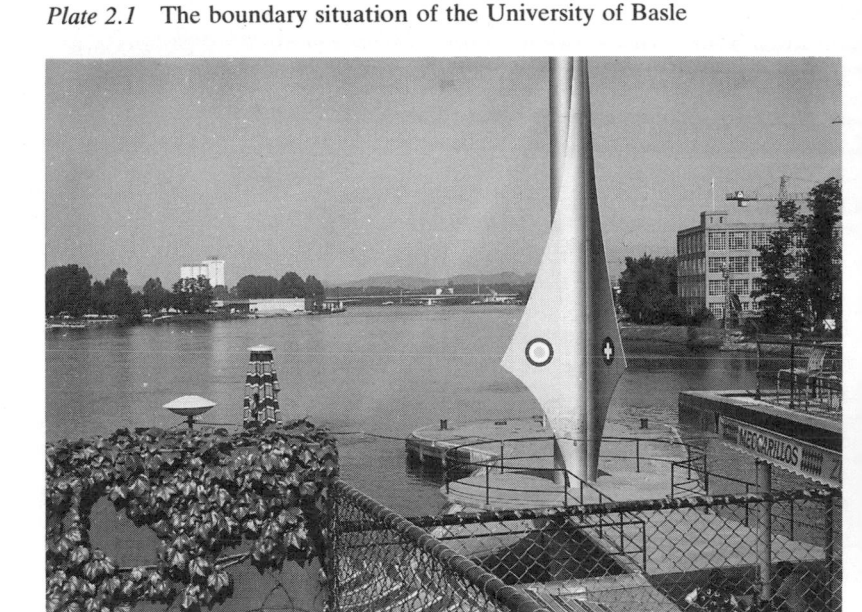

Plate 2.2   Landscape differentiation along political sub-divisions

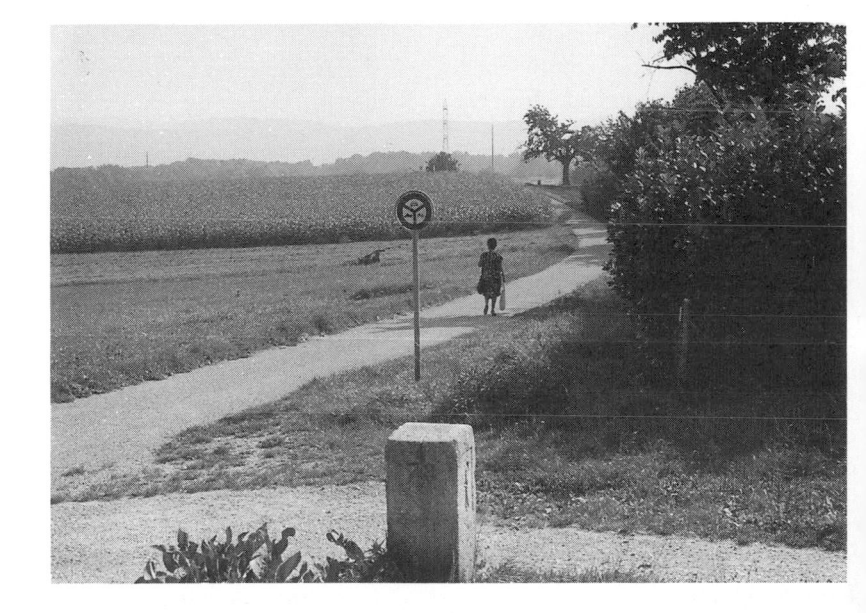

(*lebensraum*). In this respect, we do not only consider today's political boundaries between nation-states, but also other boundaries in the cultural landscape as characterised by different languages and/ or religious groups. In addition, smaller scale political sub-divisions are analysed (Plate 2.2). These current boundary situations have emerged in Central Europe as an outcome of complex territorial policies and their different phases of territorial sub-division.

As 'age' is a key factor when considering political boundaries, it is methodologically important to consider other cultural boundaries since they often represent – as in the case of language or religious boundaries – very old, but often later ignored yet in some cases 'reinstated' political boundaries. We will therefore group the following research examples according to cultural boundaries, internal political boundaries and, finally, today's nation-state boundaries.

CULTURAL AND INTERNAL POLITICAL BOUNDARIES

Aargau–Baselland boundary region

Opferkuch (1977) has investigated the impact of the state ('Kanton') boundary between Baselland and Aargau, which up to 1802 constituted the national boundary between 'outer' Austria (the Frick Valley area) and Switzerland. This 'state' boundary has since persisted as an internal political boundary, still discernible, for example, by the boundary between Protestant Baselland and the Catholic Frick Valley. An analysis of historical documents and settlement surveys shows that differentiations have diminished with the change from a national boundary to an internal boundary – that is, a continuous assimilation of both cultural landscapes has taken place. However, there are still some very persistent elements in the cultural landscape that disclose earlier differentiations, as evidenced in forest patterns, for example (Figure 2.1) or in secondary effects of historically differentiated economic processes such as the early industrialisation of Baselland with silk ribbon weaving. In general, Opferkuch comes to the conclusion that, after political boundaries, differential economic development has been fundamental in the shaping and reshaping of cultural landscapes (Opferkuch, 1977: 180).

Swiss–French language boundaries in the Swiss Jura

Research on this boundary, which is of major importance in the Swiss nation-state, required particular methodological sensitivity, especially

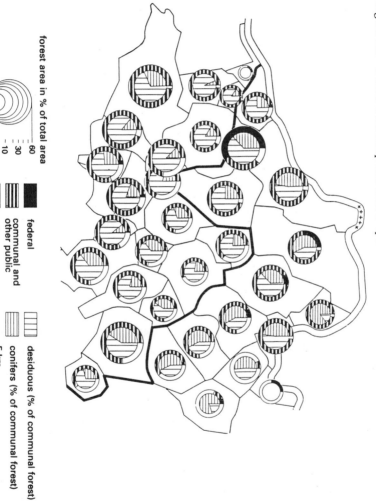

Figure 2.1 Forest ownership and timber species in communal forests

forest area in % of total area

— 60
— 30
— 10

federal

communal and
other public

private

desiduous (% of communal forest)

conifers (% of communal forest)

5 km

after the publication by Winkler in 1946 which dismissed any impact of this language boundary on the Swiss cultural landscape. Even though the German–French language boundary in the Jura developed in the early Middle Ages as a transition zone between the German-speaking colonialisation of northern Switzerland and Burgundy's occupation of Gallo-Roman western Switzerland, it remained effective for centuries within the episcopate of Basle, and (since 1815) within the canton of Berne as an internal cultural boundary. Only in 1978 was this boundary 'upgraded' to a political boundary between the newly constituted canton of Jura and the northern part of the canton of Bern.

Wasmer (1984), in charge of the investigation, concentrated his analysis on aspects of the agricultural landscape. He conducted surveys in three sets of comparable test communes on both sides of the language boundary. This much more critical study by Wasmer can certainly claim more insight than the rather cursory comment made by Winkler. Above all, as the results do not only report investigations at the commune level, but rather present a more finely disaggregated comparative study at the single enterprise and household level, it takes into consideration individual decision-making and behavioural processes. As it is not possible to fully present this amply documented work we will summarise some of the main findings:

1 The agricultural landscape of the Jura is differentiated according to the farmers' language group membership. Many of the behavioural and structural traits which were investigated can also be linked with cultural identities which in turn become visible in the landscape image (for example, through soil utilisation, or the construction type and the location of buildings).
2 German-speaking test communes indicate a high percentage of part-time farmers, whereas in the French-speaking area almost all farmers are full-time.
3 In the French-speaking test area, decision-making is directed more towards the optimisation of the enterprise and there is a stronger spirit of innovation than in the German-speaking area. Work is more capital intensive with more stress on cattle raising with the aim of practising a greater entrepreneurial rationality through the production and sale of a larger quantity of farm goods.
4 In the German-speaking test area, more work goes into the production of crops than in the French-speaking area. Capital investment for machines, buildings and cattle is less than in French-language enterprises. Economic activities remain closer to the traditional mode of subsistence farming.

5 The findings of the above research on the two language groups can be simplified and generalised as follows. On the one hand, German-speaking farmers tend to conduct their work more in a political economy-oriented and ecological style without, perhaps, even being aware of it. On the other hand, French-speaking farmers aim more for a decisively industrial management style-oriented production process.

NATION-STATE BOUNDARIES OF THE BASLE REGION

Agriculture on the French–Swiss boundary

Using similar methodology to the language boundary case, Wasmer *et al.* (1982) investigated the impact of the French–Swiss boundary on agriculture in the two neighbouring communes of Biederthal (France) and Rodersdorf (Switzerland). The study area is situated in the rural periphery of Basle, about 30 kilometres south of the city. Spatial differentiations were investigated along the nation-state boundary which has persisted for more than 400 years at the regional, communal and single enterprise scales. The major differences in the agricultural landscape can be summarised as follows:

1 There has been a strong population influx to Rodersdorf (which lies at the terminal of the Basel–Rodersdorf suburban tramway). On the other hand, there has been population stagnation in the farm commune of Biederthal which is on the other side of the boundary and not linked to the regional centre in Switzerland. This is indicative of a political accentuation of city–periphery processes.
2 The agricultural landscape in France comprises very small land parcels, whereas in Rodersdorf land enclosure can be carried out. Land development and enclosure in the French part of the border region are made even more difficult because of complicated land ownership structures (for example, land ownership by Swiss citizens).
3 With the higher income level in Switzerland and a favourable exchange rate of the Swiss franc, Swiss farmers can exploit agricultural land in France, whereas the reverse is rarely the case. As a consequence of Swiss demand, rental prices in the French boundary communes have increased.
4 In the Swiss part of the region, more machinery is used than in the neighbouring French area and this can be traced to greater capital availability and to land enclosure.

In general, it would seem that historical distinctions in agriculture either side of an international boundary will fade in the light of current political economy and urbanisation processes.

Suburban communes on the French–Swiss boundary

Within the actual suburban zone of Basle (approximately 5–10 kilometres south-west of the city), Berger (1987) has analysed the communes of Allschwil (Switzerland) and Hegenheim (France). Up to the delimitation of the international boundary in 1815, both communes belonged to the same political and cultural area which was characterised by agricultural pursuits in the fertile loess hill country and the adjacent Rhine valley basin and by the typical half-timbered buildings of the Sundgau cultural landscape. The now somewhat more than 170-year-old separation of the communes as a result of the international political boundary has become visible in the cultural landscape in the following ways (among others):

1 Starting from what was initially the same structure of cultural landscape, boundary delimitation has had a differentiating impact upon population and settlement developments.
2 Whereas in earlier times the population of both communes was about equal, the farm commune of Allschwil, now belonging to Switzerland, has turned into a Basle suburb with a population of 17,952 inhabitants (1980) as a result of urbanisation processes. On the other hand, the neighbouring commune which stayed with France has a much lower population (2,162 in 1982) with virtually no growth (Figure 2.2).
3 As a consequence of these differential processes, the built-up area of Allschwil has increased dramatically from 15 hectares to 302 hectares from 1880 to 1984. In Hegenheim, an increase from 14 hectares to 66 hectares during the same time span clearly indicates a much slower pace of development.
4 In qualitative terms, the settlement structure of Allschwil has been negatively affected by numerous new constructions, apartment houses and renovations, all of which have endangered the old stock of half-timbered houses.
5 In Hegenheim, the settlement boom is limited. In addition to the mainly conserved old buildings a few new hillside dwellings have been constructed which seem to correspond with a 'fashion trend in construction' peculiar to cross-boundary commuting workers.
6 The workforce of both communities contains more than 70 per cent

Figure 2.2   Population change in Allschwil and Hegenheim, 1920–80

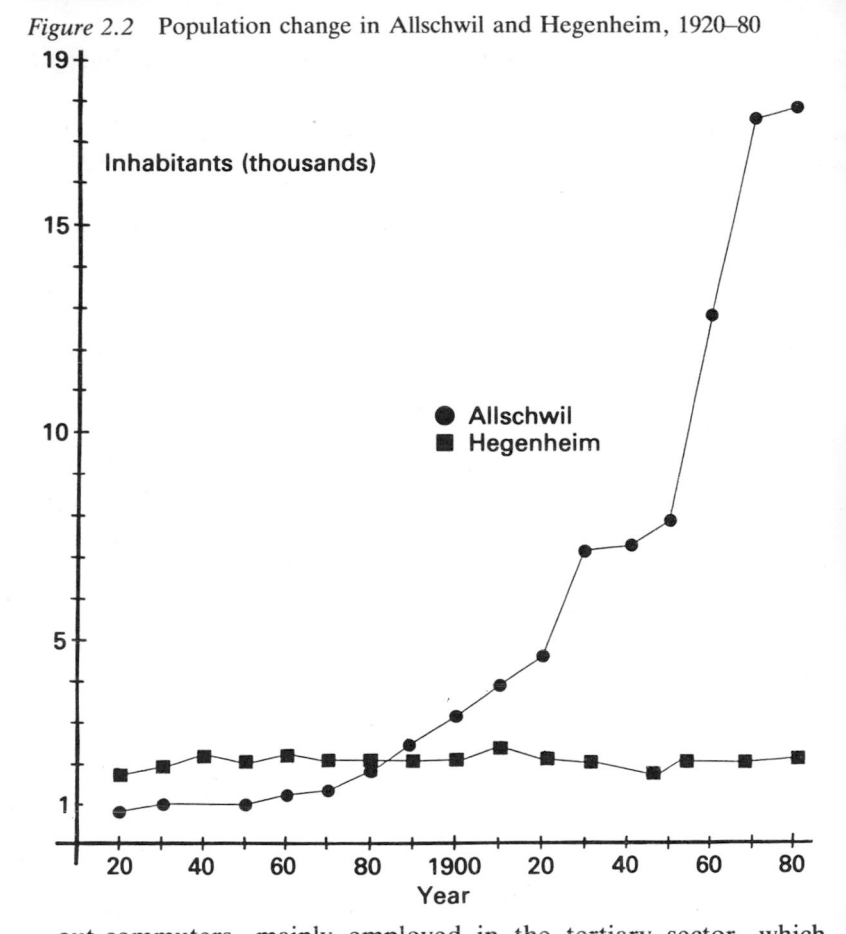

out-commuters, mainly employed in the tertiary sector, which clearly indicates a similar external economic orientation.

7 In terms of socio-cultural behaviour, in spite of the asymmetrical urbanisation process, in both communities there is a movement for the conservation of traditional culture and settlement forms (for example, the protection and reconstruction of half-timbered houses, especially in Allschwil).

THE IMPACT OF FRENCH COMMUTING TO NORTHWESTERN SWITZERLAND ON THE CULTURAL LANDSCAPE OF THE CANTON OF HUNINGUE (FRANCE)

What was investigated in the study by Berger discussed above, was at the same time examined at a larger scale by Meyer. In his thesis,

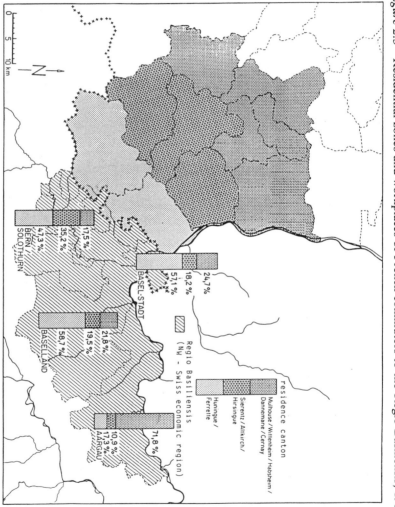

Figure 2.3 Residential zones and workplaces of French commuters to the Regio Basiliensis, 1984

Plate 2.3   Basle–Lysbuchel crossing point between France and Switzerland

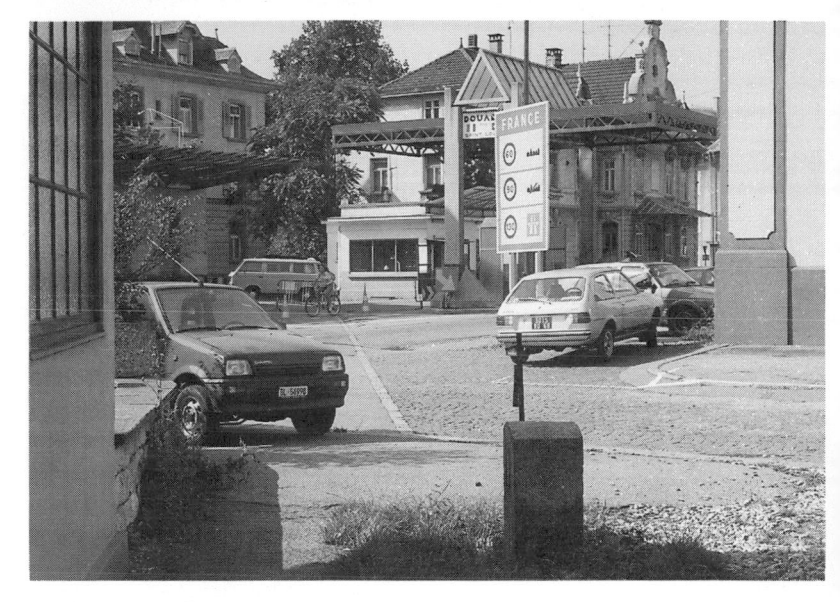

Meyer (1986) attempts to provide a more precise functional evaluation of the impact of a nation-state boundary on the lived space
(*lebensraum*) by the isolated consideration of cross-boundary commuting. In a similar manner, but with a much more refined methodological approach, Leimgruber conceptualised his 'habilitation thesis'
for the southern Ticino boundary area (Leimgruber, 1987).

The canton of Huningue makes up only a part of the total French
commuter area (Figure 2.3). The border crossing point at Basel–
Lysbuchel is one of the most important gateways between France and
Switzerland in the Regio (Plate 2.3). Of a total of 16,900 commuters
(1984) 68.4 per cent were working in Basle city, 23.6 per cent in Basle
country, 5.7 per cent in the cantons of Bern and Solothurn with the
remainder in the canton of Aargau. The results of an analysis of
statistical data and surveys (in four test communes) can be summarised as follows:

1 Since 1968, there has been a marked population influx to the rural
  canton of Huningue from other areas in the Alsace, especially from
  urban areas.
2 The region is a traditional residential area for cross-border

Figure 2.4 Construction permits in Neuwiller, 1970–84

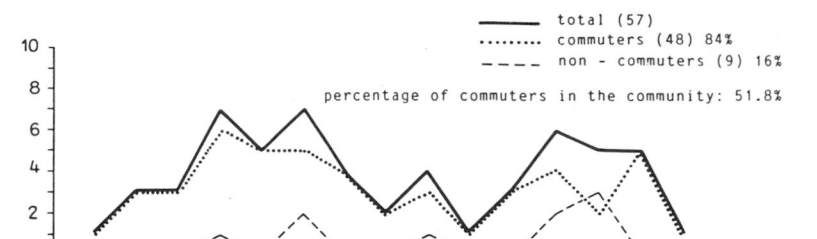

author's survey   draft: Stephan Meyer

commuters. More than 84 per cent of the commuters in the four test communes were home-owners.

3 Of the single-family houses in the test communes of the canton of Huningue, 40.2 per cent were owned or rented by commuters and 57 per cent of the homes built after 1970 had been constructed by commuters.

4 The era of the major construction boom was between 1973 and 1979 and was determined mainly by commuters (Figure 2.4). Financial institutions, when granting construction credits, take into consideration the high level of stability and security inherent in the Swiss employment sector.

5 The modern commuters' homes (bungalows with a basement garage) dominate the landscape image by their uniformity and a scattered settlement pattern.

6 In contrast to home construction developments, other infra-structure in these communes is scarcely developed. To some degree, this is compensated for by widespread car ownership and by Swiss provision of consumption and leisure time services.

7 The socio-cultural integration of the commuters into the com-munes where they live seems to be fairly limited. Most spend their free time in their own gardens and with their visibly higher living standards and urban life styles, they clearly contrast with the rest of the local inhabitants.

8 Switzerland as a 'reference' also becomes apparent by commuters' media use and by their cultivation of the German language. Only in 25 per cent of households is French only spoken, while 17 per cent of households read only French newspapers.

In summary, one can say that the boundary, with its commuting interactions has initiated a significant change in settlement structures and in social relations. This is one possible outcome of the geographical impact of a political boundary, and it is in a 'fragile' state. Commuters are not only envied by some of their compatriots, but also, in the host country, workers do not always find the expected goodwill, even though it is increasingly recognised in the Swiss part of the 'Regio' that commuters must be considered as full partners in an economically and socially interdependent region.

CONCLUSION

With this brief presentation of the methods and results of Basle's contribution to a geography of boundaries, our primary task of sharing information is fulfilled. We hope that our findings will enrich academic discussion and further the project of boundary studies in geography. Our work on boundaries in geography should not only be an objective and analytical guide to inquiry, but should also contribute to a finer consciousness of the possibilities of crossing any boundary imposed by human will.

REFERENCES

Berger, A. (1987) 'Allschwil–Hegenheim', *Allschwiler Schriften*, No. 4.
Gallusser, W. (1981) 'Grenze und Kulturlandschaft', *Regio Basiliensis*, Vol. 22, pp. 59–68.
Leimgruber, W. (1987) *Il Confine e La Gente* (Varese: Lativa).
Meyer, S. (1986) *Französische Grenzganger in der Nordwestschweiz* (Basel: Schriften der Regio 9.2).
Opferkuch, D. (1977) 'Der Einfluss einer Binnengrenze auf die Kulturlandschaft', *Basler Beiträge zur Geographie*, No. 21.
Wasmer, K. (1984) 'Landwirtschaft und der Sprachgrenze', *Basler Beitrage zur Geographie*, No. 30.
Wasmer, K., Furter, M., Vettiger, B. and Wunderlin, D. (1982) 'Die Staatsgrenze als Kulturlandschaftsgrenze – Dargestellt am Beispiel der Landwirtschaft in Biederthal (F) und Rodersdorf (CH)', *Basler Feldbuch*, Vol. 2.
Winkler, E. (1946) *Kulturlandschaft an Schweizerischen Sprachgrenzen* (Zurich: Kultur- und Staatswissenschaftliche Schriften der ETH), No. 53.

3 Boundary, values and identity: The Swiss–Italian transborder region

Walter Leimgruber

Introduction

Boundaries as human creations are an expression of territoriality, reflecting a basic human need to live in a bounded space. From this point of view, borders separate, reflecting centripetal forces within territories. However, since territories meet at boundaries, they are also points or lines of contact, favouring centrifugal tendencies. The border zone thus becomes an area where both forces are to be found side by side, visible in a variety of installations on and movements across the boundary. In addition, they are a record of different attitudes towards and evaluations of the land by the people on either side. Natural conditions for agriculture, for example, may be equal on both sides of the border, but agricultural policies may differ. Border landscapes are thus a mirror of local inhabitants' perception of regions located at the (physical) periphery of a territory.

This chapter examines these aspects first of all by referring to a land-use survey undertaken in the Swiss–Italian border area in 1981. The marked differences in land use reflect political, economic and social processes, in part dating back to the nineteenth century, in part being of more recent origin. Although the region under study forms part of the Milan agglomeration (Italy), the political boundary exercises a strong differentiating influence. In addition, reference is made to aspects of the image of the area and its population as well as to transborder shopping as one example of spatial interaction. The chapter concludes that border landscapes are not exclusively a field of political geography but find their place in the wider context of cultural geography.

In any discussion of border landscapes, however, we inevitably have to face two problems – what kind of border shall we consider, and what do we mean by landscape? The former question presents

little difficulty in so far as any kind of boundary can be studied; apart from political boundaries our considerations could therefore also bear on cultural, functional, administrative or even natural (physiographic) boundaries. In the end, it may be a problem of choice, although relevance should be a more appropriate criterion. The concept of landscape, on the other hand, is more complex. *Landschaft* has been a focus of attention in German-speaking countries for many decades. While the term seemed to have become unfashionable by the late 1960s, it experienced a comeback in the 1970s, in particular under the influence of planners and politicians in the context of landscape protection and planning. *Landschaft* has often been considered solely from a spatial point of view. It has, however, also to be seen from a temporal perspective: landscape is not only something of the past (although it does contain relics of the past), it is something of the present and even of the future, as it is constantly evolving under the influence of human action. This dynamic aspect is central to the argument of the present chapter.

I do not intend to continue the debate on the definition of *Landschaft* (Hard, 1982: 166 has shown that the term appears with at least four different meanings); for the present purpose I take a restricted view, considering landscape as cultural landscape, that is, 'the unique-individual regional result of the encounter between man and nature' (Hard, 1982).

THE BOUNDARY AS A HUMAN FACTOR

Nobody would doubt the fact that boundaries are essentially human creations. Even physiographic boundaries can be considered as such since nature rarely (if ever) draws clear border lines.[1] It is people who perceive differences and establish boundaries. By doing so we refer to territoriality which is central to human (as well as animal) existence (Raffestin, 1981; Sack, 1986). This point is made in Sack's (1986: 31ff) discussion of the ten tendencies of territoriality. The boundary is the element which communicates territoriality. Thus, properties such as 'displacement', 'impersonal relationships', 'neutral space-clearing' or 'conceptually empty places' are related to the human evaluation of space. Quite obviously, people possess a basic need to live in a bounded space as this would ensure a feeling of security and offer a certain independence of action. We cannot imagine life in a territory without external boundaries – even if they are permeable like a membrane. Environmental psychology teaches us that this phenomenon is fundamental to human beings: each has

Figure 3.1 The human shell-like spatial hierarchy

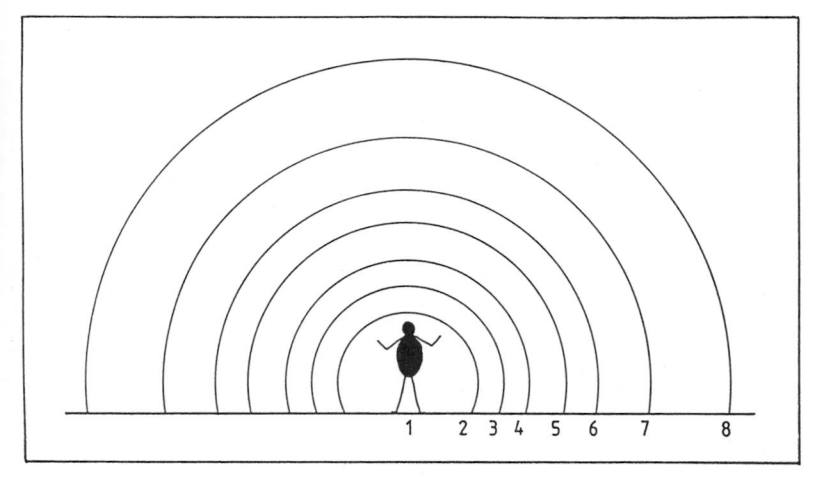

Source: after Moles and Rohmer, 1972: 41ff.
Notes: 1 The human body. 2 The range of gestures. 3 The room in the apartment. 4 The apartment/the house. 5. The neighbourhood/the village. 6 The town/the central place. 7 The region.

their different personal space (Figure 3.1) which is defined by gestures, dwelling space, activity space, and so on (Moles and Rohmer, 1972), and each constitutes a 'territory'.

Boundaries are thus social constructs, conditioned by our perception of an attitude towards space. As such, they direct human actions. A boundary of whatever type can be either repellent or attracting. It may invite or force people to stay contained in the territory or offer a chance to escape, to travel across it. On the one hand it helps to delimit structures and norms; on the other hand, it offers incentives to interactions which emanate from the different structures and norms on either side.

Border landscapes are thus characterised by both centrifugal and centripetal elements. In the case of state boundaries, the latter are represented by the control function (Plate 3.1), the former by specialisation in shops and other services as well as by the presence of border crossings. Parallel to these overt elements there are hidden ones such as differences in job opportunities and salaries or a common cultural heritage on both sides. The presence of such differences or common traits gives rise to a specific cultural landscape.

What of other boundaries, political or not? Reference has been made by a number of authors to religious boundaries (for example,

Plate 3.1 Crossing point on the Azro–Stabio road

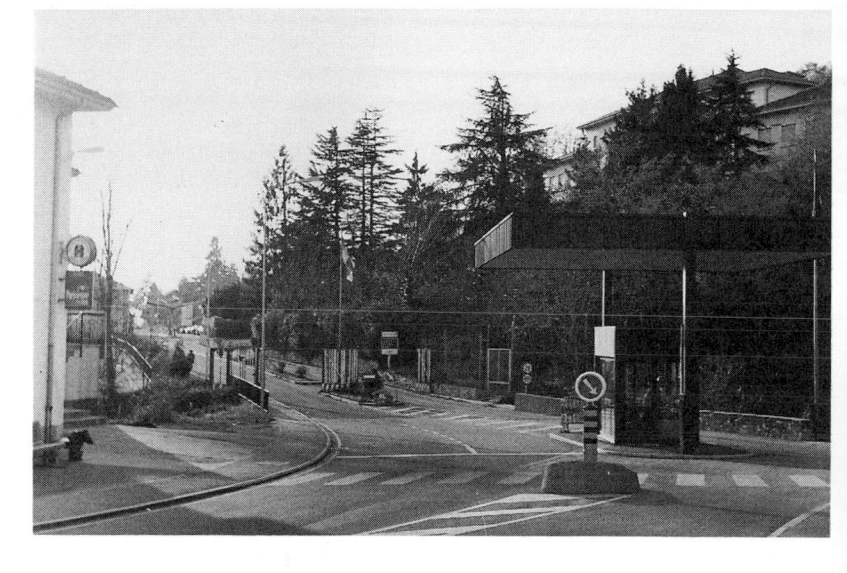

Hahn, 1950), to zones denoting a change in popular traditions (Weiss, 1947; Hager, 1982), or to linguistic boundaries (Winkler, 1946; Wasmer, 1984). Other limits or boundaries would lend themselves to similar studies, such as the limits of the hinterland of central places or the boundaries of planning or development regions. In these cases, obvious structures (customs, specialised shops and so on) are absent, and the border landscape must be viewed from a different angle – psychological rather than material aspects influence human action. However, a number of restrictions have to be recalled. Religious boundaries often coincide with political ones (religion as state ideology), and so may linguistic boundaries,[2] and the political element is not absent from the delimitation of planning regions.

More than in the case of political boundaries, border landscapes along non-political boundaries are characterised by transitional zones of varying width. Their study has therefore to use indicators rather than visible features – the physiognomy of the landscape may be almost the same, but human attitude and action will change gradually, and the spatial impact may be concealed rather than appear to be obvious.

THE BOUNDARY: STRUCTURES AND PROCESSES

As has been suggested above, boundaries both structure space and, at the same time, invite people to interact in space. This duality is one of the main characteristics of any boundary, particularly political ones. Any study of border landscapes has, therefore, to consider both functions as they are inextricably linked. The following questions may be asked:

- which elements of the (cultural) landscape are to be considered in the border region?
- which kind of regional disparities are of particular relevance in the border situation?
- how far are these disparities due to the border situation?
- to what degree do they give rise to spatial interaction?
- what kind of interaction can be observed, and to what extent are these relations due to the border situation?
- what are the attitudes of public actors towards disparities in border regions and interaction across the boundary?
- how does the population of the border region see and evaluate this region?
- is there something such as regional identity in the transborder region?
- what is the image of the border region held by the inland population (which cannot necessarily share potential benefits of the border situation)?
- how do these different attitudes vary in time and space?

The image of a border region will vary whether it is held by the population of this particular region or by people living in the interior of a country. Politicians, for their part, will have a different opinion whether they act on a regional or on a national level. The terms 'centre' and 'periphery' will then assume a different meaning. This may be expressed in the ways national and regional planning in a border area comes to be evaluated, and if transborder (international) regional planning (including development planning) is to be promoted or not. It is no accident that in Western Europe border regions tend to become central regions (regions of interaction and cooperation) whereas in centrally planned economies, the state promotes the core areas and keeps the peripheries as a sort of no-person's-land, acting as a physical separation from the neighbouring state. In the former case, the boundary becomes a focus of activity (dynamic region) while in the latter it is an area of passivity (static region).

There is, however, no reason why things should remain like this. The Yugoslav Republic of Slovenia offers an example of a region which has progressed from a centripetal to a more centrifugal attitude. This process can be illustrated by reference to the growth of industry. From 1951 to about 1978, it was essentially confined to traditional centres like Ljubljana, Kranj, Celje and Maribor (Klemencic, 1981: 225). Since then, one discovers that industrialisation has quickened its pace all along the international boundaries (with Italy, Austria and Hungary; Klemencic, 1988).

STRUCTURES AND PROCESSES: LAND USE IN THE BORDER ZONE

Preliminary remarks

The following observations summarise and discuss a number of findings from a research project carried out on the Swiss–Italian boundary (Leimgruber, 1987b). The region studied comprised the southern part of the Swiss canton of Ticino (Mendrisio district) and the north-western part of the Italian region of Lombardy (parts of the two provinces of Como and Varesse; Figure 3.2), an area characterised by easy communication across the border (there are twelve crossing points on a stretch of 26 kilometres of boundary, one every 2.2 kilometres). Situated on the periphery of the Milan conurbation, it accommodates the important railway and motorway transit routes from Germany across the Gotthard Pass to Italy. It is significant for an understanding of the canton of Ticino that the first section of this motorway to be opened was the one from Milan to Lugano (1966), that is, the link to Lombardy.[3] More than anything else this fact demonstrates the orientation of the canton towards the economic capital of Italy.

The research project did not consider macro-aspects of relations between Ticino and Italy. It was concerned, rather, with the border zone, placing it in a wider context. This micro-approach based itself on Sonnenfeld's (1972) model of nested environments, focuses on the problem of foreign workers in Switzerland and migration in Italy (indicators for the operational environment), mental maps of the border zone and sources of daily information (the perceptual environment), and transborder commuting and informal relations across the boundary (the behavioural environment). To discover spatial differentiation was not a specific aim of the study, rather it was taken for granted. However, it does illustrate a number of processes which have been occurring in recent decades.

Figure 3.2 The study area in its wider context

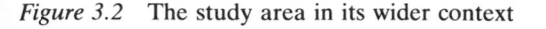

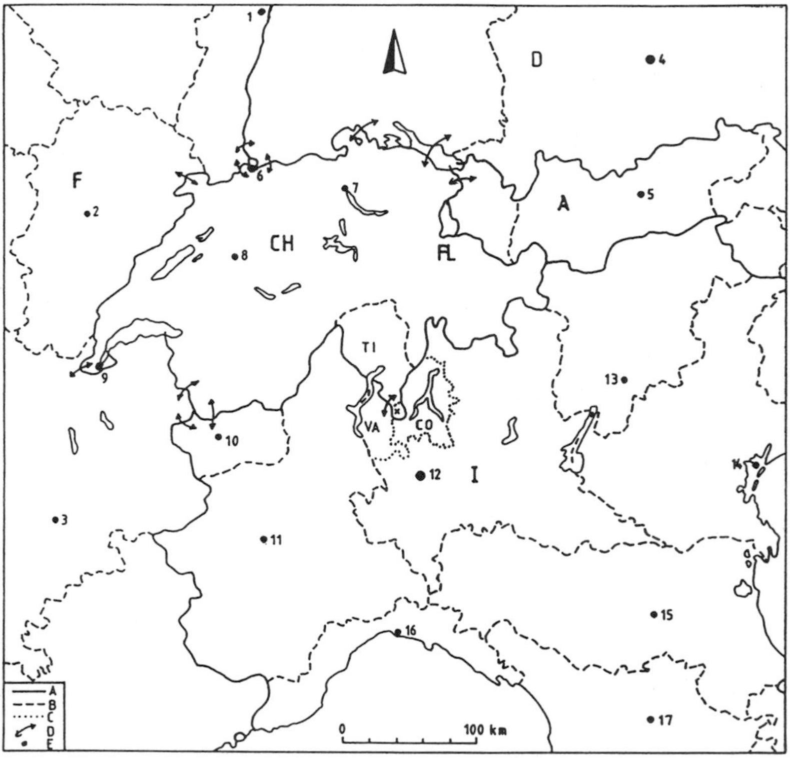

Notes: Solid lines = state boundaries; dashed lines = regional boundaries (Italy: *Regioni*; Germany and Austria: *Bundesländer*; France: *Départements*; Switzerland: *Cantons*) only as far as concerns the border area in question; dotted lines = sub regional boundaries in the study area (Italy: *Provincia*; Switzerland: *Distretto*). Arrows indicate regions of existing transborder co-operation (on Swiss border only). TI = Ticino; CO = Como; VA = Varese; x = district of Mendrisiotto. Major urban centres: 1 Strasbourg; 2 Besancon; 3 Grenoble; 4 Munich; 5 Innsbruck; 6 Basle; 7 Zurich; 8 Berne; 9 Geneva; 10 Aosta; 11 Turin; 12 Milan; 13 Trento; 14 Venice; 15 Bologna; 16 Genova; 17 Florence.

One of the most striking phenomena in the border context is the difference in land use. The spatial organisation in the border zone, as exemplified by the utilisation of the land, reflects differing attitudes to and perceptions of the environment. This in turn expresses itself in differing socio-economic processes which leave distinct imprints on the cultural landscape. The approach chosen is therefore structural, basing itself on the situation at one particular moment. The border

landscape is thus seen as a palimpsest – it contains elements of varying age and duration, modified by subsequent action and likely either to continue into the future in a modified form or to disappear at some stage. The structure always contains traces of past processes and often also indicators of future development. It is true, however, that the structure itself can tell us nothing about the processes themselves. They have to be investigated separately, a task which becomes more and more difficult the further back we have to investigate (or the further ahead we would like to look). In the case of border landscapes we are faced with the additional difficulty of the nationalist component: attitudes and perceptions are influenced by centripetal education, and in many perspectives the border zone is suspect. Rather than being a faithful part of the national territory it is often unduly influenced by ideas from 'beyond'. In addition, many decisions concerning spatial organisation are taken far away from the border area, but their impact may be decisive for the future of the region itself.

The example of the Swiss–Italian border zone: Structural differentiation through interlocking processes

The following example attempts to demonstrate how different spatial structures on either side of the boundary are not just the result of differing political systems but result from interlocking processes. By this, it is meant that the dynamics of the cultural landscape are influenced by what happens on either side of the boundary. Quite obviously, not every border region may claim a similar development model.[4] It is applicable only to areas characterised by intense transborder interaction. Regional identity may play a role, too, but it will not suffice.

In the course of the research project mentioned, land use in the transborder area along the Swiss–Italian boundary was mapped at the scale of 1:25,000. It was not possible to go into fine detail, especially since more than 25,000 hectares had to be covered. The resulting map depicts a mosaic of various land uses, dominated by agriculture, forests and residential areas (Table 3.1).

In the process of mapping (which was based on the Swiss map) it became apparent that the Italian side had undergone a considerable growth of settlements immediately south of the boundary, which had never been cartographically documented.[5] Nowadays, there is a continuous agglomeration stretching from Lake Lugano to the towns and villages south of Como as well as to the urban area of Varese

Table 3.1 Land use in the Swiss–Italian transborder region, 1981

Type of land use	hectares	%
Forests, natural vegetation	7,779	30.3
Agriculture	8,828	34.4
Abandoned	249	1.0
Water	200	0.8
Residential	5,985	23.4
Public buildings, commercial	200	0.8
Industry	1,346	5.2
Communication routes	697	2.7
Parks and open space	348	1.4
Total	25,632	100.0

Figure 3.3 Built-up areas in the Ticino–Lombardy border zone, 1981

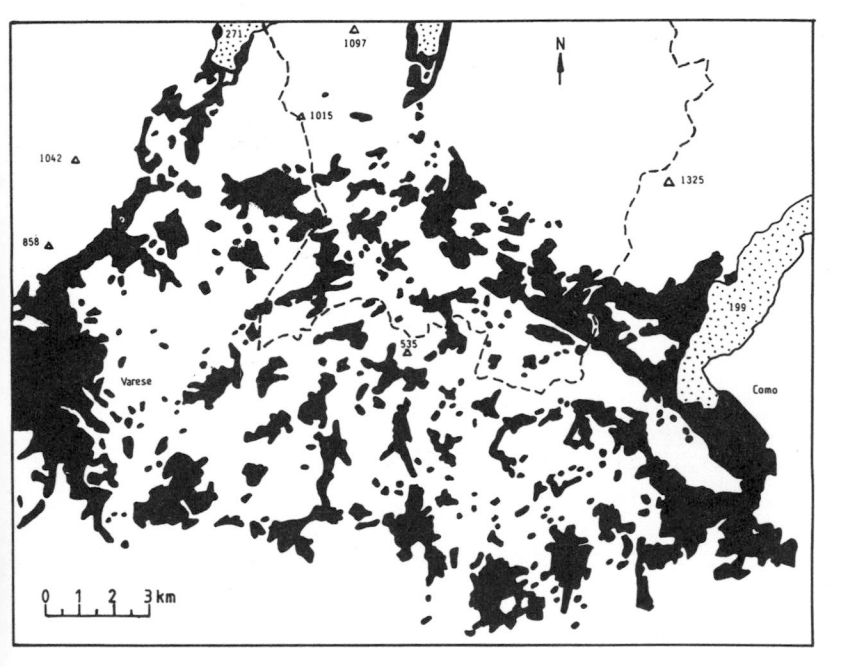

(Figure 3.3). This transborder agglomeration is, in turn, linked to the Milan conurbation, the core of which lies some 50 kilometres south of the border. This statement calls for some explanation, that is, for an investigation into the various processes at work. Two can be suggested here, although they do not stand alone. The first is

Figure 3.4 Simplified land-use map of part of the Ticino–Lombardy border area, 1981

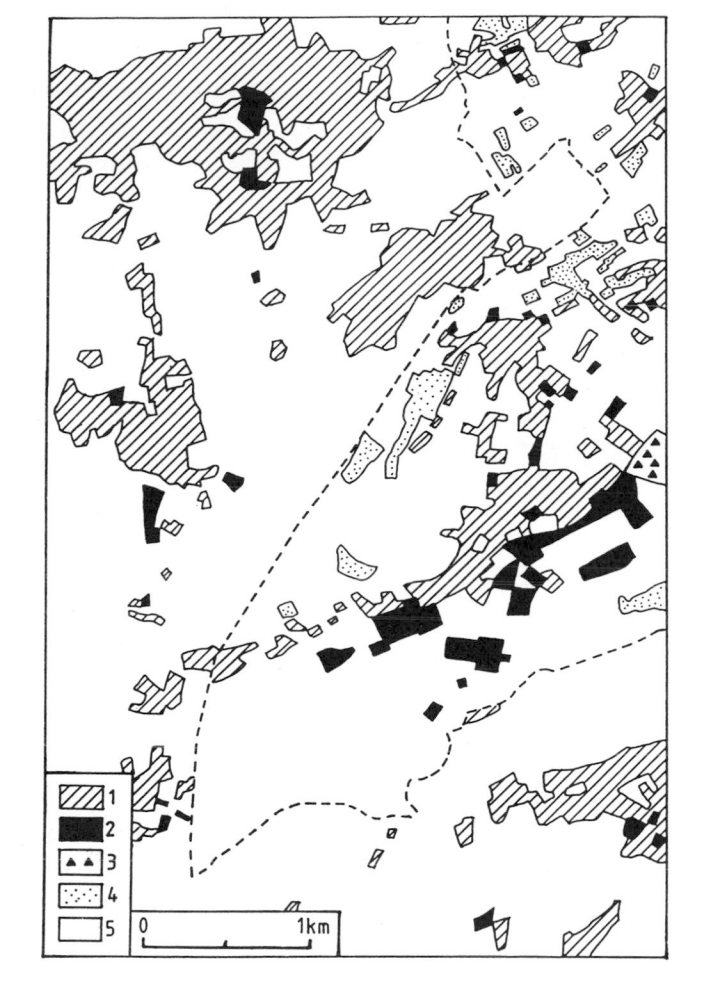

Notes: 1 Residential areas. 2 Industry. 3 Storage areas. 4 Vineyards. 5 All other uses.

intra-national migration in Italy, with the north (Lombardy and Piemont) as the most popular destinations for the destitute populations in the regions of the Mezzogiorno. This migration movement has resulted in a considerable growth of settlements, although it was for the most part the local people who built themselves new houses, while the immigrants took over the old housing stock in the village

centres. The expansion of the settlement area was thus paralleled by renovation or at least upkeep of the old nuclei. At this point, the second factor has to be introduced – the economic boom in both Italy and Switzerland. It is here that the socio-economic processes in these two countries interconnect. As will be explained below, industrialisation in the Ticino acted as an incentive for Italians in the border region to commute into Switzerland where salaries were generally higher and inflation was over many years lower than in their own country. Thus they earned enough money in relatively little time to be able to construct new houses or to renovate old buildings.

The process of industrialisation has left its imprint on the land-use pattern. Looking at the limited land resources available on the Swiss side, one notices that competition for the various uses is high. The map (Figure 3.4) gives but a scant idea of how much space industry requires. As everywhere, the areas most suitable for industry are also highly suited to agriculture. The high demand for industrial land cannot be explained by an industrial tradition. Contrary to neighbouring Lombardy, the canton of Ticino had little industry before the late nineteenth century. Its growth since the late 1870s and in particular after the Second World War is due to two distinct processes – the opening of the Gotthard railway in 1882 and the economic boom in Switzerland after the Second World War.

The construction of the Gotthard railway line (1872–82) acted as a first incentive to industrialisation because it linked the canton to the rest of Switzerland (Schneiderfranken, 1936). The effect, however, was largely offset by the supplementary tax (mountain tax) levied by the railway company on goods transported on this line and abolished only in 1926. Ticino industry thus found itself in an unfavourable situation compared to the rest of Swiss industry. Transportation costs rendered its products too expensive for the Swiss market. Foreign markets, on the other hand, were almost impossible to tap since other Swiss industries had already done so.

After the Second World War, Switzerland went through a remarkable economic boom which resulted in a considerable demand for labour. As a consequence, hundreds of thousands of Italian workers immigrated into the country[6] in the 1950s and 1960s. The political reaction (Johnston and White, 1977; Johnston, 1980) induced the federal government to adopt a number of restrictions as to the number of foreign workers that could be employed by individual firms. In 1966, however, border commuters were exempted from such restrictions. This measure rendered border regions attractive locations for labour-intensive industries (such as clothing, machines

Plate 3.2   Industrial zone of Stabio village

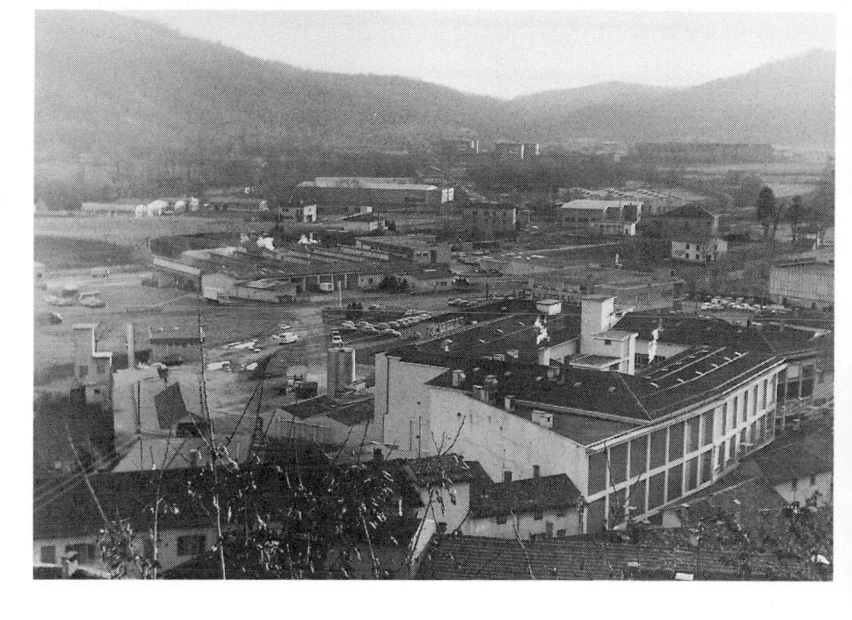

and watch-making). Foreign labourers were free to enter Switzerland as daily commuters, and as their wage expectations were below those of Swiss personnel, they found ready employment. Thus, the southern part of the canton of Ticino went through a phase of relatively heavy investment, and the number of industrial plants grew rapidly within a short time (67 new plants in the whole canton between 1966 and 1970, of which 29 were in the Mendrisio district alone) (Plate 3.2).

The Italian side suffered from this process in two ways. It saw its labour force cross the border to work in the Ticino at better salaries, depriving the native industry of workers. In addition, the border zone became an attractive residential area for immigrants from the Mezzogiorno (often via Milan or other centres) who were looking for work in Switzerland but could not get permission to enter the country except as transborder commuters. The villages along the boundary thus lived through a period of both immigration and emigration. Most of these immigrants did not work for a long time in Switzerland but carried their savings back home or tried to find work elsewhere in the Milan conurbation. This intense population movement as well as the total increase in population and the presence of a culturally

foreign population[7] led to financial problems (cost of infrastructure) and to cultural tensions (chiefly expressed by graffiti). Thus the same process (Swiss policy towards foreign workers) had quite different effects on the two sides of the boundary. The map (Figure 3.4) contains one further element of the cultural landscape which once more reflects different attitudes. It can be noted that vineyards are characteristic of the Swiss part of the area, whereas they are completely lacking on the Italian side. There is no objective reason why this should be so, natural conditions being equal on either side of the boundary. The only explanation possible is that of human evaluation, which concerns agriculture as a whole.

A more detailed survey reveals that the intensity of agriculture differs markedly between the two border areas. The land on the Ticino side is one of the relatively few areas in Switzerland where farming, horticulture and viticulture can be carried out under favourable topographic and climatic conditions. Thus there is great interest in keeping as much of the area as possible under cultivation (which is difficult given the intense land-use competition mentioned above). On the Italian side, however, things look different. What the Swiss would regard as good and suitable land, the Italians consider as inferior to other agricultural areas on a national scale (such as the fertile plain of the River Po). Viticulture in this area has suffered a severe blow from cheap (and often better) wine imported from other areas of Italy. The local wines could not compete with those from the centre and the south. Political unification in the nineteenth century has created one single market, and land use has adapted to it. The Ticino wine, on the other hand, competes successfully with other Swiss red wines, and it is protected from excessive foreign competition by duties and import restrictions.

Conclusions

The border landscape under study reveals a highly intricate pattern of processes at work on various levels or scales (Figure 3.5). What may look like a merely regional phenomenon becomes part of a national or even international network of socio-economic, cultural and political processes. Decisions taken in national capitals (political or economic) shape the spatial organisation of inland and border areas, as has been shown by the example of border commuters and industrial development and by the evolution of viticulture. In the case of the Ticino–Lombardy transborder region, this can be illustrated by yet another example – the development of the main transit route

Figure 3.5   Basic elements of the operational environment

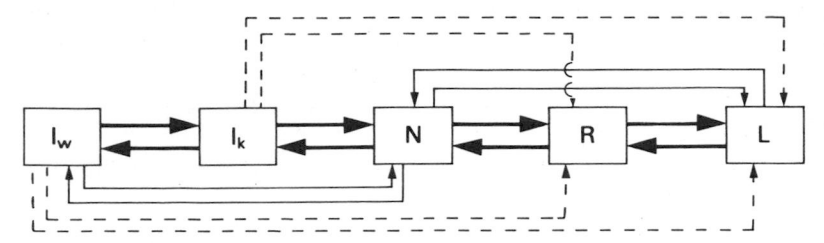

Notes: Thick arrows = strong direct influence; thin arrows = reduced direct influence; dashed arrows = weak direct influence. I_w = international elements, worldwide scale; I_k = international elements, continental scale; N = national elements; R = regional elements; L = local elements

from Italy to Central Europe. When Milan succeeded in becoming the chief railway junction between Italy and Central Europe, and the Swiss government opted for the longest possible railway transit line on Swiss territory, the line had to pass through Lugano–Chiasso in order to reach Milan. As a consequence, Chiasso became an international railway station with many forwarding agencies settling in the town. Former plans, however, had considered a direct link from Genoa to the Gotthard along Lake Maggiore, bypassing Milan. This line is now of local importance only, and the large international railway station which was built at Luino (on Lake Maggiore) seems an anachronism nowadays. However, the increase in transportation within Europe may well necessitate a revival of this single-track line, which could serve as a relief to the congested railway network around Milan.

TRANSBORDER INTERACTION: IMAGE AND REALITY

Following the spatial differentiation sketched above, one could imagine that the contrast between Ticino (the regions where there are jobs and relatively high salaries) and the Lombardian border zone (where there is a surplus of labour and salaries are low) would create tensions or at least indifference in people's attitudes towards their neighbours in the other country. The asymmetry in economic relations could then be repeated in other fields of human interaction. This hypothesis cannot be confirmed, however, and the reality is more complex. Our investigation has shown, for example, that the image people have of each other is strongly symmetrical.[8] There is almost perfect cultural homogeneity, in spite of minor differences in

Figure 3.6 Semantic profiles: auto- and hetero-images of people in the three agglomerations of Mendriso–Chiasso (M–C), Como (CO) and Varese (VA).

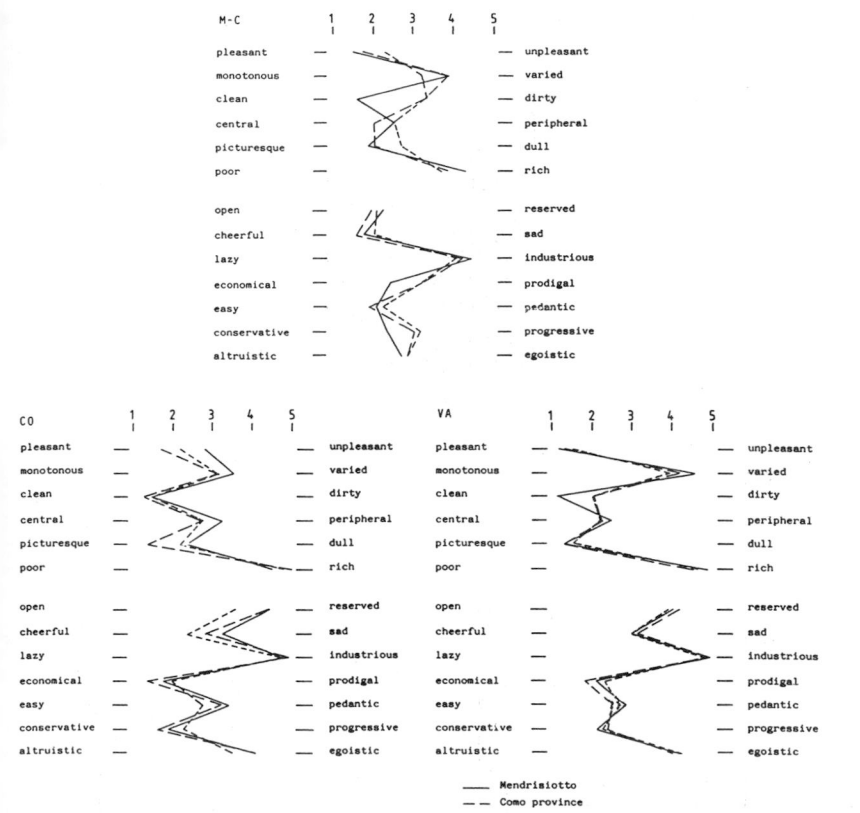

Note: The top profile refers to the region, the bottom one to the population.

the semantic profiles (Figure 3.6). The following characteristics are worth noting.

First, Mendrisiotto people judge their home region to be very clean as compared with their Italian neighbour areas, a judgement shared by the Varese respondents, but not by the Como ones. Second, the Mendrisiotto population consider themselves to be greater money-savers than their Italian neighbours, a judgement not shared by those in reverse. All three groups agree that they and their neighbours are very industrious. Such a positive image favours transborder inter-action limited not only to border commuters but encompassing also

Figure 3.7   Goods purchased across the border by inhabitants of the border agglomerations of Mendrisso–Chiasso (A), Como (B) and Varese (C)

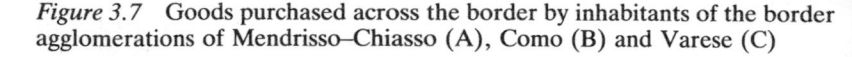

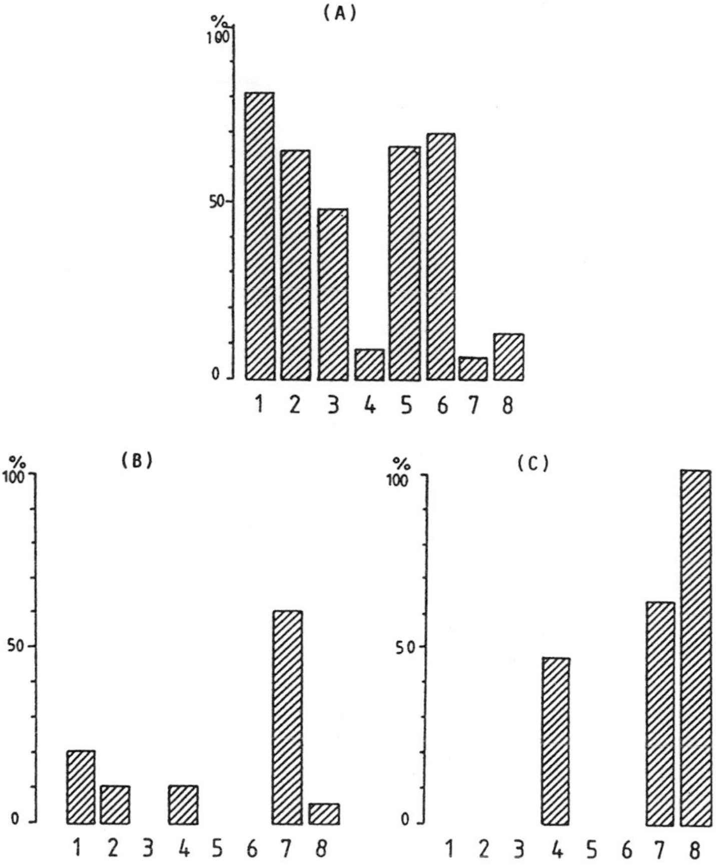

Notes: 1 Food in general. 2 Fruit, vegetables. 3 Beverages. 4 Cigarettes tobacco. 5 Papers, books. 6 Clothing, shoes. 7 Petrol. 8 Others.

informal contacts (even if our investigations have yielded poor results in this respect, due either to the absence of contacts, to errors in the sample or to a certain timidity of the persons interviewed).

Among the interactions, respondents emphasised shopping trips across the border. The places mentioned were usually situated just across the boundary, although Lugano and Milan did turn up as well. In spite of the short distances involved, the rhythm was generally irregular rather than regular, and daily–weekly shopping trips

prevailed with the Mendrisiotto respondents only. The survey also gave some insight into the contents of the shopping basket (Figure 3.7). Whereas Mendrisiotto residents purchase almost anything for sale across the border, Lombardy customers focus on certain goods which are usually much cheaper in Ticino (such as petrol, cigarettes, cigarette lighters and so on), mainly because they are not subject to such high taxes as in Italy. Apart from obvious economic reasons, personal preferences stand out clearly when people are motivated to buy abroad because of better service or greater choice. These two arguments turn up regularly both with Mendrisiotto and with Lombardy respondents. Shopping trips across the border are therefore not only a result of differences in price but also of non-measurable human factors.

CONCLUSION: THE BORDER LANDSCAPE

The boundary zone is an area where different attitudes and values meet and intermingle and where national identity is least questioned. As such, the border is not a line of separation but a zone of contact. The Swiss–Italian example has shown this by means of land use and its underlying processes; further themes (such as mental maps, information flows or personal transborder contacts) could be added. They all reveal one basic problem – the Ticino section of the transborder region has an identity problem which stems from its situation as a minority in a double sense – politically it belongs to Switzerland, yet culturally it belongs to Italy. Thus while its political allegiance is directed northwards, the demand for cultural and economic contacts is directed southwards. The Italians, in the same transborder region, do not have this problem. They belong to the Milan conurbation, and this large city is their economic, cultural and political focus (capital of the Lombardy region). Thus there is a certain asymmetry in this transborder region which is not obvious to the casual observer but which appears quite clearly once the processes behind the patterns are recognised.

Reflecting on the border landscape concept on the basis of this case study, it becomes clear that mere contrasts are not sufficient to define a transborder region. Including spatial interaction, we may arrive at a spatial definition, whereby the extent of the border region can be determined. However, such limits can be of an operational value only since it is impossible to find an objective threshold value to delimit a border zone from the non-border zone. Therefore, jurisdictional delimitations deliberately choose metric distances, although they

tend to become outdated as a consequence of the growth of private transport. Border landscapes must rather be defined using the criterion of boundary dominance. It is true that this cannot be easily quantified either, but since we are concerned with human categories, such quantification is in any case subjective. It is quite obvious that the boundary is a dominant factor in the location of industry, when 50 per cent and more of the labour employed live on the other side of the border. But where is the lower threshold? Is it 5 per cent, 10 per cent or 30 per cent? And what about other, non-visible factors (information, shopping, friends and relations ...)? There is no way out of the dilemma that the border landscape can be determined only vaguely, but that it is still a very significant type of landscape.

We have been concerned with an area on an international boundary, thus putting the problem of border landscape into a political context. However, this may be too narrow a framework within which to look at border regions. Politics has to do with social organisation and is therefore part of society but also carries the imprint of respective cultural backgrounds. Thus boundaries as human constructs have to be viewed from a human geographic viewpoint. Taking this broad outlook, we can integrate the various types of boundaries, limits and frontiers into border studies in general, forming part of cultural geography.

NOTES

1 This point is discussed by Racek (1983: 28). By way of an example he asks about the location of the boundary between a forest and a meadow. As a line the boundary cannot belong to either the forest or the meadow, thus it shrinks to something which has no extent and which, consequently, cannot exist in space. However, the boundary must exist, else there can be no objects in space.
2 In reality one must not speak of linguistic boundary lines but rather of border zones (Leimgruber, 1987a).
3 The motorway link to the rest of Switzerland was not completed until 1986, when the last section in the Ticino was finished. The Gotthard motorway tunnel, however, was opened in 1980.
4 It is possible to distinguish three types of border regions: 1. Transborder regions on 'open' boundaries with strong interaction (for example, Ticino, Geneva, Basle).
2. Border regions on 'open' boundaries with little or no interaction (for example, Sweden–Norway; compare Lunden, 1981).
3. Peripheral regions on 'closed' boundaries (e.g. Albania–Greece) These three types are by no means static but can change over time. Neeedless to say, our example is of the first type.
5 It is not possible to quantify the expansion of settlement, as we lack maps

which are precisely dated. We estimate, however, that since the Second World War the built-up areas have grown by about 300–400 per cent.

6 Italians were but the beginning of the immigration wave; they were followed by Spaniards, later on by Yugoslavs and Turks.

7 Traditionally, there is quite a difference between the Italians from the north and those from the south as a consequence of their different history (long-standing external dependence in the south versus independent states in the north).

8 This is in contrast to the results of a similar inquiry conducted in the Basle region, where differences were relatively strong and had remained so for about fifteen years (Leimgruber, 1981).

REFERENCES

Hager, A. (1982) 'Die "Brünig-Napf-Reuss-Linie" von Richard Weiss und die Verteilung der Rinderrassen in der Schweiz', *Schweizer Volkskunde*, Vol. 72, pp. 36–41.

Hahn, H. (1950) 'Der Einfluss der Konfessionen auf die Bevölkerungs – und Sozialgeographie des Hunsrück', *Bonner geographische Abhandlungen*, Vol. 4.

Hard, G. (1982) 'Landschaft', in *Metzlers Handbuch für den Geographieunterricht* (Stuttgart: Metzler) pp. 160–71.

Johnston, R. J. (1980) 'Xenophobia and referenda. An example of the explanatory use of ecological regression', *L'Espace géographique*, Vol. 1, pp. 73–80.

Johnston, R. J. and White, P. E. (1977) 'Reactions to foreign workers in Switzerland: an essay on electoral geography', *Tijdschrift voor Economische en Sociale Geographie*, Vol. 68, pp. 341–54.

Klemencic, V. (1981) 'Die Kulturlandschaft im nordwestlichen Grenzgebiet Jugoslawiens (SR Slowenien)', *Regio Basiliensis*, Vol. 22, pp. 217–31.

—— (1988) 'State border and border areas as a new geographical phenomenon in Slovenia', paper presented to the international symposium on 'Effet frontiere dans les Alpes', St-Vincent d'Aoste (Italy), 24 to 26 October 1988.

Leimgruber, W. (1981) 'Political boundaries as a factor in regional integration: examples from Basle and Ticino', *Regio Basiliensis*, Vol. 22, pp. 192–201.

—— (1987a) 'Zur Problematik der Sprachgrenze', UKPIK, *Cahiers de l'Institut de Géographie de Fribourg*, Vol. 5, pp. 109–17.

—— (1987b) *Il confine e la gente. Interrelazioni spaziali, sociali e politiche fra la Lombardia e il Canton Ticino*. (Collana dell'Istituto di Scienze Geografiche dell'Universita di Parma 7, Varese: Lativa).

Lunden, T. (1981) 'Proximity, equality and difference: the evolution of the Norwegian-Swedish boundary landscape', *Regio Basiliensis*, Vol. 22, pp. 128–39.

Moles, A. A. and Rohmer, E. (1972) *Psychologie de l'Espace* (Paris: PUF).

Racek, A. (1983) *Philosophie der Grenze. Ein Entwurf* (Wein: Herder).

Raffestin, C. (1981) 'Les notions de limite et de frontiere et la territorialité', *Regio Basiliensis*, Vol. 22, pp. 119–27.

Sack, R. D. (1986) *Human Territoriality. Its Theory and History.* (Cambridge: UP).

Schneiderfranken, I. (1936) 'Die Industrien im Kanton Tessin', Doctoral Thesis, Basle University, Munchen.

Sonnenfeld, J. (1972) 'Geography, perception, and the behavioural environment', in P. W. English, and R. C. Mayfield (eds) *Man, Space, and Environment*, (New York: OUP), pp. 244–51.

Wasmer, K. (1984) 'Landwirtschaft an der Sprachgrenze', *Basler Beiträge zur Geographie*, No. 30.

Weiss, R. (1947) 'Die Brünig-Napf-Reuss-Linie als Kulturgrenze zwischen Ost-und Westschweiz auf volkskundlichen Karten', *Geographica Helvetica*, Vol. 2, pp. 153–75.

Winkler, E. (1946) *Kulturlandschaft an schweizerischen Sprach-grenzen* (Kultur-und staatswissenschaftliche Schriften ETH, Nr. 53. Zürich).

4 Some developing and current problems of the eastern border landscape of the Federal Republic of Germany: The Bavarian example

Ulrich Ante

EDITOR'S NOTE

This chapter was submitted by the author prior to the changes between November 1989 and October 1990, during which the two Germanies were reunited and the East–West divide has functionally disappeared. The chapter has been retained as the editors feel that the methodological approach used by the author adds a unique dimension to the study of borderlands.

INTRODUCTION

This chapter will attempt to combine regional occurrences at the local level of the border region of the Federal Republic of Germany (FRG) with different levels of the hierarchical superordinate scale – the level of the state (Bundesland), the federal state of West

Figure 4.1 The scale hierarchy: The case of a border zone

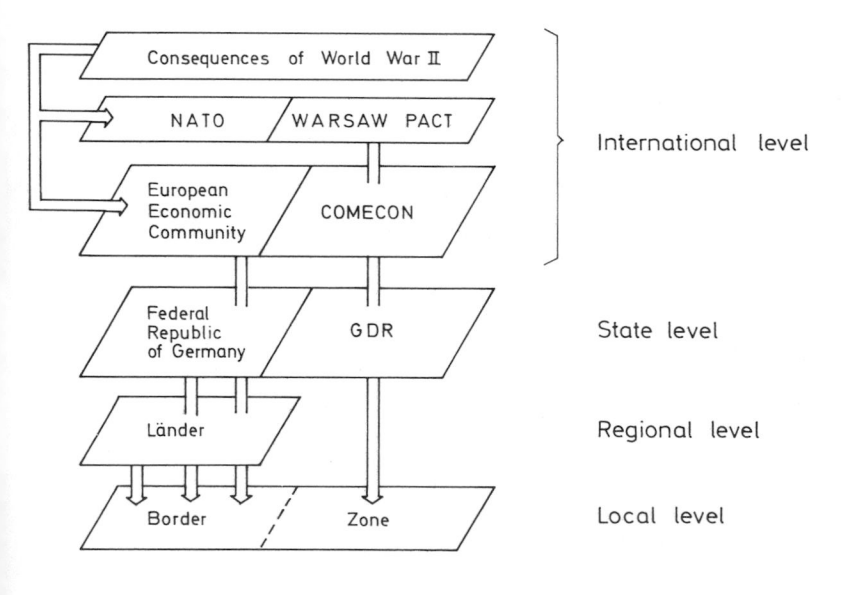

Plate 4.1   Border installations at Mödlareuth

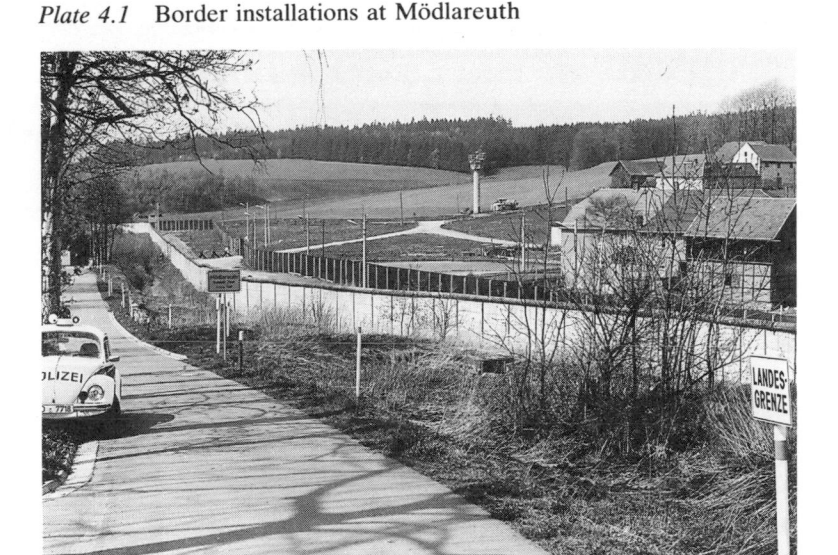

Source: Bayer. Grenzpolizei Hofls

Germany and the international level (Figure 4.1). The aim is to make clear that the spatial aspect in political geography is not only one of horizontal patterns and interactions. If the idea of the geographical continuum is to be of real value, then the vertical connections of different perspectives at each level should not be forgotten.

Typologically, the border between East and West Germany is extremely interesting because former provincial and territorial borders used for administrative purposes within the German Reich have become an external boundary (Plate 4.1). Moreover, typical for this border is its extraordinarily impenetrable character. Even though some changes have recently taken place, the character of division and friction remains, since this border not only divides Germany but is, at the same time, an ideological frontier between different political and social systems.

THE POLITICAL-HISTORICAL DEVELOPMENT OF THE BORDER

One result of the Second World War was the division of the German Reich into three parts by two borders. Up to the present, in a formal sense, they can be seen as imposed because they are not the results of a peace treaty. Moreover, these demarcation lines are in contrast to

those boundaries fixed within Europe after the First World War. One border is the so-called Oder-Neisse line. Today, it forms the boundary between Poland and East Germany–the German Democratic Republic (GDR). Poland was compensated with an area of approximately 114,500 square kilometres of German territory for the loss of its own eastern territories to the Soviet Union. The GDR, prompted by the Soviet Union, recognised the Oder-Neisse line in the 1950s. However, it was not until 1970 that an agreement was reached on its inviolability between the German Federal Republic and Poland. This boundary, however, will not be discussed here in further detail.

The second border divides the rest of Germany into the territory of the Federal Republic (including West Berlin) of 248,329 square kilometres and the area of the GDR (including East Berlin about 107,576 square kilometres). It should be stated here, that both borders are recognised by interstate agreements, even if not in the sense of international law. Being divided into four occupation zones by the Second World War allies, post-War Germany emerged with an inter-German border which originated as an administrative boundary between the Anglo-American and Soviet occupation zones. It was therefore defined and demarcated using existing regional and provincial government boundaries, even if simplified in a few cases of exclaves to make administration easier. However, this line did not take into consideration any economic and human inter-connections, and disregarded land tenure and communication patterns.

However, in the same manner as the western parts of Germany, its eastern part became integrated into the economic, political and social systems of each occupying power, and the demarcation line changed to an increasingly more closed military and political system border. This is all the more remarkable because, by 1948, the borders between the western occupation zones had been abolished. Most of all, the continuous flow of refugees, which increased when socialism and collectivism had been decided on as a way of life within the Soviet occupation zone, prompted the Soviet administration to introduce restrictive measures. In 1952 the demarcation line was closed. Since then, a border regime has been in effect. Its impact has been considerable because of the extremely elaborate fortification systems along the border (Plate 4.2). In addition to staggered installations, there is a 500-metre-wide strip parallel to the border, in which no restaurant, bar or other public meeting point is allowed. A 5-kilometre-wide zone was declared as a closed area, and people who live there have a special stamp in their identity card. Combined with fortifying this border is the interruption of existing communication

Plate 4.2   The Berlin Wall erected by the GDR in 1961

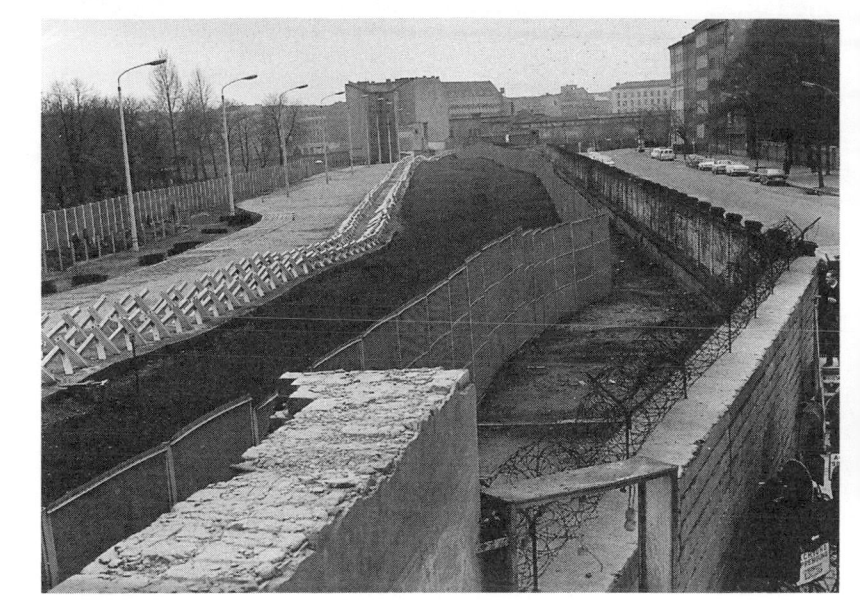

Source: Presse- und Informationsamt der Bundesregierung, Bonn

lines. Except for six railway lines, four transit roads, two inland waterways, one telephone and one teleprinter connection, all traffic and communication lines were closed.

THE POLITICAL SITUATION OF THE BORDERLAND IN 1989

Over the four decades of this borderland only limited cooperation was achieved. By a system of treaties based on the so-called 'Grundlagenvertrag' (basic treaty), a step-by-step easing occurred to some extent. In 1989 there were, on the national scale, trading connections. By these, the GDR was favoured by the Federal Government's idea of it not being regarded as a foreign country in so far as it had access to the European Community. Gradually, the formerly interrupted communication lines had been increased to around 800 cables and, since the 1970s, there had been definite improvements in traffic and visiting opportunities. From these, the GDR had received some financial advantage by way of road tolls, forced currency exchanges, and so on. The inhabitants of the border region were, by 1989, also allowed to visit the border region on the other side for up to a total of

20 days per year. There were, on the whole, some advances, but it was in no way an open border. Specifically, the inhabitants of the GDR did not have the same possibilities for crossing the border as their western counterparts. Unemployed persons were allowed to visit the Federal Republic for four weeks, while other people could go to the West only if urgent family problems required their presence there.

These improvements, however modest, were welcomed, but they did not eliminate the dividing character of this border. It was, after all, the interface between ideologically opposed parts of the world, and the insurmountable physical barriers on the eastern side were conspicuous landmarks. In contrast, on the western side there were only the usual boundary posts. Behind these, however were the contrasting ideas of the Federal Republic of Germany and the GDR about this border. The Federal Republic regarded the border only as a boundary between federal states and was endeavouring to change the border into an open one in order to create improvements for the inhabitants of the GDR. For the GDR, on the other hand, the border remained an instrument of separation and it continued to demand recognition of it in the international sense.

THE ECONOMIC-GEOGRAPHICAL SITUATION BEFORE 1945

The old territorial boundaries, which followed the German–German border, have had no importance for economic life since the foundation of the German Customs Union (Deutscher Zollverein) in 1834. Industrialisation in Germany, starting in the mid-nineteenth century with its traffic connections and economic interrelations, was independent of these boundaries and they became just an administrative instrument for organising the country. In opposition to Pounds' statement (1963), there was no basic contrast in a political, social or economic sense, but intensive interrelations existed between the eastern and western parts of Germany.

This is not only true on a general, nationwide level, but it can also be demonstrated on a smaller scale – for example, in the case of Upper Franconia, a part of Bavaria (see, for example Hofmann, 1982: 48ff.). In this north Bavarian region, the industries were not orientated to the economic region of Nürnberg, which had a more developed transportation network, but to the industrial region of Leipzig in the north. Upper Franconia was on the southern fringe of that slowly expanding region (Figure 4.2). Both areas were connected

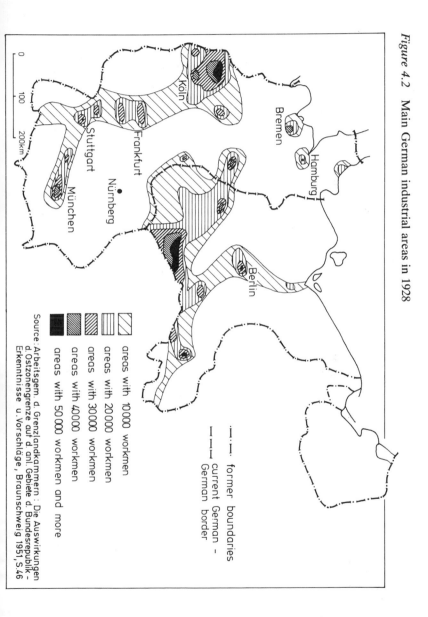

Figure 4.2 Main German industrial areas in 1928

former boundaries

current German – German border

areas with 10000 workmen

areas with 20000 workmen

areas with 30000 workmen

areas with 40000 workmen

areas with 50000 workmen and more

Source: Arbeitsgem. d. Grenzlandkammern : Die Auswirkungen d. Ostzonengrenze auf d. anl. Gebiete d. Bundesrepublik - Erkenntnisse u. Vorschläge, Braunschweig 1951, S.46

Köln

Frankfurt

Stuttgart

München

Nürnberg

Berlin

Bremen

Hamburg

0   100   200km

by flows of raw materials and semi-finished products as well as the market for industrial and consumer goods. Traffic connections to the German seaports or to the Ruhr district from the north Bavarian region passed through what was later to become the GDR. Insofar as it is worthwhile to draw a contrast between the more industrial and the more agrarian-oriented parts of the border region, the consequences of the German–German border after 1945 are significant. In general, the central locations lost the eastern part of their market areas. Agrarian-based interrelations such as access to the fields beyond the border or to market facilities were also interrupted. However, the demarcation was most disruptive for industrial spatial organisation, especially for connections between the core and the fringe of the same industrial region. In other words, if structural problems within the western border region after the demarcation of the German–German border are analysed, then demarcation tells only half the truth. Traditionally negative factors operating within the region must also be considered. Some parts of the current border region had already been on the periphery in an economic sense before 1945, while other parts became so only after 1945.

THE SITUATION AFTER 1945

The regional problems within the Federal Republic of Germany are not only influenced by contrasting natural preconditions, resources, distances to or the inaccessibility of market areas, but they are also caused by social-economic conditions creating regional differences in prosperity and by the political-geographical changes since 1945. Consequently, the border between the German countries divided what had, in previous times, been different, well-integrated regions. Thus, the communes of the eastern border area of the Federal Republic became a problem region, as noted above. A formal political region was created when the Federal Republic decided to define a strip 40 kilometres wide, generally known as the 'Zonenrandgebiet'.

Second, the federal system became the new political organisation structure of the western republic. The new Länder (federal states) – with the exception of Bavaria – were created out of the former territories. In this situation, it was important at the outset to form new identities and to build up the social market economy. As a result, and also because regional planning was generally identified with nazism and communism, they occupied a weak position within the federal and state administration.

Figure 4.3   The impact of the German–German border on spatial interaction patterns

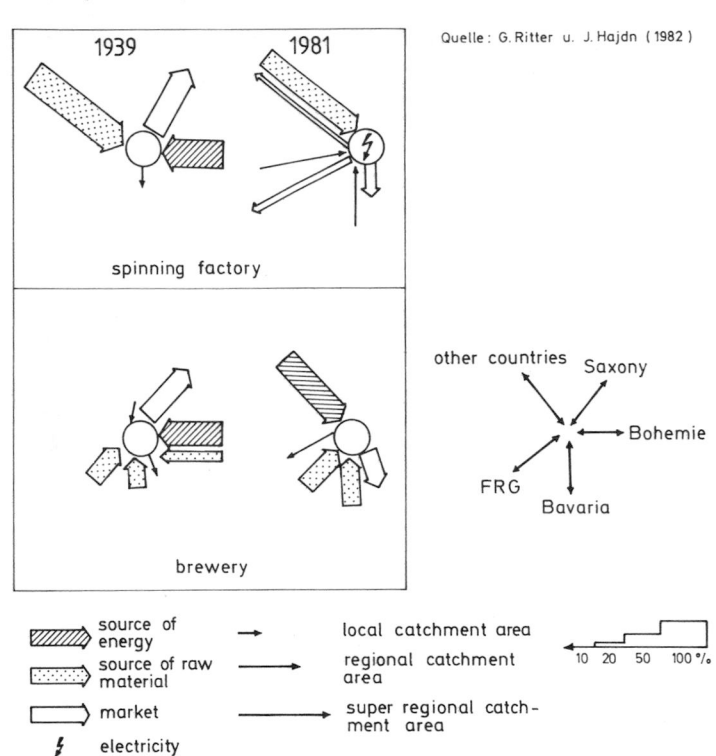

Examples of spatial interactions of manufactures in Hof

Quelle : G.Ritter u. J.Hajdn (1982)

Third, the influence of the international level is not restricted to the ideological division of Europe but also has direct consequences alongside the German–German border. Thus the eastern region became not only peripheral to the internal market but also to the European one.

For the north Bavarian part of the Zonenrandgebiet, the consequences of the closed border can be summarised as follows (Figure 4.3). The economic interrelations of this area were strongly oriented to the north and an efficient traffic network had been built up in that direction. As a result of the division of central Germany, the peripherality of the border landscape was emphasised by the lack of efficient traffic routes to the south and west. The distance to the

northern part of the Federal Republic was thus considerably increased (Table 4.1).

Table 4.1 Transport of industrial goods from northern Bavaria (for example Coburg) before and after partition in 1945

Distances from Coburg to	Before partition (km)	After partition (km)	Difference (kms)	(%)
Kassel	224	351	+127	57
Brunswick	351	495	+144	41
Hannover	350	484	+134	38

Source: Arbeitsgemeinschaft der Grenzlandkammern, 1951: 14.

After 1945, an essential task was to change the traffic system from its north–south to an east–west orientation. This has not yet been completely solved (a motorway is still under construction). In contrast, the railway administration continues to close railway lines for economic reasons. As a result, peripheral areas and the Zonenrandgebiet are strongly affected.

THE DYNAMICS OF INDUSTRIAL SITES WITHIN THE BORDER LANDSCAPE

The following periods of industrial activity within the north Bavarian border region since partition can be identified. First, between 1945 and 1949, refugees from Pommerania, Sudetenland, Silesia and Czechoslovakia founded enterprises within this area. Second, from 1948 to 1949, factories were shifted from the central parts of Thuringia and from Saxony. This reflected the beginning of political and economic change in the Soviet occupation zone. On the whole, the first and second periods strengthened the industrial facilities in the western part of the border landscape. Third, in 1952, enterprises were shifted from the immediate eastern border region to the western part. This was the result of the GDR hermetically sealing the border.

Thus, by 1952, the spatial effects of the new border can be summed up as follows. First, location within the traffic system worsened. Second, nearby raw material sites beyond the border were lost. Raw materials now had to come from more distant markets, even from abroad. The same situation applied to the energy sector. Coal, especially brown coal, was formerly obtained from central Germany, Czechoslovakia and Silesia. In summary, the mean distance of

assembling raw materials was increased from 190 kilometres to 330 kilometres, and that of fuel, from 175 kilometres to 470 kilometres. Finally, markets also had to be reorganised. This applied to the local market dissected by the border as well as to the long-distance markets within the Federal Republic. These economies suffered from additional competition as a result of an increase in transportation costs. The export industries had, in addition, lost their eastern markets. Overseas transport was burdened with higher transportation costs because of the increased distance to the sea port of Bremen, for example, by about one-third.

In the fourth period, factories were shifted out of the border region. As a consequence of the changed economic situation, attempts were made to locate first-step branch factories near raw material locations or markets. Even if the factory at first remained in the border region, the new branch factories weakened the economic potential of that region. So, after 1952, the economic peripherality of the border landscape began to be emphasised. Twenty years later, during the boom phase of the early 1970s, the peripheral character of this region was again recognisable, but then under different conditions. As manpower became scarce in the economic core areas, branch factories were relocated in the peripheral regions, including the Zonenrandgebiet, based upon the available workforce and local sites. These branches were, however, at the most, marginal ones with high rates of failure and mobility when poor site conditions prevailed (Hofmann, 1982).

In summary, the situation of the industrial sector has not been significantly improved in the border landscape since 1945, and at the most it has been stabilised. This finding appears to contradict the view projected by the intensive financial promotion on behalf of this region.

THE PROBLEM OF OFFICIAL SUBSIDIES

Because of its extreme situation and the difficulties deriving from its nature as a borderland, this region has depended on governmental subsidies since the 1950s. In the first period of so-called emergency measures (Notstandsmassnahmen) officials and interest groups at the local level urged Länder governments to help. Being short of money, the Länder turned to the federal government for aid. These subsidies to the region were motivated by political as well as economic ideals. Reunification of both Germanies and the idea of being a show case of the Western World were the political arguments. The above situation

resulted in economic arguments stemming from two socio-economic developmental processes. Within the urban agglomerations and economic core areas, economic prosperity started rather intensely because of the market economic policy and the boom caused by the Korean War. People, most of all former refugees, moved to these areas. Out of this emerged a number of pertinent expressions, such as 'the suffering border region', 'general', 'political', 'economic', 'social' or 'cultural' conditions of distress, which today sound exaggerated, but at that time seemed very real. However, these characterisations, constantly repeated, might well have caused a confusing psychological reaction, as we will see later.

In the second period, the border landscape and its financial aid were tied up in a legal system of spatial planning. The economic forces of the market did not support the expected regional pattern, but widened regional disparities. Spatial activities guided by the federal government were reinforced. However, given the very strong mistrust of planning activities, only in 1965 were the planning laws and programmes set in place. At the same time, more and more parts of the Republic were favoured by financial aid. Even though aid for the Zonenrandgebiet and Berlin had a high political ranking, they lost relative priority as a result of the new regional and sectoral subsidies (Table 4.2). In a regional political sense today, the landscape of the German–German border has become only one peripheral area among others. Its special political importance is always repeated and accentuated, but hopes for steady progress in industrialisation faded and are unlikely to be realised in the near future. This situation is based on the present trends in industrial location. Despite current financial aid, the economic situation of the border region compared with the rest of the Federal Republic has not improved, and in some parts it has become worse. The peculiar site conditions arising out of the border character prevent economic development in such a way that these special subsidies are only able to maintain the present level of reciprocal relationships between this region and the rest of the country. This is reflected in the regional structure of population (Table 4.3).

Certainly, the border is now partially open, but this relates more to human relationships within the border region rather than to improvements of its economic base. Since 1983, subsidies to the Zonenrandgebiet have once more become politically more important. Their motivation and aims deriving from the special political situation of Germany should be questioned.The instruments of regional policy traditionally fixed upon an expanding economy seem more and more

Table 4.2 Financial aid from the joint task 'Regional Economic Development'

Common projects		New jobs		Jobs to be retained		Federal Republic	
						New jobs (%)	Jobs to be retained (%)
No.	Years	N	Z	N	Z		
5	76–79	30,400	430,800	21,700	177,700	29.0	41.9
6	77–80	30,400	430,800	21,700	177,700	29.0	40.2
7	78–81	18,300	301,040	13,000	167,000	27.5	50.4
8	79–82	18,300	301,040	13,000	173,000	27.5	48.6
9	80–83	18,300	305,000	13,000	164,000	28.2	47.6
10	81–84	20,200	270,900	19,500	209,200	40.5	63.5
11	82–85	20,200	270,400	19,500	214,300	40.5	63.7
12	83–86	14,700	249,500	19,900	218,300	39.5	66.8
13	84–87	17,000	251,500	27,600	266,000	40.7	69.8

Source: Eberstein, 1971.
Note: Financial aid is of two sorts – emergency measures (N) and Federal subsidies through Zonenrandgebiet (Z).

Table 4.3 Regional structure of population

	Federal Republic	Rural areas	Bavaria	Upper Franconia West	East	Upper Palatia	Main-Rhon
Population state 1981 (in '000)	61,712.7	9,644.4	10,959.2	552.9	497.3	479.3	412.4
1981 = 100							
1985	99.7	99.9	100.4	99.9	97.7	98.0	98.5
1990	99.5	99.9	100.7	99.7	94.9	95.8	96.9
2000	98.0	99.1	99.7	98.0	89.0	91.2	93.2
Population < 20 years as a %							
1981	25.8	28.5	26.0	27.8	25.0	29.3	28.6
1985	23.2	25.7	23.5	25.2	22.8	26.6	25.8
1990	21.0	23.1	21.4	22.9	20.5	24.0	23.3
2000	21.5	23.2	21.4	22.7	20.1	23.8	23.1
Population > 60 years as a %							
1981	19.6	19.7	19.4	19.5	22.8	18.9	19.6
1985	20.2	20.4	20.0	20.2	23.5	20.1	20.8
1990	20.8	21.2	20.6	21.0	24.3	21.5	22.1
2000	23.2	23.7	23.2	23.6	26.5	24.5	25.0

Source: Stat. Jb. Bundesrepublik Deutschland, 1987.

unable to solve problems. The extensive growth in new installations or the expansion of manufacturing has found alternative sites in central regions. Furthermore, the economy is changing its structure more to the service sector and it will find its most preferable locations combined with agglomeration effects, human capital, technology access, information and communication systems within core regions, and not on the periphery.

In addition to regional policy, there are sectoral policies other than subsidies which have spatial effects. As a result of these, regional aid in general, and aid for the Zonenrandgebiet in particular, is weakened, and that means the locational situation will be worsened. The political idea of 'equivalent living conditions', questioned in recent times because of changed scientific views and instruments, seems to have been reduced to lip-service by politicians.

At present, the Commission of the European Community (EC) aims at limiting existing national applications of regional policy. New indicators and criteria of the EC are expected to abolish nearly all subsidised areas within the Federal Republic. Although it is emphasised that only those economic disadvantages caused by the division are to be counterbalanced (Article 92 (2) Treaty on the foundation of European Economic Community of 25 March 1957), the subsidies to the Zonenrandgebiet have repeatedly been under fire. This, however, is in contrast to the opinion of the federal government, which holds that subsidies to the border region are not part of regional policy but of German policy. In this context, the EC's proposal is not very favourable as subsidies could not only be granted to regions suffering structural underdevelopment but also to old industrial areas adapting to changed economic conditions. The consequences of this policy are the development of subsidised regions to the detriment of peripheral areas.

PUBLIC UTILITIES AS INSTRUMENTS FOR REGIONAL POLICY

On the whole, the current industrial pattern of locations within the Federal Republic seems to be fixed, even if the old industrial areas are taken into account. Therefore, since the 1970s, ideas were formulated not to concentrate upon industrial working places on behalf of regional planning instruments but upon those in the service sector. Private services located mostly in the large cities could hardly be expected to move their sites to central places in peripheral regions, so it was obvious that public services needed to be focused on. The

regional-political quality of state-run working places rests most of all on their reliable character as a means of improving the living and social structure of a region.

In principle, the types of decisions on sites chosen by administrators can be grouped according to the establishment of new units, mergers, relocation, expansion and closure. One general premise can be stated at the outset. Because of the federal organisation of West Germany, a relatively even distribution of institutions and state-run working places can be observed. This is most obvious to those who are familiar with the situation of a centralised country. Moreover, we have to differentiate between utilities of the federal government, of the Länder and of the communes, which have a relatively strong position in the political system of the Federal Republic. Avowedly, public utilities have not been employed intensively as a planning instrument because of the difficulties in coordinating the different political-administrative levels. The same is true for coordinating sectoral and regional planning. To this extent, public utilities seem to be a relatively inflexible instrument from which no surprises for improvements in peripheral regions are to be expected. This is supported by the fact that by reason of economic development, any significant expansion in the number of working places is unrealistic (Table 4.4). Thus, a shifting of public services from core to periphery is conceivable.

On the whole, however, the political-administrative institutions within West Germany are relatively well dispersed, at least in comparison with many other European countries. The same is not

Table 4.4 Development of jobs in public services within the Federal Republic of Germany

	1968	1976	1986
Full-time jobs in direct public services	2,767,134	3,328,631	3,567,000
Sectoral split:			
Federal government	1,068,277	1,116,880	1,037,000
of which,			
Federal authorities	276,560	295,364	1,037,000
Federal railways	400,246	404,929	285,000
Federal postal service	391,471	416,587	440,200
Federal states (Länder)	1,074,185	1,436,279	1,559,900
Communes	624,672	775,472	920,244

Source: Stat. Jahrbuch der Bundesrepublik Deutschland, different years.

true, however, for Bavaria and other Länder, in any case not for their own administrations. The shift to decentralisation as well as deconcentration of existing institutions out of the centres seems to be very difficult. There is a tendency to assign new tasks to existing authorities mostly in central locations, thus expanding them. In the periphery, staff tend to be cut mostly by rationalisation (Bundesbauministerium, 1983). The concentration (that is, the combining of existing installations) is often made in favour of the centres again, and their decentralisation is extremely difficult if the new site is planned in peripheral regions. Not every public utility seems to be equally suitable for relocation.The differences between those with local/regional and those with supra-regional tasks require different relocational procedures. Authorities of the first group serve population, where the tendency for an even locational pattern is favoured. Locations of supra-regional institutions, however, are not based on population, hence in these cases serving regional and employment aspects can be realised.

THE EXAMPLE OF THE BAVARIAN ADMINISTRATION COLLEGE IN HOF (UPPER FRANCONIA)

One of the very few examples of successful relocation of public utilities into the Bavarian part of the Zonenrandgebiet – and, therefore, one which is always praised by politicians – was the Bavarian Administration College for the General Administration of the Interior. After seven years of planning and construction, it was officially opened in 1985 for about 900 students. At that time, the college had been in operation for about three years. However, soon after the educational work was started, it became clear that there were insufficient applications for teaching positions (officials of state or community authorities or judges may be teachers at this college). In order to obtain a clearer picture of the reasons for the lack of motivation for such teaching positions, a survey of persons suitable to be teachers in Hof was conducted in 1982 by agreement with but not initiated by the Bavarian Administration of the Interior. A total of 169 usable questionnaires were returned. Answers to the following questions are of particular interest for the purposes of the present discussion:

1 What about the principal willingness to move?
2 What influences the decision to move to a new living place?
3 What conceptions are there of the region of Upper Franconia, where the College is located?

The major reason for readiness to relocate

In general, one of the more important factors seems to be related to career. The majority of interviewees – nearly 50 per cent – felt that a change of residence was not necessary. A further 21 per cent even believed that moving is not important to their professional progress. At the same time, a plurality (43 per cent) evaluated a temporary change to another sphere of activity as favourable, while only 22 per cent saw disadvantages in it (35 per cent said 'without influence' and 'I don't know').

Being strongly content with their present professional activity (81 per cent) a sectoral change would be positively viewed, but a regional one was not viewed as suitable. This basic feeling can be influenced on the one hand by younger age and resulting low wages, but on the other hand, ownership of private property hinders regional mobility. The tendency to stay put increases with the passage of time and the longer they live in one place, the less willing they are to move. Persons living for more than five years at the same place no longer have a high opinion of professional development resulting from regional mobility.

A critical factor influencing readiness for moving seems to be the employment of one's spouse. In the present sample, 39 per cent declared employed spouses (12 per cent 'no comment', 49 per cent unemployed). However, 60 per cent of the spouses are themselves employed in the public sector, so there is an additional obstacle to moving. In the opinion of the people questioned, nonetheless, the employment of their spouses is not believed to be a great obstacle. However, 40 per cent suggested a lack of readiness to move (the corresponding values for unemployed spouses are 56 per cent and 31 per cent respectively). One fine point of differentiation is worthy of note. Regardless of whether his/her spouse is employed, the readiness to move increases when it is voluntary – that is, relocation is the result of a personal decision and is not dictated by an outside authority. The inner readiness for moving is essentially determined by personal and familiar factors which quickly take effect when choosing a place to live.

Since the interviewees were informed of the background of the questioning, the special factor of employment as a teacher might have had an influence. It does not necessarily conform to the expected conception of professionalism. However, 55 per cent totally believed themselves to be suited to teaching, even if only 12 per cent considered that they possess pedagogical talent. Some 21 per cent

believed teaching is interesting and full of variety. Reasons for their unsuitability as teachers were that they did not like teaching (16 per cent) and differences to the current job (14 per cent). Only 11 per cent believed they had no pedagogical talent.

Factors influencing the decision to move to another area

To obtain some idea of those aspects influencing the decision of a potential migrant, people were asked to evaluate a range of possible factors. The data demonstrate their relative importance (Table 4.5).

Table 4.5 North-east Upper Franconia compared to the current place of residence

	Evaluation for	
	Mobilisation in general *(medians)*	*NE Upper Franconia compared to current place of residence (medians)*
Natural surroundings	1.48	2.68
Professional situation of spouses	1.87	2.79
Children's education	1.19	2.73
Shopping facilities for higher rank goods	2.51	2.73
Living conditions	1.12	2.66
Contacts with relatives and friends	1.82	3.98

Note: Medians are based upon survey responses based on a five point semantic differential scale: 1 (very positive agreement) through 3 (neutral) to 5 (very negative agreement).
Source: The author.

In addition, these characteristics were correlated with the size of the place of residence, age and family status of the interviewees. Irrespective of age, the natural environment rates 'very important' or 'important' to a great extent. However, for people living in agglomerations (cities with more than 100,000 inhabitants) this factor is somewhat less important. Their own professional situation is estimated by 98 per cent to be 'very important' or 'important'. Age and the size of the current living place does not appear to influence this factor. However, status of family and employment of spouses play a role. Of those 59 per cent to whom this characteristic is 'very important', 85 per cent are married and 9 per cent unmarried (with 6

per cent no response). Of those 38 per cent to whom this factor is 'important', 77 per cent are married and 17 per cent unmarried (again, with 6 per cent no response). If both spouses are employed, the professional situation is perceived as being less important (53 per cent) than in the one-employed case (67 per cent).

Facilities for child education are 'most important' for 70 per cent, irrespective of variables such as age, number of children and size of place of residence. In contrast, there is 'no importance' attached to shopping facilities for higher rank goods. For about 65 per cent of the interviewed persons, this is not a criterion when evaluating a new living place. Furthermore, people living in large cities tend to regard it as 'less important' (83 per cent), but 83 per cent of people in small towns think it an important factor.

Forty-four per cent of the interviewees indicated living conditions as being very important, and for 40 per cent they are important. These values increase if there are children and decrease if there are none. For home-owners, living conditions are more important (57 per cent) than for tenants (31 per cent). Finally, there are the contacts with relatives and friends – 39 per cent indicate these to be important, 30 per cent as unimportant. However, 77 per cent of persons under 30 years old estimate such contacts as important. With increasing age, this value decreases to 31 per cent.

The mental image of Upper Franconia

Finally, by selecting five indices a general idea of the conception of Upper Franconia will be attempted. To concentrate more precisely upon the situation of the location of Hof and its inherent border character, the questionnaire stated north-east Upper Franconia instead of just Upper Franconia.

(i) A locational evaluation of Hof First, the town of Hof was to be evaluated. For this, the interviewed persons had to form an opinion of several Bavarian towns from their own knowledge and conceptions using a five-point scale running from 'very good' (=1) to 'bad' (=5). The medians demonstrate clearly the different evaluations of these towns. Hof, the site of the Administration College, received the worst ranking from 45 per cent of those interviewed. This reflects not only the extreme border situation. Bayreuth, a former residence town famous for its musical events, has a rather similar location to Hof and has a better ranking. Hof, like Schweinfurt, is dominated by (textile) industries, so that the supposed lack of attraction has an additional negative influence.

(ii) Comparison between north-east Upper Franconia and the current residential location As Table 4.5 clearly demonstrates, according to our criteria north-east Upper Franconia is, without exception, estimated more negatively than the environment of the present residential area. Thus, even a neutral ranking has to be seen as a 'success' for the border landscape. Remarkable for evaluating this region is the fact that the same criteria asking for its importance in general for migration are more positive. This is clearly demonstrated by both medians on shopping facilities which are relatively similar. The large discrepancy of the criteria 'possible contacts with relatives and friends' accentuates the disfavour in which the location of Upper Franconia is held.

(iii) Comparison between north-east Upper Franconia and other Bavarian regions Compared with other Bavarian regions the result for the north-eastern Franconian border region, on the whole, is not surprising (Table 4.6). Compared with the capital Munich and its surrounding area, with the foreland of the Alps and with the Allgäu, Upper Franconia comes off worse. This reflects current conceptions of these regions with regard to culture, free-time activities and the like. These unfavourable evaluations are independent of the residential locations of interviewed persons. However, up to one-third evaluate the border region as better than the related regions, especially Munich. This should not be seen as a significant demonstration for an emerging recognition of disadvantages in agglomerations. In relation to other Bavarian regions, including in several ways

Table 4.6 North-east Upper Franconia compared to other Bavarian regions

Region	Evaluation (in %)									Median
	Positive			Neutral			Negative			
	S	N	T	S	N	T	S	N	T	
Munich	32	34	33	17	13	15	51	53	52	3.09
Alps foreland	27	20	23	7	21	14	66	58	62	3.28
Allgäu	20	20	20	21	27	24	59	53	56	3.13
Frankische Sch	14	16	15	65	53	59	21	30	26	2.59
Rhön and forel	16	18	17	64	67	66	20	14	17	2.48
Bayerischer W	11	20	16	62	57	59	27	23	25	2.56
Niederbayern	19	22	20	48	56	52	33	22	28	2.54

S = People from southern Bavaria; N = people from northern Bavaria; T = total. For the meaning of positive, neutral and negative see the note on Table 4.5 on p. 79. The values have simply been converted into a percentage figure of the sample for each region on the scale. The heading of the last column is the median on the five point scale for each region.
Source: The author.

the comparable Rhön region, neutral values are dominant. However, in no case is Upper Franconia evaluated better than a comparable area.

(iv) The importance of distance   Calculating the travel time for the journey from Hof to Munich by car would give remarkable insight into the mental map of distance, thus demonstrating how familiar the interviewed persons are with spatial relations. It is not unrealistic to expect a normal travel time of about 2 hours 40 minutes by motorway for the roughly 280 kilometres distance in question. The responses are summarised in Table 4.7. Most of all, more than half the persons have very incorrect perceptions of travel time and distance. Thus the accessibility of north-east Upper Franconia (Hof), is evaluated more on ignorance than on fact. Indeed, persons living in northern Bavaria estimate accessibility rather better, but there is no fundamental difference between them and those living in southern Bavaria. The largest discrepancies of both groups are in the same 'time-groups'. Even if 82 per cent state that they had visited Upper Franconia before, this fact does not significantly alter the result.

Table 4.7 Calculation of travel time for the journey from Hof to Munich

| | | Values of travel time (%) | |
Time	Total	S	N
Up to 2 hours	8	11	6
2–2 hr 29 min	15	12	17
2 hr 30 min–3hr	28	26	30
More than 3hr	49	51	47
	100	100	100

S = People from southern Bavaria; N = people from northern Bavaria.
Source: The author.

(v) Conceptions of north-east Upper Franconia   Finally, the sample was confronted with thirteen statements about Upper Franconia, partially exaggerated.These statements were formulated with a negative viewpoint which would not be verifiable in reality. The interviewed persons were to evaluate from 'full agreement' to 'rejection' on a five-point scale. The data indicate that two groups can be differentiated – those mostly agreeing with the statements and those mostly disagreeing with them (Table 4.8).

It seems that people from northern and southern Bavaria evaluate the border region in almost the same way, but the rate of agreement

Table 4.8 Reactions to statements on the mental image of north-east Upper Franconia

Statements	Total sample Rejection/ acceptance	Median	Rejection/acceptance N. Bavaria	S. Bavaria
Statements mostly rejected				
1. Population slow to accept new ideas	48%	2.94	49%	47%
2. Region lacks proper leisure infrastructure	48%	2.91	48%	49%
3. Hardworking people without interests	52%	3.10	48%	56%
4. Old/badly fitted flats/ houses implies decay	46%	2.87	47%	44%
5. Lack of kindergardens and educational facs.	49%	2.92	52%	46%
6. Inadequate health services	44%	2.81	45%	42%
7. Border region culture and history uninteresting	69%	3.91	72%	66%
Statements Mostly Accepted				
8. Older pop./emigration of younger people	53%	1.90	60%	46%
9. Politicians think Munich region is isolated	64%	1.36	73%	54%
10. Nearby border is politically weak and negative	48%	2.14	50%	45%
11. Isolated situation in traffic network	63%	1.63	69%	56%
12. Low living costs and low wages	49%	2.06	52%	45%
Neutral				
13. Border region is not dynamic	36%/ 34%	2.47	45%/ 31%	27%/ 38%

Note: The percentage values have been calculated according to the system outlined in the notes to Table 4.5 on p. 79.
Source: The author.

of people living in the northern part of the country is between 4 per cent and 19 per cent higher than that of the south Bavarian people. This is true with two exceptions for agreement as well as disagreement. The statements accentuating north-east Upper Franconia as a political and traffic problem area have the strongest agreement,

which indicates the 'isolated' situation of this region. The negative statements about the population in this border region (nos 3 and 7) are clearly rejected, remarkably more intensely by people from southern Bavaria.

In a similar way, all statements are rejected which accentuate an unsatisfactory infrastructure. Both the factual space and structures and their evaluation conform. Only the statement about the border region lacking dynamism in an unspecified sense is an exception. It is neither clearly accepted nor rejected. People from north Bavaria agree with it in a higher rank (45 per cent) than those of south Bavaria (27 per cent) [rejection: north Bavaria 31 per cent; south Bavaria 38 per cent].

CONCLUSION

One general point should be emphasised. Today, the problems of the border region – without regard to industrial problems – are mainly problems of the region's mental image. Although many facts are seen correctly, they are evaluated negatively. The idea should not be dismissed out of hand that due notice should be taken of the complaints of politicians and others living and working in the border region who are working to strengthen the positive feelings of others living outside. It is no coincidence that of those 23 teachers starting education in Hof, 48 per cent were born in northern Bavaria, and 87 per cent had worked before in north Bavaria. This, I believe, is hardly surprising. In addition, it is also not surprising that today (summer 1988) in a staff consisting of 63 full-time positions, every fourth one is vacant. This is officially explained by the difficulties of recruitment.

ADDENDUM

Starting in October 1989, revolutionary events have led to rapid changes in the internal situation in the GDR and hence also in its relations with the FRG, with dramatic impact on the border region between the two neighbours. With the agreement announced in January 1990 easing circulation between the two Germanies, and following the currency union making the Deutsche mark the basic currency in the GDR in July 1990, it was possible to observe regional consequences on both sides of the border as the boundary reversed its function from being a closed border to an open one. The initial

borderland effects were economic in nature, but events have since entered a new dimension as the political border between the two Germanies was dissolved on 3 October 1990.

REFERENCES

Ante, U. (1981) 'Politische Geographie – Braunschweig', *Das Geographische Seminar*.
—— (1982) 'Der Beitrag der Politischen Geographie zur Untersuchung von Grenzräumen mit Beispielen aus Nordbayern', 18, *Deutscher Schulgeographentag Basel 1982*, Tagungsband, pp. 59–66.
Ders. (1983) 'Das historische Raumgefüge als Verständnisgrundlage des gegenwärtigen Regionalbewußtseins am Beispiel von Oberfranken', *Würzberger Geogr. Arbeiten*, Vol. 60, pp. 287–97.
Arbeitsgemeinschaft der Industrie – und Handelskammern des Zonenrandgebietes u.a. (Hrsg.) (1984) *Zentrale Fragen und Perspektiven der Zonenrandförderung*.
Bayerisches Staatsministerium f.Landesentwicklung und Umweltfragen (Hrsg.) (1984) *Erfahrungsbericht über Behördenverlagerung vorwiegend in europäischen Ländern, unter Berücksichtigung der für den Freistaat Bayern verwertbaren Ergebnisse* (München).
Bayerische Staatsregierung, *Grenzlandbericht*. – versch. Jahrg.
Boesler, K.-A. (1985) 'Das Zonenrandgebiet', *Geogr. Rundschau*, Vol. 37, pp. 380–4.
Bundesforschungsanstalt f. Landeskunde u. Raumordnung '(Hrsg.)' (1979) 'Themenheft Behördendezentralisation' *Informationen z. Raumentwicklung H 5*.
Bundesminister f. Raumordnung, Bauwesen u. Städtebau (Hrgs.) (1983) *Falldokumentation zur Standortproblematik bei neugegründeten und verlagerten Behörden* (Bonn).
Eberstein, H. H. (Hrsg.) (ab1971) *Handbuch der regionalen Wirtschaftsförderung* (Köln).
Hartke, St. (1985) '"Endogene" und "exogene" Entwicklungspotentiale, dargestellt für unterschiedliche Teilräume des Zonenrandgebietes', *Geogr. Rundschau*, Vol. 37, pp. 395–9.
Hofmann, A. (1982) 'Industrie in peripheren Grenzräumen, unter besonderer Berücksichtigung der industriellen Zweigbetriebe, dargestellt am Beispiel der Räume Coburg-Kronach und Cham.', *Würzburger Geogr. Arbeiten 55*
Mellor, R. E. H. (1978) *The Two Germanies: A Modern Geography* (London: Macmillan).
Pounds, N. J. G. (1963) *The Economic Pattern of Modern Germany* (London: Murray).
Ritter, G. and Hajdu, J. (1982) 'Die deutsch-deutsche Grenze', *Köln Geostudien 7*.
Voppel, G. (1985) 'Industrie im Zonenrandgebiet', *Geogr. Rundschau*, Vol. 37, pp. 385–94.

5 Geographic problems of frontier regions: The case of the Italo–Yugoslav border landscape

Vladimir Klemencic and Milan Bufon

Introduction

The present Italian–Yugoslav boundary runs through a region which underwent extensive transformation in the political-geographic delimitation of the border, profoundly affecting the contemporary development, the socio-economic transformation and the function of the region. The international political boundary, which used to run between Austria and Italy, was moved further to the east and, after the First World War, divided the new Yugoslavia from Italy, thus shaping a special border area which emphasised a military-strategic function. Italy only partially encouraged the economic development of this region, but took great pains to ethnically 'improve' it, which resulted in significant emigration of the nationally aware autochthonous Slovene and Croatian population into the neighbouring country and overseas, while the remaining non-Italian populace had to deal with strong pressure to assimilate.

After the Second World War the boundary between Italy and Yugoslavia was again moved to the west, thus causing extensive emigration of the population in the entire border area because it divided two countries with two different socio-political systems. It also caused additional conflicts insofar as it ran mostly over the Slovene ethnic area.

In the last two decades and in accordance with the European trend towards international cooperation, the functioning of the Italian–Yugoslav boundary has changed somewhat. For example, economic cooperation between border areas has been encouraged by many Italian–Yugoslav agreements which have also tended to enhance cooperation in the cultural, political and ecological fields, and in which the Slovene minority in Italy and the Italian minority in Yugoslavia are becoming more involved. In this way, a special type

of border landscape is being shaped around the Italian–Yugoslav political boundary. Both physiognomy and function of the region now straddle the political boundary and have joined both sides into an interdependent spatial unit. The border has thus ceased to be a geographic and strategic dividing line but has become a factor of regional connectivity.

BORDER DISPLACEMENT AS AN ELEMENT IN THE FORMATION OF THE 'INTER-BORDER' REGION

The international political boundary between Italy and Yugoslavia is undoubtedly one of those in Europe which has undergone the greatest changes over the past century in terms of demarcation, morphology and function. In modern times – that is, the period from 1900 to the present – we witnessed a characteristic shift of the old Austro-Italian border after the First World War far to the east, thus allotting the former Austrian regions of Gorizia (Gorica) and Trieste (Trst) as well as a portion of Dalmatia (Dalmacija) and, after 1924, also the city of Rijeka (Fiume), to Italy. Furthermore, at the northern end of this new border, dividing the kingdom of Italy and the newly-formed kingdom of Serbs, Croats and Slovenes (SHS), Tarvisio (Trbiz) with the valley of Kanalska dolina were annexed to Italy. Although at the time the principle of nationally 'pure' countries was predominant, it was not applied in this case. In addition, the new border disrupted the economic, communication and transportation balance inside the former Austrian regions of Carinthia (Korosko), Gorizia (Gorica), Trieste (Trst) and Carniola (Kranjsko). Due to the suppression of ethnic minorities and economic autarchy, the border region after the First World War was underdeveloped and of marginal importance.

Following the Second World War, several new demarcation proposals for dividing the republic of Italy and the socialist federal Yugoslavia were put forth at various international peace conferences (Figure 5.1). These proposals varied considerably in terms of territory, and at the same time represented various demarcation 'philosophies'. Territorially the most favourable for Yugoslavia was the Soviet proposal, which was in fact a version of the former Austro-Italian frontier based on ethnicity and functional relations. For Italy, the most advantageous was, of course, the Italian proposal, which re-established the 'classical' geographic and strategic demarcation in the sense of the so-called 'natural' boundaries.

It is surprising that the Yugoslav demarcation proposal was less

Figure 5.1   Boundary proposals and changes in the Italo–Yugoslav frontier region

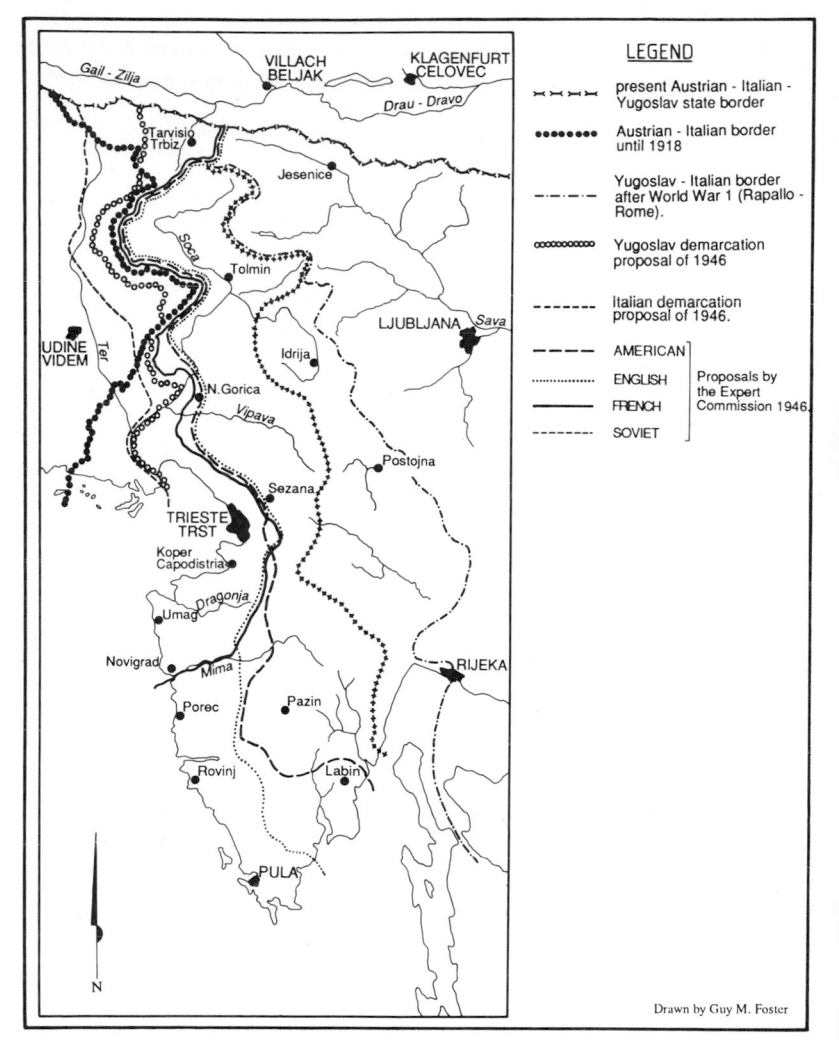

LEGEND

⊶⊷⊶⊷   present Austrian - Italian - Yugoslav state border

●●●●●●●   Austrian - Italian border until 1918

–··–··–   Yugoslav - Italian border after World War 1 (Rapallo - Rome).

∞∞∞∞∞∞   Yugoslav demarcation proposal of 1946

– – – –   Italian demarcation proposal of 1946.

– – – –   AMERICAN ⎤

············   ENGLISH ⎟ Proposals by the Expert Commission 1946.

———   FRENCH ⎟

– – – –   SOVIET ⎦

Drawn by Guy M. Foster

favourable than the Soviet one in terms of territorial size, since it was based on a 'pure' ethnic concept, with a single exception. The Yugoslav proposal included the larger nationally mixed cities of Trieste and Gorizia in Yugoslav territory.[1] In the end, the French

compromise proposal was accepted. In the north, it once again awarded the valley of Kanalska dolina with Tarvisio to Italy and from there followed the former Austro-Italian border to Gorizia. Problems arose along the southern stretch of the border where larger urban centres are located. The French proposal solved the problem by awarding both cities to Italy on the basis that the Italian nationality represented the majority of citizens in both cases. The principle of inseparability of the city with its hinterland, advocated at the beginning of the century by Lenin as well as Wilson, was thus abandoned, because the French proposal gave both cities only a minimal share of their historical or 'natural' hinterland, reducing it to a mere corridor enabling nothing but transportation and communication links with the mother state. The new boundary therefore completely destroyed the former organisation of the region, which gravitated towards the two respective centres of Trieste and Gorizia. The separation of both centres from their historic hinterlands was particularly felt among the Slovene national community for which these two cities played an important social role. It is precisely these inconsistencies between the 'gravitational' and ethnic demarcation concepts, if we ignore the international strategic and political factors which contributed to this decision, that have also contributed to the fact that the southern section of the new boundary remained for such a long time the scene of problems and conflicts. This situation was temporarily resolved at the international level by the formation of the Free Territory of Trieste, which was immediately divided into two parts: the Trieste part was administered by the Allied troops, and the Istrian part by the Yugoslav army. The issue was partly solved by the London Treaty of 1954, which granted Zone A with Trieste to Italy and Zone B with the Istrian coastal towns to Yugoslavia, with the recommendation that all outstanding questions be settled by the two concerned parties. The 'Trieste question' was thus removed from the international scene, and was not definitely resolved until 1975 when Italy and Yugoslavia signed the so-called Ozimo Accords, and opened the door for a new phase in the relations between the two states.

This history of conflict along the Italian–Yugoslav boundary has had innumerable socially and territorially significant consequences. In terms of culture, it created among the population of the entire region between the old Austro-Italian border and the post-First World War border between Italy and SHS a sense of a common historic and geographic affiliation and a common 'destiny', as well as strong inter-ethnic conflicts. The roots of these conflicts in this

'inter-border' strip of land go back even further, originating at the time of the nineteenth century national movements. However, after the formation of both neighbouring states, these conflicts acquired a suitable political base. Modifications of the boundary have also produced a number of social changes, which have markedly contributed to the reshaping of the former ethnic make-up of this typical 'inter-border' or frontier region.

The new demarcation and political system, set up after the First World War in Italy, forced thousands of non-Italians to emigrate, particularly the autochthonous Slovene population along the Italian frontiers. Emigration was mostly politically and economically motivated. Political emigration was mainly directed toward Yugoslavia and economic emigration towards South America. Slovene emigrants were replaced by civil servants of Italian extraction from the interior of the country, especially in the social services and education. Furthermore, a considerable decrease in minority population took place at this time due to prevailing assimilation policies. The most telling example of the changes in the ethnic make-up of the population in this frontier or 'inter-border' region is the valley of Kanalska dolina, where an autochthonous Slovene population had been living up to the mid-nineteenth century. At that time the relative size of the German population rapidly began to increase, especially due to assimilation and a tendency to create ethnically 'pure' frontier regions. The same factors were at work in this region, when, after the First World War it was annexed to Italy. After that time, the previously almost non-existent Italian population in this area became predominant, while the German population moved to their mother country, Austria.

Similar migrations were experienced by post-Second World War Istria after the signing of the London Treaty, when the majority of Italian inhabitants emigrated to Italy, namely to the Trieste area, for political or economic reasons. At the same time, a new wave of Italian and Slovene nationals emigrated from Trieste to Australia, so that the city did not experience any significant population growth. Gorizia presents a different case, since the loss of the centre of the region of Gorizia brought about the creation of a 'surrogate' regional heart on the Yugoslav side of the border. With its name of Nova Gorica, it drew attention to the continuity of the earlier regional situation.

All of these migration fluctuations,[2] which do not take into account the 'normal' migration from the peripheral areas to the urban centres, which itself was undoubtedly strongly encouraged by the new

and old demarcations, caused a series of changes in the social and ethnic structure of the frontier population. These changes, in turn, brought about changes in the physiognomy and function of the cultural landscape. For better or for worse, it also caused the integration and mixing of the population in the entire 'inter-border' strip, which has become, perhaps reluctantly, a region of linguistic multiculturalism and economic interdependence.

PHASES AND FORMS OF BORDER COOPERATION

The structure of the new Italian–Yugoslav boundary, especially its southern section as it runs through densely populated urban and nationally mixed territory, necessitated a special policy of economic frontier cooperation between the two neighbouring states. This is despite the fact that the two countries have remained for some time on the verge of latent or explicit political conflict owing to the different forms of relations at the international level, differential internal social and political organisation and conflicting territorial claims.[3] It is precisely this example of the Italian–Yugoslav border that demonstrates how a border does not represent merely a kind of abstract political dimension, but rather a functional means of a broader form of territorial coordination and organisation, particularly when these forms are traditionally consolidated. In our case, this was a concrete question of establishing international transportation links and maintaining ties between the two cities and their traditional hinterland.

In this spirit, the first post-War economic agreements of a trade and financial character were signed as early as 1947. Of special significance was the signing of the new economic accords in 1955, which not only provided for 'regular business', but also directed much attention to the aforementioned forms of communication links and economic cooperation. This type of agreement was afterwards renewed twice, and in 1967 an agreement swung the doors of trade between the two countries wide open. In addition to these agreements, the two countries also signed 200 various agreements on mutual cooperation, among which the most significant are the following: an agreement on fishing rights in the Adriatic signed in 1969 and subsequently amended and ratified; a technical cooperation agreement in 1956; a tourism agreement in 1967; agreement on joint delimitation on shale plates in 1967; agreement on scientific cooperation in 1966; a convention on social security in 1957; and agreement on technical and industrial cooperation from 1964. A number of

proposals for mutual cooperation are also contained in the Ozimo Accords from 1975 – a project on a unified road system; a project on an industrial tax-free zone on the border; water management along the border; a feasibility study on a navigable route from Trzic to Gorizia to Ljubljana; cooperation among the ports of the northern Adriatic; protection of the Adriatic against pollution; instigation of economic cooperation in the frontier region; and the honouring of school certificates issued by each state. Finally, the 1988 Italian–Yugoslav programme of development cooperation will certainly further boost international interaction and exchange along the border.

Direct cooperation along the border was already instigated by the signing of two important documents in 1955. The first document concerns trade between Trieste and its hinterland, while the other involves exchange activities between the other two near-border regions. These agreements are being updated and amended on a yearly basis. The same year, an agreement on near-border exchange, providing for special benefits for border crossing of inhabitants and goods of frontier regions, was signed in Udine (Videm). For this purpose, a substantial number of special, so-called 'near-border crossings' have been opened along the entire length of the border and not only in the vicinity of Trieste and Gorizia, as it had been initially planned. This was in fact the first agreement of its kind in Europe, ensuring total freedom of passage between two states with different social and political systems, while elsewhere this difference still presented a major obstacle to concrete international and near-border cooperation. This agreement is also being renewed on a yearly basis, and was supplemented and expanded in 1982.

Regional cooperation has been further enhanced with the decentralisation of power, which, on the Italian side, brought about the formation of the autonomous region of Friuli-Venezia Giulia (Furlanija Julijska krajina) in 1964, while on the Yugoslav side many international business deals were entrusted to Slovenia and its communities. The region of Friuli-Venezia Giulia soon established a number of concrete contacts with the neighbouring Yugoslav Republic of Slovenia. These contacts were institutionalised and developed into a broader Central European context with the foundation of a regional 'work community' of Alpe-Adria in 1978. Within this work community there are three particularly active committees, namely, the committees on ecology, economy and culture.[4] The near-border cooperation between Italy and Yugoslavia has been further enhanced in recent years by an internal policy which

Table 5.1 Yugoslav trade with Italy, 1960–81 (in $US '000*)

Year	Imports	Exports	Balance	Imports as % of exports
1960	74,770	95,150	−20,380	78.6
1961	70,343	132,717	−62,374	53.0
1962	96,340	104,593	−8,253	92.1
1963	158,330	112,956	+45,374	140.2
1964	131,936	174,472	−42,536	75.6
1965	144,248	137,536	+6,716	104.9
1966	173,048	168,488	+4,560	102.7
1967	225,080	228,032	−2,952	98.7
1968	176,528	268,624	−92,096	65.7
1969	229,641	319,647	−90,006	71.8
1970	254,589	378,000	−123,411	67.4
1971	226,059	396,294	−170,235	57.0
1972	308,059	400,000	−91,941	77.0
1973	466,235	530,706	−64,471	87.9
1974	428,712	890,630	−461,918	48.1
1975	371,890	868,877	−496,987	42.8
1976	596,000	760,438	−164,438	78.4
1977	664,000	1,029,425	−365,425	64.5
1978	531,014	826,630	−295,616	64.2
1979	716,081	1,145,678	−429,597	62.5
1980	833,114	1,116,740	−283,740	74.6
1981	1,011,941	1,290,916	−278,975	78.4

* Converted from dinars according to prevailing official exchange rates.
Source: Statistical Yearbooks of Yugoslavia for the appropriate years.

pays particular attention to the internationalisation of this frontier region, particularly in view of economic integration within the European Community (EC) in 1992. Hence, the Italian Parliament and the Regional Council of Friuli-Venezia Giulia have already initiated proposals to promote the development of peripheral regions and equip them for near-border and international cooperation.

Several indicators can be utilised to gauge the intensity of near-border contacts. The most elementary indicator is goods trade between Italy and Yugoslavia (Table 5.1). A chronological survey of this indicator clearly indicates the positive impact of the Ozimo Accords on the volume of exchange. Although international exchange is often dependent on conditions closer to the border, in this case the role of frontier conditions is extremely significant, since it has been demonstrated that they are an indispensable stimulator of exchange. Of an entirely local nature is 'compensation goods trade' between the neighbouring countries on the basis of the Trieste and Gorizia agreements (Table 5.2), in which all the near-border factors are

Table 5.2 Trends in frontier trade after the Trieste and Gorizia agreements (in billions of lira)

	Trieste			Gorizia			Total		
	Imports	Exports	Total	Imports	Exports	Total	Imports	Exports	Total
1973	4.9	8.1	13.0	1.5	1.6	3.1	6.4	9.7	16.1
1974	5.5	8.6	14.1	0.5	2.4	2.9	6.0	11.0	17.0
1975	9.2	9.4	18.6	2.8	2.9	5.7	12.0	12.3	24.3
1976	12.3	16.0	28.9	6.5	4.7	11.2	18.8	21.3	40.1
1977	19.6	12.3	31.9	9.2	5.1	14.3	28.8	17.4	46.2
1978	15.9	18.7	34.6	5.1	4.8	9.9	21.0	23.5	44.5
1979	29.6	28.7	58.3	12.6	7.7	20.3	42.2	36.4	78.6
1980	40.8	35.6	76.4	13.3	7.0	20.3	54.1	42.6	96.7
1981	68.0	63.1	131.1	29.9	25.8	55.7	97.9	88.9	186.9
1982	132.4	130.1	262.5	54.1	59.7	113.8	186.8	189.8	376.3
1983	249.4	251.7	501.1	116.0	95.3	211.3	365.4	347.0	712.4
1984	317.4	282.3	599.7	141.6	141.6	283.0	459.0	423.7	882.7
1985	231.6	264.1	495.7	106.0	123.3	229.3	337.6	387.4	725.0
1986	192.6	156.7	349.3	93.0	81.0	174.0	285.6	237.7	523.3
1987	332.8	307.2	640.0	143.4	121.2	264.6	476.2	428.4	904.6

Source: Servizio Commercio Estero del Commissariato del Governo nella Regione Friuli-Venezia Giulia and Banca d'Helia.

Table 5.3 Trends in border crossings between Italy and Yugoslavia by the frontier population according to region

	1984			1985		
	A	B	C	A	B	C
Trbiz	1,329	323	24.3	2,793	377	13.5
Cedad	556	408	73.4	784	569	72.6
Gorica	6,429	5,111	79.5	8,634	5,966	69.1
Trst	22,815	10,837	47.5	31,319	13,154	42.0

A = total crossings (in '000).
B = number of crossings by frontier population (in '000).
C = B as a percentage of A.

involved. The significance of the narrow border cooperation is clear, since these exchanges are not attaining a large portion of the total trade between the countries, but in recent years have been increasing rapidly in an absolute as well as a relative sense.

The intensity of near-border ties can also be measured by the number of border crossings and by the volume of border-crossing passenger transport. The latter can be further broken down into 'near-border' traffic and international traffic volume of persons

permanently residing in the near-border region and traffic volume of persons from the interior of both states (Table 5.3). Although in the latter case the across-the-border flow is intensive, it does not have a decisive impact upon the border region, even though it does influence the structure of the transportation network and services. Near-border traffic, on the other hand, is inextricably tied to the frontier region, since it starts and ends within this region. It essentially supports the functional integration of both frontier zones into a unified frontier region, insofar as it enables the fulfilment of essential needs of the frontier population such as supplies and leisure-time activities. In the narrow border area, the social and territorial organisation is adapted to these two facts, especially in the vicinity of larger urban centres.

In several research projects, data on the number of bilateral across-the-border contacts have been analysed to measure near-border contacts.[5] These contacts were maintained by politicians, businessmen, athletes and persons involved in the arts and culture. It was established that economic ties developed from local contacts which were established first. These contacts were later followed by social contacts (sports, cultural), and only then political, which were strengthened and 'normalised' as late as 1966. It must be stressed, however, that the majority of these contacts are maintained above all by the Slovene nationality in Italy and its Italian counterpart in Yugoslavia, which have at their disposal their own means of mass communication, cultural institutions and numerous social as well as economic organisations. Thus across-the-border cooperation is not only of vital importance for the existence and growth of the two communities, but represents also an important element in their integration into the social fabric in which they exist, and into the broader international arena. In Trieste and Gorizia, for example, there are over 300 foreign trade companies, and business directed to Yugoslavia accounts for 50 per cent of their total trade. In this way, the frontier regions account for about one-third of the total trade between the two neighbouring countries. About half of the foreign trade companies are in the hands of minority organisations, which are very successful in this line of business, mainly due to their bilingual skills and familiarisation with the respective cultures and living habits. On the instigation of the minorities, several joint Italian–Yugoslav ventures have been carried out involving smaller industrial companies, which were established throughout the near-border area of both states.

REGIONAL ASPECTS OF THE ITALIAN–YUGOSLAV BOUNDARY

The general orientation of the Italian–Yugoslav boundary is north–south, encountering diverse geographic regions along its path. The northern portion of the frontier region between Tarvisio and Cividale (Cedad) is characterised by limestone alpine terrain, and the boundary here coincides with the watershed between two hydrographic systems, the Soca river basin on the Yugoslav side and the Tagliamento (Tilment) river basin on the Italian side. The borderline thus runs over the mountaintops and with rare exceptions offers little possibility for border-crossing transportation links. This section of the border of about 50 kilometres possesses only three international crossings, of which the one between Tarvisio and Kranjska gora on the northernmost point by the Austrian border is somewhat more important, particularly for tourist traffic (approximately 2.5 million persons). It does not come close to the importance of the nearby Italian–Austrian border crossing, since the Tarvisio area registers over 10 million border crossings yearly.

In its central section, the border runs over pre-alpine and sub-alpine or sub-mediterranean, mainly flysch landscape, characterised by relatively easily negotiable, hilly topography. The political boundary follows the watershed (but not consistently) between the tributaries of the Soca and the tributaries of the Torre (Ter) and the Natisone (Nadiza) and divides the dense network of settlements, considerably depopulated, on the south slope from the sparsely populated northern slopes on the Yugoslav side. Since the terrain here is more indented, it creates more potential for transverse connecting lines. Thus 56 kilometres of the borderline are interrupted by seven crossings of various categories. They are all poorly frequented; the only international border crossing in this area registers fewer than 200,000 crossings annually.

In the vicinity of Gorizia, the border between Italy and Yugoslavia first swings in an east–west direction and divides the flysch, sub-mediterranean wine-growing district of Brda, then crosses the river Soca and swings southward over the limestone-covered plateau of Karst. Here the borderline runs over densely populated suburban districts of Gorizia. Only the city centre was awarded to Italy, while its eastern sections belonged to Yugoslavia and were subsequently incorporated into the city of Nova Gorica. On a stretch of 40-kilometre-long border there are as many as seventeen border crossings of various categories, of which five are 'urban' border crossings

ensuring direct ties between the two cities. Most of international traffic flows through the two crossings, which jointly register over 5 million personal crossings annually.

In the vicinity of Trieste, the borderline runs over karst terrain, except on its southern portion, where it separates the suburbs of Trieste from its Istrian hinterland. This area has characteristics similar to those of Gorizia, since its main function is precisely in the connection of Trieste with its traditional 'historical' hinterland. There are seventeen border crossings of different categories dotting a stretch of about 55 kilometres of border, of which as many as six are international crossings. The total traffic flow of this portion of the border is over 30 million people annually.

To sum up, along the northern portion of the Italian–Yugoslav border the ties between the two regions are restricted to local exchange and national transit, while the major traffic flow is oriented towards ties between Italy and Austria, which have been further strengthened following the completion of the motorway (about 7 million metric tons of goods trade). Nevertheless, Tarvisio represents for the Yugoslav side a significant commercial centre, while the nearby Yugoslav areas provide attractive alternatives for Italian tourists.

Due to the lack of natural connection and shortage of larger economic centres on both sides, across-the-border activity is lowest along the central section of the Italian–Yugoslav border, although more recent tendencies indicate that in the future, ties between the two sides will improve, particularly thanks to the construction of several small enterprises and closer ties among the inhabitants along the border. In the Gorizia area, the local aspect of near-border ties comes to the fore, although after the signing of the Ozimo Accords and the opening of another international border crossing and truck terminal connected with a motorway (over 100,000 trucks annually), this region is becoming increasingly important at an international level. The intertwining of its local and international function is most pronounced in the Trieste region. The former enables Trieste to be tied to its hinterland, and the latter ensures trade between Italy and Yugoslavia, or the EC and Central Europe and the Near East, as well as the flow of tourists from Central Europe to the Yugoslav coast. To facilitate the volume of traffic following the signing of the Ozimo Accords, a truck terminal was built on the Italian as well as on the Yugoslav side to handle a volume of about 150,000 trucks and about 2 million metric tons of goods annually. In addition, a motorway system project, stipulated in the same accords, is at the planning stage.

It is obvious that the various regions along the border differ considerably, conditioned mainly by the differences in the regional traffic systems and different territorial and gravitational location of regional centres, as well as certain historical factors. The most intensive are, of course, the border-crossing ties along the southern stretch of the Italian–Yugoslav border, although the situation in the Trieste and Gorizia regions differs in one significant respect – while the ties between the border-divided regions take place on a more-or-less equal footing, thanks to the two very similar urban centres, the dominant role in the Trieste region belongs undoubtedly to the city of Trieste itself, simply because there is no urban centre of the same calibre in the vicinity (Ljubljana lies 100 kilometres from Trieste). This region is thus characterised primarily by a very strong traditional international function, to a large degree caused by the presence of this city, but is partly also independent of the city (seasonal flow of tourists). The narrow frontier area is mainly characterised by the intervention of the urban population in the surrounding area, because the Italian territory around Trieste is too narrow to satisfy every spatially important social activity. Hence, the Yugoslav near-border region functions as a recreational and supply centre for the urban population, while Trieste is a shopping destination for the Yugoslav population and partly also a place of study.

FACTORS OF REGIONAL DEVELOPMENT ALONG THE ITALIAN–YUGOSLAV BOUNDARY

The current situation along the Italian–Yugoslav border is expressed as a kind of conglomerate of diverse forms of frontier connections. These conditions undoubtedly underlie certain elements of territorial and social organisation from before the Second World War, which the subsequent development of international and Italian–Yugoslav relations transformed to varying degrees. The freest passage across the Italian–Yugoslav border is at three points: in the north in the valley of Kanalska dolina; in the central section in the vicinity of Gorizia; and near Trieste in the south. In the north, border crossing is favoured by a suitable geographical configuration, establishing transportation links for a broader region (the pass of Tarvisio is the lowest-lying pass in the eastern Alps). The facility of border crossing in the other two cases has been fostered particularly by the presence of two major urban centres in their immediate vicinity, for which the relative openness of the border was of vital importance. In addition, the nationally mixed population along the entire stretch of the

border, and especially along its southern section, further contributed to its openness. Trieste and Gorizia are the homes of a large and well-organised Slovene minority, while on the Yugoslav side there is an Italian national minority in Istria, which is less numerous and less active owing to post-War emigration, but nevertheless represents a significant tie between Trieste and its southern hinterland, which is at the same time the destination of many of its emigrants.

The regions of Gorizia and Trieste, therefore, offered potentially the largest possibilities for border-crossing cooperation, but these potentials encountered serious political obstacles, triggered by the undefined political border and ideological and national conflicts among the population. The political border in this area was only precisely delimited in 1975, while economic exchange did not completely emerge before 1980 with an agreement between the EC and Yugoslavia. This 'macro' level of frontier cooperation has continuously fostered the fundamental 'micro' level, which blossomed as early as 1955 with complete openness of the border to personal traffic. In this way, the 'Berlinisation' of both major urban centres along the border was avoided. A closed international border would undoubtedly have had a traumatic effect on both cities, since they would have had to make do without the hinterland with which they developed very close ties during the Austrian administration.

Of particular importance is the growth of the central section of the Italian–Yugoslav border, where the traditional local links among the population had been severed already in the period of agrarian society with the new demarcation between Italy and Austria in 1866. With the annexation to Italy, the Slovenes in the region were being intensively assimilated, while all economic and communication links were redirected to the west towards the large Piedmont communities, which brought about the fall of traditional society and excessive depopulation of this mountainous frontier territory, particularly after the Second World War. Precisely for this reason, the restoration of 'normal' forms of across-the-border cooperation proved to be extremely difficult. It was necessary to wait for the transformation of the population from a rural to an industrial society, for the propagation of a new orientation towards the decentralisation of a variety of forms of economic and social organisation, for improvements in education, for a decrease in national bias, and for the initiation of the development of peripheral regions.

The current predominant attitude is that a true and comprehensive development of these regions does not only involve the usual territorial exchange between Italy and Yugoslavia, but calls for these

areas to become actively involved in the exchange as instigators and maintainers of cooperation at the national and regional levels. This natural creative and instigative role can be promoted especially through a multilingual and multicultural environment. This kind of environment, which is more developed in the other frontier regions along the Italian–Yugoslav border, is becoming a reality even in the most remote corners of the central portion of this border, particularly thanks to the ever-increasing interest in Friulian economic circles for international trade and joint ventures. The greatest obstacle on the way to an intensification of relations in this frontier region is the lack of a suitable larger urban centre on the Yugoslav side of the border. In the southern part of the border, a true 'frontier region' was created. In the vicinity of Trieste and Gorizia, the border provides the dominant imprint on the landscape of this region (transportation, service infrastructure and business structures). It also has a major impact on the way of life of the local population which comes in contact on a daily basis with the border and the neighbouring territory, either in terms of work, recreation, supply, information, or cultural exchange. The valley of Kanalska dolina in the north represents another type of frontier region in a non-urban environment, where three states, cultures and nations shake hands.

CONCLUSION

The Italian–Yugoslav boundary has given rise to a special type of border landscape and border region. A range of agreements on cultural, economic and political cooperation between Italy and Yugoslavia, cooperation between companies of these neighbouring states and cooperation on the level of local institutions have each contributed to a connection of both border areas into a tightly-linked region, differing from the other regional types in the interior of both countries. The presence of infrastructure and work organisations in this border area, which enable over-the-border cooperation gives a special tone to the region. A knowledge of both the languages and national intertwining of the population provide for more sophisticated forms of social and cultural cooperation. The typical example is of a strongly urbanised area on both sides of the border in the region of Nova Gorica and Gorizia and in the Trieste area. Here, not only is there heavy international traffic, flows of goods and personal interaction, but there is also elaborate mutual communication exchange maintained by the minorities on both sides of the border.

NOTES

1 It must be stressed that no 'pure' ethnic region exists as the previous demarcation proposals and the ever-increasing connection between the countryside and the city encouraged the intermingling of different nationalities in the greater area around the historic ethnic borderline.

2 According to estimates, from the present Italian–Yugoslav border area more than 300,000 inhabitants emigrated after the Second World War: 200,000 from Istria and the Kvarner islands (of which two-thirds were Italian and the rest Croats and Slovenes), while from the area between Trieste and Tarvisio (Trbiz) about 100,000 persons moved out due to the post-War economic crisis which affected the area.

3 Italy is a NATO and EC member; Yugoslavia, on the other hand, is one of the founders of the non-aligned movement and has developed its own brand of socialism in the post-War period based on workers' self-management.

4 In addition to the two mentioned regions along the Italian–Yugoslav border, the members of the community include the Yugoslav Republic of Croatia, the Italian regions of Veneto (Benecija) and Lombardy (Lombardija), the Austrian regions of Upper Austria (Oberosterreich, Zgornja Austrija), Carinthia (Koroska), Styria (Stajerska) and Salzburg (Solnograsko) as well as West Germany's Bavaria (Bavarija).

5 See Boileau, A. M. and Sussi, E. *Dominanze e minoranze*, 1981.

REFERENCES

Aerobrot, F. H. (1982) 'On the Structural Basis of Regional Mobilisation in Europe', in *Boundaries and Minorities in Western Europe* (Milano).

Battisti, G. (1982) 'La collaborazione economica del Friuli-Venezia Giulia con la Jugoslavia e le prospettive di sviluppo', Atti del 8 Convegno scientifico internazionale Alpe-Adria, Graz.

Benedetti, G. (1980) 'Flussi migratori: un'analisi regionatta dell'esperienza del Friuli-Venezia Giulia', *Rivista Italiana di Economia Demografica e Statistica*, No. 2–3.

Boileau, A. M. and Sussi, E. (1981) *Diminanza e minoranze* (Udine).

Bufon, M. (1987) 'Regionalni razvoj in narodnostno vprasanje' (Regional development and the nationality question), *Geografski obzornik*, No. 2.

Clavora, F., Mattelig, R. and Ruttar, R. (1987) *Liberazione, il nuovo nome dello sviluppo* (Circolo culturale Studenci, Udine).

Instituto Gramsci (1986) *Il Friuli-Venezia Giulia nell'economica e società Italiana* (Friuli-Venezia Giulia, Udine).

Gallusser, W. (1981) 'Grenze und Kulturlandschaft', *Regio Basiliensis*, Vol. 22.

Gosar, A. (1977) 'Specificnost migraćij za zacasno delo v tujino iz obmejnih regij SR Slovenije na primeru obcin ob italjansko-jugoslovanski meji' (Specificity of migrations to temporary employment abroad from the frontier regions of SR Slovenia – the case of communes along the Italian–Yugoslav border), *Geographica Slovenica*, Vol. 6, Ljubljana.

Gottman, J. (1982) 'The basic problem of political geography: the organisation of space and the search for stability', *Tijdschrift voor Economische en Sociale·Geographie*, Vol. 73.

102　Vladimir Klemencic and Milan Bufon

Grandinetti, R. (1983) *Modelli di sviluppo di un'economica periferica : il caso del Friuli, La Benecia ad una svolta: emarginazione o sviluppo?* (Atti del 10 Ciclo degli Incontri culturali della Benecia, S. Pietro al Natisone).

Hansen, N. (1977) 'Border region: a critique of spatial theory and a European case study', *Annals of Regional Science*, Vol. 11.

Heigl, F. (1982) 'The border as a sociological, social or national phenomenon – the anthropogenous region', in *Cooperation and Conflict in Border Areas* (Milano).

Jazbec, B. (1987) *L'internazionalizzazione dell'economica nelle aree di frontiera : La specificita del Friuli-Venezia Giulia in una perspettiva generale* (Trieste).

Jersic, M. and Klemencic, V. (1973) *Topical Problems of Open Boundaries – the Case of Slovenia* (Confini i regioni, Trieste).

Johansson, R. (1982) 'Boundary conflict in a comparative perspective: a theoretical framework', in *Cooperation and Conflict in Border Areas* (Milano).

Keohane, R. V. and Nye, J. S. (1970) *Transnational Relations and World Politics* (Cambridge: Harvard University Press).

Klemencic, V. (1974) 'Odprta meja med Italijo in Jugoslavijo in vloga manjsin (The open border between Italy and Yugoslavia and the role of minorities), *Teorija in praksa*, No. 9–10.

—— (1977) 'Regionalna preobrazba s Slovenci poseljenega obmocja ob Italijansko–jugoslovanski meji v Italiji' (Regional transformation of the Slovene-populated region along the Italian–Yugoslav border in Italy), *Geografski vestnik*, Vol. 49.

—— (1978) 'Grenzregion und nationale Minderheiten, Socialno-geografski problemi obmestnih in obmejnih obmocij, *Geographica Slovenica*, Vol. 8, Ljubljana.

—— (1979) 'Urbanizzazione spaziale e minoranze etniche nel Centro Europa', Conferenza internazionale sulle minoranze, Trieste.

—— (1981) 'Die Kulturlandschaft in nordwestlicher Grenzgebiet Jugoslawiens (SR Slowenien)', *Regio Basiliensis*, Vol. 22.

—— (1984) *Geographische Probleme der Grenzraume Sloveniens, Osterreich in Geschichte und Literatur mit Geographie* (Wien).

—— (1987) 'Drzavne meje na obmocju SR Slovenije in obmejna obmocja kot nov geografski fenomen' (State borders on the territory of SR Slovenia and frontier regions as a new geographic phenomenon), *Revija za narodnostna vprasanja, Razprave in gradivo*, No. 20.

Klemencic, V. and Piry, I. (1982) 'The elements of regional integration in border areas', in *Cooperation and Conflict in Border Areas* (Milano).

Lacasse, J. P. (1974) 'Les nouvelles perspectives de l'etude des frontiers politiques', *Cahiers de geographie de Quebec*, Vol. 18.

Leimgruber, W. (1980) 'Die Grenze als Forschungsobjekt der Geographie', *Regio Basiliensis*, Vol. 21.

Luhmann, N. (1982) 'Territorial borders as system boundaries', in *Cooperation and Conflict in Border Areas* (Milano).

Malchus, V. (1981) 'Bedentende Initiativen der Europaraten zum Verbesserung der grenzuberschreintenden Zusammenarbeit', *Regio Basiliensis*, Vol. 22.

de Marchi, B. (1982) 'A sociology of language research in Friuli-Venetia

Julia, a multilingual border area', in *Boundaries and Minorities in Western Europe* (Milano).
de Marchi, B. and delli Zotti, G. (1985) *Cooperazione regionale nell'area alpina* (Milano).
Meier, J. (1983) *Grenzen und Raumforschung – eine Problemskizze, Staatsgrenzen und Einfluss auf Raumstrukturen und Verhaltensmuster (I. Teil – Grenze in Europe)* (Beireuth).
Moodie, A. E. (1945) *The Italo–Yugoslav Boundary: A Study in Political Geography* (London: Philip and Son).
—— (1950) 'Some new boundary problems in the Julian March', *Transactions*, Institute of British Geographers, No. 16, pp. 83–93.
Pak, M. (1981) 'Geografska problematika demografskega razvoja, industrije in oskrbnega omrezja v obmejnem obmocju zahodne Slovenije' (Geographical problems of demographic development, industry, and services infrastructure in the frontier region of western Slovenia), *Geographica Slovenica*, Vol.12, Ljubljana.
—— (1982) *Socialnogeografski razvoj podezelja v obmejnih predelih zahodne Slovenije, Geografske znacilnosti preobrazbe slovenskega podezelja* (Social-geographic development of rural areas in the frontier regions of western Slovenia: Geographic characteristics of the transformation of the Slovenian countryside) (Ljubljana).
—— (1987) 'Meja kot faktor razvoja obmejnih obmocij' (The border as a factor in the development of frontier regions), Zbornik radova sa naucnog simpozijuma, Geografski problemi pogranicnih regija nase zemlje, Vranje.
Prescott, J. R. V. (1978) *Boundaries and Frontiers* (London: Croom Helm).
Prost, B. (1974) 'Frontière et individualité regionale: la frontiere Italo-Yugoslave et la formation de la Slavia friulana', *Etudes geographiques sur la montagne,* Actes du 99e Congres national des societes savantes, Besancon.
Raffestin, C. (1974) 'Elements pour une problematique des regions frontalieres', *L'Espace geographique*, Vol. 1.
Ratti, R., Bottinelli, T., Cino, T., Marci, A. (1982) 'Gli effetti socio-economici delle frontiere: il caso del frontaliarato nel Cantone Ticino', *Quaderni URE*, 15, Bellinzona.
Rokkan, S., and Urwin, D. W. (1983) *Economy, Territory, Identity* (London).
Strassoldo, R. (1979) *Temi di sociologia delle relazioni internazionali* (Gorizia).
Strassoldo, R. and Gubert, R. (1973) 'The boundary : an overview of its current theoretical status', *Confini e regioni*, Gorizia.
Valussi, G. (1973) *La funzione internazionale del confine Italo–Jugoslavo* (Estratto de i Quaderni del Centro Studio Economico, Trieste).
—— (1978) Friuli-Venezia Giulia, Il quadro generale, Atti del Convegno di studi sui fenomeni migratori in Italia, Piancavallo.
Vrsaj, E. (1975) *La cooperazione economica Alpe-Adria* (Trieste).

6 The impact of sovereignty transfer on the settlement pattern of Sakhalin Island

Shinsuke Minamide

INTRODUCTION

The main purpose of this chapter is to discuss the ways in which Russian and Japanese settlement policies represented different evaluations of the southern part of Sakhalin Island from the latter part of the nineteenth century to the early part of this century. In particular, the chapter will present a classification of settlement types in two southern river basins and discuss the contrasting landscape impact of settlement policy as a consequence of sovereignty transfer. In order to pursue these aims, the chapter will rely principally upon cartographic data and on literary accounts as aids to landscape reconstruction.

Sakhalin Island, situated on the east of the Asian continent, extends over 46–54 degrees north latitude, and is 78,200 square kilometres in area. The population of the aboriginal group, the Ainu, is approximately 15,000, the Oroko group is 600, and there are several minority races. They live by hunting, fishing, and by gathering various kinds of plant (Habar, 1939; Kindaichi, 1930). From the nineteenth century, the Japanese came to this island for the purpose of trading with the indigeneous peoples (Bassin, 1988) and at that time called it either 'Kita-ezo' (northern part of the Barbarian land) or 'Karafuto' (Funakoshi, 1976). Subsequently, the Russians came and settled the island. In the first Friendship Treaty between Russia and Japan in 1855, the question of the claim to Sakhalin Island was tentatively shelved.

In Japan, the last feudal government of the Tokugawa-Bakufu was overturned in 1867, and the Meiji era, which was the first of the modern period, was initiated the following year. As the imperialistic policy of the new government was implemented, conflict occurred again between Russia and Japan (Stephen, 1971; Yasukawa, 1973).

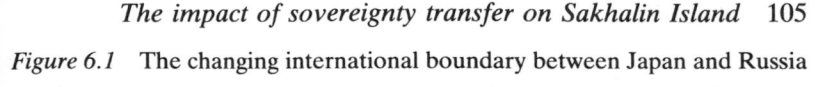

Figure 6.1   The changing international boundary between Japan and Russia

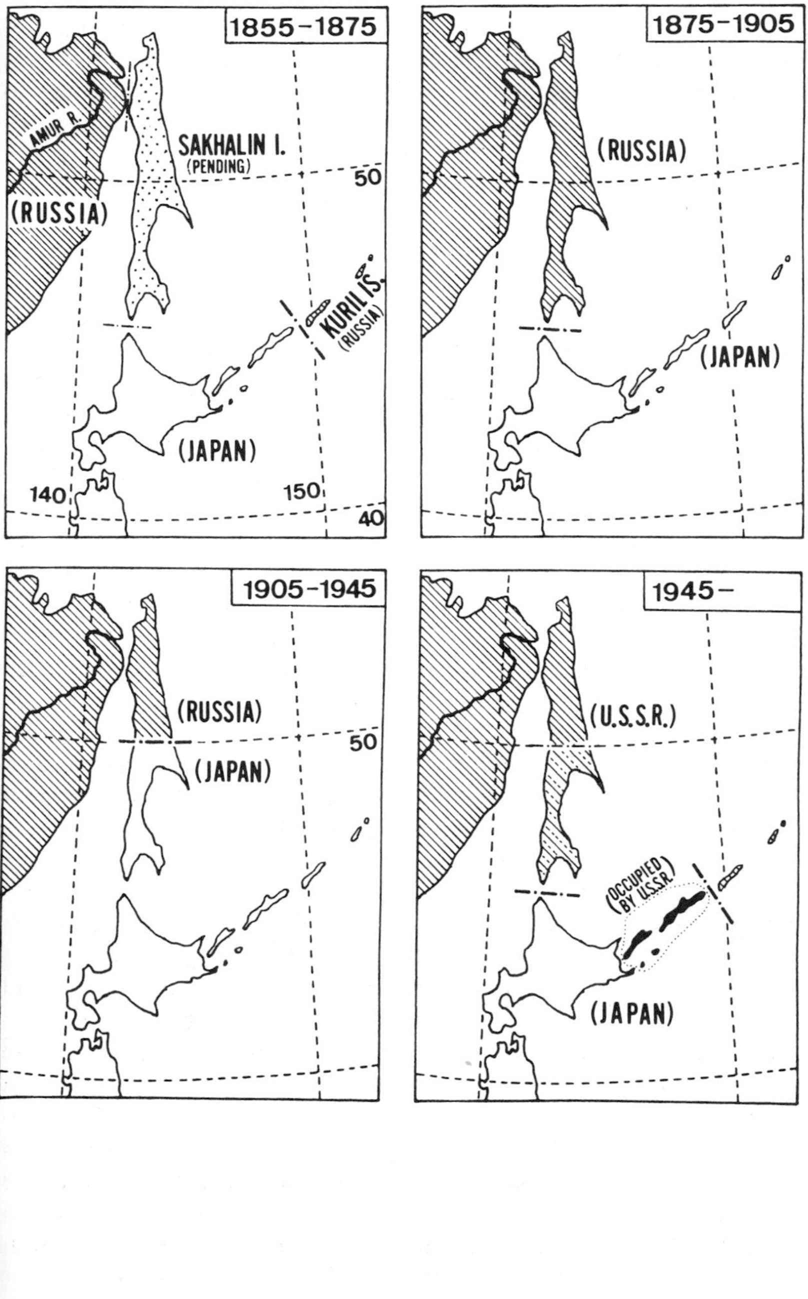

The St. Petersburg Treaty (the Chisima-Karafuto Exchange Treaty) was necessarily concluded to delimit a clear boundary between Russia and Japan in 1875. As a result of this treaty, the whole of Sakhalin Island was brought under Russian jurisdiction, and, in exchange, the whole of the Kuril Islands (the Chisima Islands) to the east of Etorofu Island were controlled by Japan. However, the confrontation between the two imperialisms finally caused the military conflict of 1904–5. Russia was defeated in this war and was obliged to transfer to Japan the Sakhalin Island region south of 50 degrees north latitude.

After the Second World War, Japan was forced to renounce the territories which had been gained by military power since the Meiji era. The Soviet Union broke the Non-Aggression Treaty of 1941 and invaded to the south of the 50 degree north parallel a mere week before the end of the War. Since then, the Soviet Union has substantially occupied not only this territory, the claim to which is still undecided in a strict sense, but has also occupied the islands of Etorofu, Kunashiri, Shikotan, and Habomai which had been agreed to be Japanese territory in the Treaty of 1855 (Rees, 1985). From such an historical perspective, the southern half of Sakhalin Island is a very interesting region where both Slavic culture and Japanese culture have interacted with aboriginal culture (Figure 6.1).

Following the treaty of 1855, the Russian government made an attempt to settle Sakhalin Island as an exile colony. It was in 1859 that a convict settlement was established based on coal mining near Port Alexandrovskii, which was located on the north-west coast of Sakhalin Island and served as the main ferry terminal to the continent (Mitsul, 1873; Panov, 1905; Takumu-Sho, 1942). In this region the climate was cold and foggy even in summer, and, in addition, the peaty soils were poorly drained like the tundra areas in Siberia. This meant that some of the early attempts to develop agriculture failed. Consequently, food supplies were dependent on provisions being imported from the mainland government. The southern lowland district, which, in contrast was rather warm, came to be noticed for its potential for agricultural colonisation. About one hundred 'free immigrant' applicants, who had been emancipated from serfdom, were sent to settle in the Takoe Valley (Figure 6.2) in 1869 (Takumu-Sho, 1942: 55–60). This region was not necessarily the best location for agricultural colonisation, since the settlers had to avoid the southernmost areas where the Japanese had already occupied. In fact, the indiscrete establishment of agricultural lands and indiscriminate cultivation without proper preparation for farm machinery or for

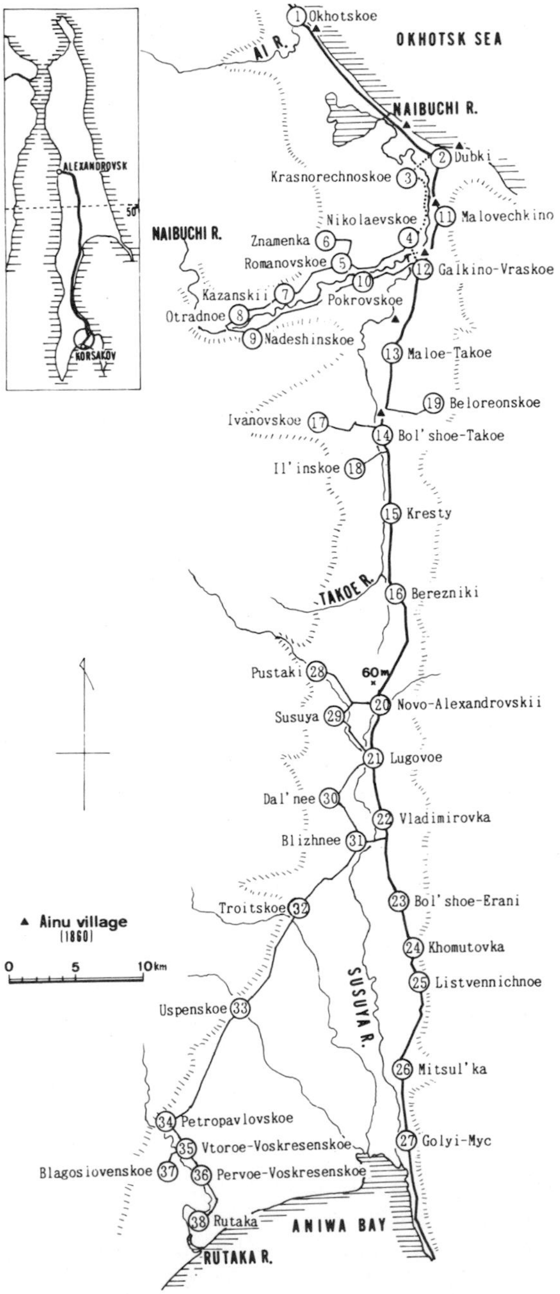

Figure 6.2 Russian settlements in the southern lowland district

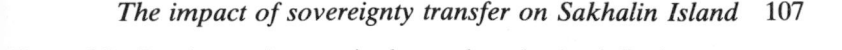

cattle meant this attempt failed. The flood hazard of 1875 finally reduced that settlement to ruins.

Since that year, following the incorporation of the southern half of Sakhalin into Russia, many convict settlements were founded for grain growing. Not only from the continent, but also from the Due Prisons near Alexandrovskii, many people who had served out their sentences were despatched to this region (Takumu-Sho: 1942, 124–5). In spite of this advance in agricultural colonisation, just a few decades later, the 1904–5 war took place and the vast majority of these settlements were deserted.

There were a number of particular problems with these settlements which will be mentioned below. The southern lowland is a narrow fault valley opening on to two bays. The Susuya River flows to the south into Aniwa Bay, and the Naibuchi River flows to the north, into the Sea of Okhotsk. The dividing region is very flat and low, contains many river branches forming complex fans and is only 60 metres above sea level.[1] In the lower basins there are many complex meanders with numerous crescent lakes and marshes. In the period under Russian rule, the main military postroad ran through this valley at the foot of the mountains, and led to the Korsakov Fortress in front of the Aniwa Bay facing the Japanese boundary (Takumu-Sho, 1942: 138–42).

It is possible to identify the location and morphology of 38 settlements in the southern lowland from three kinds of maps published by Japanese surveys:

1 The 1:50,000 scale temporary topographical map prepared by the Rikuchi-sokuryo bu (Japanese Ordnance Survey) in 1909 and published in 1911. This map shows the ruins of the uninhabited Russian settlements just after the 1904–5 war. Russian settlement names still remain and are shown in Japanese phonetic symbols on this map.

2 A regular topographical map at the same scale and published during 1928–33. This shows the shapes of the new settlements reorganised by the Karafuto-cho (Karafuto Government Office or KGO). Settlement names have already replaced with Japanese words.

3 The 1:25,000 planning map prepared for selected areas and published by the KGO from 1928 to 1930. This shows the strictly reorganised plan of housing lots on the abandoned settlements just before (2) was made. The KGO undertook a field survey of these settlements in 1905, and published a report – *Karafuto*

shokuminchi sentei hobun (Survey Report of Colonial Karafuto) – in 1910 which included statistical data both of numbers of houses and of acreages under cultivation. In addition, Anton P. Chekhov's detailed report, *Ostrov Sakhalin* (Sakhalin Island) of his trip in 1890 is also available (Chekhov, 1890). Chekhov recorded not only the condition of but also population data on each of the settlements he visited.[2] The location and structure of the thirty-eight settlements can be reconstructed mainly from these maps and data (Figure 6.2 and Table 6.1).

SETTLEMENTS IN THE NAIBUCHI RIVER BASIN

There were nineteen settlements in the Naibuchi River basin. Among them, eight were located along the main military postroad. Okhotskoe (settlement serial No. 1), which was situated at the north end of the southern lowland district, facing the Sea of Okhotsk was isolated from the other settlements (Figure 6.2). However, this settlement is regarded as one of the planned settlements in this district. Not having been exactly located along the postroad, the built-up area of this village assumed a compact morphology and appeared as a regularly shaped 'T', on the map of 1909 (Figure 6.3a). There were never any regularly shaped settlements to the north of Okhotskoe in the southern half of Sakhalin Island. Needless to say, neither the Japanese nor the Ainu developed any settlement like this. According to the appendix chart of the accounts of the exploring expedition by S.Suzuki, there was a small Ainu village near the mouth of the Ai River (Suzuki, 1860). The shape of it is thus also marked on the map of 1909. The map of 1932–3 shows the Russian village already having been replaced by the new dispersed village planned by the KGO (Figure 6.3b). According to the KGO report of 1910, the abandoned settlement comprised twenty houses and a total cultivated area of only 6 hectares (Table 6.1).

The KGO first made an attempt to adopt the dispersed village plans as a kind of township settlement system in the colonisation of Sakhalin Island, similar to that of Hokkaido which had not been cultivated on a large scale before the Meiji era. According to the reminiscences of S.Takakura, it had been easy to lay out plans in Hokkaido Island because the Ainu as the former inhabitants now lived mostly near water, and thus had developed no agricultural settlement on a large scale inland. However, on Sakhalin Island the dispersed village plan was not always possible where Russian

Table 6.1 Structure of the thirty-eight settlements in the southern lowland district

No.	Russian Settlement Name	Found	1890 House-holds	Popula-tion m.	f.	Form	1905 Houses	Fields (ha)	Fields/ House (ha)	Japanese Settlement Name
1	Okhotskoe					T	20	6.0	0.30	(Aihama)
2	Dubki	1886	30	31	13	T	26	10.0	0.38	Kashiwahama
3	Krasnorechnoskoe					I	16	34.0	2.13	---
4	Nikolaevskoe					I	52	78.0	1.50	---
5	Romanovskoe					T	38	50.0	1.32	Watase
6	Znamenka					I	8	16.0	2.00	Yamanaka
7	Kazanskii					I	25	26.0	1.04	(Fukakusa)
8	Otradnoe					I	14	7.0	0.50	Kawakita
9	Nadeshinskoe					I	21	30.0	1.43	Kawaminami
10	Pokrovskoe					I	15	36.0	2.40	(Kurokawa)
11	Malovechkino					I	7	6.0	0.30	(Aho)
12	Galkino-Vraskoe	1884	45	50	24	T	52	68.0	1.31	(Ochiai)
13	Maloe Takoe	1885	35	37	15	I	28	50.0	1.79	Kotani
14	Bol'shoe-Takoe	1884	47	56	15	I	45	38.0	0.84	Otani
15	Kresty	1885	52	63	27	I	47	40.0	0.85	Miyuki
16	Berezniki		140	142	17	I	40	30.0	0.75	Tomioka
17	Ivanovskoe					I	33	38.0	1.15	Maruyama
18	Il'inskoe					*				---
19	Beloreonskoe					*	18	36.0	2.00	Shirakawa
20	Novo-Alexandrovskii	1884	42	95	16	I	72	124.0	1.72	Konuma
21	Lugovoe	1888		69	5	I	17	68.0	1.45	Kusano
22	Vladimirovka	1881	46	55	36	I	60	51.0	0.85	Toyohara
23	Bol'shoe-Erani	1888	30	32	8	I	25	36.0	1.44	Osawa
24	Khomutovka	1886	25	25	13	I	37	76.0	2.05	Kiyokawa
25	Listvennichnoe	1886		15	0	I	15	20.0	1.33	Karamatsu
26	Mitsul'ka	1884	10	16	9	I	12	10.0	0.83	Nakasato
27	Golyi-Myc	1889		24	0	*				(Shinba)
28	Pustaki					H	31	76.0	2.45	Hon-kawakami
29	Susuya					L	73	55.0	0.75	Suzuya
30	Dal'nee					H	78	114.0	1.46	Ikusagawa
31	Blizhnee					T	55	80.0	1.45	Oiwake
32	Troitskoe					I	102	78.0	0.76	Namikawa
33	Uspenskoe					T	30	21.6	0.72	Nakasawa
34	Petropavlovskoe					T	27	17.0	0.63	Kosato
35	Vtoroe-Voskresenskoe					I	30	37.6	1.25	Kita-hirano
36	Pervoe-Voskresenskoe					I	27	29.6	1.10	Minami-hirano
37	Blagoslovenskoe					T	30	28.6	0.95	Kohara
38	Rutaka	1886	33	37	16	T	32	14.8	0.46	Rutaka
	Totals		535	747	214		1285	1536.2		
	Averages		44.6	49.8	14.3		35.7	42.7	1.20	

* =indistinct, --- =abandoned, ( ) =replaced

Figure 6.3 The settlement of Okhotskoe, 1909–33

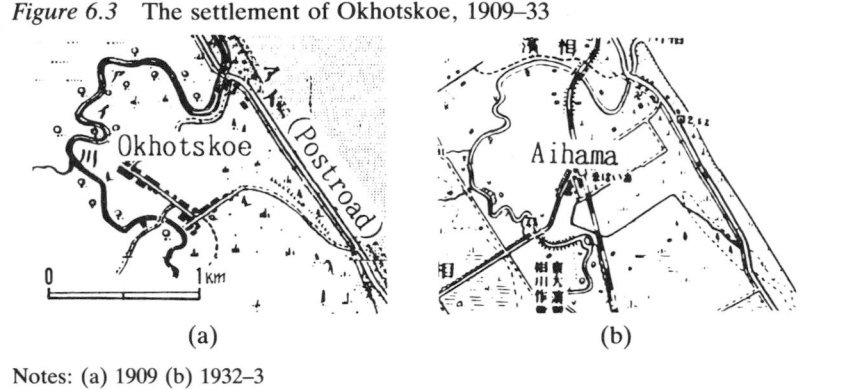

(a)   (b)

Notes: (a) 1909 (b) 1932–3

settlement had already been firmly established, and consequently the linear-form village remained. It was probable that the village of Okhotskoe was believed to be of little value for development by the KGO and that the dispersed village plan was adopted over the ruins of the abandoned settlement.

According to the quotation from Mitsul in Chekhov's report, a depot village had been set up on a sand dune area near the mouth of the Naibuchi River in 1866 (Nakamura, 1953: 287). There had been 18 houses, a chapel, and a grocery shop when Mitsul had visited, but they were already abandoned when Chekhov went through there in 1890. On the chart by S. Suzuki (1860), an Ainu village was formerly located near there (Figure 6.2). Hence, the Russian depot village could be interpreted to have been, not an agricultural settlement, but one of the trading points founded near the Ainu villages facing water. The Russian village would likely have supplied food and goods for the early colonisation of the Takoe Valley from 1869.

The next settlement to the south – Dubki (No. 2) – was established in 1886 (Chekhov, 1890), was located at the corner of the postroad and was also a regularly shaped 'T' similar to Okhotskoe. In detail on the map of 1909, an Ainu village was situated 1.5 kilometres east of Dubki. The main axial street of Dubki seems to have been the road which formerly connected the Ainu village with Krasnorechnoskoe (No. 3) beyond the river (Figure 6.4a). This seems to indicate that the postroad was joined to this former road and consequently developed into a 'T'. The map of 1932 shows that the postroad was replaced by a new road which ran through the higher terrace to the south of Dubki (Figure 6.4b). Although Chekhov must have gone through Malovechkino (No. 11), 4 kilometres to the south of Dubki, he merely recorded its place-name as the name of a small stream where

Figure 6.4   Settlements in the lower Naibuchi Valley

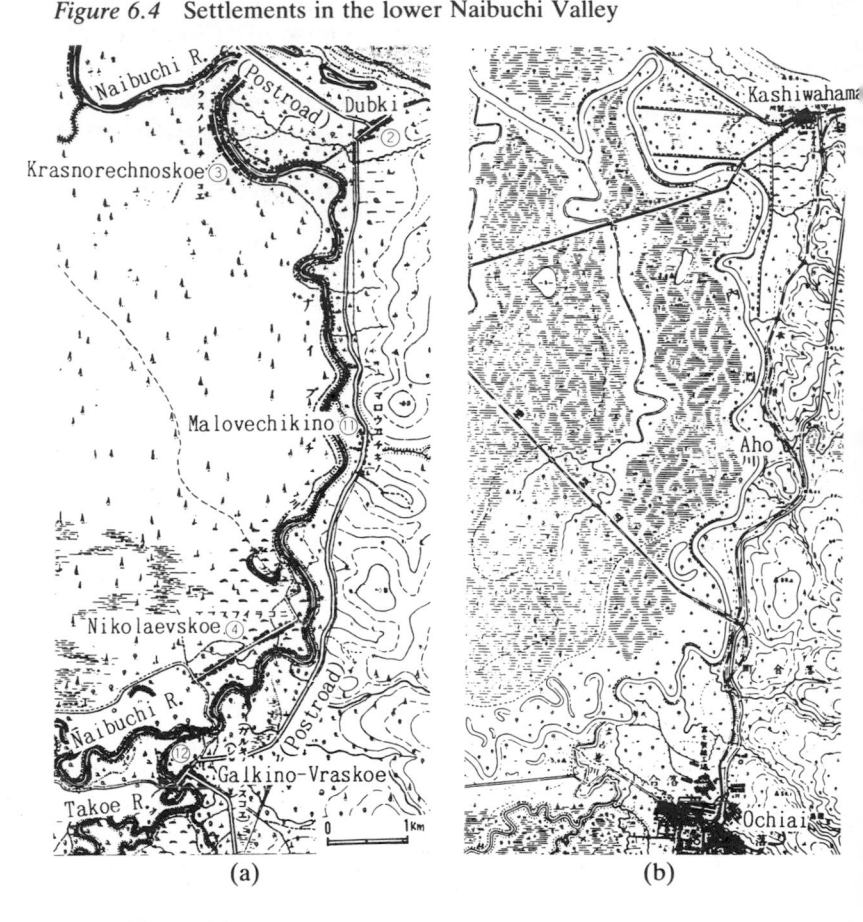

(a)   (b)

Notes: (a) 1909 (b) 1929–32

convicts often fished. According to the chart by Suzuki (1860), an Ainu village had once been there (Figure 6.2). The number of houses in the Russian settlement was only seven (KGO, 1910) although it may not have been completed by that time. However, once the postroad was replaced, the settlement was abandoned (Figure 6.4a).

A further 4 kilometres south of Malovechkino, Galkino-Vraskoe (No. 12) was located at the confluence of the Takoe and the Naibuchi (Figure 6.2).There had been an Ainu village – Shants – consisting of eight houses (Suzuki, 1860) prior to the Russian settlement being established in 1884 (Chekhov, 1890). The latter was a regularly shaped 'T', with one of its axial streets set in the opposite direction to

the sites of the two rivers. The postroad seems to have been curved and to have been joined to this street afterwards (Figure 6.4a). Although there was a bridge at the confluence, the rivers were often flooded and people were forced to go over inundated ground by a small Ainu boat (Chekhov, 1890). New settlement – Ochiai – ('confluence' in Japanese), was reconstructed on the higher terrace some distance from the riverside (Figure 6.4b). Hence these settlements, which were situated along the main military postroad in the lower Naibuchi basin, are considered to have served as ferries and as trading points with the Ainu, irrespective of the flood hazard. There seems to have been minimal conflict in relations between the Russians and the Ainu.

In addition to these villages, four settlements were located along the postroad which runs through the Takoe Valley to the south of Galkino-Vraskoe. Maloe ('small') Takoe (No. 13) was established in 1885 subsequent to Bol'shoe ('great') Takoe (No. 14) which had been established before 1884 (Chekhov, 1895). These two settlement names imply that the 'small' was derived from the 'great'. In fact, in terms of the number of houses and population size, Bol'shoe Takoe was comparatively large (Table 6.1). Chekhov records that there was a ruin of the early settlement of 1869 alongside the postroad between Maloe-Takoe and Bol'shoe-Takoe (Chekhov, 1895) which cannot be identified on the map of 1909. There had also been an Ainu village – Takoi – near Bol'shoe Takoe (Suzuki, 1860). The reason why the Russians preferred the proximity of the Ainu village may be due not only to trading but also to ease of access. Kresty (No. 15) was founded in 1885. Although the year of establishment of Berezniki (No. 16) is unclear in Chekhov's report, it seems to have been relatively early since its population was among the largest and because its four streets had already been completed by the time of his visit. All such settlements were situated at regular intervals and were of a similar-sized linear form and are considered to have served principally as stations (Figure 6.5a). Later, the postroad and these settlements were retained by the KGO and were occupied by Japanese settlers (Figure 6.5b).

According to Chekhov's report, Berezniki had an especially large population (159) and a large number of households (140). However, based on KGO data, the number of houses in Berezniki was only 40. This was not larger than any of the other settlements along the postroad (Table 6.1). It was unthinkable that the houses of Berezniki were suddenly reduced to one-third between 1890 and 1905. Accordingly, data from Chekhov's report are interpreted to have meant not

114   *Shinsuke Minamide*

Figure 6.5   Settlements along the postroad in the Takoe basin

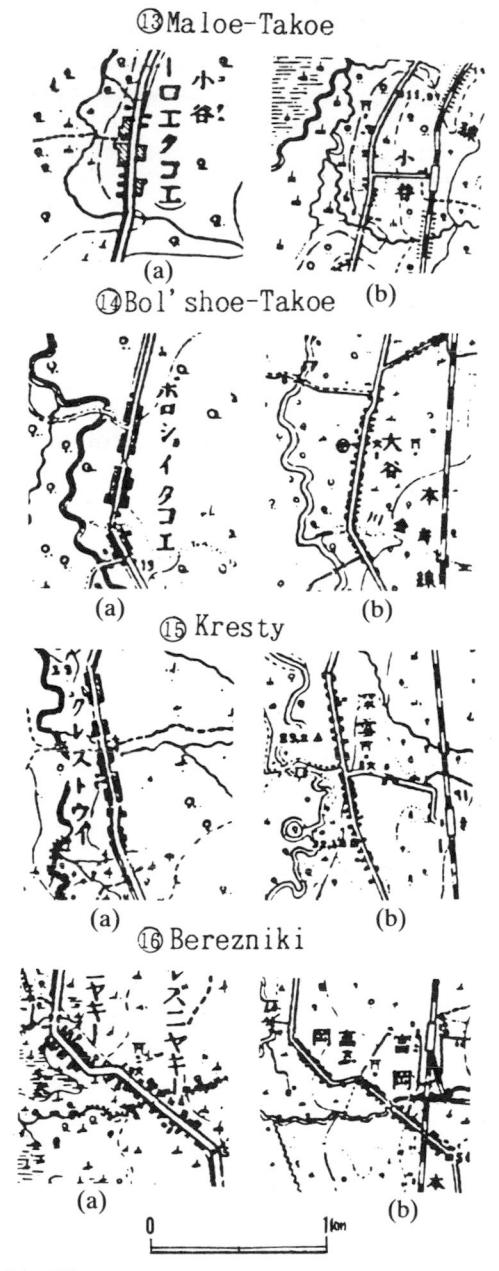

⑬Maloe-Takoe

(a)   (b)

⑭Bol'shoe-Takoe   (b)

(a)   (b)

⑮Kresty

(a)   (b)

⑯Berezniki

(a)   (b)

0   1km

Notes: (a) 1909 (b) 1929

the number of the built-up houses but the whole number of house-holds including many bachelors living together in a common house. This settlement, situated on the uppermost part of the Takoe Valley, may well have served as an advanced base for colonisation.

In contrast, the settlements of Ivanovskoe (No. 17), Il'inskoe (No. 18), and Beloreonskoe (No. 19) were situated on complex fans where floods were few, some distance from Bol'shoe-Takoe. Having not visited these settlements, Chekhov did not report anything about them. Ivanovskoe seems to have been a linear-formed village of thirty-three houses (Table 6.1). In terms of acreage under cultivation per house, there was little difference between Ivanovskoe and other settlements along the postroad. On the other hand, Il'inskoe seems to have comprised only three dispersed houses on the map of 1909. The KGO did not record any data on the settlement since it was still extremely small at that time and it may have been evaluated to be of little use. The other, Beloreonskoe, consisted of eighteen houses and had 36 hectares of fields (Table 6.1). For some reason, the mor-phology of this village was not linear but irregularly agglomerated, which was rare in the southern lowland region. Subsequently, Il'inskoe was abandoned and Beloreonskoe was reorganised into a linear village. It was extremely unusual for an irregularly agglomer-ated Russian village to be subsequently transformed into a linear-shaped village by the Japanese.

In the main Naibuchi Valley itself, other settlement types were evident. In the lower basin, for example, Krasnorechnoskoe (No. 3) and Nikolaevskoe (No. 4) were located on the left bank of the river, and each was a long-shaped village which extended for 1.5 kilometres (Figure 6.4a). In particular, the latter, which had rectangular corners at both ends of the village, seems to have been constructed according to a very precise plan. In cases discussed above – Dubki and Galkino-Vraskoe, for example – the main axial streets were laid out in the direction of those settlements beyond the river. This suggested that the settlements on the left bank were older than those on the right bank, and that the former had been laid out before the main military postroad was constructed. They are considered to have been founded in locations convenient to water transportation. It is known that early colonisation very often proceeded along river valleys in Sakhalin Island, and that small boats could row up to Nadeshinskoe (Figure 6.2, No. 9) on the Naibuchi.

Settlers clearly initially preferred vacant ground along rivers to thick forests where they were forced to work extremely hard in order to prepare the soil for farming. However, humid flood plains, which

Figure 6.6   Settlements along the Naibuchi River

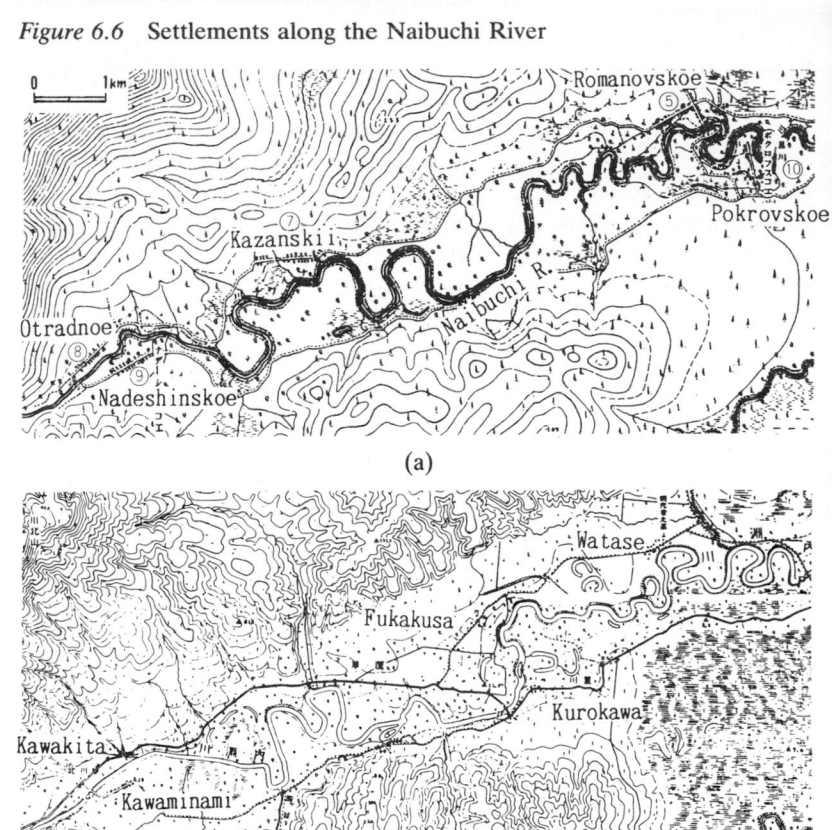

(a)

(b)

Notes: (a) 1909 (b) 1929–32

included marshes and lakes, were of poorly drained peaty soils, and were naturally unsuitable for farming. The two settlements on the left bank were completely abandoned until 1929 and nothing remained of them (Figure 6.4b).

There were a further six settlements above Nikolaevskoe in the Naibuchi River valley. Romanovskoe (No. 5) was located on the left bank and had two axial streets which met at right angles to each other (Figure 6.6a). The built-up area seems to have been 'T'-shaped with another road branching at the mid-point of the longer side of the 'T'. This road is believed to have been added to the 'T' at a later date. The shorter side of the 'T' was extended to the ferry terminal. Such an arrangement of streets illustrates the obvious point that this

settlement was established to take advantage of river transportation. Though Romanovskoe partly remained, Pokrovskoe (No. 10), which was located on the opposite bank, was completely abandoned for similar reasons to the cases of Krasnorechnoskoe and of Nikolaevskoe. The new dispersed village, Kurokawa, was located to the west of Pokrovskoe (Figure 6.6b). Similarly, Kazanskii (No. 7) a linear-shaped village located 5 kilometres above Romanovskoe, was also abandoned and replaced by a new dispersed village, Fukakusa to the east of the old one. Both Otradnoe (No. 8) and Nadeshinskoe (No. 9) were located at the uppermost point of small boat navigation. These villages were partly retained by the KGO. Lastly, Znamenka (No. 6) was situated on a small branch of the Naibuchi, 3 kilometres to the north of Romanovskoe. Its linear-shaped village was partly retained for the new settlers to advance colonisation into the interior.

It is possible to group the locations of the nineteen settlements discussed above into three main categories as follows: (1) located along the main military postroad; (2) located on a well-drained fan, and (3) located on the bank of a river meander in the flood plain. Type 1 settlements can be sub-divided into two groups. The first contains settlements located in the flood plain (Table 6.1, Nos 1, 2, 11 and 12). These were founded to serve as ferry terminals or as trading points before the postroad was completed, and mostly were of a 'T'-shaped village. The 'instability' of their location meant that all of them were abandoned or were removed as part of the subsequent KGO settlement plan. The other sub-group comprises settlements in the Takoe Valley (Nos 13–16). They were situated at similar intervals along the postroad, and may have served as stations. The villages were of a linear form, the number of houses was similar and they seem to have been mature, stable and fully occupied. Rigid built-up areas took their place in the time of Japanese settlement.

Type 2 settlements were distributed on the complex fans spread around Bol'shoe-Takoe (Nos 17–19). Though they are considered to have been established primarily for agriculture, the villages were small, unplanned or immature, and were consequently abandoned or were converted to new planned villages by the KGO. Type 3 settlements were established to take advantage of water transportation and for ease of soil preparation (Nos 3–10). The villages were linear-shaped or 'T'-shaped and one of the streets necessarily faced to the river. In this sense, Type 3 settlements may fall into the same category as the former sub-group of type 1 settlements. Similar to these cases, the majority of type 3 villages were abandoned or were reorganised into dispersed villages on a higher terrace with minimal flood hazard.

Figure 6.7   Novo-Alexandrovskii and Lugovoe

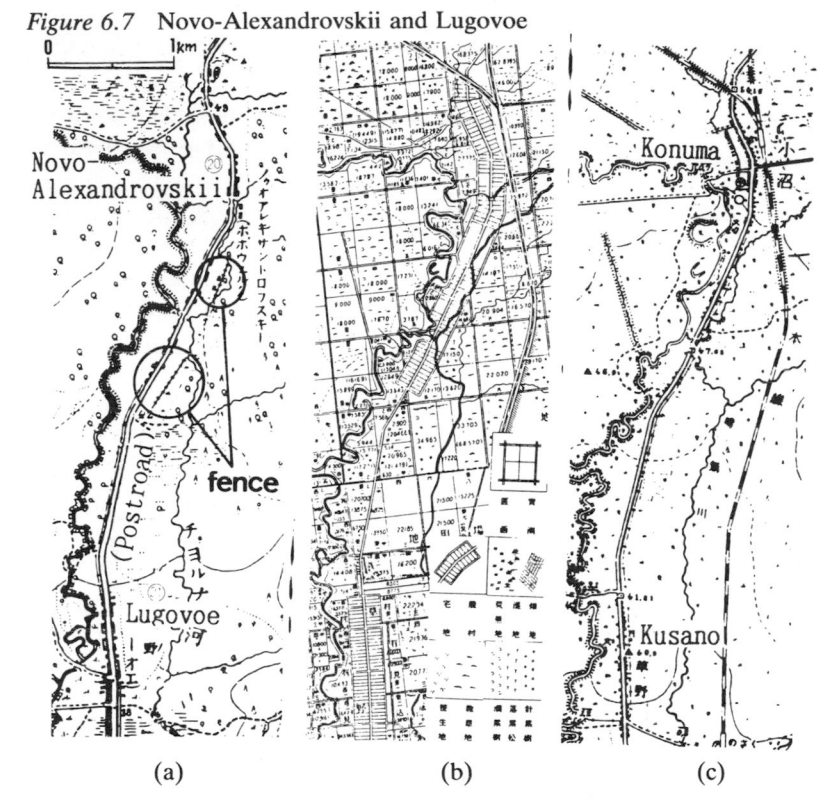

(a)   (b)   (c)

Notes: (a) 1909 (b) early 1920s (c) 1929

SETTLEMENTS IN THE SUSUYA RIVER BASIN

In the Susuya River basin, the location and morphology of the other nineteen settlements was similar to the case of the Naibuchi River basin. To the south of the dividing region, which is very flat and is only 60 metres above sea level, eight settlements were located along the main military postroad. Novo-Alexandrovskii (No. 20), established in 1884, was of a gently curved slender shape extending over 2 kilometres. This settlement had the largest population next to Berezniki in Chekhov's report, and had the largest area under cultivation according to KGO data. It was likely that the original small village gradually grew larger and consequently curved along the road. As is discussed below, larger settlements were mainly established on complex fans in the upper Susuya River valley.

Planning maps, which were made partly for the more promising settlements in this region, show the reorganised plans of housing lots in each village. From the 1928 map, for example, in the case of Novo-Alexandrovskii, each housing lot can be measured in terms of a frontage of about 25–30 metres and a depth of about 100 metres (Figure 6.7b). This size approximates to the rough data discussed by Takakura (1947) – 15 ken (27 metres) by 60 ken (108 metres) – and may be approximately converted into Russian units – 12.5 sazhen by 50 sazhen.[3] In the detail of the map of 1909 (Figure 6.7a), fences enclosing the backs of the housing area were partly retained, which implies that the depth of housing lots on the reorganised plan conformed to the former limit which separated house garden from pasture. Such housing lots may have been one of the normal plans in Russian villages. The landscape of this village indeed resembled examples in Siberia in the latter part of the nineteenth century. However, each lot had not always been filled with a house in the case of Novo-Alexandrovskii, because the number of lots amounted to more than 100 on the planning map in spite of the number of houses being only seventy-two (KGO, 1910). In terms of the housing lots, the village is thus not considered to have been fully occupied.

Lugovoe (No. 21) was 4 kilometres to the south of Novo-Alexandrovskii. This settlement was established in 1888, and, as was usual in such new settlements, there were very few women – only five women in contrast to 69 men (Table 6.1). The next village to the south, Vladimirovka (No. 22), was among the earliest, having been established in 1881. Although it was not large, this village occupied the best position in order to be able to communicate with settlements on the opposite side of the Susuya River. From 1905, the Japanese began to construct the new town of Toyohara to the south of Vladimirovka to contain the government office (KGO) and, after the Second World War, the town was renamed Yuzno Sakhalinsk and became the capital city of Sakhalin province.

Five settlements were located along the main military postroad to the south of Vladimirovka, each of which was of the linear type, except for Golyi-Myc (Figure 6.8). At about 6 kilometres from Vladimirovka, Bol'shoe-Erani (No. 23) was founded in 1888. Again in this new settlement men outnumbered women 32 to 8 (Table 6.1). South of Bol'shoe-Erani was Khomutovka (No. 24) which was established in 1886. This settlement seems to have been already mature in 1890, since there were 13 women compared with 25 men at that time which was a reasonably good ratio in such settlements. Though the establishment year of Listvennichnoe (No. 25) cannot be

Figure 6.8   Settlements along the postroad in the Susuya basin

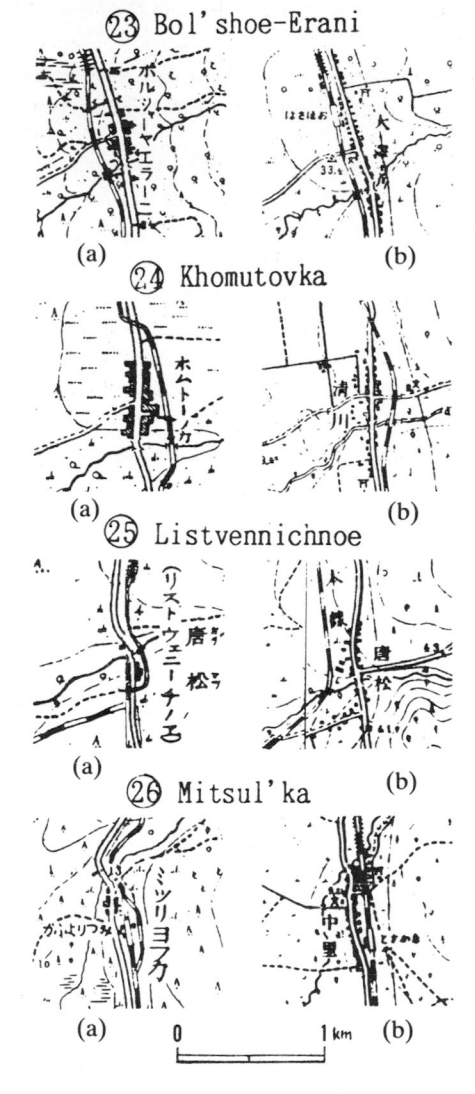

Notes: (a) 1909 (b) 1928–9

identified from Chekhov's report, it is regarded as new because there were no women. Mitsul' ka (No. 26) , on the other hand, was an older settlement established before 1884. Chekhov reported that Mitsul'ka had formerly served as a station and that new immigrants were

prohibited after 1885. He also reported that Golyi-Myc (No. 27) was not mature, houses were still under construction, and all residents were men. Indeed, Golyi-Myc was located in a marshy valley near the river mouth and seemed to have been unsuitable for farming. Even the shape of the village was obscure on the map of 1909. It is a noteworthy fact that the older settlements established before 1886 and the younger settlements established after 1888 were located alternately to each other. This suggests that the younger settlements were established between the neighbouring older settlements which were already fully occupied. All such settlements, except for Golyi-Myc, were retained for Japanese settlers.

To the south of Golyi-Myc, several other settlements were located near to the coast. Solov'evka, for example, was established in 1882 (Chekhov, 1890). There were 37 men and 37 women living in this settlement and a total of 26 households. From its location, Solov'evka may have been regarded as being more appropriate for fishing than agriculture. Between Solov'evka and the Korsakov Fortress, which was the end of the main military postroad, three small settlements of Trech'ya-Pad', Vtoroe-Pad', and Pervoe-Pad' were located respectively on narrow sea terraces. The Russian words *trech'ya*, *vtoroe* and *pervoe* mean 'third', 'second' and 'first'. These names clearly indicate that the settlements were established in that order counted from the Korsakov Fortress. Each settlement had 17, 6 and 3 households respectively. In addition, the total population of the three settlements was only forty-six (Chekhov, 1890). These settlements are clearly distinguishable from the thirty-eight settlements in both the Naibuchi and the Susuya.

On the western side of the upper Susuya Valley, four large settlements were located on complex fans where there were well-drained and fertile soils. Chekhov did not go through these settlements and reported nothing about them. On the maps of 1909, however, each of these villages shows a unique shape. Pustaki (No. 28) was a regularly shaped 'H', Susuya (No. 29) was 'L', Dal'nee (No. 30) was also 'H', and Blizhnee (No. 31) was 'T' (Figure 6.9). Though they were connected by road to each other, these settlements were located away from the main military postroad (Figure 6.2). Furthermore, the rivers near them were not navigable. It is unthinkable that these settlements were originally established in relation to convenient road or river access. They are thus considered to have been located solely for agriculture despite unfavourable transportation conditions. The Russian words *dal'nee* and *blizhnee* mean 'far' and 'near', and these settlements were named in their order from

Figure 6.9   Settlements in the upper Susuya basin

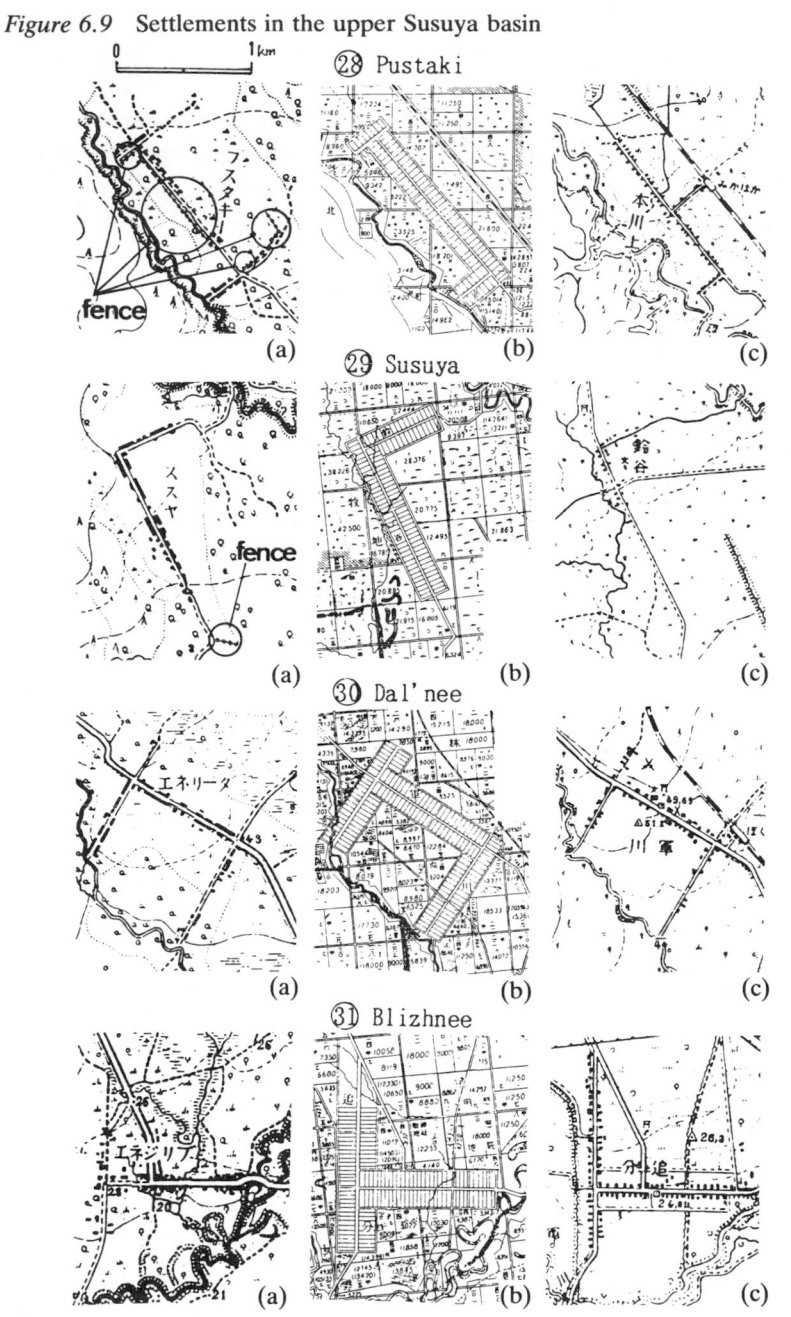

Notes: (a) 1909 (b) early 1920s (c) 1928–9

Vladimirovka to the west, for they were founded after Vladimirovka was completed in 1881.

On the map of 1909, both Pustaki and Susuya show traces of fences similar to the case of Novo-Alexandrovskii (Figures 6.7a and 6.9a). Such long fences were erected for cattle and accordingly indicated that land was clearly divided and that suitable areas for dairy farms and fields were operated in them. Pustaki had 31 houses (KGO, 1910) though approximately 90 housing lots can be determined from the planning map (Figure 6.9b). Many vacant lots were evident in this village, which was succeeded with a little transformation by a Japanese village (Figure 6.9c). Similarly, in the case of Susuya, there are about 130 lots compared to 73 houses. In Dal'nee, which had the largest area of fields next to Novo-Alexandrovskii, there were about 140 lots compared to 78 houses; and in Blizhnee, the number of lots was about 100 with 55 houses. The KGO planned these lots in order to maximise the capacity of housing area and it is retroactively suggested that the Russian linear village had not always achieved this goal.

The extension of the south side of the 'T' in Blizhnee was another main road, which connected Vladimirovka with the port, Rutaka (Figure 6.2, No. 38), and which ran through the foothills on the west side of the Susuya Valley. Along this road, about 5 kilometres from Blizhnee, Troitskoe (No. 32) was located. This village consisted of two parts of a linear built-up area, the total length of which extended over 2 kilometres (Figure 6.10a). There were 102 houses, making it the largest of all settlements in this district. Although there were 150 housing lots on the planning map, the lot plan included a wide vacant space between the two built-up areas (Figure 6.10b). Apart from this vacant space, both sides of the road seem to have been almost filled with houses in this village. The lots planned on the vacant space were fully occupied until 1928 (Figure 6.10c). These settlements may be identified not as settlements located along main roads, but rather as one of the large-sized settlements originally established solely for agriculture, as mentioned above.

Uspenskoe (No. 33) was situated beside this main road about 8 kilometres south of Troitskoe. The axial street of this village made a right angle with the straight main road and was consequently 'T'-shaped which implies that the village branched from the main road. The land around Uspenskoe was marshy and seems to have been unsuitable for farming. The type of this settlement must be strictly distinguished from that of Troitskoe in terms of its location and morphology. Petropavlovskoe (No. 34) was located on the 'T'

Figure 6.10   Troitske

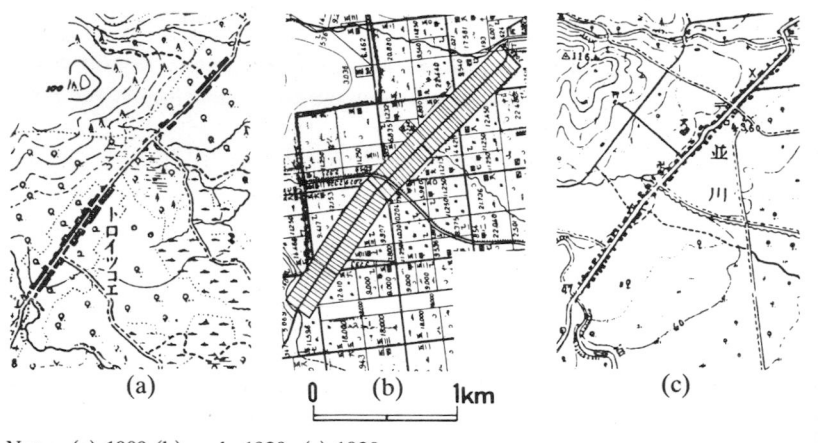

(a)   0   (b)   1km   (c)

Notes: (a) 1909 (b) early 1920s (c) 1928

corner turn toward Rutaka (Figure 6.11a). Between Petropavlovskoe and Rutaka, there were several settlements very similar to those in the lower Naibuchi basin (Figure 6.4a). Both Vtoroe-Voskresenskoe (No. 35) and Pervoe-Voskresenskoe (No. 36) were of a long linear village type located along the main road on the east bank of the Rutaka River. As was noted above, the Russian words *vtoroe* and *pervoe* mean 'second' and 'first'. These two settlements must have been established in the order of their names starting from Rutaka. It is suggested that colonisation was advanced from the river mouth to the upper interior. In detail on the map of 1909, a dotted line, which corresponded to a small road took a short cut across the plain on the western side of the river (Figure 6.11a). This road ran across Blagoslovenskoe (No. 37) and connected the west end of Petropavlovskoe with Rutaka by the shortest distance. The road may have been older than the one on the eastern bank.

Lastly, Rutaka, located on the left bank of the river of the same name, was the ferry terminal to both Solov'evka and Korsakov beyond Aniwa Bay. Rutaka may have served as a trading point with the Ainu who lived near the village, similar to Dubki and Galkino-Vraskoe (Figure 6.4a). Chekhov did not visit Rutaka, however, although his survey at the branch office in Korsakov recorded the fact that Rutaka was established in 1886 and that there were 37 men, 16 women and 33 households. From KGO data, the number of houses was almost identical, 32. From these data it appears that all settlements along the Rutaka River had a similar number of houses. In

Figure 6.11 Settlements along the lower Rutaka River

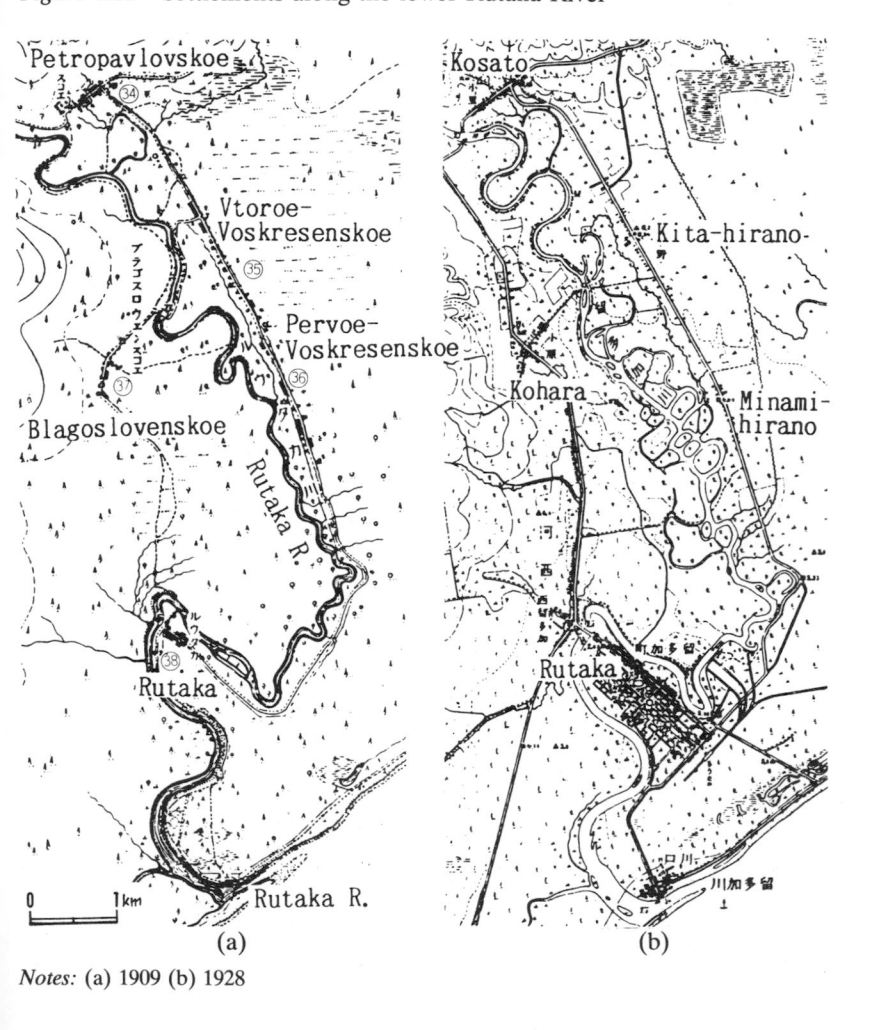

(a)   (b)

Notes: (a) 1909 (b) 1928

order – Petropavlovskoe (27), Vtoroe-Voskresenskoe (30), Pervoe-Voskresenskoe (27), Blagoslovenskoe (30) and Rutaka (32) (Table 6.1). These data clearly suggest a standard size for these settlements. After 1886, they may have been strictly established under the allotment scheme which regulated village size to 30 houses.

The 19 settlements in the Susuya basin discussed above can be classified into three groups similar to the case of the Naibuchi basin. First, is a group of settlements located along the main military postroad (Table 6.1, Nos 20–7). The location and morphology of

these generally resembles the situation in the Takoe basin. However, they may be broken into two sub-groups. The first is those settlements established before 1886 and the other comprises those settlements established after 1888. Women were comparatively few in number in such new settlements. Among them, the rigidly planned settlements in the upper basin grew larger and became Japanese settlements. On the other hand, Golyi-Myc, which was the youngest settlement in the lower basin, was removed. The second is a group of large settlements constructed on well-drained and fertile complex fans (Nos 28–32). These settlements were originally established for farming and were regularly shaped 'H', 'L', 'T', or 'I'. Both prudent selection of lands and strict village plans may have been prepared for them, in contrast to the similar type in the upper Takoe Valley. And last is the group of settlements located beside the lower Rutaka River (Nos 33–8). Even though the location of these resembles the case of the lower Naibuchi basin, they were considered to have been constructed under a certain regulation after 1886, and were not abandoned.

CONCLUSION

From the cases of the Naibuchi basin and of the Susuya basin, three types of the location of the thirty-eight settlements have been identified and discussed. Among them, sixteen settlements were of type 1, which located along the main military postroad. The majority of this type were of a linear-formed village, while some of them were 'T'-shaped in cases where the postroad joined the main axial street of that settlement. All occasionally served as stations, and, in the cases that they located near water, they often served as ferry terminals and as trading posts with the Ainu. In spite of wide variations in village sizes, type 1 settlements were mostly retained and were occupied by Japanese settlers, except for those settlements on the lower flood plains.

Eight other settlements fell into type 2, which located on well-drained and fertile fans. They were originally established for farming despite the difficulties of cutting thick forests and transportation inconvenience. In the upper Takoe Valley, three settlements of this type were relatively small and immature, and they were abandoned or were later removed. On the other hand, in the upper Susuya Valley, five large settlements of this type were constructed after the major settlements along the postroad had been completed. Tolerable areas of dairy farms and fields were there, and the villages were

regularly shaped 'T ', 'H' , and so forth. It is not too much to suggest that they were model settlements in the southern lowland district. The KGO mainly preserved them and strictly reorganised housing lots in each village.

Lastly, the other fourteen settlements were of type 3, which located near the rivers in the lower flood plains. They were constructed on vacant land with little difficultiy in preparing the soil. In the lower Naibuchi basin, the river often overflowed and inundated the settlements. Such a process of land selection implied that they were not planned very carefully. In spite of their various sizes and forms, which were 'T'-shaped in some cases, these settlements were almost all abandoned or were replaced by a new dispersed type of village on the higher terraces away from the flood hazard. However, the five settlements along the lower Rutaka River were more firmly established, since they were built according to regulation, and were never abandoned.

Whichever of the three types, these settlement plans originated in the Slavic concept of agricultural settlement.[4] They were adapted to this district despite considerable natural and social environmental problems – climate, soils, transportation and the allocation of convicts. Furthermore, these settlements had to be built in a short period. In a sense, their suitability for such an environment emerges in the variation of the three types and in the continuity of the Japanese settlements. The KGO first made an attempt to adopt in Sakhalin Island the dispersed village plan following the township settlement system which had prevailed in nearby Hokkaido. However, on the strength of the field survey, the mature and sturdy Russian villages were retained as they were. This outcome may retroactively indicate the suitability of the Russian settlements to this island in border east Asia. Today, all have been reorganised and modernised.

ACKNOWLEDGEMENT

The structure of this chapter principally derives from an earlier article by the author entitled, 'Teisei rosia-ki ni okeru Saharin kaitaku shuraku no ricchi to keitai' (Settlement Patterns in Sakhalin Island in Imperial Russia), *Journal of the Faculty of Liberal Arts*, Saga University, Vol. 13, 1981, pp. 61–86.

NOTES

1 According to the 1:50,000 scale topographical maps published by the Rikuchi sokuryo-bu (the Japanese Ordnance Survey), 1928–33.

2 The items of the personal interview on his field survey was as follows: (1) standing; (2) name; (3) age; (4) religion; (5) native place; (6) coming year; (7) job; (8) literacy; (9) marriage; (10) subsidy. Those original individual data were not presented in his report.

3 The Japanese unit, 1 ken equals 1.8 metres. The Russian unit, 1 sazhen, is equivalent to 2.1 metres.

4 For example, the three types of settlements discussed in this chapter are similar to the settlement types identified by S. A. Kovalev. He classified the location patterns of the Russian settlements into three categories. According to him, first type settlements were located on small vacant lands in thick forests; the second type were along the main road, and last type were on wide open lands. See Kovalev, S. A. (1963) *Selsnoe rasselenie* (Agricultural Settlement) (Moskva), page 166.

REFERENCES

Bassin, M. (1988) 'Expansion and colonialism on the eastern frontier: views of Siberia and the Far East in pre-Petrine Russia', *Journal of Historical Geography*, Vol. 1, pp.3–21.

Chekhov, A. P. (1890) *Ostrov Sakhalin* (Sakhalin Island) (Moskva). Translated into Japanese by Nakamura, T. (1953) *Saharinto* (Tokyo: Iwanamishoten), 2 volumes.

Funakoshi, A. (1976) *Hoppozu no rekishi* (History in Maps of Northeastern Asia) (Tokyo : Kodansya).

Habar, A. M. (1939) *Ainu syakai keizaishi* (Socio-Economic History of the Ainu) (Tokyo: Hakuyosya).

Karafuto-cho (1910) *Karafuto shokuminchi sentei hobun* (Survey Report of Colonial Karafuto) (Toyohara).

Kindaichi, K. (1930) *Karafuto Hokkaido no jinshu* (Races in Karafuto and Hokkaido), in *Nihon Chiri Taikei* (The Complete Regional Geography of Japan), Vol. 10 (series of Hokkaido and Karafuto) (Tokyo: Kaizosya), pp. 470–97.

Mitsui, M. S. (1873) *Ocherk ostrova Sakhalina v seleskokhoziaistvennom otnoshenii* (Report in Relation to Agricultural Economics in Sakhalin Island) (St. Petersburg), quoted in Panov A. A. (1905) *Sakalin kak kolon'ya* (Sakhalin as Colony) (Moskva), and translated into Japanese by Takumu-Sho (The Japanese Colonial Office) (1942) *Shokuminchi to site no Sagaren* (Tokyo), p. 55.

Rees, D. (1985) *The Soviet Seizure of the Kuriles* (New York: Praeger).

Stephen, J. J. (1971) *Sakhalin: a History* (Oxford), translated into Japanese by Yasukawa, K. (1973) *Saharin: nicchuso koshi* (Tokyo: Harashobo).

Suzuki, S. (1860) *Karafuto nikki* (Travel Diary in Karafuto), Edo (Tokyo).

Takakura, S. (1947) *Hokkaido takushoku-shi* (History of Colonisation in Hokkaido) (Tokyo: Hakuyoshoin).

Yasukawa, K. (1973) *Saharin: Nicchuso Koshi* (Tokyo: Harashobo).

7 Society, state and peripherality: The case of the Thai–Malaysian border landscape

Dennis Rumley

INTRODUCTION

This chapter has two principal aims. First, it explores the relevance of the concept of peripherality to an understanding of the creation of border landscapes. It is argued that it is possible to discern the existence of 'peripheral characteristics' along international political boundaries irrespective of the type of state structure of contiguous states. It is suggested, however, that the configuration of these characteristics can only be fully comprehended with reference to the particular geographical and historical context along the border region.

Second, the chapter seeks to begin to address past inadequacies in border landscape research, which has tended to be overly concerned with static interstate differences in the overt functions of political boundaries and border regions rather than with comparative intra-state differences in conflict and power which become manifest in the border zone or which are likely to become evident at some future date.

The case of the Thai–Malaysian border region (Figure 7.1) was chosen to pursue these two aims for four main reasons. First, the contiguous states possess different state structures. Thailand is a highly centralised state officially containing 53 million people of which 5.5 million live in the capital Bangkok (National Statistical Office, 1987: 20). In 1970, the Bangkok metropolitan area had a population more than 30 times that of the second largest city, Chiang Mai (Keyes, 1987: 13). In addition, Thailand is politically dominated by the military, contains relatively few inherent participatory institutions and the level of political consciousness among the Thai people is generally relatively low (Bunbongkarn, 1987). Malaysia, on the other hand, has a population of 16.5 million and possesses an elected

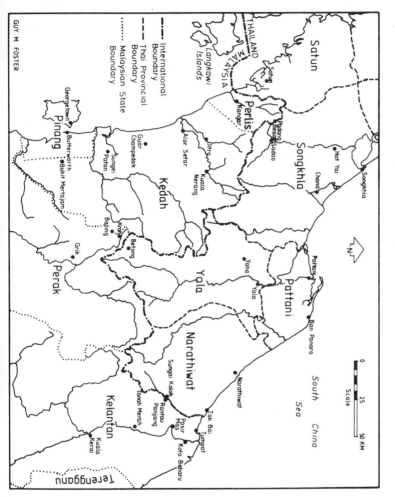

Figure 7.1 The Thai–Malaysian border region

federal government. Regular federal elections have been held every four or five years since the first full parliamentary election in 1959. However, wide variations in the population size of federal electoral districts, the present virtual monopoly parliamentary hold of the Barisan Nasional coalition, curbs on the freedom of the press and relatively recent attempts to emasculate the judiciary all raise serious questions about the true democratic welfare of the Malaysian federation. Importantly, in the 1986 state and federal elections, one of the major concentrations of opposition political party support was to be found in the border states of Kedah, Kelantan, Perak and Terengganu (Hanafiah, 1987: 284).

A second reason for choosing to examine the Thai–Malaysian case relates to the different ethnic and religious structure of each state, their geographical variation and the respective state policies regarding these structures which tend to be highlighted in the border region. In Thailand, official census data mask considerable ethnic, language and religious diversity (Keyes, 1987: 14). In particular, there exists a very considerable Malay Muslim minority in the four southern provinces of Narathiwat, Pattani, Satun and Yala (Haemindra, 1976). In Malaysia, on the other hand, Malays comprise about half of the total population, although there are significant minorities of Chinese (about one-third) and Indians (about 10 per cent) but there is considerable cultural diversity within these groups (Carstens, 1986: 1). There is also a significant geographical variation in the distribution of the groups with four of five of the border states (Terengganu, Kelantan, Perlis and Kedah) having the highest peninsula proportions of Malays, for example. The other border state, Perak, contains significant concentrations of Chinese and Indians and consequently the Malays are in a minority in that state (Shafruddin, 1987: 120). Both Thailand and Malaysia possess an overt nationalist policy based on a pre-eminent ethnic and religious code of behaviour, and in combination these policies have important future implications for the Thai–Malaysian border region. Thailand's policy is based on the pre-eminence of Thai culture and of the Buddhist religion, while Malaysia's policy is based on the pre-eminence of Malay culture and of Islam. These policies interrelate along the Thai–Malaysian border region with economic development policies, communal politics and incipient Islamic fundamentalism. Furthermore, the Thai–Malaysian border is the only complete international land boundary meeting place of Islam and Buddhism.

A third reason for an examination of the Thai–Malaysian case is historical. Unlike Malaysia, Thailand did not enjoy European colonial

rule. In Malaysia, however, British colonial ideas of centralisation and uniformity of control were built into a federation which was designed to accommodate the legacy of the Malay states and the institution of the Sultanate rather than to accommodate communalism or size as in many other federal systems (Shafruddin, 1987). In Thailand, on the other hand, the lack of any political alternative to authoritarian rule has been seen as virtually a by-product of the avoidance of colonial control (Cady, 1974: 422). The differential legacy of British colonial rule is thus an important ingredient in the understanding of the Thai–Malaysian border region. Currently, Thailand is seen as a 'semi-democracy' (Chai-anan, 1989), and Malaysia is perceived to be a 'quasi-democracy' (Zakaria, 1989).

A fourth and related reason for being concerned with the Thai–Malaysian case derives from the historically strategic importance of the Malay peninsula and its relationship to emergent Thai and Malay nationalism in the twentieth century. This relationship is brought into sharp focus along the Thai–Malaysian border region. It has been noted, for example, that, given its location approximately half way between the civilisations of India and China, that the peninsula has always been a barrier to trade. Partly as a consequence of this factor it has functioned as a region of contact between different peoples for many centuries. For example, the Malay peninsula played a key role in the dissemination of Indian culture to northern South-East Asia (Wheatley, 1961: 194). Furthermore, Arab traders were especially evident from the eighth century (Hall, 1981: 221). From the sixteenth to the eighteenth century there developed a European contest for the peninsula. First, the Portuguese took Malacca in the sixteenth century, the Dutch in the seventeenth century and the British in the eighteenth century (Wheatley, 1961). The beginning of the nineteenth century saw the reawakening of the Greater Siam concept and the revival of Siam's ancient claims over all of the peninsula (Hall, 1981: 553). For more than half of the twentieth century, in addition to British colonialism, there existed a number of strategies to incorporate the whole Malay peninsula into a larger political-economic entity. In the 1920s, for example, members of the 'Greater Indian Society' saw the South-East Asian states as being 'ancient Indian colonies' (Hall, 1981: 16). Japan's explicit goal of a Greater East Asia Coprosperity Sphere continued into 1944 (Cady, 1974). The expansion of Malaya itself to incorporate North Borneo can be seen not only as an attempt to 'balance' the Singapore Chinese but also as a response to Indonesia's Maphilindo concept and the 'crush Malaysia' campaign of the 1960s (Means, 1976: 318).

The Thai nationalist emergence in the twentieth century has been closely linked with Buddhism since the patriotism of those belonging to other religions has been called into question (Hall, 1981: 769). Such a situation has the potential to push the Muslim minority along the southern border internationally towards other Islamic states and even closer to neighbouring Kelantan across the border. Nationalism in Malaysia is an even more recent and more fragile phenomenon, and it appears that policies designed to favour Malay and/or Muslim groups will inevitably alienate the other major sections of the population (Carstens, 1986: 87). In addition, one of Malaysia's several strategic concerns has been that communalism may well be exploited by Sino-Soviet rivalry, and, among other things, lead to renewed communist guerrilla activity along the Thai–Malaysian border (Poh Ping, 1986).

HISTORICAL EMERGENCE OF THE THAI–MALAYSIAN BORDER REGION

At the international scale, it is possible to view the Thai–Malaysian border region as an historically peripheral region East–West as well as from a North–South perspective. The region has been peripheral to both Indian Arab and Chinese traders. It has been peripheral to European colonialists. It has been peripheral to Java and to Malacca and, traditionally at the national scale, the region has been peripheral to Thailand and to the Malaysian federation. From the earliest times to the final delimitation of the Thai–Malaysian boundary in 1909, the people of the region have been subject to the manipulation and control of outside political and economic forces. Evidence of early states in the Malay peninsula goes back to the second century (Hall, 1981: 24). For example, the Hindu kingdom of Langasuka was founded on the east coast close to what is now the Thai province of Pattani and lasted until the sixteenth century (Wheatley, 1961).

Indian contact dates at least from the fourth century and the later Chinese contact meant that the peninsula was not only a point of departure but a region which was used to cross from the South China Sea to the Indian Ocean (Wheatley, 1961). The Buddhist state of Srivijaya emerged in the seventh century based primarily on trade and was commercially important until the twelfth century after which the Tai kingdom began to expand (Hall, 1981: 50–72). The original settlements of the Tai were in southern China (for example, in Szechwan and Yunan) but they were forced south and displaced the

Khmer who controlled most of what is now Thailand, and the Khmer in turn fled to Cambodia (Syukri, 1985: 7–8).

The first Thai claim for suzerainty in the Pattani region dates from the late thirteenth century (Pitsuwan, 1985: 16). It appears, however, to be debatable as to whether Thai influence over the southern part of the peninsula was restricted by Javanese expansion (Wheatley, 1961: 301). At that time, Kedah had been incorporated with a colony of Malays from Malacca (Newbold, 1971). Malacca had become an important trading centre by the fifteenth century and came under European control in 1511. At its greatest extent the kingdom included much of present Kedah and Kelantan (Wheatley, 1961: 310). It was the most important commercial centre in South-East Asia and the main point of diffusion of Islam. Islamic penetration was seen in part as a political weapon against Buddhist Siam (Hall, 1981: 227–9).

In the early sixteenth century, Siam claimed suzerainty over the whole of the Malay peninsula but agreed to a treaty with the Portuguese over trade. The Dutch capture of Malacca in the seventeenth century led to a treaty with Siam which guaranteed Dutch free trade with the Malay states under Siamese suzerainty (Hall, 1981: 371).

From a Pattani Muslim-Malay nationalist viewpoint, three historical periods have been identified (Dulyakasem, 1981). First from 1785 to 1867 which saw the present territory incorporated in a Thai expansionist phase during the reign of King Rama I. The British acquisition of the island of Penang from the Sultan of Kedah in 1786 was important for naval strategic reasons (Hall, 1981: 539). In 1818, Perak was overrun by troops from Kedah who had invaded on behalf of the King of Siam. In 1821 Kedah itself was 'conquered and devastated by the Siamese'. The Anglo-Siamese treaty of 1826, however, allowed the Rajah of Perak to govern in his own right. After this, at first, Siam appeared to abandon any real attempt to gain the west coast Malay states and transferred its interests to Kelantan and Terengganu (Hall, 1981: 559). Siamese designs on Kelantan, however, caused that state to seek British protection. Meanwhile, Pattani was finally conquered by Siam in 1832 and was divided into seven states (Newbold, 1971).

In 1839 Kedah itself was divided into four principalities and Perlis was separated from Kedah as a state in its own right (Salleh, 1974: 54). In 1852, the conquest by the British of lower Burma led to the creation of an Anglo-Siamese Border Commission to determine political boundaries. For the first time in their history Siamese

rulers had to think in terms of territorial boundaries (Keyes, 1987: 49).

A second period in Pattani Malay-Muslim history was from 1868 to 1931 which saw the introduction of a system of provincial administration (Dulyakasem, 1981: 62). The British gained control over Perak in 1874 and it became the first of the 'Protected Malay States' (Roff, 1974). In 1896, the formation of the Federated Malay States (FMS) saw the joining of only one of the present border states, Perak, with Negri Sembilan, Pahang and Selangor. The other four border states were part of the Unfederated Malay States (UMS) where British rule was 'indirect' (Shafruddin, 1987).

During the nineteenth century, the large-scale 'invasion' of Chinese tin miners and Indian immigrants to exploit rubber facilitated a major change in the racial composition of the Malay peninsula in one generation (Hall, 1981: 606). Towards the end of that century Britain had adopted a 'forward policy' in the same area of the peninsula as Siam. The *Boundary Agreement* of 1899 defined the frontier between 'British' and 'Siamese' Malaya (Salleh, 1974: 35). In 1901 the seven Pattani states were grouped into one administrative unit. However, there has been a Malay-Muslim 'struggle for survival' since the formal incorporation of Pattani into the Thai state in 1902 (Pitsuwan, 1985: 4). The cession by Siam of the Malay states of Kedah, Kelantan and Terengganu, on the other hand, was made on the grounds that these remote 'Siamese Malay States' were a source of irritation and danger to Bangkok. Britain's aim, on the other hand, was to enlarge trade and protect naval interests (Salleh, 1974: 52).

Before and after border treaties, however, there was constant conflict between the British and Thai authorities until the *Anglo-Siamese Treaty* of 1909 formally ceded territory to the British and established the present international boundary (Figure 7.2). Britain had earlier argued that, on geographical and cultural grounds, Satun was a part of Kedah and the Malay states of Pattani were closely connected to Kelantan (Numnonda, 1967). The Thai government thereafter adopted a policy of gradual assimilation of the Malay minority in Pattani especially during the third period of Pattani Muslim–Malay history following the change from an absolute to a constitutional monarchy in 1932 (Dulyakasem, 1981: 72). The only other temporary border change since 1909 occurred during the Japanese occupation in the Second World War when the territory which was earlier ceded was returned to Thailand (Pitsuwan, 1985: 94). These annexations were returned as part of the 1946 peace treaty (Cady, 1974: 9). However, even though the boundary has not

Figure 7.2 Thai–Malaysian boundary changes, 1909

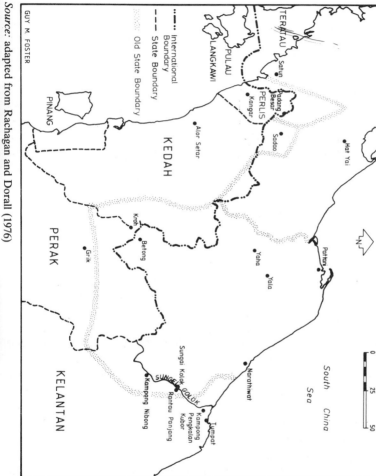

International
Boundary
State Boundary
Old State Boundary

GUY M. FOSTER

Source: adapted from Rachagan and Dorall (1976)

changed since 1946, there have been recurrent protests against the manner of Thai control (Pitsuwan, 1985: 271).

In Malaysia, in contrast, the Japanese occupation was associated with a communist-led rebellion in 1943 (Cady, 1974: 13). After the War, the initial British policy of attempting to emasculate the power of the hereditary sultans and attempts to accord equal citizenship rights to all Malay-born and recent immigrants became associated with the beginnings of Malay nationalism. This, in turn, was increasingly anti-Chinese and had a strong religious orientation (Hall, 1981: 871). In 1946, the United Malays National Organisation (UMNO) was founded as a broad coalition of Malay politicial organisations opposed to the British proposal for a Malay Union and which was eventually transformed into Malaya's largest political party (Barraclough, 1988: 93).

In 1948, the year of the federation of Malaya, a Moscow-led policy of 'overt rebellion' against imperialism encouraged a mainly Chinese communist revolt. Many of the communist insurgents based themselves in the jungle in the rugged sections of the Thai–Malaysian border landscape and the conflict reached a peak in 1951. At independence, the government was faced with a major long-term 'problem' of resettling some 500,000 peasant Chinese living along the edges of the jungle (Cady, 1974: 76–7).

The Malaysian Chinese Association (MCA) was founded during the Emergency in 1949 to represent the more wealthy Chinese and became a political party in 1952. In the same year, MCA entered into an electoral arrangement with UMNO to contest municipal elections, and this together with the Malaysian Indian Congress (MIC) became the basis of the Alliance Party which ruled the Malaysian federation from 1959 until the formation of the Barisan Nasional in 1973 (Barraclough, 1988), The Barisan Nasional, which was formed to try to increase the support base of the Alliance vote by encouraging greater non-Malay support, easily won the federal elections in 1974, 1978 and 1982, and in 1986 won 152 of the 177 contested seats, much of the opposition party support, especially at the state level, being concentrated in the border states (Hanafiah, 1987: 284).

THE THAI–MALAYSIAN BORDER LANDSCAPE IN ITS REGIONAL SETTING

The Thai–Malaysian international boundary is geographically more peripheral to Thailand than it is to Malaysia. From the federal capital of Kuala Lumpur, for example, the straight-line distance of the

boundary is approximately 300 kilometres. In contrast, the international boundary is about twice that distance from Bangkok.

The use of physical features as 'natural boundaries' appealed to colonial powers, especially in South-East Asia, due to their apparent simplicity in boundary delimitation. Inevitably, however, their delimitation paid scant regard to cultural homogeneity or traditional economic and social organisation (Rachagan and Dorall, 1976: 47). The 512-kilometre-long Thai–Malaysian boundary thus follows the watersheds from the Straits of Malacca west of Kangar in Perlis, east and south between Kroh and Betong, and then north-east to the level alluvial plain of the Sungei Kolok where it follows that river 94 kilometres to the South China Sea, with the remaining 6 kilometres being located in coastal waters (Figure 7.1). The central section, which is the northern extension of the main Malaysian ranges, comprises a series of rugged summits rarely exceeding 1500 metres covered in dense tropical forest while the western section bordering Perlis averages about 600 metres (Prescott *et al.*, 1977).

In terms of the reconstruction of past human occupance from visible evidence, the tropical Thai–Malaysian border region is much more problematic than the temperate areas of Western Europe, for example. The collective impact of climate and insects ensures that no organic material survives for more than a few years and masonry disintegrates in decades (Wheatley, 1961). Visual landscape evidence is therefore hard to find assuming that problems of access arising out of transportation limitations and security restrictions can be overcome in any case. Secondary data are thus at a premium combined with limited observations and feasible discussions.

The present Thai–Malaysian border region consists of the five southern Thai provinces of Narathiwat, Pattani, Satun, Songkla and Yala and the five northern Malaysian states of Kedah, Kelantan, Perak, Perlis and Terengganu (Figure 7.1). In 1980, the total populations of the border zone political units in Thailand and Malaysia was virtually the same (2 million). In Thailand, populations range from 818,000 in Songkla to 156,000 in Satun. In Malaysia, the smallest border state is Perlis with 24,000 and the largest is Perak with 902,000, although in the case of the latter the northern-most border district of Ulu Perak has a relatively low population.

The population density in the rugged central border section from eastern Perlis to western Kelantan is low save for the town of Betong in Yala where the main road crosses the boundary to Kroh in Perak. The eastern coastal plain along the Sungei Kolok in contrast offers relatively easy access between Thailand and Malaysia via road and

rail and the region is relatively densely populated (Rachagan and Dorall, 1976: 49). Thus, Yala province has a population density of 52 per square kilometre compared with 102 in Narathiwat and 214 in Pattani. As was noted above, four of the five Malaysian border states contain the highest peninsula proportions of Malays while the fifth (Perak) has significant percentages of Chinese and Indians. The Thai Muslim population is highest in the border province of Narathiwat (78 per cent) while Pattani is 77 per cent Muslim, Satun 70 per cent and Yala 60 per cent. Indeed, in the latter, 70 per cent of the population cannot speak Thai and 25 per cent of the population is illiterate (Vannaprasert *et al.*, 1986: 16). The largest concentrations of urban population in the border region are contained in Malaysia. Apart from Kota Baharu, the state capital of Kelantan, which has a population of approximately 168,000 and Alor Setar, the state capital of Kedah, which has a population of 69,500, the border region contains only a few relatively small urban settlements. There are three occurrences of the 'twin town' border phenomenon – Sadao–Padang Besar (Songkla–Perlis), Betong–Kroh (Yala–Perak) and Sungai Kolok–Rantau Panjang (Narathiwat–Kelantan). In all three cases, the Thai towns are significantly larger than their Malay counterparts, even though the total Thai border zone urban population is smaller. Thus, Sadao has a population of 11,000 compared with its Malaysian 'twin' Padang Besar which has 2,500. Second, Betong in Yala, which is predominantly Chinese, has a population of 36,000 compared with 4,500 in Kroh. The third, Sungai Kolok in Narathiwat, has 21,000 compared with Rantau Panjang's 5,000.

All three Malaysian 'twin towns' contain a majority of Malays – Padang Besar (58 per cent), Kroh (54 per cent) and Rantau Panjang (90 per cent). In all other border zone towns, apart from those in Kelantan, the urban Malay population is a minority. In Kangar, for example, which is the state capital of Perlis and has a population of 13,000, the Malay population is 46 per cent and in Alor Setar it is 43 per cent. In Kelantan, on the other hand, Tumpat has 91 per cent Malays in its 10,000 population and Kota Baharu is 85 per cent Malay.

Overall, however, the border economy is predominantly rural and agricultural and is dominated by rice cultivation (for example, in Pattani and in Kedah) and by the production of rubber (for example in Yala). In the five Thai border provinces, employment in the agricultural sector ranges from a low of 67 per cent in Songkla to a high of 77 per cent in Pattani (National Statistical Office). It has been

estimated that 80 per cent of Malay-Muslims in Southern Thailand are involved in rice farming and rubber plantations, all on relatively small average landholdings (Pitsuwan, 1985: 19). In northern Malaysia, on the other hand, Perak and Terengganu have had a traditionally greater emphasis on mining and manufacturing compared with the other border states which are predominantly agricultural (Pryor, 1978: 64).

In both Thailand and Malaysia the border landscape is one which reflects economic peripherality. In Malaysia, contributions to the Gross Domestic Product of the three most important industrial sectors (agriculture, manufacturing and mining and wholesale and retail trade) show that Perak is the only border state with an above average contribution in all three sectors. Of the remaining four states, in the main, all have significantly below average GDP contributions with the exception of Kedah for agriculture (Fifth Malaysian Plan, 1986: 174–5). In Thailand, the agricultural economy of the border provinces has been in relative decline since the Second World War. This is a direct reflection of the national shift in the contribution made by the various sectors to economic growth in the country. From 1951 to 1984, for example, the contribution to economic growth made by the agricultural sector declined from 50.1 per cent to 19.9 per cent without any corresponding shift from agricultural to non-agricultural occupations. The most rapid growth, on the other hand, has been in the industrial sector (Keyes, 1987: 154).

POLITICAL CONFLICT IN THE THAI–MALAYSIAN BORDER LANDSCAPE

The interaction of economic, cultural, political and geographical peripherality along the Thai–Malaysian border region has resulted in at least five ongoing political conflicts – the location of the international boundary; the Thai Muslim minority; Malaysian opposition party support; Chinese resettlement and economic development policies.

The location of the international boundary

As was noted above, the Thai–Malaysian international boundary was finalised through the 1909 agreement between Siam and Britain. The coincidence of a physical boundary with a political boundary was assumed to facilitate the process of delimitation and control. However, there have been a number of ongoing disputes in the central

Figure 7.3 The international boundary at the mouth of the Sungei Kolok, 1955–71

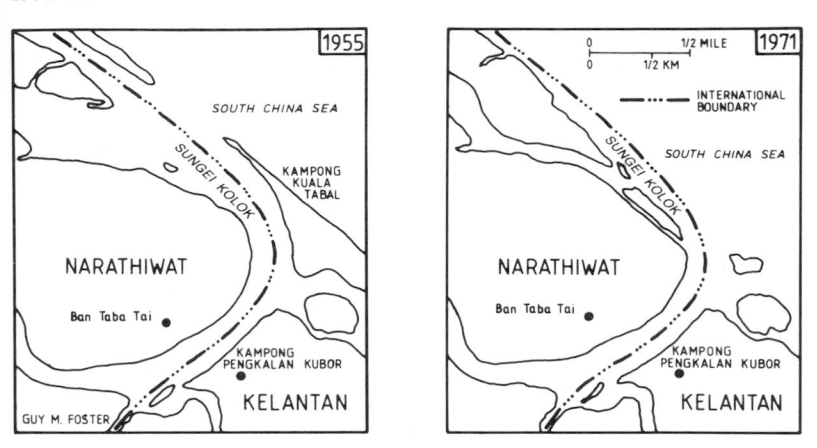

Source: adapted from Rachagan and Dorall (1976)

jungle regions and in the western section over the precise location of boundary markers. Overall, on both sides of the boundary security is very tight, but perhaps more so on the Malaysian side. The erection of a large wall by the Malaysians at the Kroh crossing and the walled compound patrolled by Malaysian guards at Pedang Besar is evidence of this. However, Thai border security, in general, appears to increase from west to east and is especially tight in Narathiwat partly associated with smuggling which is an endemic component of the Thai–Malaysian border economy.

Among the most problematic sections of the boundary in terms of physical delimitation and control is the eastern section between Narathiwat and Kelantan which runs along the Sungei Kolok. There are at least two aspects to this physical problem. First, the determination of the boundary is problematic close to the river mouth since the location of small islands can change both seasonally and yearly. Islands which are visible in the dry season, for example, can disappear in the wet. Furthermore, the location of river mouth islands from 1955 to 1971, for example, has changed and this makes the identification of the boundary very difficult (Figure 7.3). These issues have become associated with local conflicts over land use, fishing rights, river pollution and the movement of goods and people (Rachagan and Dorall, 1976: 54).

This leads to the second aspect of this problem which is more

Plate 7.1   Illegal crossing point of Sungei Kolok

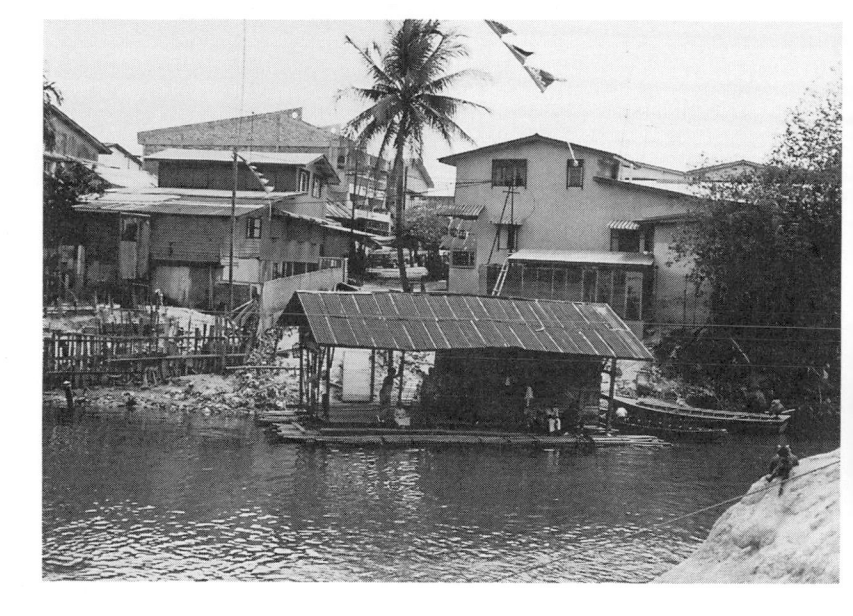

evident upstream. In the vicinity of the twin towns of Sungai Kolok and Rantau Panjang, for example, the Kolok River at times is very narrow and easy to cross. Control of river crossings and hence smuggling is very difficult if not impossible to police. Although there is only one 'official' crossing point, fifteen illegal crossing points are known to the local inhabitants in Sungai Kolok (Plate 7.1). Furthermore, in Malaysia and Thailand it is illegal to maintain dual citizenship. However, due to the comparative ease of crossing the boundary and the uncertainty of home location, it is possible for border residents to maintain dual citizenship. Pattani Malays from Thailand have even been known to vote in Kelantan state elections! (Rachagan and Dorall, 1976: 55).

The Thai Malay-Muslim minority

The Malay-speaking Muslims of southern Thailand do not possess any innate linkage to the Thai nation. Residents on both sides of the international boundary have relatives on the other side. This is reflected in the estimated interaction across the boundary by customs officials for the purpose of visiting relatives – more than 100 per day

at Sadao, 300 per day at Sungai Kolok and more than 300 per month at Ban Taba Tai. It appears that Thai state policy regarding the minority to a certain extent has exacerbated regional alienation (Keyes, 1987: 131). This degree of alienation, in turn has been politically expressed in different ways.

At least four political groups have sought to represent the cultural, economic and political aspirations of the Malay-Muslim minority (Dulyakasem, 1981: 91–8). The first group to be organised was the Barisan Nasional Pembasan Pattani (BNPP) or National Liberation front of the Pattani Republic. This group emerged in 1949 and its HQ is believed to be in Kota Baharu. Its tactics have involved ambush, terrorism and indoctrination. A second group is known as the Barisan Revolusi Nasional (BRN) or National Revolution Front and is thought to have been organised in the early 1960s. This group has an Islamic socialist platform and aims to establish an independent state of Pattani. It reportedly has a loose alliance with the Communist parties of Malaysia and Thailand. The third group, which is believed to be the largest, is the Pattani United Liberation Organisation (PULO) which was set up in 1968, has its HQ in Mecca and whose aim is to set up an independent Islamic State of Pattani. The rugged central jungle region of the Thai–Malaysian border is the guerrilla base for PULO which purportedly has its own refugee village near Kroh in Perak. The fourth group is Sabil-illah ('path of God'), which is an urban terrorist group formed in 1975.

Any separatist groups are an embarrassment to Malaysia in that, on the one hand, Malaysia cannot be seen to support them in order to maintain good relations with Thailand, and, on the other hand, Malaysia cannot be seen to condemn them for fear of alienating sympathetic Kelantan Malays (Keyes, 1987: 132). Thailand, on the other hand, has pursued a policy of recruiting Malaysian and Indonesian help to deny PULO a voice at Islamic forums (Pitsuwan, 1982: 39).

Political opposition to Barisan Nasional

The federal elections of May 1969 marked a turning point in Malaysian democracy. Support for the ruling alliance fell 9.5 per cent to 48.5 per cent and the party lost twenty-two seats in the parliament (Shafruddin, 1987: 270). Basic factors of political and economic competition reinforced by long-standing cultural and ethnic differences resulted in bloody communal violence shortly after the elections (Cady, 1974: 185). With the help of a fragmented opposition, the

alliance continued to govern, eventually via emergency rule, determined both to promote national unity on the one hand, and prohibit discussion of communal conflict on the other (Milne, 1981: 50). Malay nationalism, however, is far from a uni-dimensional concept. Indeed, three variants have been identified – Islamic, radical nationalist and elitist-administrative.

Whereas UMNO was the political variant of elitist-administrative Malay nationalism, the Islamic Party of Malaysia (PAS) is seen as embodying the other two variants (Kessler, 1974). A central aim of PAS is the creation of an Islamic state in Malaysia. However, traditionally its support has been regional with strong bases in Kelantan, Terrengganu and Kedah, all peripheral border states, all historically underdeveloped, all former Unfederated Malay States and almost totally Malay in composition (Shafruddin, 1987: 271). Indeed PAS has previously controlled the state governments of Terengganu (1959–62) and Kelantan (1959–69) and in the 1986 state elections was the only opposition party in parliament in those states and Kedah (Hanafiah, 1987).

One of the most serious threats to the internal security of Malaysia has been seen to be the revival of the communist party of Malaysia guerrilla movement in the mid-1970s (Milne, 1981: 190). The CPM membership, which is predominantly Chinese, is based along the central rugged jungle section of the Thai–Malaysian border and the estimated US$40 million border wall is also meant to contain that group. Some Malaysian officials believe that the CPM has received US arms from the Thai army. However, since the revival of guerrilla activity, there has been considerable Thai and Malay cooperation against the CPM including the ability to engage in 'hot pursuit'.

Chinese resettlement

Both the Thai and Malaysian governments have had different relationships with the Chinese community *vis-à-vis* resettlement policies for actual or potential communist sympathisers. Late in 1986, the Thai government decided to offer an amnesty to CPM members in an attempt to curtail guerrilla activities along the Thai–Malaysian border. As a result, several hundred former Chinese guerrillas have been resettled on the Thai side of the border in 'Friendship Villages' (Plate 7.2). Four of these villages are located on the western side of the Yala–Betong road which was regarded as the territory of the 12th regiment (Figure 7.1). Villages 1 and 2 are about 15 kilometres from Betong and each houses approximately 200 and 100 residents

Plate 7.2 Piyamit Friendship Village, Thailand

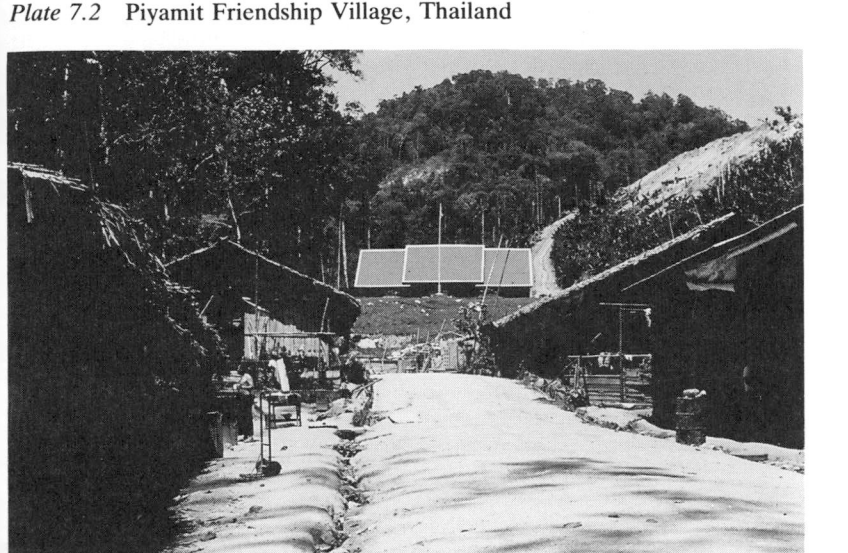

respectively and is 'guarded' by Thai soldiers. The fifth village is close to Sadao in Southern Songkla. Village 1 (Piyamit Friendship Village) opened on 28 April 1987. The local people grow much of their own food, and, although each person receives a small daily allowance from the Thai government, finance is regarded as the main problem among the villagers.

Of course, the concept of 'new village' is not new along the Thai–Malaysian border, since many such settlements were set up in Malaysia between 1949 and 1953 in an attempt to overcome the communist insurgency. In particular, the resettlement policy was aimed at preventing the inhabitants or 'squatters' being either the victims or the supporters of communist guerrilla activity. The largest number of people (32 per cent) and villages (30 per cent) were relocated in Perak, while significant relocations also occurred in Johore (25 per cent people and 22 per cent villages) and in Selangor (18 per cent people and 9 per cent villages) (Voon and Khoo, 1986: 39–42). In most cases, squatters were resettled within 3–8 kilometres from their original location, although in some cases longer-distance moves were required. By the end of the Emergency, the barbed wire fences which had surrounded the earlier villages had been removed

and by the 1960s many new villages had developed into prosperous settlements (Sandhu, 1964). However, basic facilities often were poorly developed, and it took until the mid-1980s for most villages to be able to have proper water, electricity and schools. By 1985, the total new village population had reached 1.8 million (Fifth Malaysian Plan, 1986: 91–6). Whereas the Chinese villages in southern Thailand are 'guarded' by Thai soldiers, for the most part in the Malaysian case, policy stations are presently Malay 'outposts' in areas inhabited primarily by Chinese (Zakaria, 1987: 121).

Economic development policies

The Thai–Malaysian border region is economically peripheral to its respective states on any measure. However, economic development policies applied to similar groups on either side of the boundary clearly reflect different national goals. In Malaysia there is a well-defined communal complexion to income disparities between 'rich' and 'poor' states, with the Malays being heavily concentrated in the relatively poor states of the border region with the possible exclusion of Perak (Table 7.1). In 1985, the degree of poverty in the border states ranged from 20.3 per cent in Perak to 39.2 per cent in Kelantan compared with a total of 18.4 per cent for all of peninsular Malaysia (5MP, 1986: 88). Furthermore, unemployment is consistently above the national average in the five border states (5MP, 1986: 170–1). The New Economic Policy (NEP) enunciated following the 1969 riots in Malaysia is committed both to an eradication of poverty as well as to a 'restructuring of society' (5MP, 1986: 3). In effect, what this means is that Malays are theoretically more likely to benefit from national economic development policies. Since the border states have among the highest proportions of Malays in the federation, this has potentially significant implications for the Malaysian border region. Disproportionate allocations to one favoured group in an economically peripheral context, however, may well lead to considerable resentment and conflict on the part of other groups.

Of total Malaysian federal development allocations for 1986–90, 72.3 per cent is for 'economic' developments and 27.7 per cent is for 'social' developments (5MP, 1986: 551). For the 1986–90 economic development allocation, all border states except Perak received above average allocations per head of population and two of the largest allocations went to two of the poorest states, Kelantan and Perlis (Table 7.1).

In the Thai border provinces, on the other hand, the context of

economic development policies is fundamentally different. The Thai border region, like that in Malaysia, is economically peripheral. The average unemployment rate in the Thai border provinces in 1980 was 12.5 per cent compared with 7.1 per cent for the Malaysian border states. However, this economic dimension is overlain by and interacts with a significant cultural dimension of peripherality. The Malay-Muslim minority in Thailand has lagged behind in terms of education and health provision, for example (Syukri, 1985: 75). In Thailand as a whole, per capita incomes have declined from 1960 to 1983 as a proportion of the national average in all three peripheral regions (north, north-east and south). However, in relative terms the rate of decline in the south has been faster than for any other region (Keyes, 1987: 159). Government development policies which have been aimed at export-led development have tended to favour industrial over agricultural developments (Keyes, 1987: 330), and thus, by implication have tended to exacerbate rural–urban inequalities. This combination of cultural peripherality and relative economic decline has potentially serious implications for the Thai border provinces, especially when it is associated with secessionist political organisations and when relatives across the international boundary are seen to be treated preferentially.

Table 7.1 Malaysian GDP and resource allocations by state 1986–90 (ringgit)

State	GDP/capita 1985	% Contribution to national GDP 1985	Fed alloc/hd econ devel	% Fed econ devel allocs
Federal Territory	7,783	15.1	618	3.0
Johore	3,324	10.4	1,123	8.8
Kedah	2,358	4.8	1,471	7.6
Kelantan	1,740	3.0	2,327	10.1
Malacca	2,765	2.3	598	1.3
Negri Sembilan	3,846	4.1	1,201	3.2
Pahang	3,495	5.9	2,572	10.9
Penang	3,649	7.3	726	3.2
Perak	3,194	10.4	897	7.4
Perlis	2,604	0.7	2,420	1.7
Sabah	3,572	7.7	1,677	9.1
Sarawak	3,085	8.0	1,236	8.1
Selangor	4,963	15.2	715	5.5
Terengganu	4,719	5.1	1,741	4.7

Source: Fifth Malaysian Plan 1986–90, Government of Malaysia, Kuala Lumpur, 1986.

CONCLUSION

It has been argued that an understanding of the emergence and present structure of the Thai–Malaysian border landscape is enhanced by a consideration of its cultural, political, economic and geographical peripherality. It has been suggested that five main types of conflicts can be seen to be caused by the interaction of these elements of peripherality. For the future, from a cultural viewpoint, it seems that most Thai people would like to see the three state 'pillars' (monarchy, Buddhism and the Thai people) being able to support a more open structure which allows for a greater diversity of peoples (Keyes, 1987: 205). Politically, in Malaysia, for the federal system to function more effectively requires a leadership which is more tolerant of political diversity (Shafruddin, 1987: 358). It is possible that economically peripheral militant Islamic groups pose a threat both to the Thai state and to the Malaysian federation. However, in the case of Malaysia, the aims of the New Economic Policy are clearly designed to favour the Malay majority and thus the border states. The actual outcomes of this policy, on the other hand, are less than clear. It has been suggested, for example, that one of the main consequences of the NEP is that wealth has been accumulated into fewer hands (Mehmet, 1986: 157). It may well be, therefore, that the 'nightmare scenario' of the NEP which promotes the interests of the Malay elite and the middle class (Snodgrass, 1980: 284) is in the process of becoming a reality. In Thailand, on the other hand, economic development policies designed to reverse the apparent relative economic decline in the south coupled with policies aimed at integrating the region into the highly centralised Thai state are extremely sensitive and important long-term issues.

ACKNOWLEDGEMENTS

The research on which this paper is based is part of a long-term project on the human geography of southern Thailand. Its completion would not have been possible without the generous assistance provided as part of the sister relationship between the Prince of Songkla University and the University of Western Australia. I would like to thank sincerely all of those in the Faculty of Humanities at PSU Pattani campus who helped in so many different ways, especially Rangsie Hansopa, Perm Nilrat, Pichai Kouwsomram and Phanngam Gothamasan. In Malaysia, I was also helped by Voon Phin Keong and Sothi Rachagan of the Department of Geography, University of Malaya.

REFERENCES

Annandale, N. (1900) 'The Siamese Malay states', *Scottish Geographical Magazine*, Vol. 16, pp. 505–23.

Barraclough, S. (1988) *A Dictionary of Malaysian Politics* (Singapore: Heinemann).

Bee, O.-J. (1975) 'Urbanization and the urban population in peninsular Malaysia, 1970', *Journal of Tropical Geography*, Vol. 40, pp. 40–7.

Bunbongkarn, S. (1987) *The Military in Thai Politics 1981–6* (Singapore: Institute of South-East Asian Studies).

Cady, J. F. (1974) *The History of Post-War SouthEast Asia* (Athens, Ohio: Ohio University Press).

Carstens, S. A. (ed.) (1986) *Cultural Identity in Northern Peninsular Malaysia* (Athens, Ohio: Centre for International Studies).

Chai-anan, S. (1989) 'Thailand: A stable semi-democracy', in L. Diamond, J. J. Linz and S. M. Lipset (eds) *Democracy in Developing Countries, Volume Three, Asia* (Boulder: Rienner), pp. 304–46.

Cosgrove, D. and Jackson, P. (1987) 'New directions in cultural geography', *Area*, Vol. 19, pp. 95–101.

Cragg, K. and Speight, R. M. (1988) *The House of Islam* (Belmont: Wadsworth).

Crouch, H. (1982) *Malaysia's 1982 General Election* (Singapore: Institute of SE Asian Studies).

Department of Statistics (1986) *Population and Housing Census of Malaysia 1980* (Kuala Lumpur).

Dhiravegin, L. (1984) 'Local government systems and democratic development in Thailand', *Monograph Series*, Faculty of Political Science, Thammasat University.

—— (1985) 'Nationalism and the state in Thailand', *Monograph Series*, Faculty of Political Science, Thammasat University.

Dulyakasem, U. (1981) 'A Study of Muslim-Malays in Southern Siam', PhD Dissertation, Stanford University.

Fifth Malaysian Plan 1986–90 (1986) (Kuala Lumpar: Government Printer).

Gale, B. (ed.) (1987) *Readings in Malaysian Politics* (Petaling Jaya: Pelanduk).

Gellner, E. (1987) *Culture, Identity, and Politics* (Cambridge: Cambridge University Press).

Girling, J. L. S. (1981) *Thailand: Society and Politics* (Ithaca: Cornell University Press).

Gottmann, J. (ed.) (1980) *Centre and Periphery: Spatial Variation in Politics* (Beverly Hills: Sage).

Great Britain (1909) *Parliamentary Papers* (Cd. 4703).

Gullick, J. and Gale, B. (1986) *Malaysia: Its Political and Economic Development* (Petaling Jaya: Pelanduk).

Haemindra, N. (1976) 'The problem of the Thai-Muslims in the four southern provinces of Thailand (Part One)', *Journal of SouthEast Asian Studies*, Vol. 7, pp. 197–225.

—— (1977) 'The problem of the Thai-Muslims in the four southern provinces of Thailand (Part Two)', *Journal of SouthEast Asian Studies*, Vol. 8, pp. 85–105.

150   *Dennis Rumley*

Hall, D. G. E. (1981) *A History of SouthEast Asia* (London: Macmillan).
Hanafiah, A. M. (1987) 'The Malaysian general election of 1986', *Electoral Studies*, Vol. 6, pp. 279–85.
Kessler, C. S. (1974) 'Muslim identity and political behaviour in Kelantan', in W. R. Roff, (ed.) *Kelantan: Religion, Society and Politics in a Malay State* (Kuala Lumpur: Oxford University Press), pp. 272–313.
Keyes, C. F. (1987) *Thailand: Buddhist Kingdom as Modern Nation-State* (Boulder: Westview).
Koch, M. L. (1977) 'Patani and the development of a Thai state', *Journal of the Malaysian Branch of the Royal Asiatic Society*, Vol. 50, pp. 69–88.
Legal Research Board (1986) *Election Laws of Malaysia* (Kuala Lumpur: International Book Services).
Leinbach, T. R. (1974) 'The spread of transportation and its impact upon the modernization of Malaya, 1887–1911', *Journal of Tropical Geography*, Vol. 39, pp. 54–62.
London, B. (1980) *Metropolis and Nation in Thailand: The Political Economy of Uneven Development* (Boulder: Westview).
Maxwell, W. G. and Gibson, W. S. (1924) *Treaties and Engagements Affecting the Malay States and Borneo* (London: Truscott).
Means, G. P. (1976) *Malaysian Politics* (London: Hodder and Stoughton).
Mehmet, O. (1986) *Development in Malaysia: Poverty, Wealth and Trusteeship* (London: Croom Helm).
Milne, R. S. (1981) *Politics in Ethnically Bipolar States* (Vancouver: UBC Press).
—— and Mauzy, D. K. (1986) *Malaysia: Tradition, Modernity and Islam* (Boulder: Westview).
Morell, D. and Chai-anan, S. (1981) *Political Conflict in Thailand: Reform, Reaction, Revolution* (Cambridge, Mass.: Oelgeschlager, Gunn and Hain).
National Statistical Office (1987) *Population and Housing Census* 1980 (Bangkok: Office of the Prime Minister)
Newbold, T. J. (1971) *Political and Statistical Account of the British Settlements in the Straits of Malacca* (Kuala Lumpur: Oxford University Press).
Numnonda, T (1967) 'Negotiations regarding the cession of Siamese Malay states 1907–1909', *Journal of the Siam Society*, Vol. 55, pp. 227–35.
Oceana Publications (1964) *Catalogue of Treaties 1814–1918* (New York).
Pitsuwan, S. (1982) 'Some issues affecting border security between Malaysia and Thailand', *Monograph Series*, Faculty of Political Science, Thammasat University.
—— (1985) *Islam and Malay Nationalism: A Case Study of the Malay-Muslims of Southern Thailand* (Bangkok: Thai Khadi Research Institute).
Poh Ping, L. (1986) 'The Indo-Chinese situation and the big powers in SouthEast Asia: The Malaysian view', in B. Gale (ed.), *Readings in Malaysian Politics* (Petaling Jaya: Pelanduk), pp. 285–93.
Prescott, J. R. V. (1987) *Political Frontiers and Boundaries* (London: Allen and Unwin).
Prescott, J. R. V., Collier, H. J. and Prescott, D. F. (1977) *Frontiers of Asia and SouthEast Asia* (Melbourne: Melbourne University Press).
Pryor, R. J. (1978) 'Internal Migrants in Peninsula Malaysia', *Journal of Tropical Geography*, Vol. 46, pp. 61–75.

Rachagan, S. S. and Dorall, R. F. (1976) 'Rivers as international boundaries: the case of the Sungei Golok, Malaysia–Thailand', *Journal of Tropical Geography*, Vol. 42, pp. 47–58.

Roff, W. R. (ed.) (1974) *Kelantan: Religion, Society and Politics in a Malay State* (Kuala Lumpur: Oxford University Press).

Rokkan, S. (1970) *Citizens, Elections, Parties* (Oslo: Universitetsforlaget).

Salleh, M. B. N. M. (1974) 'Kelantan in transition: 1891–1910', in W. R. Roff (ed.) *Kelantan: Religion, Society and Politics in a Malay State* (Kuala Lumpur: Oxford University Press), pp. 22–61.

Sandhu, K. S. (1964) 'Emergency Resettlement in Malaya', *Journal of Tropical Geography*, Vol. 18, pp. 157–83.

Seton-Watson, H. (1977) *Nations and States: An Enquiry into the Origins of Nations and the Politics of Nationalism* (London: Methuen).

Shafruddin, B. H. (1987) *The Federal Factor in the Government and Politics of Peninsular Malaysia* (Singapore: Oxford University Press).

Snodgrass, D. R. (1980) *Inequality and Economic Development in Malaysia* (Kuala Lumpur: Oxford University Press).

Suhrke, A. (1970) 'The Thai Muslims: Some aspects of minority integration', *Pacific Affairs*, Vol. 43, pp. 531–47.

Suwannathat-Pian, K. (1984), 'The 1902 Siamese-Kelantan Treaty: An end to traditional relations', *Journal of the Siam Society*, Vol. 72, pp. 95–139.

Syukri, I. (1985) *History of the Malay Kingdom of Patani* (Athens, Ohio: Center for International Studies).

Teeuw, A. and Wyatt, D. K. (1970) *Hikayat Patani: The Story of Patani* (The Hague: Martinus Nijhoff).

Torsvik, P. (ed.) (1981) *Mobilization, Centre-Periphery Structures and Nation-Building* (Bergen: Universitetsforlaget).

Van Der Kroef, J. M. (1981) *Communism in South-East Asia* (London: Macmillan).

Vannaprasert, C., Rahimmula, P. and Jittpoosa, M. (1986) *The Traditions Influencing the Social Integration between the Thai Buddhists and the Thai Muslims* (Pattani: Prince of Songkla University).

Vasil, R. K. (1980) *Ethnic Politics in Malaysia* (New Delhi: Radiant).

Voon, P. K. and Khoo, S. H. (1986) 'The New Villages in Peninsular Malaysia: A socio-economic perspective', *Malaysian Journal of Tropical Geography*, Vol. 14, pp. 36–55.

Wheatley, P. (1961) *The Golden Khersonese* (Kuala Lumpur: University of Malaya Press).

—— (1983) 'Nagara and Commandery: Origins of the SouthEast Asian urban traditions', University of Chicago, Department of Geography, *Research Paper*, nos 207–8.

Zakaria, H. A. (ed.) (1987) *Government and Politics of Malaysia* (Singapore: Oxford University Press).

Zakaria, H. A. (1989) 'Malaysia: Quasi democracy in a divided society', in L. Diamond, J. J. Linz and S. M. Lipset (eds) *Democracy in Developing Countries, Volume Three, Asia* (Boulder: Rienner), pp. 347–81.

8 The Indonesia–Papua New Guinea border landscape

Ronald J. May

INTRODUCTION

Indonesia and Papua New Guinea share a common border of some 750 kilometres, separating the province of Irian Jaya from Papua New Guinea. The border itself has not been one of contention, but it has been a source of tension in the relations between the two countries as a result of the movement of Organisasi Papua Merdeka (OPM or Free Papua) guerrillas in the border area, occasional incursions into Papua New Guinea by Indonesian military personnel and aircraft, and a sizeable inflow of Irianese refugees into Papua New Guinea. This chapter examines some of these problems, the administrative arrangements created to deal with the problems, and their effectiveness in creating harmonious relations between the two countries.

THE BORDER LANDSCAPE

The land boundary between Indonesia and Papua New Guinea stretches for some 750 kilometres, following the 141st east meridian of longitude from the north coast to the Fly River bulge, thence, after a stretch of about 50 kilometres defined by the thalweg of the Fly River, extending to the mouth of the Bensbach River, a fraction of a degree to the east of the 141st meridian, on the south coast (Figure 8.1). In the south, the boundary line passes through dry savannah and swampy rainforest before ascending into the precipitous limestone ridges of the rain-soaked Star Mountains. North of the Star Mountains it traverses the Sepik floodplain, another series of formidable limestone ridges and raging mountain streams, and a thickly forested swampy plain before rising again into the Bougainville Mountains which ultimately fall, in a succession of limestone cliffs,

Figure 8.1 The Indonesia–Papua New Guinea boundary

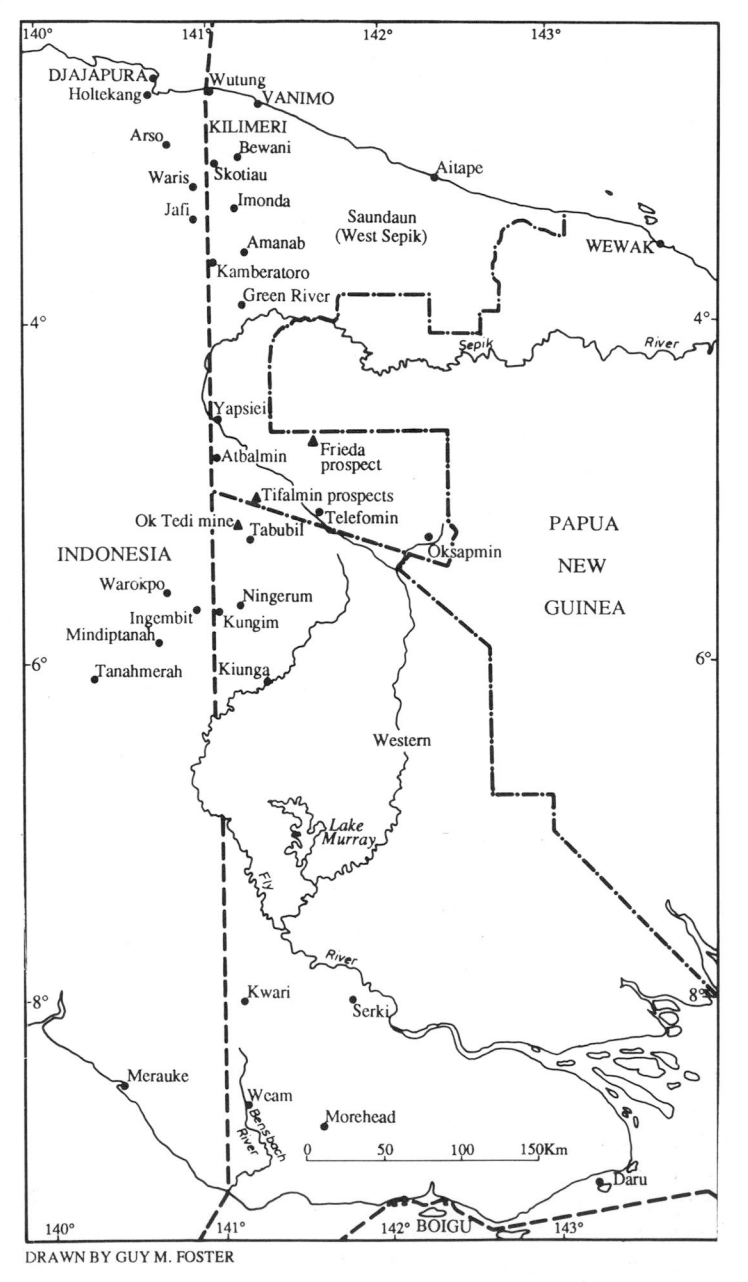

DRAWN BY GUY M. FOSTER

into the sea at Wutung. The international boundary itself is poorly defined. Until recently, there were only fourteen markers along the entire length of the boundary, but additional markers are being added as the result of recent survey and demarcation.

Except for parts of the border area roughly from the Fly River bulge to 100 kilometres north of it, the region is sparsely populated by people who are shifting cultivators with small groups of predominantly hunter-gatherers. In the north and south respectively taro and yam provide the main staples, and in the higher altitudes some depend on sweet potato; for the rest sago is the main staple, supplemented by hunting. As in other countries whose borders are the product of arbitrary decisions made by past colonial regimes, language groups and traditional rights to land as well as relations of kin and of trade extend across the border (Figure 8.2). Indeed, border surveys during the 1960s established that the boundary ran right through the middle of at least one village and that several villages which had been administered by the Dutch were in fact in the Australian territory. As recently as 1980, a village included in Papua New Guinea's national census was found to be inside Irian Jaya. The situation is made more complex for administering authorities by the tendency, among these shifting cultivators, for whole villages to shift, reform and disappear over time. (A recent population survey of the border census divisions of Western Province by the Papua New Guinea IASER or Institute of Applied Social and Economic Research (Pula and Jackson, 1984) provides some documentation of this fluidity.)

The land boundary is defined by an Australian–Indonesian border agreement of 1973, and is the subject of an agreement between Indonesia and Papua New Guinea concerning administrative border arrangements. The latter was originally drawn up in 1973 (when Australia was the administering authority in Papua New Guinea, though the agreement was signed by Michael Somare as Chief Minister), and has been renegotiated, with minor but significant amendments, in 1979 and 1984. The agreement contains a number of provisions relating to the definition of the border area, the establishment of a joint border committee, consultation and liaison arrangements, border crossings for traditional and customary purposes and by non-traditional inhabitants, customary border trade and the exercise of traditional rights to land and waters in the border area, border security, quarantine, navigation, exchange of information on major construction, major development of natural resources, environmental protection, and compensation for damages. There is,

Figure 8.2 Border area: Language groups and population density

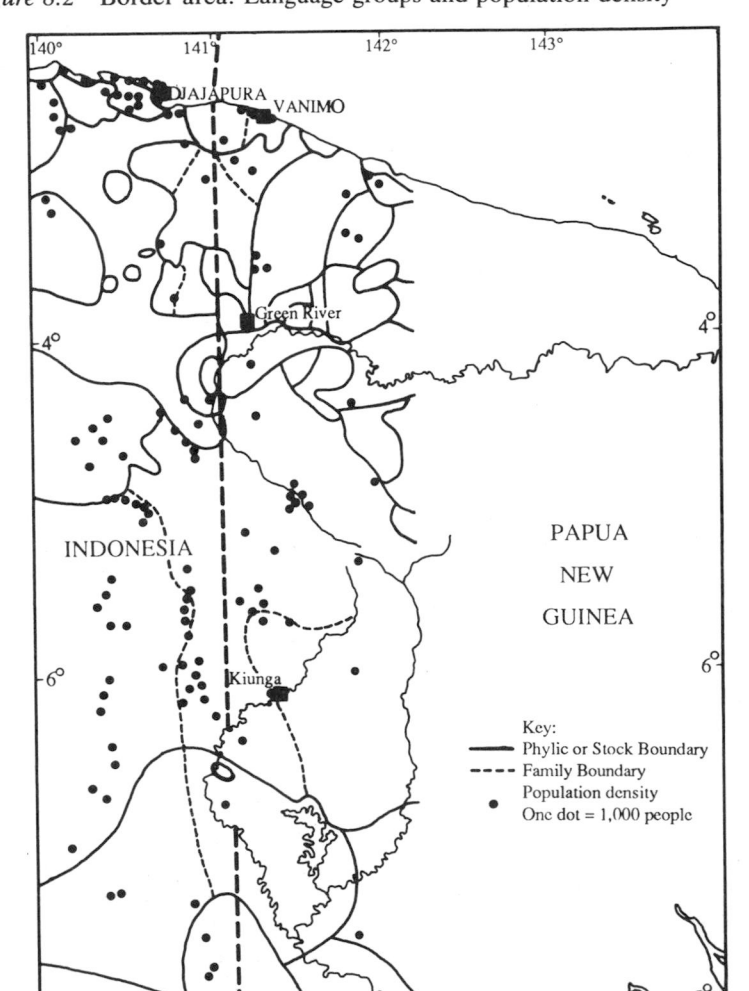

DRAWN BY GUY M. FOSTER

however, no provision for hot pursuit across the border, and Papua New Guinea has repeatedly resisted proposals for joint military patrolling of the border.

BORDER PROBLEMS

Since the earliest colonial times, New Guinea's borders have been an occasional source of friction between the neighbouring administrations. In recent years, problems between Papua New Guinea and Indonesia over the border have arisen from four sources – border crossers, the OPM, border violations and border development.

Border crossers

In principle, one can distinguish four broad classes of border crossers. First, there are villagers from the border area who cross from time to time, as they have always crossed, to make sago, to hunt, or to visit kin. Provision is specifically made for such traditional movement in the border agreement. Traditionally, such movement was two-way and sometimes, in response to drought or disputes for example, was more or less permanent. Within comparatively recent times, there has been continuous substantial movement across the border. During the Dutch period many Papua New Guinean villagers from the border area travelled across into what was then Dutch New Guinea, attracted by the superior facilities available, especially at centres such as Hollandia, Mindiptanah and Merauke. Lately, it seems, movement has tended to be in the opposite direction, though greater formality of border administration and the existence of different *lingue franche* has inhibited such movement. The IASER survey referred to above has documented extensive cross-border ties for the people of Western Province. In the North Ok Tedi and Moian census divisions, for example, 47.8 and 30.3 per cent respectively of adults surveyed were Irian Jaya-born (Pula and Jackson, 1984: 35). In view of the frequency of movement in the past, the IASER report ventured the opinion that 'a good proportion of these border-crossers (that is, those who crossed into Papua New Guinea during 1984) could have good claim to PNG citizenship' (Pula and Jackson, 1984: 33). Much the same situation exists in West Sepik (Sandaun) Province. In 1984, the Sandaun premier, Andrew Komboni, accused the Australian, Indonesian and Papua New Guinean governments of ignoring the 'family aspects' of the situation created by border crossing – 'the traditional ties among the border villages in the

northern sector have not changed since the white man declared an invisible border line', he said; 'a good number of the current refugees ... have run this way with the natural inclination to seek family refuge. It must be shocking ... to see blood relatives being jailed or being held at camps' (*Post-Courier*, 12 April 1984). As the IASER report observed:

> As time has passed and as the rule of national laws has reluctantly spread to the border area so people going about their business as they have done for centuries are slowly being made into law-breakers at worst or 'problems' at best. (Pula and Jackson, 1984: 32)

Secondly, there has been a relatively small number of Irianese nationalists seeking political asylum in Papua New Guinea. Some of these have been allowed to resettle in Papua New Guinea but increasingly in recent years those granted refugee status have been passed on, with the assistance of the United Nations High Commissioner for Refugees (UNHCR), but lately with considerable difficulty, to third countries such as Sweden and Greece. Thirdly, from time to time as a result of military activity in Irian Jaya, groups of Irianese villagers have crossed over into Papua New Guinea seeking temporary refuge – often with kin or wantoks. Fourthly, OPM guerillas operating in the border area have on occasion crossed over into Papua New Guinea seeking refuge from Indonesian military patrols. This, however, is a special class of border crosser and will be considered in more detail below.

Papua New Guinea policy on border crossers was established during the colonial period. As I described it some years ago:

> People crossing the border are required to report to one of the several patrol posts along the border and state their reason for crossing. If their purpose is 'traditional' (the most common is sago making) they are normally allowed to stay until they have finished what they came to do and are then expected to return across the border. If they apply for political asylum they are held until a decision is taken and then either granted permissive residence or told to return. In all other cases they are told to return. If they refuse, they are arrested and charged as illegal immigrants, after which they may be deported. (May, 1979: 98–9)

The essential features of this policy have not changed since the 1960s, though in early 1984, in an apparent effort to discourage movement across the border, all adult male border crossers were

charged as illegal immigrants. In practice, as I noted in 1979, the stringency with which this policy has been applied has varied since 1962. However the available evidence suggests that from about 1972, when the first Somare government came to office, Papua New Guinea has taken an increasingly hard line against border crossers, in all of the above categories (May, 1979, 1986a).

With regard to numbers, before 1984 the best estimate of Irian-born residents in Papua New Guinea was around 2,000–3,000. Many of these must have slipped across the border, some prior to 1962, and taken up residence in villages or towns without acquiring formal residential status. Of this number, 217 have been granted citizenship in Papua New Guinea – 157 in 1976 and another 60 in 1977. No Irian-born person has been granted citizenship since 1977.

I began this section by saying that 'in principle' border crossers could be classified into four categories. In practice, of course, border crossers are not always so easily distinguishable. Up to 1984, the number of border crossers was sufficiently small that this was not a major problem. In 1984 this changed. Following an abortive local uprising by Irianese nationalists in Jayapura (Djajapura) in February, and a subsequent military crackdown, hundreds, and eventually thousands, of Irianese began to pour across the border into Papua New Guinea. By the end of 1984 there were some 12,000 border crossers in camps along the border, few of whom showed any inclination to return, and many of whom could claim traditional land rights.[1] Most of these people were 'refugees' in the broad sense that they crossed the border to take refuge from conditions they found threatening. The Papua New Guinea government was reluctant to refer to them as refugees, however, because of what this implied with regard to the UN 1951 Convention and 1967 Protocol Relating to the Status of Refugees. It preferred to see them as Indonesian citizens who would soon return to their own side of the border. Border crossers themselves, especially those from the border area, were also reluctant to have themselves classified as refugees for fear that, like earlier border crossers, they might be sentenced to resettlement in Sweden.

The refugee problem became a salient issue in Papua New Guinea politics in 1984–5, and it remains such. The handling of the refugee situation during 1984–5 has been documented elsewhere (May, 1986b; Smith and Hewison, 1986). It is a story which does not reflect well on either Indonesia or Papua New Guinea, nor on regional neighbours who have shown no willingness to help resettle those who are eventually granted refugee status. The Papua New Guinea

administration tried, but with little success, to persuade groups of border crossers to return to Irian Jaya – even forcibly repatriating some – in the face, initially, of strong domestic reaction. Following a change of government in late 1985, attempts to negotiate repatriation were strengthened. In the following year, the new government acceded to the UN Convention and Protocol Relating to the Status of Refugees and sought increased UNHCR involvement in the screening of 'genuine refugees' and arranging the repatriation of others, though without much conspicuous gain. Over the past twelve months or so some success has been achieved in persuading groups of border crossers to return, and some 3000 people from camps along the border have been resettled to the east at East Awin where they are at present developing subsistence gardens and will eventually become part of an integrated rural development programme. The Blackwater camp, just outside Vanimo, at which most of the more politically active Irianese were located, was closed down in 1988, though a pro-OPM group refused relocation and is currently camped on the beach at Vanimo in defiance of the government's action (Figure 8.1).

The Indonesian government, having initially refused to acknowledge that an influx of border crossers had occurred, hampered efforts at repatriation by its reluctance to give a formal undertaking regarding the safety of returnees, its refusal, for some time, to agree to UNHCR involvement in repatriation, and its insistence that Papua New Guinea provide a list of names of the border crossers. Former Foreign Minister Mochtar Kusumaatmadja was even reported as saying: 'The biggest problem of these Irianese ... is ... they want to go through life doing nothing at all. We don't need people like that' (*Sydney Morning Herald*, 16 August 1985). Since 1985, however, Indonesia appears to have adopted a more conciliatory approach, though several thousand border crossers have chosen to remain in the Western and Sandaun Provinces, at considerable cost and with evidence of increasing tension in the relations between the border crossers and local villagers.[2]

The OPM

Since the early 1960s, groups of Irianese nationalist rebels have operated in the border area of Irian Jaya, in the name of the Organisasi Papua Merdeka (OPM), and have occasionally crossed over into Papua New Guinea for 'R and R' or to escape Indonesian military patrols. There have also been isolated instances of OPM sympathisers within Papua New Guinea seeking to materially assist

the OPM, but usually without effect. (The two notable cases have been a rather naive letter of 1981 seeking arms from the Soviet Union, which was returned – and intercepted – because the address ('Mr George, c/o Poste Restante, Turkey') was insufficient, and an unsuccessful attempt in 1984 to obtain weapons through an Australian mercenary soldier.)

Successive Papua New Guinea governments, however, have consistently reiterated their denial of Papua New Guinea soil to OPM rebels and Papua New Guinean police, military and administrative personnel patrol the border area in an effort to discourage movement across the border in general and to deny the use of the border area to OPM guerrillas in particular. In 1983 and again in 1984 budgetary allocations for police and military border patrols were increased and it was announced that an infantry company would be stationed at Kiunga. In addition several Irianese granted permissive residence in Papua New Guinea have been deported for violating their undertaking, as a condition of their residence in Papua New Guinea, not to engage in political activity relative to their nationalist sentiments. Indeed, since the late 1970s, the Papua New Guinea government's actions against OPM supporters have brought retaliatory threats from the OPM. For example, in 1984, in protest against planned repatriation of border crossers, specific threats were made against the Ok Tedi mining project and against individual Papua New Guinean politicians and bureaucrats, and in 1985 government officers were pulled out of refugee camps in the Western Province following threats from the OPM's regional commander, Geradus Thommy.

Notwithstanding this, Papua New Guinea has occasionally been accused of not devoting to the task of 'sanitizing' the border the resources it might. Whether or not Papua New Guinea should spend more on border patrolling depends on judgements about priorities. Personally, given the nature of the terrain and the small number of OPM guerillas involved, I see little reason why a country whose main concerns are with the economic and social development of its people should divert scarce resources away from development in an attempt to deal with a problem of internal security which a large, militaristic neighbour has been unable to resolve. This is especially so when that neighbour has in turn denied that there is conflict in Irian Jaya, has told Papua New Guinea that affairs in Irian Jaya are none of its business, and denied the existence of the OPM itself. But whatever one feels on this issue, it is simply not accurate to accuse Papua New Guinea of not taking firm action against the OPM.

Border violations

Although it has occasionally been proposed by Indonesia, Papua New Guinea has stopped short of the sort of border agreement which Indonesia has with Malaysia, which allows 'hot pursuit' across the border, and on a number of occasions Papua New Guinea has indicated its unwillingness to enter into joint military patrols along the border.

On several occasions since the late 1960s, however, Indonesian troops or aircraft have crossed the border, intentionally or unintentionally. In mid-1982, for example, Indonesian military patrols crossed into Papua New Guinea on seven occasions, despite Papua New Guinea protests, and a helicopter flying the regional military commander to Wamena, 240 kilometres south-west of Jayapura, landed 'off course' at a mission station 10 kilometres south-east. In March 1984, two Indonesian aircraft appear to have violated Papua New Guinea's air space over Green River station, and the following month there were three border violations, during one of which Indonesian troops destroyed houses and gardens in a hamlet on the Papua New Guinea side of the border.

Such incursions are perhaps inevitable given the nature of the terrain, the poor demarcation of the border, and the circumstances of a guerrilla campaign. But such 'incidents' have been magnified rather than minimised by the refusal of the Indonesian government, or the inability of its civil and military elements, to deal credibly with Papua New Guinea's representations. In the instance of the 1982 border violations, for example, the Indonesian government denied that the incursion had occurred, saying that some Indonesian hostages taken in an OPM raid had been recovered from the Papua New Guinea side of the border by Irianese villagers and accusing Papua New Guinea of not honouring its obligations under the border agreement. In fact, the hostages, who had been held on the Indonesian side of the border, were subsequently released to Irianese villagers who escorted them across to Papua New Guinea for repatriation. In the case of the 1984 air violations, the Indonesian Ambassador in Papua New Guinea initially denied that the planes were Indonesian (despite the fact that the Antara News Agency had already reported an exercise by the Indonesian air force in the vicinity of Jayapura), and though the possibility of an unintentional incursion appears to have been admitted privately in Jakarta (*Far Eastern Economic Review*, 12 August 1984; *Niugini Nius*, 30 March 1984), a belated official response to Papua New Guinea's diplomatic protests again denied

that an incursion had taken place. And with respect to the military incursions of mid-1984 (which occurred during military exercises in the border area, of which – despite earlier Indonesian assurances – Papua New Guinea had not been informed), in the face of all evidence General Murdani denied the violation, suggesting that perhaps the offenders were OPM guerrillas in Indonesian army uniforms. About the same time the Governor of Irian Jaya was reported (*Times of PNG*, 31 May 1984) as saying, 'There have never been any clashes between the Indonesian defence forces and the OPM rebels. There have been no clashes, never'.

Such responses to legitimate concerns of the Papua New Guinea government have created avoidable tensions in the relations between the two countries. By mid-1984, Papua New Guinea's then Foreign Minister (the present Prime Minister) was saying that, while Papua New Guinea did not want to interfere in Indonesia's internal affairs, the border crossers were not simply internal affairs of Indonesia, that they had direct effects on Papua New Guinea, and that Papua New Guinea therefore had an immediate interest in the way in which Irian Jaya was governed and developed (*Times of PNG*, 24 May 1984; *Post-Courier*, 24 July 1984), and in late 1984, frustrated and 'bloody angry', the Foreign Minister expressed his dissatisfaction with the border situation in a speech to the UN General Assembly. The Indonesian ambassador in Washington, it was reported, was 'painfully surprised'.

Border development

From time to time, joint border development has been proposed as the solution to problems of Irianese separatism and of border crossers. Indeed in 1983, before thousands of Irianese began flooding over the border into Papua New Guinea, Peter Hastings observed that Papua New Guineans from the Vanimo area were visiting Jayapura and suggested that greater development efforts on the Irian Jaya side could soon produce a situation where the predominant flow of border crossers was from Papua New Guinea to Irian Jaya (*Sydney Morning Herald*, 2 May 1983). In fact, however, border development programmes on the Papua New Guinea side, and it seems on the Irian Jaya side, have not made much progress and since 1984 the Papua New Guinea government has been more concerned with sustaining (and eventually getting rid of) border crossers than with providing the improved conditions along the border which might attract more crossers.

Except perhaps at its northern extremity, the border area is poorly endowed and poorly developed. On the Papua New Guinea side, apart from the fortuitously placed Ok Tedi mine (Figure 8.1), what 'development' there has been – a little basic infrastructure (schools, aid posts, minor roads) – is largely the result of the attention the border area has received during periods of OPM–Indonesian military confrontation (Herlihy, 1986). Agricultural development has been inhibited by the government's policy on quarantine. A modest border development programme was included in Papua New Guinea's 1980–3 National Public Expenditure Plan but the allocation for border development was cut in 1983 as a consequence of declining revenue from domestic sources and Australian aid. In 1985, the UNDP initiated proposals for a feasibility study for a joint border development programme. The Papua New Guinea government welcomed the proposal but approaches by the UNDP to the Indonesian government seeking the latter's participation in a study mission 'were not fruitful' (UNDP, 1986: II-5). In late 1986, the Papua New Guinea government was presented with a consultant's report on the development of the border area (UNDP, 1986), but to date there is no evidence of the government's intention to act upon its recommendations.

On the Irian Jaya side, the construction of the trans-Irian Jaya highway and the transmigration programme are seen as major contributions to development and there have been announcements of plans to improve communications in the border area (including, according to one report, colour TV sets) in the hopes of persuading Irianese border dwellers to stay on their side of the border. More recently it was reported that under a three-year border development plan commencing in 1986, Indonesia would spend about A$66 million on highway construction, airstrips, health and education services, industrial and agricultural developments and the establishment of trading centres to improve living conditions in the border area. A further A$2 million was to be spent on border security, including an army base. However, little seems to have come of the proposals.

In the longer term there is some concern in Papua New Guinea that if large-scale transmigration to Irian Jaya takes place, and unless it proves more successful than it has to date in Irian Jaya, this could aggravate the problems of border crossing.

RELATIONS BETWEEN INDONESIA AND PAPUA NEW GUINEA

Since 1975, relations between Indonesia and Papua New Guinea have been largely dictated by developments along the border, and have followed short cycles of tension and self-conscious cordiality. Behind the fluctuations lie two important elements of the broader relationship between the two countries. One concerns the question of balance between a relatively large, militaristic Asian state and a comparatively small and sparsely settled Melanesian country. The broad defence and security aspects of Indonesia–Papua New Guinea relations have been fully discussed elsewhere (Mackie, 1986; Crouch, 1986). The informed consensus seems to be that Indonesia does not have expansionist ambitions towards Papua New Guinea (past expansionist ventures being the product of particular historical circumstances which cannot be projected onto the Papua New Guinea case), though there are imaginable circumstances – the emergence of a hostile (communist sympathetic) regime in Papua New Guinea or some kind of breakdown in Papua New Guinea's political system, perhaps caused by regional dissidence – which Indonesia might see as a threat to its national security and thus a cause for intervention in one form or another.

Undoubtedly, there is some perception of a threat from Indonesia among Papua New Guineans. In 1982, Defence Minister Epel Tito was relieved of his portfolio after expressing the view, to an Australian audience, that an Indonesian invasion of Papua New Guinea was a future likelihood, and, in the same year, former Defence Force Chief Ted Diro (the same Diro who in 1987 accepted a contribution of some K200,000 towards party campaign expenses from Indonesia's General Murdani) was quoted as saying that Indonesia probably had plans for the takeover of Papua New Guinea 'one day'. More pragmatically, Michael Somare, as PNG Chief Minister, in 1973 advised members of parliament that Papua New Guinea was 'living with a lion' and therefore should not create disputes (May, 1979). However, while a feeling of imbalance in the relationship, especially perhaps on Papua New Guinea's part, does influence the nature of the relationship, I do not believe either that fear of an Indonesian invasion is widespread in Papua New Guinea or that it is a major determinant of relations between the two countries.

Secondly, there has existed in Papua New Guinea what I have described elsewhere as a 'tension' between public attitudes – expressed in the acceptance, reaffirmed by successive Papua New Guinea governments, of Indonesia's sovereignty in Irian Jaya and

private feelings, expressed by a number of Papua New Guinea's political leaders over the years, of broad sympathy for the demands of Irian Jaya's Melanesian nationalists (May, 1979). Recognising this 'tension', Indonesia's leaders have sometimes been moved to express doubts about the extent of Papua New Guinea's commitment to denying the OPM territorial access and an outlet for propaganda. The recent formation of a Melanesian Spearhead Group (comprising Papua New Guinea, Solomon Islands and Vanuatu) has increased Indonesian anxieties about the possibilities of a planned Melanesian movement supporting the West Papua cause.

Shortly after coming to power in late 1985 in PNG, the Wingti government announced its intentions to establish a more stable formal relationship with Indonesia. In October 1986, the Foreign Ministers of the two countries signed a Treaty of Mutual Respect, Friendship and Co-operation. Under the terms of this treaty the two have agreed not to threaten or use force against one another and not to cooperate with others in hostile or unlawful acts against each other or allow their territory to be used by others for such purposes. Provision is made also for consultation and negotiation in the event of any dispute. The treaty was regarded by President Suharto as 'another milestone in the history of both countries', while Papua New Guinea's Prime Minister and Foreign Secretary said it would give direction for the future and inspire confidence in Papua New Guinea and its regional neighbours (*Niugini Nius*, 28 October 1986). More sceptical opinion, however, observed that there was nothing in the new treaty which had not either been the subject of earlier and repeated verbal assurances or was already adequately provided for in the existing agreement on border administration. Some opposition politicians in Papua New Guinea went further, describing the treaty as 'naive and misconstrued', 'sinister', and 'an exercise in hypocrisy' (*Post-Courier*, 29 October 1986; *Times of PNG* 31 October–6 November 1986). The doubts of the sceptics might have been reinforced by the fact that, in the same week as the Treaty of Mutual Respect, Friendship and Co-operation was signed, a Joint Border Committee meeting in Bandung broke up after four days, having failed to reach agreement on proposals for joint search-and-rescue operations in the border area. Indeed, the history of relations between the two countries since 1975 would support the argument that the more immediate concerns in Indonesia–Papua New Guinea relations have to do not with possible invasion or intervention or covert support of the OPM but with the problems arising over administration of the common border.

Administration of the border takes place within the framework of the border agreement and in the context of a mutual commitment to good relations. Since 1981, there have been annual Joint Border Committee meetings, irregular meetings of a Border Liaison Committee, and a number of meetings of technical sub-committees. When 'incidents' have occurred, the machinery of border liaison has generally proved ineffective. For example, when in 1983 it was discovered that Indonesia's trans-Irian Jaya highway crossed into Papua New Guinea at three points, it took more than three months to secure an acknowledgement that the incursion had taken place and sixteen months before the offending sections of road were closed off. (Incidentally, the incursion might have been established several months earlier had Indonesia not withdrawn from a joint survey exercise because of inadequate funds.) Again, in February 1984, with refugees flooding across the border, Indonesian officials told the Papua New Guinea Foreign Minister that they knew nothing of reported events and assured him that things in Jayapura were 'normal', even though residents on the Papua New Guinea side of the border confirmed that Jayapura was in darkness and its government radio station silent. At this time there had not been a border liaison meeting for over a year – allegedly because of lack of funds and the Vanimo–Jayapura 'hot-line' had been out of service for several months. And when in April 1984 Papua New Guinea sought a meeting of the Joint Border Committee, to attempt to achieve some resolution of the situation, its Foreign Secretary found himself sitting down with a local *bupati* who was apparently uninformed on the subject of the border crossings and had no authority to make decisions. A scheduled meeting the following month was cancelled at short notice when the Irian Jaya Governor withdrew from the Indonesian delegation due to 'over commitment'. This sort of situation, combined with evasive responses to Papua New Guinea's protests over border violations, discussed above, did much to generate the strains which characterised Indonesia–Papua New Guinea relations throughout most of 1984–5.

There has been a tendency among distant commentators on Indonesia–Papua New Guinea relations to refer to the problems, and to offer solutions, as though the Indonesia–Papua New Guinea relationship was symmetrical. Obviously it is not: apart from the huge disparities in size and military capacity between the two countries, border crossing has been essentially one way; border violations have been entirely at Papua New Guinea's expense; Papua New Guinea does not have a domestic insurgency problem overflowing its border;

it has been Papua New Guinea rather than Indonesia which has had to seek explanations for external disturbances, and the frequent ineffectiveness of liaison machinery has been largely, though not exclusively, on the Indonesian side.

CONCLUSION

It has been argued that disputes over boundaries are less a cause of conflict between nations than a symptom of underlying tensions (Prescott, 1986). In the Indonesia–Papua New Guinea case, however, this does hold. Despite apparent goodwill on both sides, at least at the govemmental level, the problems of administering the border have tended to dictate relations more generally. Indonesian policies in the province of Irian Jaya have not only failed to win over the Melanesian population, attempts to assimilate the people of the province into the larger Indonesian society and to supress sub-nationalist sentiments have ensured the survival of a dissident movement in the province and abroad, and have prompted the movement of people across the border into Papua New Guinea. At the same time, a sense of broad ethnic solidarity between Papua New Guineans and the Melanesian population of Irian Jaya has encouraged the acceptance of such movement and has prevented the sort of military cooperation across the border which Indonesia has achieved with Malaysia. Compounding this is the fact that what for Papua New Guinea is an issue of considerable importance, is for Indonesia a comparatively minor matter. This partly explains Indonesia's frequent insensitivity to Papua New Guinea's concerns over border-related issues. The Treaty of Mutual Respect, Friendship and Co-operation represents the most recent attempt to place relations between the two countries on a firmer footing. However, while the problems of the border remain – and they seem unlikely to go away – we can expect to see continuing cycles of tension and cordiality.

NOTES

1 It is difficult to measure the exact number, since quite large groups of people appear to have moved back and forth across the border. In late 1984 'about 12,000' was the official estimate. Following the change of government in Papua New Guinea in late 1985 the figure generally quoted officially was 10,000 (though there was no apparent reason for the reduction, except perhaps an earlier Indonesian claim, never verified, that 2,000 border crossers had returned to Irian Jaya).

2 The financial cost of maintaining the border camps has been met in part by the UNHCR, with funds mostly provided by the Australian government, and in part by church organisations. The Indonesian government has contributed only about A$50,000 for the support of its citizens. According to a former Papua New Guinea Foreign Minister, 'most of our requests have gone unanswered' (*Post-Courier*, 20 August 1984).

REFERENCES

Crouch, H. (1986) 'Indonesia and the security of Australia and Papua New Guinea', *Australian Outlook*, Vol. 40, pp. 167–74.

Herlihy, J. M. (1986) 'Border development: a "political necessity" again', in R. J. May (ed.) (1986) *Between Two Nations. The Indonesia–Papua New Guinean Border and West Papuan Nationalism* (Bathurst: Robert Brown and Associates), pp. 175–99.

Mackie, J. A. C. (1986) 'Does Indonesia have expansionist designs on Papua New Guinea?', in R. J. May (ed.) (1986) *Between Two Nations. The Indonesia–Papua New Guinean Border and West Papuan Nationalism* (Bathurst: Robert Brown and Associates), pp. 65–84.

May, R.J. (ed.) (1979) *The Indonesia–Papua New Guinea Border: Irianese Nationalism and Small State Diplomacy* (Research School of Pacific Studies, Australian National University, Department of Political and Social Change, Working Paper No. 2).

—— (1986a) *Between Two Nations. The Indonesia–Papua New Guinean Border and West Papua Nationalism* (Bathurst: Robert Brown and Associates).

—— (1986b) 'East of the border: Irian Jaya and the border in Papua New Guinea's domestic and foreign politics', in R. J. May (ed.) (1986) *Between Two Nations. The Indonesia–Papua New Guinean Border and West Papuan Nationalism* (Bathurst: Robert Brown and Associates), pp. 85–161.

Prescott, J. R. V. (1986) 'Problems of international boundaries with particular reference to the boundary between Indonesia and Papua New Guinea', in R. J. May (ed.) (1986) *Between Two Nations. The Indonesia–Papua New Guinean Border and West Papuan Nationalism* (Bathurst: Robert Brown and Associates), pp. 1–17.

Pula, A. and Jackson, R. (1984) *Population Survey of the Border Census Divisions of Western Province* (Port Moresby: Papua New Guinea Institute of Applied Social and Economic Research).

Smith, A. and Hewison, K. (1986) '1984 : Refugees, "holiday camps" and death', in R. J. May (ed.) (1986) *Between Two Nations. The Indonesia–Papua New Guinean Border and West Papuan Nationalism* (Bathurst: Robert Brown and Associates), pp. 200–17.

United Nations Development Program (1986) *Draft Final Report Preparatory Mission on Development of the Border Area (PNG/86/011).Western and West Sepik Provinces of Papua New Guinea* (Port Moresby: UNDP).

9 Coastal islands on an international boundary: Dauan and Parama in the Torres Strait

George Ohshima

INTRODUCTION

The international boundary between Australia and Papua New Guinea runs curiously close to the Papuan side – only about a mile or so off the coast of the mainland. Before the independence of the Republic of Papua New Guinea on 16 September 1975, the boundary was essentially an administrative division line separating the State of Queensland, Australia, from the Territory of Papua New Guinea as both were controlled by Australia. Near to the international boundary, several coastal or offshore islands were divided into two different administrative systems, though the peoples of these coastal islands were highly integrated and possessed strong traditional ties. From west to east the islands are Boigu, Dauan and Saibai of Queensland, Australia, and Daru, Bobo (Bristow) and Parama which are part of the Western Province of Papua New Guinea. These islands include five which are inhabited while the other (Bobo) has since been abandoned. The three Australian islands comprise the northernmost western islands of the Torres Strait group, while the other three Papuan islands are part of the Kiwai Island group along with some others in the Fly River delta (Figure 9.1). The aim of this chapter is to describe and analyse the impact of the international boundary in this region, especially upon the social and economic life of the people of Dauan Island, Australia, and of Parama Island, Papua New Guinea. The data to be used derive from six field visits to the region from 1974 to 1983, and especially from intensive research of the two islands.

These two islands are quite different from a physical geographical standpoint. Dauan Island is a tall rocky island formed by orogenic movement which stands prominently near the coastline of mainland Papua just opposite Mabaduan which itself is a rocky hill and significant landmark on the south Papuan coast. The names '*dauan*'

Figure 9.1   Proposed boundaries between Queensland and PNG

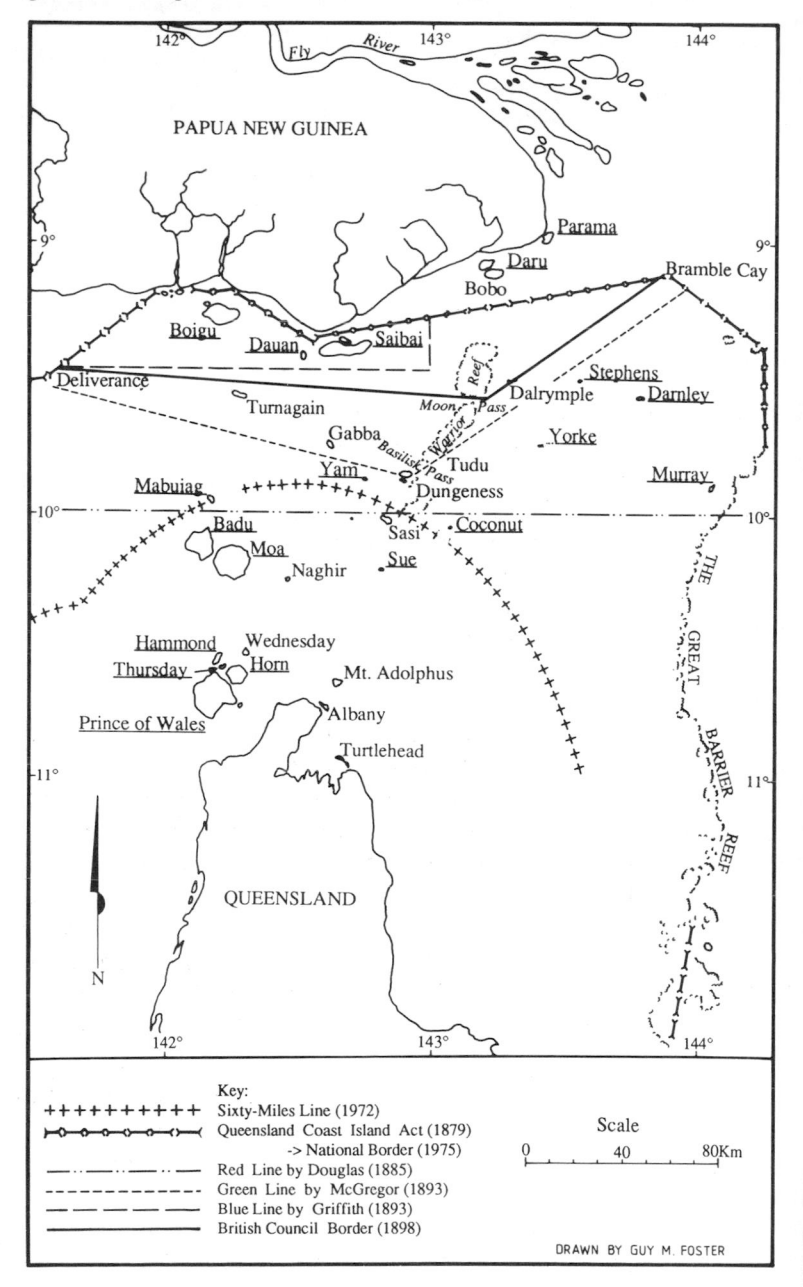

PAPUA NEW GUINEA

Key:
+ + + + + + + + +   Sixty-Miles Line (1972)
)–o–o–o–o–o–o–(Queensland Coast Island Act (1879)
                      -> National Border (1975)
—–·—–·—–··—   Red Line by Douglas (1885)
– – – – – – – – –   Green Line by McGregor (1893)
— — — — — —   Blue Line by Griffith (1893)
———————   British Council Border (1898)

Scale
0   40   80Km

DRAWN BY GUY M. FOSTER

and '*duan*' of Mabaduan, in local tongue, mean rock or rocky. The first European navigator to pass through the Strait by these two 'gateposts' in 1606 was Luis Vaez de Torres, vice captain of the *San Pederico*, a Spanish ship which arrived at this very island in the middle of July, after sailing westward from the Pacific Ocean along the southern Papuan coastline.

Parama Island, on the other hand, is a low, flat and muddy island of alluvial soil deposited by several streams running down from the plateau of the southern Fly. The island is covered with thick mangrove forest which requires enormous effort to clear either for housing or for farming. Consequently, it is very difficult to find any substantial area of cultivable dry ground. People from the mainland coastal villages often used to commute here for seasonal fishing or for crocodile hunting. In addition, as the location of the island is excellent for navigating, the island became important in traditional trading routes.

The two islands, however, possess some common human geographical characteristics. For example, the population size and numbers of houses are similarly small compared with other islands. The current population of each island is at least one hundred occupied in about twenty houses. The physical environment is harsh on the local people – very rough terrain in Dauan and an unhealthy damp environment in Parama. Only one small area on each island has been chosen for settlement.

HISTORY OF INTERNATIONAL BOUNDARY DELIMITATION

It is necessary to give a brief outline of the history of the international boundary drawn through the Torres Strait since it has seriously influenced the lives of peoples on both sides. Generally, a political boundary located in a Strait between two different administrative systems is delimited by the relative strengths of two opposing powers. If the two have almost the same power, then the boundary is likely to be located in the mid-point of the Strait, while, if the one is more powerful than the other, the line might be pushed closer to the weaker state in order to maximise territorial control on the part of the other. The international political boundary in the Torres Strait is drawn on the basis of this principle. Indeed, it is located extremely distant from mainland Australia and very close to the Papuan coast (Figure 9.1).

Historically, it reflects the policy or strategy of the government on the Queensland side which originally was not concerned with Papua and

paid little regard to the island people in the Strait (Farnfield: 1974, 66–72). In 1859, Queensland became a Crown Colony and was separated from New South Wales. It extended to Cape York Peninsula at the time, but it was not initially concerned about any coastal issues. However, in 1864, the first (initially temporary) administrative office was established at Somerset, at the northern tip of Cape York Peninsula opposite Albany Island, and this became an outpost for governing the coastal region including Torres Strait. In 1872, Arthur Palmer, the Premier of Queensland, declared territorial possession over the coastal area within 60 miles of mainland Queensland. This was the first line to be drawn in the Strait, but it was clearly a very rough dividing line since some islands and reefs were cut in half by it, even those which were populated or fully used by native people, such as Mabuiag, Yam and Coconut (Figure 9.1).

The Queensland Coast Island Act was passed in 1879 and proposed a boundary from Deliverance Island in the north-west to Bramble Cay in the north-east, which was intended to include almost all islands in the Strait. This line was very important because it became fixed after several proposals to delimit an alternative had been rejected. The line now assumes an even greater significance, which was not realised at that time, since it is now the international political boundary. However, one of the principal problems of its delimitation in 1879 was that the line was drawn without due regard to the cultural and ethnic characteristics of the people of all of the inhabited islands.

The British declared the south-eastern part of New Guinea a protectorate in 1884 and, as a result, John Douglas came to hold the dual roles as a Queensland Resident on Thursday Island, to where the administrative facilities moved from Somerset five years before, and Special Commissioner in Port Moresby. He was also the Premier of Queensland when the Queensland Coast Island Act was proclaimed. After assuming both positions, Douglas still had to impartially consider the border problem. He knew the region extemely well on account of his accumulated experience, and weighing all of the facts, he decided to propose a balanced solution in 1885, which was to cut the Strait in half along the 10 degree south line of latitude. This line is known as the Douglas Line or, more commonly as the 'Red Line'. According to this plan, Badu and Moa would remain in Queensland while Mabuiag would be separated from these two closely related islands. In addition, Sue and Coconut would be on the southern side separated from Tudu, Yam and Yorke (Figure 9.1).

In addition to the Douglas plan, two further suggestions were proposed in 1893 as amendments to the earlier proposals. The one

was drafted by Sir William MacGregor, the first Governor-General of the newly created British New Guinea, as a revision of the Douglas Line, and added a little more northern water to Queensland. The other, proposed by Sir Samuel Griffith, Premier of Queensland after Douglas, was rewritten with minimal changes in the 1879 Act. The MacGregor boundary became known as the 'Green Line', connecting Deliverance Island to Dungeness Island in the west, bending by the Basilisk Pass at the south end of Warrior Reefs and then northeastward to Bramble Cay (Figure 9.1). It resulted in the retention by Queensland of Mabuiag, Yam and Yorke as well as Darnley, Stephens and Murray. All of these recovered waters were recognised as being valuable for pearling, which was just beginning to be a prosperous industry in the Torres Strait (Beckett, 1977: 77). This boundary also guaranteed the Warrior Reefs for the Papuan side as traditional fishing grounds for native inhabitants.

On the other hand, the Griffith boundary, commonly known as the 'Blue Line', was designed to transfer only the offshore islands of the Papuan coast to British New Guinea, on the basis of what he believed to be their close relationship with mainland Papua (Moore, 1979). However, the people of the offshore islands – Boigu, Dauan and Saibai – did not feel particularly close to the mainland villages. For a European official like Griffith, it might appear as if people of a similar culture were living around the area from the mainland to coastal islands. An examination of Griffith's papers shows that he partly misunderstood the real situation. Peoples of the mainland and the islands were often commuting and involved in traditional trading yet were also often fighting one another.

In the event, all of the earlier boundary proposals were never sufficiently discussed at the time, either in Queensland or in New Guinea, and only Queensland's Act of 1879 became effective until the end of the nineteenth century, notwithstanding any alternative suggestions. Indeed, after these alternative boundaries had been proposed, the British Council itself discussed the problem during the process of forming the new Federation, the Commonwealth of Australia. The Council provided another medium line as a boundary for the new state. It was a little north of MacGregor's 'Green Line' and south of Griffith's 'Blue Line', running from Deliverance Island to Bramble Cay via the Moon Pass. As a result of this boundary, the Warrior Reefs, the most important fishing ground in the strait, would be impartially divided between states and the offshore islands such as Boigu, Dauan and Saibai would be transferred to the British Protectorate with New Guinea. However, Turnagain and Gabba

would remain in Australia (Figure 9.1). Although these two islands were not very important, the waters around them were exceptionally good for the pearl fishery (Ohshima, 1988: 163). The bill was proclaimed in 1898, and was entrusted to the Queensland government for its endorsement. After every effort had been made to expedite proceedings, the last but indispensable one was not completed by the Queensland government before the formation of the new Federation in 1901. This boundary proposal was therefore never realised.

About a century after the first delimitation of the boundary by the Queensland Coast Island Act, another new country, Papua New Guinea, celebrated its independence day in 1975. Prior to that day, the boundary problem had been discussed in the Australian Federal Parliament (Griffin, 1976). Some Torres Strait Islanders feared a rumour that the boundary might be relocated to the 10 degree south line of latitude – the 'Red Line'. By chance, the author attended a public hearing about the border problem held by a Member of Parliament at Yorke Island, a little north of the 10 degree south line. It was concluded that no change was wanted by the island inhabitants, even though several families in Yorke had relatives in Parama of Papua. To the author's surprise, one Papuan-blood female explained that she did not want her island to be transferred to Papua New Guinea. At the time, a large propaganda board was hoisted at the pier of Saibai Island, only 2 kilometres from mainland Papua, with an appeal, 'Queensland Border Will Not Change', and also, close to the board, a monument was erected praising a Saibaian hero who fought and fell in battle against Papua one hundred years earlier. Nothing had changed on the border in that time until the division line between State (Queensland) and Territory (Papua New Guinea) was elevated to international boundary status of a new country.

VILLAGE STRUCTURES OF DAUAN AND PARAMA

As was mentioned above, the islands of Dauan and Parama are physically quite distinct. Dauan Island is known by an English name, Cornwallis Island, in Australian charts (Figure 9.2). Mount Cornwallis, which was named by Captain Bligh in 1792 (Simagal Pad is the original local name) is the highest peak in the Strait, 296 metres above sea level. The island appears like a triangular cube at the northern end of the Great Dividing Range. The sides of the island are not easily accessible since there are steep cliffs on the eastern side and fallen rocks and stones on the west coast. Only the northern side is

Figure 9.2 The village of Dauan, Australia, 1979

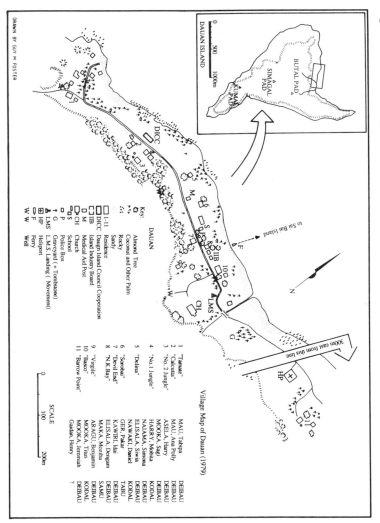

DRAWN BY GUY M FOSTER

DAUAN ISLAND

0   500   1000m

BUTAL PAD

SIMAGAL PAD

KUMAG PAD

DAUAN ISLAND

to Sai Bai Island

300m east from this line

N

Key:

	Almond Tree
✶✶	Coconut and Other Palm
⸱⸱	Rocky
⸳⸳	Sandy
1-11	Residence
DICC	Dauan Island Council Cooperation
IIB	Island Industry Board
M	Medical Aid Post
CH	Church
S	School
P	Police Box
G	Graveyard (+ Tombstone)
LMS	L.M.S. Landing (Movement)
HP	Heliport
F	Ferry
W	Well

Village Map of Dauan (1979)

1	"Tamait"	MAU, Tabipa	DEIBAU
2	"Calcutta"	MAU, Ana Polly	DEIBAU
3	"No. 2 Jungle"	ASELA, Harry	DEIBAU
4	"No.1 Jungle"	MOOKA, Sagi	DEIBAU
		HARRY, Mobia	KODAL
5	"Delina"	NAIAMA, Simona	DEIBAU
		ELISALA, Siwia	DEIBAU
		NAWAKI, Daniel	KODAL
6	"Sorobai"	GER, Pakar	TABU
7	"Devil End"	KAWIRI, Idai	DEIBAU
8	"N.K.Bay"	ELISALA, Dengan	DEIBAU
		MAKA, Moziba	SAMU
9	"Virgile"	ARAGU, Benjamin	DEIBAU
10	"Basso"	MOOKA, Tius	KODAL
11	"Barrow Point"	MOOKA, Jeremiah	DEIBAU
		Gaidan, Henry	?

SCALE

0   100   200m

Figure 9.3 The village of Parama, PNG, 1979

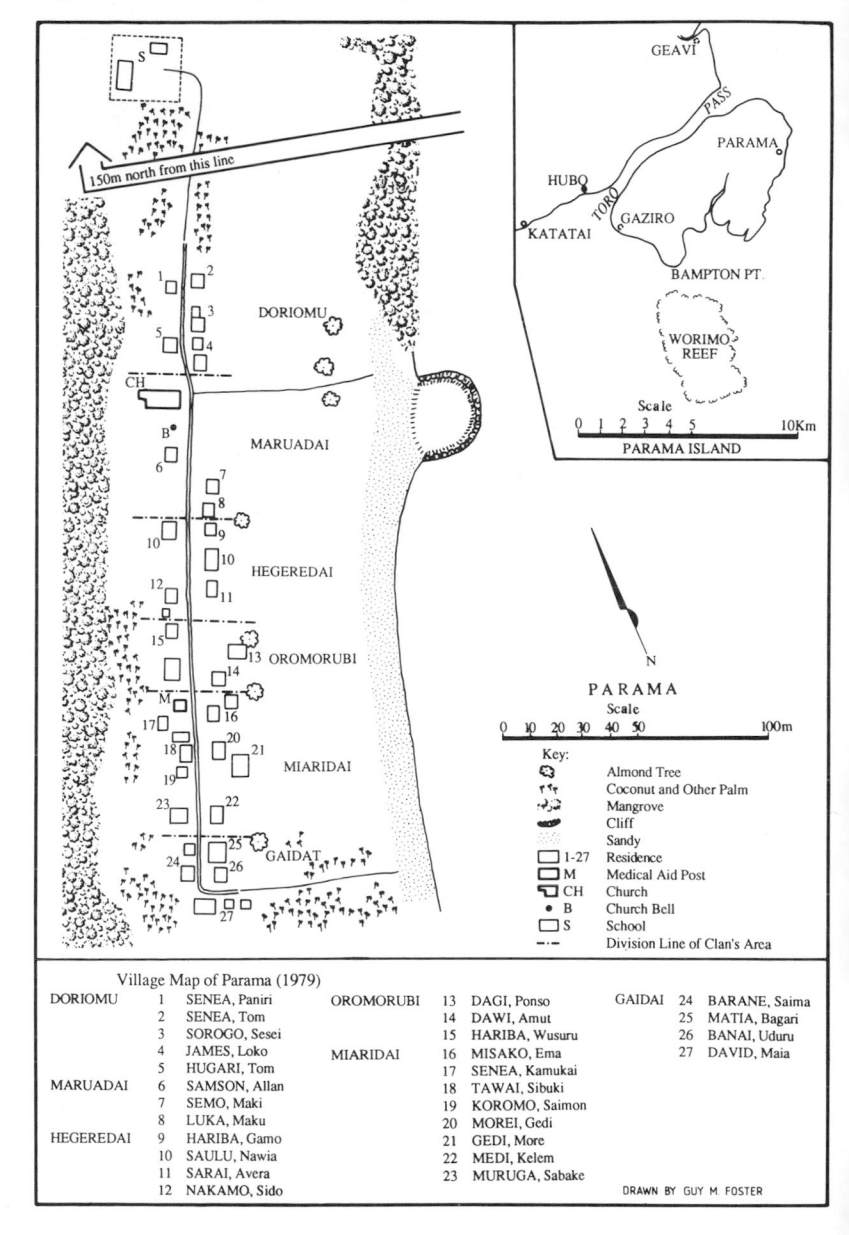

Village Map of Parama (1979)

DORIOMU	1	SENEA, Paniri	OROMORUBI	13	DAGI, Ponso	GAIDAI	24	BARANE, Saima
	2	SENEA, Tom		14	DAWI, Amut		25	MATIA, Bagari
	3	SOROGO, Sesei		15	HARIBA, Wusuru		26	BANAI, Uduru
	4	JAMES, Loko	MIARIDAI	16	MISAKO, Ema		27	DAVID, Maia
	5	HUGARI, Tom		17	SENEA, Kamukai			
MARUADAI	6	SAMSON, Allan		18	TAWAI, Sibuki			
	7	SEMO, Maki		19	KOROMO, Saimon			
	8	LUKA, Maku		20	MOREI, Gedi			
HEGEREDAI	9	HARIBA, Gamo		21	GEDI, More			
	10	SAULU, Nawia		22	MEDI, Kelem			
	11	SARAI, Avera		23	MURUGA, Sabake			
	12	NAKAMO, Sido						

DRAWN BY GUY M. FOSTER

somewhat flat and has a narrow sandy beach, along which the sole village of Dauan extends from west to east, facing to the north, 10 kilometres from mainland Papua, opposite the small village of Sigabaduru on the coast.

Parama Island, known by its English name of Bampton Island, has a rectangular shape and is 9 kilomteres long and 4 kilometres wide. Its coastline is covered with thick mangrove and swamp forest along a marshy waterway, shown on the Australian topographical map as a dotted line. It is the southernmost delta of the Fly River (Figure 9.3). It is separated from mainland Papua by a narrow channel, the Toro Pass, which is 500 metres wide and which is the most important sea route between the Kiwai Islands Group around the mouth of the Fly. The inner part of the island is like a complex labyrinth of stagnant water, repelling any kind of human activity except crocodile hunting, which attracted white people and which was to the benefit of the native people who sold crocodile skin. The only available settlement sites on the eastern coast facing the open sea of the Gulf of Papua are to be found behind the low sand dunes with broad sandy beaches and a wide coral reef in front. The delta continues to develop, and, as one villager pointed out, the sandy beach is fortunately growing forward, thus gradually enlarging the available area for the village.

Before the era of contact with white people, almost all of the islands in the Strait were more thinly populated. Before this century, white people as voyagers or explorers appeared here at first, then pearl-seekers and missionaries, and lastly public administrators. In this century, government and missionaries pursued a policy or strategy of resettling the people for reasons of public welfare and especially for the prevention of epidemics. As a result, several islands were forcibly abandoned. Bobo (Bristow Island in English) and Naghir (Mount Earnest), which were important nodal points in traditional trading routes, and Tudu (Warrior) and Aureed (a little south of Yorke), feared for their pirates or 'head-hunters', were depopulated. Today, the number of inhabited islands in the Strait is nineteen (in Figure 9.1, all inhabited island names are underlined), and among them, fourteen islands on the Australian side are designated as reserves for the Torres Strait Islanders. Thursday Island, as the administrative centre of the Strait, Horn Island, which has an airport facility, and Prince of Wales Island, for holiday homes, are open to all people.

Dauan village

After concentrating on several limited islands of better circumstance as the next stage of the strategy the dispersed small hamlets on each island were reorganised into one compact village with a church, a school and even a small shop which supplied the usual goods for daily village life. Overall, the traditional style of native life was completely reformed during this century. In Dauan Island, there were several hamlets either on the west side at a somewhat dangerous site of falling rocks, or even on the east side at the foot of a sharp gradient, in earlier times. One such hamlet, Burugud, on the west side, is known as the 'New Garden' and was used by the villagers for family picnics or even for overnight trips. The village of today is situated along the north coast and is about 600 metres long. Only one road penetrates the village in a snake-like curve along flat ground as much as possible. The front of the village was, in earlier days, the west end of this village road, at a site known as 'Tamate', and had regularly planted coconut trees on both sides. Today, a ferry, which anchors on the shore of the central part of the village, connects Dauan to Saibai Island, 5 kilometres to the east, the district centre of the Top Western Islands. Located behind there are grouped all of the public facilities including the school, MAP (Medical Aid Post, which is a frontier post defending the Island against malaria from Papua), the IIB shop (Island Industrial Board of Queensland to which the Papuan coastal people used to come for shopping and which takes both currencies) and the police station. The new DICC (Dauan Island Coordinating Council) building stands a little apart to west, on a raised area beside the village road (Figure 9.2).

The ferry boat anchorage is remembered as the first landing place of the London Missionary Society (LMS) on 6 July 1871, five days after 'Light Coming Day' on Darnley Island. Behind the monument at the LMS landing an Anglican Church by the name of Holy Cross is located with an open place at the foot of the mountain, Butai Pad, on the left bank of the short stream, Warzid Kusa. Beyond the stream, about sixty tombstones stand in a village cemetery all in Christian style with the oldest date being 1908. This is almost the east end of the village with the exception of two more houses in one plot 300 metres away which was cleared by a family who came back to the island after the Second World War. Next to this plot there is a newly opened heliport for commuting which connects Boigu and Saibai.

The houses in Dauan village are neat and tiny with light-coloured wooden board on supporting metallic piles known as the 'federal

Plate 9.1 Neat and tiny Dauan house: 'federal type' with metallic piles

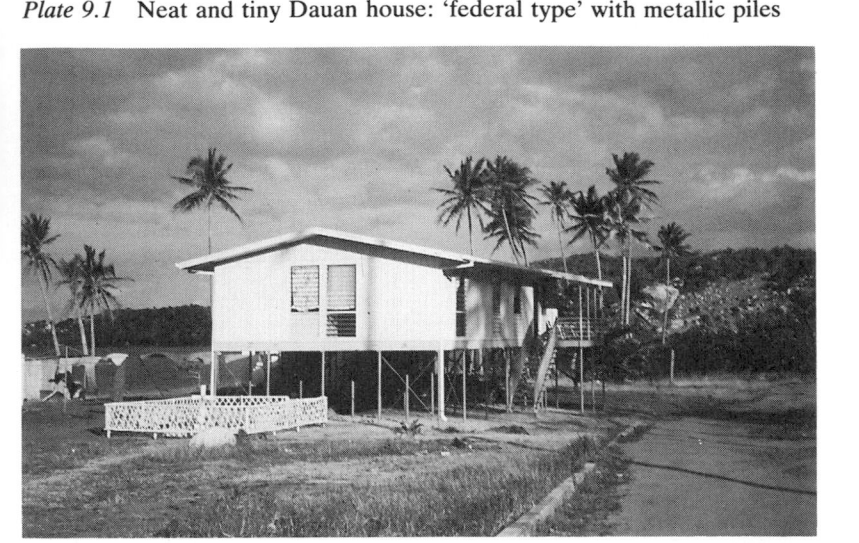

type' in Australia and which is very popular throughout the Strait (Plate 9.1). Since the village road curves irregularly, so the disposition of houses is also irregular. It is difficult to observe the landscape of the whole village by walking along the main road. In the village eleven of the houses containing sixteen households appear to be randomly scattered. They are not located according to any regulation, traditional clan group, or even by blood relation. The villagers of Dauan Island are well known for their *augud* or totem clan system still which today consists of five clan groups. The clan names are, Tabu (snake), Deibau (yam), Kodal (crocodile), Umai (dog) and Samu (cassowary). Before the 'Light Coming Day', the people of the Torres Strait Islands lived in segregated clans. Haddon's report of Saibai Island, just next to Dauan, records the segregated location of two groups of houses, the one consisting of Tabu-Deibau (Daibau in Rivers' record) and the other being Kodal-Umai-Samu (Sam in Rivers) as '*buai*', totemic communities, separated by an open space from the other group (Rivers, 1904: 174). Today there is no longer any evidence of such segregation on Dauan Island. Clean houses of somewhat European style are located according to people's wishes.

Parama village

The case of Parama village is quite different from that of Dauan (Figure 9.3). It is believed that the first settler on Parama came from Geavi, on the south-western coast of mainland Papua, 5 kilometres north of Parama Island. In a legend, the story is as follows (Hashimoto, 1983: 249–50). A man of Geavi planted mangrove saplings on a muddy delta at first, which was bare at that time, as a mark of his possession of a block of land. Several months later, he came again and found it had grown and so he stayed. The population of the new settlement of Parama increased rapidly, and so some people resettled at Gaziro on the south-western corner of the island, which was actually a small islet separated from Parama. However, owing to a shortage of drinking water at Gaziro, the people had to move again to Hubo and to Katatai across the Toro Pass. Thus, the people of Parama and Katatai have the same lineage, and Geavi, Gaziro and the abandoned Hubo all belong to the people of Parama and Katatai for temporary gardening. Hubo was destroyed by a flood-tide in 1939. The southern corner of Parama Island is known as Bampton Point, which is a good base for fishing on the Worimo Reef. People stay at Gaziro for seasonal gardening and fishing and live in '*hupo moto*' or temporary huts.

It is incredible that the population of Parama was estimated to be 773 in the 1964 census. Actually, it included 504 absentees who were working in Daru, the provincial capital town, or in other places inside or outside of Kiwai district, and even as far afield as Thursday Island. The author checked three volumes of the 'Village Register Book' of Parama Island from 1949 to 1964 and two volumes of the 'Tax census sheets' from 1966 and 1971. All of these official publications indicate that the population of Parama was between 334 at its smallest in 1950 and 773 at its largest as mentioned above in 1964, of which only a half to a quarter were permanent village inhabitants.

Today, in Parama, nipa-leaf thatched and high-floored houses stand inside the low sand dune, in two lines along both sides of the village road (Plate 9.2). It is easy to observe the entire village by walking along the road. This road is straight and wide enough to use as an unfloored and unroofed stage for the '*sin-sin*' show, the tribal dance contest on festival day. Here the twenty-seven dwelling houses are aligned north–south, with a church and a MAP (Medical Aid Post). The church is still known as the LMS church, though it now actually belongs to the United Church of Papua New Guinea and the Solomon Islands. The houses in the village are segregated into six

Plate 9.2   Parama house of Nipa-leaf thatched type with flags

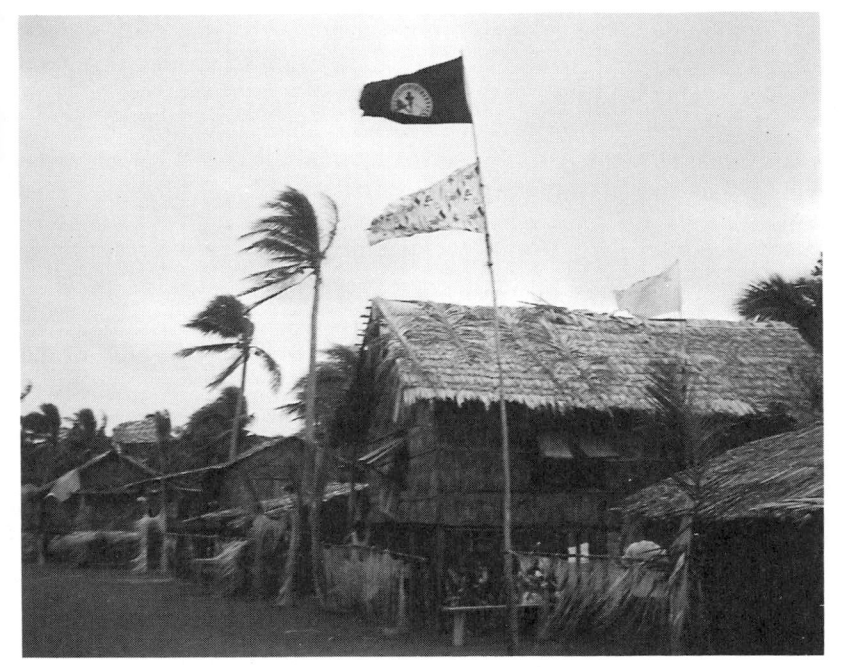

divisions – namely, from the north, Doriomu (shark, and in the old census book, Tebere) clan of five houses, Maruadai (cassowary) of three houses, Hegeredai (dingo or wild dog) of four houses, Oromorubi (dog) of three houses, Miaridai (crocodile) of eight houses and Gaidai (eagle) consisting of four houses (Figure 9.3). The Parama church is located in the Maruadai division due to its dominant position for viewing from outside of the island from the eastern open sea. This is the only exception of location which is not related to any specified person of the clan. The MAP, known to the villagers as the hospital, is situated in Miaridai division, because the hospital orderly or manager, Ema Misako, is a member of this clan and lives just opposite. The other public facility, the school, was reopened in 1977 about 150 metres north of the original village in an area formerly covered in thick bush but which was cleared by all of the villagers. The place does not belong to any clan of the village. Two small shops are privately managed by villagers at their own residences. The names of the totem clans are different from Dauan owing to different local languages, but some of the clan objects are

common – for example, Maruadai compared with Sam in Dauan, Oromorubi compared with Umai and Miaridai with Kodal.

Clan territorial boundaries are not distinctly recognisable by outsiders, although all of the villagers know them well. Village school children told the author of some of the boundary landmarks, such as a 'tall almond tree' or certain coconut palms. However, there are plenty of tall almond trees and innumerable coconut palms in the village, so that the author could not confirm clan boundaries by himself.

Clan groups occupy not only the inner part of the village for residential purposes but also the slight sand dune slope for cultivating cassava or other vegetables, and the broad beach for keeping their canoes. They say that clan boundaries extend even to the edge of the coral reef where villagers must pass in or go out using their own area. Visitors to Parama Island must also strictly abide by this rule. For example, a guest of the Gaidai clan, as the author himself was, must come into the reef using the Gaidai entrance and pass through the Gaidai's sand dune and garden area. The only exception which is allowed is for an ambulance boat, which can sail in from any part of the reef edge.

Register books mentioned above consisted of families listed according to six clans. It is surmised that the clan system in Parama is still dominant and convenient for administration. It may well be maintained in the future by the government of Papua New Guinea or at the least by the district office of Western Province. In contrast, no kind of segregation is now seen on the Australian islands of the Strait. Instead of segregation, in Dauan Island, every house has its own house name (Figure 9.2). For example, 'Tamate' is a nickname of the former favourite missionary of the LMS, Reverend James Chalmer, who stayed a while but was killed at the mouth of the Fly River in 1901 (Lockley, 1972: 8–9). 'Calcutta' was named as a memorial place where missionaries might often talk because the headquarters of the LMS was settled then. 'Delina' is also a place-name near Yule Island close to Port Moresby, from where a missionary's boat once came. These were named a generation ago as memories of the early LMS mission work. 'Basco' is the name of a pearling company, while 'NK Bay' is shortened from New Castle Bay, also where a pearl culturing farm was located. Family heads happily went to work on these pearl farms and earned a good income which enabled them to build their own houses. 'Devil End' was named by its resident, a policeman, as a joke about his occupation. House names were originally village names, and each village consisted of '*baradar*' (yard) and '*arp*'

(garden). Each yard and garden was located separately and surrounded by a hedge. The custom of naming the village and then the house was suggested by a missionary or school teacher (known as 'White Teacher') who stayed there in the early days. This new custom contrasted with traditional custom which, from an ideological viewpoint, white people considered ought to be changed.

The house flags of Parama Island are also visible characteristic signs of tradition. They are designed symbolically, hand made by each family and are hoisted on festival days. Each is a means of identification even within the same clan. Dauan Island, on the other hand, has an island flag instead of house flags, which was designed by Kabai Mau, a man of a noble family on the island. The design of the island flag is divided diagonally into two parts. One side is coloured with light blue, Dauan Island's colour, surrounding a five-pointed star symbolising harmony among its five clans, while the other side is striped with three colours representing the blue sea, white beach and green hill of beautiful Dauan. The island flag does not occur on every island in the Strait and is to be found mainly in the northern region. It represents a symbol of island integration in contrast to modern individualism.

DIVERSITY OF STRATEGY: GOVERNMENT AND MISSIONARY

In order to understand the emergence of the landscape in this region it is essential to refer to the opposing strategies of the two ruling administrative systems and the two missionary groups operating there. As was discussed earlier, the boundary between the two areas has remained without alteration since 1879, and its influence on the two areas has been significant. Throughout this time, Dauan Island has belonged to Queensland even though overall governmental control was transferred from Great Britain to the Commonwealth of Australia in 1901. On the other hand, Parama Island throughout the same time period has belonged to the Papuan side. It was part of the British Protectorate of New Guinea in 1884, which became British New Guinea in 1888. Then following the formation of the Commonwealth of Australia the Papuan Act transferred it from Britain to Australia in 1905. Following the era of Australian Trust Territory from 1945 it finally became a part of the Western Province of the new Republic of Papua New Guinea in 1975.

The systems of control of the governments of contiguous states are invariably different. In Queensland's case, several islands of the Strait, including Dauan, were designated as reserves, and were

provided with social welfare, financial support, an education system and so on. The administration of the resources for these facilities was first undertaken by DNA (Department of Native Affairs), then by DAIA (Department of Aboriginals' and Islanders' Advancement) and later by changing the official title of the people from Torres Strait Natives to Torres Strait Islanders. In the twentieth century, policies for the Torres Strait have differed in detail between Brisbane (Queensland State Government) and Canberra (Federal Government), and thus the people of the Strait were given benefits from two administrations. As a result, every island on the Australian side of the international boundary came to enjoy a European life style either materially or mentally. In each island, there were neat tiny houses with a school and kindergarten, a public clinic provided by MAP and even a public shop via the IIB organisation. Inside the village, a road was provided, together with water supply, sanitary system and other public facilities. Outside of the island, the wharf and jetty to take bigger ferry boats was reinforced. An airstrip or heliport for inter-island transportation has also been constructed and telephone cable laid below the sea. In short, all of the inhabited islands became very convenient and comfortable to live in during this time.

In the Papuan islands, on the other hand, everything is less well developed than in the Australian islands even though the method of government is not fundamentally different, having been under the same policy of the British in the early days and of the Australian administration later on. Houses of European style are very seldom without a church, and the traditional life style is dominant, even in the schools.

It is important to emphasise the influence of missionaries upon the process of modernisation through Christianisation. Several missionary groups worked around the Strait, but among them, two of the British boards have been historically dominant. The one is the London Missionary Society (LMS) founded with several voluntary laymen and led by pastors of the Congregational Church, and the other is the Anglican Church which, as the official religion of England, worked in every British colony in the world as an accompaniment to imperial colonial policy. In Australia, the Australian Board of Missions (ABM) was organised for mission work to aboriginal people.

There is one particularly interesting matter which is noticeable in the titles of books referring to the missionary activities of these two boards in the Strait. The work of the LMS has been discussed in two books written by the first missionary himself entitled, *Journal of a*

Missionary Voyage to New Guinea (McFarlane, 1873), and, *Among the Cannibals of New Guinea* (McFarlane, 1888). On the other hand, the history of the work of the ABM is summarised by a bishop in *Cross over Carpentaria, Being a History of the Church of England in Northern Australia from 1865–1965* (Bayton, 1965). These are contrasting and symbolic titles.

The LMS worked in the Torres Strait en route to New Guinea, and missionary workers recognised the islands in the Strait as adjacent to New Guinea, referring to them as New Guinea Islands and considered them as jumping off points to New Guinea (Walker, 1972). The ABM began its work in the Strait in the Diocese of Carpentaria as part of a programmed strategy for Northern Australian natives, aboriginals and islanders. The mission centre at that time was located in Darwin.

The strategy used by the LMS was unique with its successful experience in the South Pacific prior to its work in New Guinea. Everywhere, LMS trained so-called 'native evangelists' at its base station. Lifu Island in the Loyalty Islands was choosen as a frontier station for this programme in New Guinea. From here, two pastors, Reverend Archibald W. Murray, veteran missionary in the Pacific, and Reverend Samuel McFarlane, a young and able person, started on the mission work accompanied by eight couples of 'native evangelists', on the ship *Surprise* on 30 May 1871. They arrived at Erub (Darnley Island) on 1 July, which has since become a very important memorial day ('Light Coming Day') throughout the Torres Strait region. During this voyage, after landing at Darnley, they stopped at Tudu, Tauan (miswritten version of Dauan), Saibai and even Katau, a coastal village on mainland Papua. These islands were thought of as links in a network of traditional trading with the Papuan people. The reason for the selection of Tudu was its relation with Bampton Island, the English name for Parama, and Dauan was considered as the last step to mainland Papua.

After this 'light coming' voyage, several despatches of 'native evangelists' followed as school teachers in addition to their original mission work, and became known as 'Samoan Teachers' in the first stage of education on each island prior to governmental 'White Teachers' in government schools. A new Institute of Higher Education (Papuan Institute) was established at Darnley Island for training native evangelists for the New Guinea mission work. In this way the education system was first established by the LMS. Resettling or concentration of people on several islands was a strategy of the LMS for creating a new order by cutting off some of the old prestigious

islands such as Tudu and Aureed while promoting islands such as Yam and Yorke. The LMS policy was carried into effect very strictly and puritanically and it was felt by the islanders to be so serious that nobody could joke in daily life (Beckett, 1971: 33). After proceeding to the last destination of Papua New Guinea itself, tribal custom and the old order were respected by the LMS and rapid reform was avoided to maintain the peace.

In 1914, the Church of England took over the mission work in the Strait from the LMS since the latter could not conduct its work due to shortage of funds. The successor organisation, the ABM, did not like to change the policy of mission work quickly and so the island people had no clear impression of any 'hand over' from LMS to ABM.

The reorganisation to one settlement in each island was planned mostly after 1914, with the cooperating mission (ABM) and the government (Queensland State), both having their main offices on Thursday Island. The ABM intended to give cordial treatment to people in order that old customs might be forgotten. Christianisation was complete following a few decades of mission work carried out in two stages by the LMS and the ABM. Throughout the Strait, every island church was filled with villagers for Sunday morning service, and every tombstone became carved with Biblical verses ending in the words 'Rest in Peace'.

On the Papuan side, though the missionary work of the LMS ended when a new United Church organisation was formed, many people of the present generation still favourably remembered its work. As was explained above, Parama Church is known as the LMS Church in a corrupted pronounciation of Pidgin English, 'Elemis'. All villagers also attend church, and even on a church memorial day, people enjoy a whole night's *'sin sin'* prior to the festival of holy communion at the following Sunday morning service. Today, old customs and new religion completely coexist.

CONCLUSION

Overall, it is clear that the international political boundary divides the area into two different regions, although basically it is not a political division but mainly a strategic difference between two main missions which has caused diversity within the Torres Strait. In terms of the visible landscape of two islands of Dauan and Parama a number of particular differences can be highlighted:

1 All houses in Dauan are built in the European style, but in Parama almost all houses are built in a traditional manner with the only exceptions being the church and the MAP.

2 A segregational disposition is still strictly maintained in Parama but is not taken into consideration in Dauan.

3 Identification is shown by a house flag in Parama as a common characteristic of tribal tradition. On the other hand, integration is symbolised by the island flag in Dauan in order to unite all villagers' consciousness.

4 Christian life is appreciated fully in both islands, but in Dauan it is a part of a modern European life style, while in Parama it still coexists with a traditional tribal way of life.

REFERENCES

Bayton, John (1965) *Cross Over Carpentaria : Being a History of the Church of England in Northern Australia from 1865–1965* (Brisbane: Smith and Paterson).

Bayton, John (1971) *The Coming of the Light* (Stanmore: Australian Board of Missions).

Beckett, Jeremy R. (1971) 'Rivalry, competition and conflict among Christian Melanesians', in L. R. Hiatt, and C. Jayawardena, (eds) *Anthropology in Oceania: Essays Presented to Ian Hogbin* (Sydney: Angus and Robertson), pp. 27–46.

—— (1977) 'The Torres Strait Islanders and the pearling industry: a case of internal colonialism', *Aboriginal History*, Vol. 1, pp. 77–104.

—— (1978) 'Mission, church and sect: Three types of religious commitment in the Torres Strait Islands', in J. A. Boutilier *et al.* (eds) *Mission, Church and Sect in Oceania* (Ann Arbor: University of Michigan Press), pp. 209–29.

Farnfield, D. Jean (1974) 'The moving frontier: Queensland and Torres Strait', *Lectures on North Queensland History* (James Cook University), pp. 63–72.

Fisk, E. K. (ed.) (1974–5) *The Torres Strait Islanders*, Vols 1–5, Department of Economic, Research School of Pacific Studies (Canberra: Australian National University).

Fisk, E. K. and Tait, Maree (1974) 'Rights, duties and policy in the Torres Strait', in E. K. Fisk, (ed.) *The Border and Associated Problems, The Torres Strait Islanders*, Vol. 5 (Canberra), pp. 1–27.

Griffin, James (ed.) (1976) *The Torres Strait Border Issue: Consolidation, Conflict or Compromise?* (Townsville: Townsville College of Advanced Education).

Haddon, Alfred C.(ed.) (1901–35) *Reports of the Cambridge Anthropological Expedition to Torres Straits*, Vols 1–6, (Cambridge: Cambridge University Press).

Hashimoto, Seiji (1983) 'Katatai-mura, Kadawa-mura', in George Ohshima (ed.) *Torres Kaikyo no Hitobito, sono Chirigakuteki, Minzokugakuteki Kenkyu* (Tokyo), pp. 248–56 (in Japanese).

Lockley, G. Lindsay (1972) *From Darkness to Light: The London Missionary Society in Papua 1872–1972* (Port Moresby: The United Church in Papua New Guinea and the Solomon Islands).

McFarlane, Samuel (1873) *The story of the Lifu Mission, and, Journal of a Missionary Voyage to New Guinea* (London: James Nisbet).

—— (1888) *Among the Cannibals of New Guinea* (London: London Missionary Society).

Moore, David R. (1979) *Islanders and Aborigines at Cape York* (Canberra: Australian Institute of Aboriginal Studies).

Murray, Archibald W. (1872) *Voyage from Loyalty Islands to Cape York* (Microfilm in History Department, University of Papua New Guinea, Port Moresby).

Ohshima, George (1980) 'Acculturation and Christianisation in Torres Strait Island', *Kwansei Gakuin University Annual Studies*, Vol. 29, pp. 47–58.

—— (1983) 'Land use and sea surface use of coral islands, *Kwansei Gakuin University Annual Studies*, Vol. 32, pp. 43–57.

—— (1986) 'Between Australia and New Guinea: Ecological and cultural diversity in the Torres Strait with special reference to the use of marine resources', *Geographical Review of Japan*, Vol. 59 (Ser.B), No. 2, pp. 69–82.

—— (1988) 'Pearl culture and the islanders' society of the Torres Strait', *GeoJournal*, Vol. 16, No. 2, pp. 157–68.

Rivers, W. H. R. (1904) 'Totemism', in Haddon, Alfred C. (ed.) *Sociology, Magic and Religion of the Western Islanders, Reports of the Cambridge Anthropological Expedition in Torres Straits*, Vol. 5 (Cambridge), pp. 129–77.

Walker, D. (ed.) (1972) *Bridge and Barrier: The Natural and Cultural History of Torres Strait* (Canberra: Department of Biogeography and Geomorphology, Research School of Pacific Studies, Australian National University).

White, Gilbert (1917) *Round about the Torres Strait: A Record of Australian Church Missions* (London: Central Board of Missions and Society for Promoting Christian Knowledge).

10 Inter- and intra-regional conflicts in Pakistan's border landscape

Mohammed Ismail Siddiqi

INTRODUCTION

Border landscapes in Pakistan present a variety of physical features with tribal and rural settlements in valleys and on plains. Nomadic tribes, particularly on the western borders, move from season to season in mountain valleys stretching on both sides of the border. The south-eastern part of the border area is covered by desert, with irrigated lands in the centre and further north and north-east are the mountainous regions of the Himalayas. The total length of all of Pakistan's international political boundaries is 6560 kilometres, forming on three fronts common boundaries with the following neighbouring states (Figure 10.1):

	kilometres
North and north-west with Afghanistan	1920
North and north-east with China	560
South-west with Iran	720
North-east, east and south-east with India including the borders of Jammu and Kashmir	2530
The southern coastal boundary running close to the 24th parallel	830
Total boundary line	6560

Tribal warfare and inter-regional conflicts are the most prominent in the north and north-west of the borderland with Afghanistan. Inter-regional conflicts are ancient issues, not yet properly acknowledged by earlier regimes of the numerically weaker nation, although most of the issues were settled through the delicate policy of the British Raj with properly documented treaties. Soviet and Indian interest in the region has kept the political conflict alive, however,

Figure 10.1 The Pakistan–Afghanistan borderland

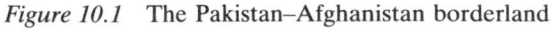

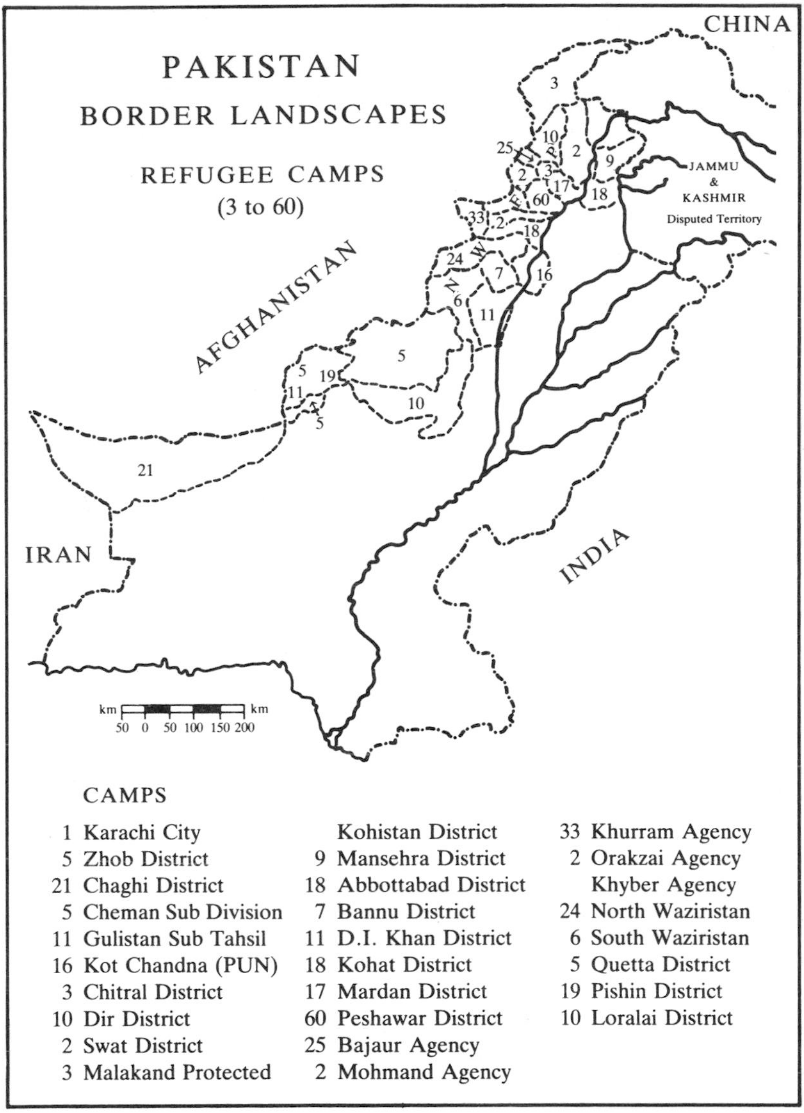

PAKISTAN
BORDER LANDSCAPES
REFUGEE CAMPS
(3 to 60)
CHINA
AFGHANISTAN
IRAN
INDIA
JAMMU
&
KASHMIR
Disputed Territory
km
50 0 50 100 150 200
km
CAMPS
1 Karachi City
5 Zhob District
21 Chaghi District
5 Cheman Sub Division
11 Gulistan Sub Tahsil
16 Kot Chandna (PUN)
3 Chitral District
10 Dir District
2 Swat District
3 Malakand Protected
Kohistan District
9 Mansehra District
18 Abbottabad District
7 Bannu District
11 D.I. Khan District
18 Kohat District
17 Mardan District
60 Peshawar District
25 Bajaur Agency
2 Mohmand Agency
33 Khurram Agency
2 Orakzai Agency
Khyber Agency
24 North Waziristan
6 South Waziristan
5 Quetta District
19 Pishin District
10 Loralai District

and thus the border landscapes in the region have been constantly changing. In general, ethnic identity has had the greatest effect on the political life of the border regions of Pakistan. The importance of religion as a common identity and the fostering of national integration among the various groups are currently undergoing significant internal changes independent of feelings of attachment to ethnolinguistic group. These changes extend from the level of the sub-tribe to the tribe to the larger and socially more heterogeneous linguistic communities.

Pakistan's total population in 1985 has been estimated to be in the order of 95 million people. This represents an annual increase of 3 per cent from 65 million in 1972. The population comprises numerous ethnic groups, especially in the border regions. Many ethnic group members are 'transborder people' – that is, groups are divided between neighbouring states. They have developed a landscape oriented more to other ethnic groups of their own state, despite having a common ethnic identity with the people of the borderland who live on the other side of the boundary under different sovereignty. From an ethnic point of view, the Punjabis live on both sides of the eastern border. Furthermore, Baluchi settlements are located on both sides of the common borders of Pakistan, Iran and Afghanistan. Similarly, the Pushtuns on the north-western borders are separated by a political boundary yet live in many districts. Their continuity of occupation of the land beyond the international boundaries of Iran and Afghanistan makes that boundary 'weak' and politically vulnerable. The political influence of the Pushtuns compared with other tribes in this region (as well as in the capital of Afghanistan) is considerable, although they are not as economically powerful as the Pushtuns of Quetta and Peshawar.

The problems of the western political boundaries of Pakistan and their associated landscapes in mountain systems and passes form the main theme of this chapter (Figure 10.1). As was noted earlier, the boundary which divides Pakistan and Afghanistan covers a distance of some 1920 kilometres along a series of rugged, broken mountains with intermittent passes. These borders are relatively 'porous' and local people are allowed to cross them whenever they wish without the usual permission. This long-standing practice remains even to this day, although an agreement was signed between Afghanistan and India during British rule.

POLITICAL CONTROVERSY AND INTER-REGIONAL DISPUTES

The border landscapes within Pakistan and the boundary line west of the whole region located between Pakistan and Afghanistan was internationally recognised during the British period, despite the fact that there were many unsettled political problems between the local people and the British administrators. The area which extends north-eastward from the point at which the Gowmal River crosses into Pakistan from Afghanistan is a stretch of mountainous country approximately 360 kilometres long. All of the valleys and some low mountain terraces have been occupied by an agglomeration of Pathan tribes, held together by tribal custom and by the informal control of a tribal Jirga (council). Social contacts, on the other hand, are rigidly controlled and the tribe is violently opposed to any infringement of its liberty in terms of thought or action. However, the group is divided and split by a devastating blood feud and is united only in its fierce determination to defend itself and its land from all forms of external pressure (Adamec, 1967). The total population of the Pathans living on both sides of the boundary was 20 million in 1984. Some 11 million live on the Pakistan side of the border and the remaining 9 million live on the Afghan side (Rahman and Qureshi, 1981). At present, due to the war in Afghanistan, some 2 million out of 9 million are living temporarily in Pakistan as refugees.

The Pushtun tribes are generally classified into four major groupings. The Durranis and Ghilzais occupy the central and eastern parts of Afghanistan, while a number of independent tribes straddle the northern part of the Pakistan–Afghan border, and several tribes including the Khattaks and Bannuchis are centred in the North West Frontier Province of Pakistan. Several thousands of Pushtuns, not far from the border, who have been long settled in urban and semi-urban areas, especially in the Peshawar Valley, have to a degree detribalised, even though the tribal hold is still fairly strong throughout Pushtun society. The Pushtun tribes regard themselves as members of a single interrelated kinship group in spite of endemic conflict among different groups. Their notion of ethnic and cultural unity is symbolically complex and has great potential for political unity.

Inter-regional conflict

Successive Afghan governments, following the partition of the sub-continent in 1947 and the creation of Pakistan in the region, have

tentatively tried to question the legality of the international boundary which was artificially delimited by the British. In recent times, they have advanced fresh and intriguing arguments in support of their claims designed, in addition, to create confusion in the minds of the Mujahideen. In the past, the political situation of the hill tribes has been uncertain even though, in reality, they were independent by virtue of a remaining part of the Empire of Ahmad Shah Durrani. In effect, what this meant was that the Afghan claim to all territory lying west of the Indus was relinquished when the British took some of it by force and some by agreement. Afghanistan's inability to enforce its rule over the region following the fall of the Durrani Empire meant that the tribes became known in succeeding years for their independence. On numerous occasions, due to political differences, the hill tribes fought against the British and made peace. During the thirty year period between the British occupation of the frontier and the second Afghan war, thirty-seven expeditions were sent across the administered borders. With the introduction of British rule, the border became relatively tranquil. However, the whole country had been studded with forts in narrow mountain valleys. Examples of those landscape features still exist in some parts of the region which have not yet been influenced or altered by recent developments. For a range of political reasons, the British were not serious about capturing the hill tracts. It was in British interests to keep the peace in that tract of the border which they had dominated in order to enforce their 'forward policy'. The tribes were allowed to move freely not only in their borderlands but also within British territory for trade purposes. The inter-regional dispute and internal political contro-versy created a situation which was quite unfavourable to the British. Consequently their 'forward policy' to occupy the borderlands was given up in favour of peace and compromise (Tyler, 1950). This resulted in giving freedom to a brave and a very independent people, and at the same time, interposed a buffer between the two states while reducing the friction which was inherent among the borderland peoples.

Since the growth of civil conflict in Afghanistan and following the Soviet intervention in 1979, population movements have increased significantly and the landscape on the Pakistan side of the border has been severely degraded. The continuous and accelerated movements of refugees during the period from 1979 to 1988 as recorded on 30 April was 324,906 (Government of Pakistan, 1988a). Many are temporarily housed in some 343 camps located in the border regions of Pakistan. Twenty-two per cent of the refugees live within 8

kilometres of the border, another 20 per cent within 16–20 kilometres, and a further 54 per cent more than 30 kilometres from the
border (*Dawn*, 1988). The number of refugees has been increasing by
about 6000–8000 per month and several hundred thousand still await
registration. Refugee camps are scattered throughout twenty-seven
border districts and political agencies. Mianwali in Punjab and
Karachi in Sind are the only two districts where the urban context can
provide a new source of income.

The mass migration of Afghan refugees along with their cattle has
resulted in some significant, though localised, effects upon the
natural environment, including deforestation, overgrazing, grain
pests and pollution. In addition, the removal of organic matter has
had a negative impact upon soil fertility. In summer, due to the high
temperatures, the refugees have been allowed to move into the
forested mountainous areas of Parachinar, Razara, Galyath, Kaghan,
Swat and Dir. As a direct consequence of this policy, a large
proportion of the region has been deforested. In the North West
Frontier Province (NWFP) many types of grasses have been con-
sumed or removed to erect mud houses in refugee settlements.
Generally, most of the tent villages have been located away from
forested regions in saline or dry mountainous areas. In order to
afford some protection from the heat, the refugees tend to plant fast-
growing shade trees nearby. The species of tree planted, where
possible, is adjusted to local environmental conditions (Hussain,
1982).

Border landscapes of the Pakistan–Afghan frontier region

The western borderlands of Pakistan present a variety of physical
features with many sub-regions of smaller size enclosed by lofty
mountain ranges, some in a longitudinal direction and others in a
latitudinal direction. As a result, some valleys are entirely dry while
others are green, resulting in a very distinctive and variegated
physical landscape. The western frontier district extends across the
Hindukush and the Pamir and Karakoram Mountains which run in a
north-east to south-west direction, and fall from 8400 metres to the
north of Chitral to 1700–2000 metres in the Mahmand Hills and
Malakand Ridge which separates the Swat Valley from the Vale of
Peshawar. All human links from the deep narrow valleys of these
mountains are via the passes to the south, thus maintaining a series of
longitudinal linkages, the most important of which are Chitral,
Kunar, Tarkhun, Panjkora and the upper Swat Valley.

Further to the south, the north-east to south-west trend of the mountains is interrupted by the Safed Koh ranges which run in a west to east direction, resulting in the formation of a structural depression, known as the Peshawar Valley. It gradually falls from the west from a height of 5200 metres to between 1000 and 1700 metres in the Kohat Hills. The whole area between the Safed Koh and the Tochi River is made up of arid hills rising up to about 1700 metres. The same general trend is present in the southern flanks where two more valleys – the Tochi (Bannu) and the Gomal (Dera Ismail Khan) – have been developed. The dominance of a hill culture has produced distinctive human values, and the people who settled in this region are known as Pathans, the Hindco of the Peshawar zone.

In the extreme south of Waziristan on the western border close to the international boundary run the Toba-Kakar ranges, generally about 300 metres high, towards the south-west up to Cheman. From the south-eastern side of the Waziristan the Sulaiman ranges run, forming a great series of inclined ridges which rise to over 3400 metres at Takha-e-Sulaiman, but in general the summits are in the order of about 2000 metres high. From there, they swing westward, join with the Bugti Hills and then again turn towards the north-west to the Quetta nodes. The physiognomy of the border landscape in this section consists of a broken series, and in between the Toba-Kakar range and the Sulaiman ranges lie the basins of Zhob and Beji with innumerable small plateaus, mesas and steep outcrops. The complex of the Quetta nodes consists of two variegated heights – over 3600 metres at Zerghum and in the Khilafat Mountains – while further south, along the Pakistan–Afghan boundary, are the Sarlat Hills in the east to Koh-e-Malik-Siah in the west, a distance of about 560 kilometres.

The actual territorial layout of the frontier districts provided by this mountain system is an important factor in influencing population characteristics, which, in turn, is affected by the obvious difficulty of assimilating the local tribes, commonly known in the region as the Afridis, Mohmands, Masuds, Orakzais, Waziris, Yousufzai Shinwari, Bangash, Jaji Bangal, Zardan, Daur, Bhittani and many others. It seems possible that the differences are in part associated with the physical background, more massive in Baluchistan, yet more fragmented in the northern frontier hills. The tribes in the north are more oligarchic and are based on a feudal system practised in between the higher and bolder topographic outlines of Chitral, Dir and Swat. The group which settled in Chitral is not from the common Pathan stock but the Pathan name implies a tribal rather than racial status but

speaking a Pushtu dialect. Numerous Pathan and Baluchi tribes are settled in tribal areas, each of which has a more or less clearly defined territory and generally possesses a peculiar form of dress, speech and manner which distinguishes it from its neighbour.

Independence is not sacrificed at the cost of economic advantage although economic development on their own terms is encouraged and the opening of schools and welfare services is seen to be highly desirable. In some of these regions, these facilities are already provided but their maintenance has become difficult due to insufficient regional resources. In order to develop this region it will be necessary to coordinate all projects on a national basis.

The most isolated and barren hills have been occupied by the Masud, Mohmands and the Afridis tribes. The latter group successfully manufacture and export guns as well as operate a profitable trucking business in the tribal agency of the Khyber Pass. Generally, however, the hill tribes are agricultural, with animal husbandry being a side occupation. All of the settlements are located in fertile lowlands and valleys from where they can control the border posts and obscure passes.

Politically, the whole of the western border region falls into the provinces of Baluchistan and the North West Frontier and the centrally administered tribal agencies of Pakistan. The federal government is directly concerned with the development of the tribal areas including social, cultural, economic and other general tribal activities. However, one of the very significant complicating factors in this process in recent years has been the impact of Afghan refugees in the border provinces and tribal agencies.

AFGHAN NOMADS AND REFUGEE CAMPS IN THE BORDERLAND

For centuries, Afghan nomads have sought refuge eight months of every year close to the eastern border of Afghanistan and four months in Pakistan. Before the major revolution of 1979 in Afghanistan, around 60,000 nomads (locally known as Povindas) came into Pakistan but have never returned. They penetrated deep into NWFP, Sind and Baluchistan with their livestock and are a source of seasonal labour during harvest time. Drought and lack of resources in the borderland have forced them to move further east into regions of a different character. In addition, hundreds of royalists fled to Pakistan with their movable urban resources through the border via Peshawar when Zahir Shah, the Afghan Monarch, was

removed from power by Daud in 1973. Refugee numbers swelled in Pakistan again in 1978 through many mountain border passes when the Soviet-backed People's Democratic Party toppled the government of Sardar Daud. Since then, the movement of Afghans towards Pakistan as refugees or as nomads has not just been seasonal, but is rather intermittent with large increases when the tempo of military action in Afghanistan increases and people are forced to flee over the mountains and across the deserts. The large-scale influx of refugees began when Noor Mohammad Tarakki succeeded in staging a bloody coup in April 1978. In September 1979 Amin took over the government as Prime Minister following another revolution. Later on, Amin was killed in unknown circumstances and Babrak Karmal was installed with the support of a foreign power, the Soviet Union.

During this period of revolution, the number of refugees in this Pakistan borderland had risen to 386,916. The entire nation was thrown into chaos and the movement of population towards Pakistan sharply increased. Within a few days of the Soviet intervention with a force of about 80,000 men from the northern borders, as many as 150,000 Afghans were pushed into the western border region of Pakistan. By the middle of 1980 the number had reached one million. Refugees were continuously coming in from all points of the border of Baluchistan and the NWFP, and by the end of June 1982 their number had increased to almost three million, 48 per cent of whom were children, 28 per cent women and 24 per cent men. Many of the adults were old and crippled. Most of them had belonged to villages which had been completely destroyed and helpless women and children, if caught, were killed indiscriminately. According to some refugee estimates, close to 500,000 Afghans were killed in 1980. In the Afghan border province of Laghman, according to one eye witness, 650 persons were buried alive in 1980 by local members of the leftist party (Rahman and Qurashi, 1981: 24). As a result of these events there was a mass influx of refugees, and by the end of 1983, the number had increased to three million. At the same time one and a half million had entered Iran from the other side of the border.

The refugee influx into Pakistan included people from all walks of life and many religious denominations based on the Islamic faith, mainly from the north-eastern and south-eastern regions of Afghanistan. Among them were tribes speaking Pushtu, Persians mainly from the regions of central Afghanstan and from the border areas of Soviet Central Asia. In addition, multilingual minorities such as the Nooristani, Turkomans, Uzbecks, Tajiks and many others were uprooted and forced to flee to Pakistan. Many young people

from these groups joined the 'freedom fighters' commonly known as the Mujahideen in the name of Janad against their government and the Soviet Union.

Border routes

The majority of the Afghan refugees did not enter Pakistan through well-defined routes. A number of Afghan people living on both sides of the 2400-kilometre-long border have very intimate and historic links with the two border provinces of Pakistan. From Baroghil Pass in Chitral to the Chagi district of Baluchistan, there are countless potential routes in difficult mountain terrain. Of these, about 180 have been actively used by people of both sides over many centuries in search of food and pastures for their goats, sheep and cattle. It was surprising to learn from the refugees that as many as 320 routes were used, all of them located in extremely difficult terrain, and some as high as 3500 metres above sea level. These latter were so remote and in such difficult terrain that they were known only to those who had lived in the mountains all their lives. On entering Pakistan, the refugees would seek out those of their own clan, and, after registration for relief assistance and proper verification, would be taken to the border camps. During the summer months, it was found that action against the rural population was more intense compared with winter. Moreover, all exit routes are across the high passes where the journey becomes more difficult and hazardous under the cover of snow.

Borderland refugee camps

Refugees are lodged with all the necessary facilities in 343 camps scattered over twenty-seven districts and agencies in the two border provinces of Pakistan (Table 10.1). One-third of these camps are located in the tribal areas. Their relocation to other provinces was disallowed despite the fact that the language and culture of the other provinces might provide better longer-term prospects. However, many rich Afghan traders obtained a residence of their own in Pakistan's major cities. Furthermore, Karachi, a city of Sind, accepted a camp and provided labour for construction. At present, on average, the ratio of refugee to local population in the border provinces is approximately one to five or six. In regions of high population density in the province of Baluchistan even a 1:1 ratio has been recorded. The official government data do not include any

Plate 10.1   Refugee tentage village close to the border

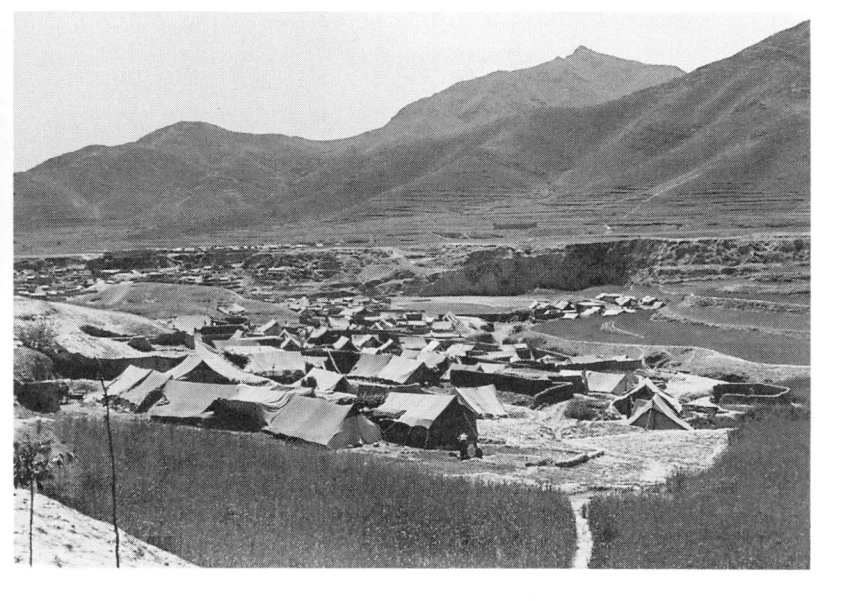

residential facilities provided in the neighbouring tribal areas of Pakistan next to the Afghan border. The largest concentration of refugees is to be found in the 155 camps in the frontier provinces which had a total registered population of 2,231,229 on 30 April 1988 (Table 10.1). In government literature, the camps are referred to as Refugee Tentage Villages (RTVs) indicating the freedom of movement within their confines (Plate 10.1). The 155 camps contain 244,553 families with 518,085 men, 590,128 women and 112,016 children (Government of Pakistan, 1988a). The largest number of camps (60) is located in the Peshawar district and the city of Peshawar accommodates 50,000–60,000 refugees who have either drifted into the city during the days before the camps were set up, or have chosen for other reasons to live away from camp life. Such people relinquish their entitlement to the generous rations and other benefits which are provided to each refugee from 'general funds. Other high-density areas in the border frontier provinces include the Kurram Agency, Kohat, North Waziristan, Mardan, Abbottabad, Bajaur and Dir (Table 10.1). The camps were located as far as possible along the canals to ensure a continuous water supply. In areas where water is not easily available, it is supplied from a fleet of water trucks.

Table 10.1 Population and refugees in the Pakistan–Afghan borderland

Districts and tribal areas	Area (km²)	Population ('000) 1972	Population ('000) 1981	Registered refugees	Refugee camps
North West Frontier Province (NWFP)					
Chitral	14,850	159	208	38,559	3
Dir	5,282	529	767	89,691	10
Swat	8,788	888	1,253	14,370	2
Malakand	952	180	257	55,042	3
Kohistan	7,581	205	465	no data available	
Mansehra	5,957	887	1,066	72,004	9
Abbottabad	6,565	977	1,169	143,525	18
Bannu	4,391	567	710	73,344	7
D. I. Khan	9,005	473	635	87,813	11
Kohat	7,012	581	758	231,347	18
Mardam	31,137	1,206	1,506	106,839	17
Peshawar	4,001	1,711	2,281	505,856	60
Tribal Areas					
Bajaur	1,290	364	289	197,158	25
Mohmand	2,296	382	163	14,928	2
Khurram	3,380	279	294	347,754	33
Orakzai	1,538	284	359	13,356	2
Khyber	2,576	378	284	no data available	
N. Waziristan	4,707	250	238	184,525	24
S. Waziristan	6,619	307	309	55,118	6
Baluchistan Province					
Quetta	2,653	252	382	114,715	5
Pishin	11,112	249	379	168,503	19
Loralai	19,071	188	388	105,041	10
Zhob	27,129	172	362	55,228	5
Chaghi	50,545	65	120	169,185	21
Cheman	3,293	64	93	41,638	5
Gulistan	no data	76	96	165,106	11
Kot Chandna	5,403	1,095	1,377	180,587	16
Karachi (Sind)	1,362	3,606	5,437	18,674	1

Source: Government of Pakistan, 1988b.

As noted earlier, one southern province of Pakistan which has a common border with Afghanistan is Baluchistan. Its physiognomy is similar to the NWFP, but the mountains are not as high and have a different orientation. Here the refugees are mainly concentrated in Gulistan, Pishin and in Quetta. Seven RTV centres were established in districts close to the border in Pishin, Gulistan, Chagai, Quetta, Loralai, Zhob and Chaman. Altogether, some sixty-five camps have been established accommodating 130,718 families and a total population

of 819,424 (Table 10.1). This includes 196,669 men, 229,437 women and 393,318 children (Government of Pakistan, 1988a). In Baluchistan, the largest number of camps is located at Chagai, Pishin, Gulistan and Loralai. Quetta is situated in a small structural depression and, being the capital city of Baluchistan, is not in a position to easily accommodate large numbers of refugees, similar to Peshawar. It is a place of intense commercial activity between the people of Pakistan and Afghanistan. During this critical period of uncertainty there has been an 'invasion' of rich Afghan traders for permanent settlement due to the frequency of business exchange between Quetta and Karachi. The rest are mostly farmers and herders who live in the RTV centres with their families.

Pastoral activities are more prominent in the districts of Zhob and Loralai in Baluchistan. The physical landscape in this region is broken by circular hills and narrow ridges. The mountain slopes have been utilised by the locals for raising cattle and sheep. Once the refugee camps had been established, herders with their livestock along with their families were allowed to live close to the cattle areas. Other essential services and basic amenities of life, such as health services, educational facilities and vocational training are provided by special arrangement with the assistance of United Nations agencies. The temporary Refugee Tentage Villages may not be located where they will be in the future, but for the present the barren lands of parts of the Pakistan borderlands have been turned into an area of human habitation.

CONCLUSION

The western border landscapes of Pakistan, made up of compartmentalised valleys, have played an important role throughout history in shaping the destinies of many peoples, even though the area is basically known as a region of temporary transit. Those who have settled in the region have remained at a relatively low level of economic development. The influx of refugees through a variety of routeways as well as by the more clearly defined routes such as the Khyber and Bolan Passes, indicates the seriousness of contemporary boundary problems. The imposition of restrictions, such as those which exist between North and South Korea, is not possible in this region. This is partly a result of historical tradition and partly due to the nature of the physical landscape. In order to maintain harmony among the border provinces and agencies, what is required is the implementation of a policy of equal development taking into account

local tribal sentiment. The direct involvement of the Soviet Union in the political affairs of Afghanistan between 1979 and 1988 created a new dimension to the whole border problem by consequentially jeopardising the security situation in Pakistan.

REFERENCES

Adamec, L. W. (1967) *Afghanistan, 1900–1923* (Berkeley: University of California Press).
Alvi, S. A. (1988) 'Karachi Master Plan: Expanding horizon', *Landmark*, Vol. 5, p. 34.
Dawn, daily newspaper, Karachi, April 1987.
Embree, A. T. (ed.) (1979) *Pakistan's Western Borderlands* (Royal Book Company).
Government of Pakistan (1962) *Twenty Years of Pakistan, 1947*.
Government of Pakistan (1972) *District Population, Census Reports*.
Government of Pakistan (1981) *Pakistan Statistical Yearbook*.
Government of Pakistan (1985) *Statistical Pocketbook of Pakistan*.
Government of Pakistan (1988a) *Report of Chief Commissioner for Afghan Refugees* (Islamabad).
Government of Pakistan (1988b) *Handbook of Population Census Data, Baluchistan Government*.
Hussain, F. (1982) 'The possible ecological impact of Afghan refugees on the natural vegetation of NWFP (Pakistan)', *Central Asia*, No. 2.
Rahman, F.-U. and Qureshi, B. A. (1981) *Afghans Meet Soviet Challenge* (Peshawar: Institute of Regional Studies).
Tyler, F. W. K. (1950) *Afghanistan: A Study of Political Development in Central Asia* (London: Oxford University Press).

11 The Gulf of Aqaba coastline: An evolving border landscape

Alasdair Drysdale

INTRODUCTION

The boundaries of four countries – Egypt, Israel, Jordan and Saudi Arabia – converge at the northern end of the Gulf of Aqaba, access to which was a major contributing factor behind Arab-Israeli wars in 1956 and 1967 (al-Hakim, 1979; Khouri, 1976). This border region has a high potential for producing conflict because of its strategic setting but, equally, it presents exceptional opportunities for co-operation (Figure 11.1). Currently, there is almost no land traffic between the four countries within the immediate region. The importance of the Gulf to each of the four riparian states differs greatly, resulting in a complex, varied border landscape. These differences can largely be explained by reference to the broader political-geographic environment – such disparate events as the Lebanese civil war, the Iran–Iraq war, the Iranian revolution, the closure of the Suez Canal, the oil price explosions of 1973 and 1979, and the state of relations between Syria and Lebanon, Jordan, and Iraq have all had a profound, but differential, impact on the upper Gulf region, particularly its two ports at Aqaba in Jordan and Eilat in Israel, which are located a few kilometres apart on either side of the Jordanian–Israeli border. Sharp and sudden fluctuations in the importance of these 'geopolitically-located' border zone ports can be attributed almost entirely to political events and to their geographical context (Drysdale, 1987; Stern and Hayuth, 1984). The Gulf, therefore, has been a very sensitive barometer of political relations in the wider region. This chapter will briefly describe the evolution of the boundaries in the upper Gulf of Aqaba region and explain why the border landscapes of the four riparian states differ so greatly. Particular emphasis will be given to explaining why the Jordanian sector is notably more developed than the others.

Figure 11.1   The Gulf of Aqaba region

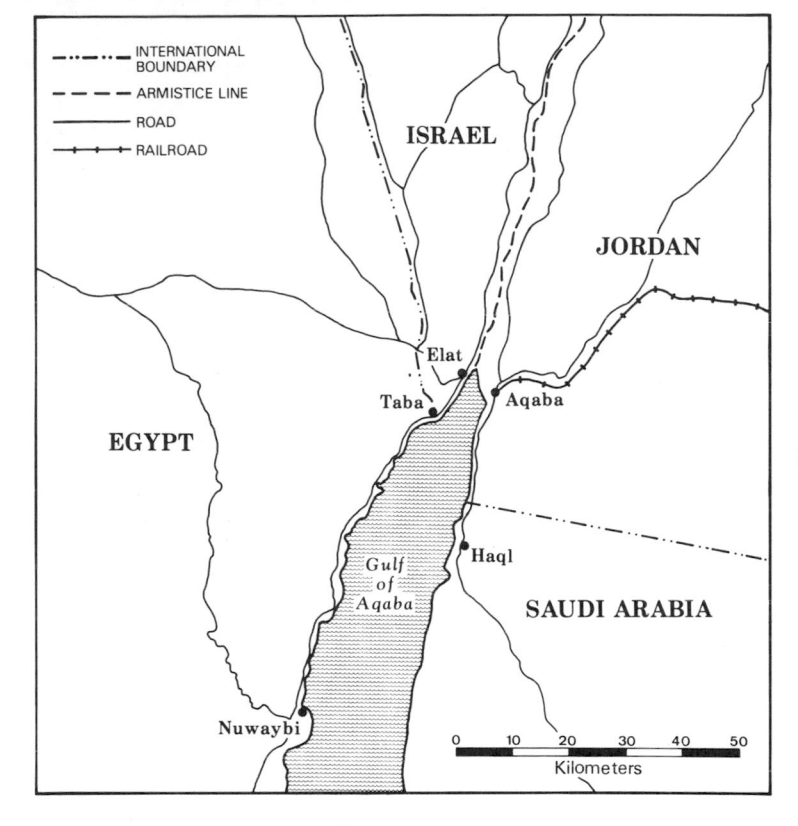

BOUNDARY EVOLUTION

The Gulf of Aqaba is unevenly divided: Egypt accounts for roughly 200 kilometres of its 385-kilometre coastline and Saudi Arabia for another 150 kilometres, leaving Jordan with 25 kilometres and Israel with only 10 kilometres.

Egypt–Israel

The boundary between Egypt and Israel was first delimited in 1906 by Britain and the Ottoman Empire, under British pressure, and originally separated the Ottoman province of the Hijaz, the governate of Jerusalem, and the Sinai peninsula (Kliot, 1987; Warburg, 1979).

The allocation of territory reflected British imperial might, which was marshalled to place as much distance between the Turks and the Suez Canal (with the Sinai peninsula as a buffer) and to protect the vital sea route between Britain and India. In addition, the placement of the boundary near the northern end of the Gulf of Aqaba was designed to discourage the Turks from building a military base at Aqaba. With the dismemberment of the Ottoman Empire in the First World War and the division of the central Middle East into British and French spheres of influence and control, the line became a border between British-controlled Egypt and British-controlled Palestine and Transjordan. Talks were held between 1918 and 1922 on the precise demarcation of the boundary, which became an armistice line between Egypt and Israel in 1949, shortly after the latter's birth in what had been Palestine. Hostilities along the heavily fortified border were common until 1967, when Israel occupied the Sinai peninsula and ended Egypt's riparian status in the Gulf of Aqaba.

Although Israel withdrew from Sinai in 1982 following the signing of a peace treaty with Egypt, the two countries were unable to agree about the position of the boundary where it meets the Gulf of Aqaba. The dispute involved Taba, a 700-metre stretch of sand. Egypt contended that the boundary should be where it was during the Palestine mandate period and before the Israeli occupation of 1967, and pointed out that Israel accepted its claim to Taba by returning it after the 1956 war. Israel asserted that the survey map giving Taba to Egypt was inaccurate and forged and that the original agreement between Anglo-Egyptian and Ottoman negotiators placed the boundary running through Taba itself. However, a British military survey carried out in 1915 produced a map showing the boundary running less than a kilometre to the north-east. The head of the survey team, T. E. Lawrence, subsequently admitted that he had 'invented' certain details of the map, acting under instructions. The Israelis contended that the 1906 agreement should be the basis for the boundary, whereas Egypt asserted the 1915 map was definitive (Hazan, 1988; Raafat, 1983; Lapidot, 1986).

The dispute was complicated by the presence of a luxury resort hotel built with the permission of the Israeli government during the Israeli occupation. The owner of the hotel, noting that guests could see four countries from their balconies, observed that tourists visited Taba in part 'because we are an international problem. ... How many people get to stay at an international problem?'

Before Israel's final withdrawal from the Sinai peninsula in 1982,

Israel and Egypt agreed that Taba should be placed under the temporary control of a multinational peacekeeping force pending further negotiations on the issue. The Taba dispute, however, proved to be a major impediment to improved relations between the two countries. The Israeli government eventually agreed in January 1986 to accept binding arbitration, but the two parties could not reach agreement on the arbitration procedure until September 1986. An arbitration panel consisting of an Israeli, an Egyptian, a Swiss, a Swede, and an American met for the first time in Geneva in December 1986. In the meantime, US soldiers from Observer Group Egypt, established by United Nations Truce Supervisor Organization (UNTSO), operated an observation post in Taba to monitor compliance with an agreement not to introduce arms or troops into the area during the arbitration talks. In September 1988, the arbitration panel ruled in favour of Egypt, but left it up to the two countries to decide the exact placement of the boundary for some 150 metres between the last marker and the Gulf. Currently, Egypt and Israel are negotiating a final settlement.

Israel–Jordan

The Israeli–Jordanian boundary was fixed in 1922 as a line partitioning two areas under British mandatory control, Palestine and Transjordan, although details were not worked out until 1929. North of the Gulf of Aqaba, the boundary was defined as running along a line connecting the lowest parts of the Arava, the southern extension of the Jordan–Dead Sea Rift Valley. This line was not always clear, resulting in some border incidents in the 1950s. Technically, the boundary is an armistice line dating from the first Arab–Israeli war of 1949. Nevertheless, the position of the line itself at the head of the Gulf of Aqaba is not disputed; should Israel and Jordan sign a peace treaty, the boundary between them in this region would in all probability follow the armistice line.

Jordan–Saudi Arabia

The Jordanian–Saudi Arabian boundary in the Gulf of Aqaba region remained in dispute until 1965 (Blake, 1989; Schofield and Blake, 1988). Saudi Arabia initially asserted that the boundary ran from 30 to 80 kilometres north of Aqaba, coinciding approximately with the northern limit of the former Ottoman province of Hijaz, which in 1925 was incorporated into what became Saudi Arabia. Such a

boundary, of course, would have left Jordan landlocked. Britain, as the mandatory power, and Saudi Arabia defined Transjordan's eastern boundaries by treaty, but left its southern boundary undefined. Consequently, Britain unilaterally drew a line slightly to the south of Aqaba, giving Transjordan access to the sea. Saudi Arabia opposed this action but agreed to accept the status quo pending a final solution. Although the line gave Jordan access to the Gulf of Aqaba, it left it with only 8 kilometres of coastline, which seriously limited the potential for port and urban development. Because the Gulf of Aqaba coastline was of little use or interest to Saudi Arabia, in a 1965 boundary treaty it agreed to give Jordan approximately 18 kilometres of coastline; in return, Jordan ceded some desert in the interior to Saudi Arabia. The exchange was of vital importance to Jordan, permitting large-scale expansion and industrialisation of its port at Aqaba to proceed.

BOUNDARY LANDSCAPES

The importance of the Gulf of Aqaba, particularly the region where Egypt, Israel, Jordan and Saudi Arabia meet, varies greatly to each of the four riparian states, which accounts for the differences in the evolution of their respective border landscapes.

Saudi Arabia

This sector of the border remains almost completely undeveloped. The settlement, economic and political cores of Saudi Arabia are located far to the south, around Jiddah–Mecca–Medina, Riyadh, and Dahran, and the country's major ports all lie on the Red Sea and Persian/Arabian Gulf. The willingness of Saudi Arabia to cede some of its territory along the Gulf of Aqaba coastline is a measure of its relative unimportance. Haql, the only Saudi settlement in the region, will likely remain a small, remote village, without serious prospects for economic growth. Should Saudi Arabia decide to develop the region, Jordan's port at Aqaba would be the likely beneficiary. At present, little crosses the Jordanian–Saudi border here; virtually all traffic between the two countries passes through other crossing points. Strategically, Saudi Arabia has been much more concerned with what happens in the Persian Gulf. Should the Saudi monarchy be overthrown and replaced with a regime that played a more active role in the struggle against Israel, however, Saudi Arabia's close proximity to Eilat would assume a new strategic

significance and might contribute to the militarisation of the border landscape.

Egypt

Egypt, historically Israel's most formidable foe, has always recognised the immense strategic importance of the Strait of Tiran at the mouth of the Gulf of Aqaba. Through its control of the Strait, Egypt was able to prevent Israeli access to the Gulf before 1956. Indeed, one of Israel's objectives in attacking Egypt in 1956 was to open the waterway to Israeli vessels, a *sine qua non* to the development of a port at Eilat. Israel withdrew from the Sinai peninsula in 1957 only after Egypt permitted UN forces to be stationed at Sharm al-Shaykh, at the entrance to the Gulf, and after the right of innocent passage through the Strait was assured. A decade later, Egypt's request that these UN forces be withdrawn and its closure of the Strait to ships bound for Eilat was a major contributing factor to the 1967 Arab–Israeli war, one of whose outcomes was Israel's occupation of the Sinai peninsula until 1982. For fifteen years, Egypt lost all control of its Gulf of Aqaba coastline. During that period, Israel attempted to develop the region's tourist industry, especially at Sharm al-Shaykh. Because of its strategic importance, Sharm al-Shaykh was one of the last places from which Israel withdrew in 1982. Significantly, the 1979 Egyptian–Israeli peace treaty provided for the stationing of an international peacekeeping force in a demilitarised zone that included Sharm al-Shaykh and formally pronounced the Strait of Tiran and the Gulf of Aqaba as 'international waterways open to all nations'. The peace treaty also strictly limited the number and location of Egyptian troops and military installations in the Sinai peninsula.

Before 1967, Egypt had little economic interest in its Gulf of Aqaba coastline, particularly the upper section, which remained essentially undeveloped (Melamid, 1957). Since Israel's withdrawal from the Sinai in 1982, however, Egypt has begun to exploit the modest economic potential of the region. As long as the status of Taba was disputed, development of the upper Gulf region was postponed. There has been very little movement across the Egyptian–Israeli border at this point – almost all land traffic between the two countries crosses by Rafah, near the Mediterranean. With the resolution of the Taba dispute, border traffic and tourism can be expected to increase. Nevertheless, Taba is likely to remain an isolated, small, and unimportant outpost in view of the concentration

of people and economic activity in the Nile Valley and Delta. Should Israel and Jordan reach peace and the border between Eilat and Aqaba be opened to land traffic, Taba's importance would increase significantly. For the first time in over forty years it would be possible to travel by land between the western and eastern parts of the Arab world. Taba could become a major crossing point, although most traffic would presumably pass through Jerusalem and the West Bank. In 1984, Egypt and Jordan introduced a ferry service between Nuwaybi, 60 kilometres south of Taba, and Aqaba. This land–sea link between the two countries has become a major route for the vast number of Egyptian migrant workers employed in Jordan, Iraq and the Arabian peninsula. In 1981, 77,000 people entered Jordan through Aqaba; by 1985, 423,000 did so.

Israel

Israel's main ports are at Ashdod and Haifa, on its Mediterranean coastline, where over 80 per cent of the population lives. Nevertheless, Eilat is clearly an important maritime outlet, both economically and strategically, and Israel's Gulf of Aqaba coastline, short though it is, has undergone significant development since the mid-1950s (Orni and Efrat, 1971). Before Egypt and Israel signed a peace treaty in 1979, Egypt would not allow Israeli vessels or cargoes to transit the Suez Canal. Since most of Israel's trade in the 1950s was with Europe or North America, this initially was not a major problem. However, as Israel's desire to trade with Asia, Australia, and East and South Africa grew, so too did its interest in developing a port at Eilat, which would eliminate the need to circumnavigate the Cape of Good Hope. As previously noted, Egypt's closure of the Strait of Tiran to Israeli shipping, which prevented the development of Eilat, was one of the reasons Israel went to war in 1956. Thus, the first port facilities at Eilat were not constructed until 1957. In that year, also, a pipeline was completed between Eilat and Haifa to transport oil from Iran, Israel's chief supplier at that time. Without this pipeline, Iranian oil would have had to go around Africa and through the Mediterranean, an expensive, lengthy detour. Until the mid-1960s, traffic at Eilat remained light, consisting mainly of oil tankers or vessels exporting phosphates and potash from the Negev region to Asia. Because of its peripheral location, some 300 kilometres from the core of the state, Eilat suffered from considerable locational disadvantages compared to Ashdod and Haifa, which limited its growth despite various government incentives to use the port and to locate businesses in the town.

However, Eilat's importance grew after the 1967 Arab–Israeli war and the closure of the Suez Canal to all traffic, which resulted in the port becoming a link in the international trade system, as well as a port that served Israel. Israel quickly recognised that, with the canal closed, the Negev could serve as a land bridge between the Gulf of Aqaba and the Mediterranean and obviate the need for cargo moving between Asia and Europe to circumnavigate the Cape of Good Hope. The so-called Negev Continental Bridge succeeded in attracting some transit container traffic through Eilat, which experienced a sharp increase in traffic. Between 1967 and 1975, when the canal remained closed, cargo handled at the port increased more than fourfold from approximately 200,000 tons to 900,000 tons. Nevertheless, by the mid-1970s, Eilat still handled only about 10 per cent of all Israeli cargo. Furthermore, the reopening of the Suez Canal in 1975 and peace between Israel and Egypt in 1979 adversely affected Eilat. For the first time, Israeli cargo and vessels could use the canal. Despite increased transit fees, transportation through the canal is cheaper (and much faster) than using Eilat (Gradus and Stern, 1977; Stern *et al.*, 1983).

Events in Iran also diminished the usefulness of Eilat. In 1970, a 260-kilometre oil pipeline was completed between Eilat and Ashkelon on the Mediterranean to transport up to 20 million tons of oil annually, by-passing the closed Suez Canal. The flow of oil through the line was limited by the fact that no Arab country would use it; virtually all shipments came from Iran. In addition, Egypt constructed a large-capacity pipeline between the Gulf of Suez and the Mediterranean that also by-passed the canal and removed whatever temptation may have existed for some countries to use the Israeli line. Eilat's role as an oil port, which depended on Iranian oil, ended abruptly after the 1979 Iranian revolution, one of whose many consequences was the severing of relations between the Islamic Republic and Israel. As a result, total cargo handled at the port declined from approximately 1.2 million tons in 1979–80 to roughly 800,000 tons in 1981–2.

Eilat's role as a port has always depended on political factors. In the current regional political environment, the port has lost some of its usefulness. However, Eilat does not only depend on its port functions: its tourist industry is thriving, especially in the warm winter, when it is a destination for European package tours.

Jordan

Without question, Jordan is most reliant on the Gulf of Aqaba, and this is clearly expressed in the landscape: the Jordanian portion of the upper Gulf of Aqaba coastline is by far the most developed and is the sector with the greatest potential for continued growth. This difference is not hard to explain: whereas the Gulf of Aqaba accounts for only a tiny, peripheral portion of the total coastlines of the other riparians, it provides Jordan's only maritime access. Jordan, along with Iraq, has the poorest access to the sea of any Middle Eastern state, being virtually landlocked because of its geographical configuration. Moreover, Jordan's alternative routes to the Mediterranean, through other countries, have been closed or unreliable. Historically, Jordan's natural outlets were Haifa and Jaffa, on the Mediterranean. After the creation of Israel in 1948 in what had been Arab Palestine, Jordanian use of these ports ceased completely and all economic links between Israel and the Arab world were severed. The Arab boycott of Israel cost Jordan dearly. Whereas Amman, the capital, was only 150 kilometres away from Israel's Mediterranean ports, it was some 350 kilometres from Beirut in Lebanon, which is the closest alternative. In addition, road and rail links with Beirut were far from satisfactory, resulting in long delays and expensive transportation costs for Jordanian cargoes. A truck journey between Jerusalem and Jaffa took an hour or two. Between Jerusalem and Beirut, it took several days.

The biggest drawback to using Beirut, however, was the vulnerability of this northern route to political disruption. Jordanian cargoes had to transit Lebanon and Syria, two countries that have suffered acute political instability at various times. During the civil war in Lebanon in 1958 the port of Beirut was virtually paralysed, which had serious economic consequences for Jordan. Since 1975, Beirut's port has been more or less unusable because of the turmoil associated with the Lebanese civil war. In Syria, frequent *coups d'état*, expecially between 1949 and 1963, occasionally resulted in border closures and travel delays. In addition, Jordan suffered whenever there were disputes between Lebanon and Syria. Jordan thus found itself at the mercy of political events that were beyond its power to control. Syria, particularly, exploited its location to gain political leverage over Jordan and on several occasions impeded or disrupted transit trade. For most of the past forty years, Jordan and Syria have been at odds on most major issues in the region, the former being governed by a conservative, pro-Western monarchy,

the latter generally by radical, neutralist or pro-Eastern republican regimes. On several occasions they have almost come to blows and their border has been closed or traffic disrupted, most notably in 1958–9 (when Syria united with Egypt and Jordan united with Iraq), 1970–2 (when Syria briefly intervened in the Jordanian civil war on behalf of the Palestinian guerrillas) and 1980 (when Syria threatened to attack anti-regime Muslim Brotherhood sanctuaries inside Jordan) (Drysdale, 1987).

Because of the vulnerability of the northern route to frequent political disruption, developing a port at Aqaba on Jordan's short coastline became a national priority. However, Aqaba possesses many disadvantages, most notably its peripheral location some 350 kilometres south of Amman, around which roughly 90 per cent of Jordan's population lives. In the early 1950s, land communications between Amman and Aqaba were considerably worse than those between Amman and Beirut. In addition, port facilities at Aqaba were meagre until 1960. Had Aqaba competed freely with Beirut and the northern route been more reliable, the port might never have survived. But the Jordanian government, to increase its viability and to divert trade away from Lebanon and Syria, levied a 20 per cent *ad valorem* tax on goods imported through all ports other than Aqaba.

Aqaba also had certain political-geographical disadvantages. Most obviously, it is extremely vulnerable to Israeli attack, situated as it is, virtually on the Israeli border (Eilat, of course, is equally vulnerable, but it is not Israel's sole port). Road and rail links to Aqaba could also easily be cut in time of war. Second, access to Aqaba, as to Eilat, is via the Strait of Tiran, which Israel controlled between 1967 and 1982. Although Israel has never attempted to prevent access to Aqaba, the threat that it might enables it to exert some leverage over Jordan, a key frontline state in the Arab–Israeli conflict. Third, the shortness of Jordan's original coastline – 8 kilometres – and Aqaba's site – on a narrow coastal plain flanked by high mountains – imposed severe space restrictions on the port. This problem was not solved until Saudi Arabia ceded approximately 18 kilometres of its coastline to Jordan in 1965, as noted previously. Finally, a large portion of Aqaba's trade passes through the Suez Canal, which was closed in 1956–7 following the Anglo–French–Israeli invasion of Egypt and in 1967–75, when it served as a ceasefire line between Egypt and Israel following the latter's occupation of the Sinai peninsula. Both closures resulted in a precipitous decline in traffic at Aqaba because, with the canal closed, all vessels from Europe and the Americas had to sail around southern Africa. Whereas 219 vessels docked at the port in

1955, only 95 did so in 1957. The blocking of the canal in 1967 was even more serious. When the canal was open, the voyage from western Europe or the eastern seaboard of the United States to Aqaba took only two days longer than to Beirut (12–14 days). With the waterway closed, it took vessels between 45 and 60 days to sail from London to Aqaba. In 1966, 666 vessels called at Aqaba; in 1968, only 275 did so. In the same period, the share of Jordan's non-oil imports arriving through Aqaba dropped from 75 per cent to 35 per cent. Inevitably, Jordan's reliance on the northern route through Syria and Lebanon increased greatly.

Even with the canal closed, Jordan continued to develop Aqaba and to encourage its use in order to reduce dependence on transit through Syria and Lebanon. During the 1970–2 crisis in relations between Syria and Jordan, when the Damascus regime temporarily closed the border, Aqaba became Jordan's lifeline. During the crisis, three-quarters of Jordan's non-oil imports came through Aqaba, an extraordinarily high proportion with the Suez Canal closed.

Several other events combined to increase Aqaba's importance in the early 1970s. First, the port of Beirut suffered serious congestion, with delays of twenty days to berth, as a result of the massive surge of imports for the oil-producing states in the Arabian peninsula following the oil price explosion of 1973. Consequently, the gap between the delivery time for goods imported to Jordan through Beirut and those imported through Aqaba narrowed considerably, in spite of the detour around the Cape of Good Hope. Second, the Lebanese civil war in 1975–6 made use of Beirut virtually impossible. Although some of Beirut's traffic was diverted to Syria's ports at Tartus and al-Ladhiqiyah, the turmoil in Lebanon re-emphasised to Jordan the importance of having a secure outlet of its own.

Since the mid-1970s, Aqaba has experienced explosive growth. First, the reopening of the Suez Canal in 1975 resulted in a sharp increase in traffic, from 299 vessels in 1974 to 1064 in 1976. In the same period, imports grew from 370,000 tons to 1,370,000 tons. Second, in 1975 a railway was completed between the port and the phosphate mines at al-Hasa, which permitted a large increase in exports (phosphate shipments increased from 850,000 tons in 1975 to 5.6 million tons in 1985). The sudden growth of traffic at Aqaba created serious congestion by 1976, prompting a significant expansion of facilities over the next five years.

However, the greatest impetus to Aqaba's growth was the Iran–Iraq war. Even before the outbreak of fighting in 1980, Iraq had begun to import through Aqaba to relieve congestion at its own ports

of Basra and Umm Qasr in the Persian/Arabian Gulf. Traditionally, some Iraqi trade passed in transit through Syria and Lebanon, the most direct route from Europe, but antagonism between the Ba'thi regimes of Syria and Iraq compelled Iraq to look at the Jordanian route as an alternative after the Suez Canal reopened. Shortly after the Iran–Iraq war began, Iraq's ports were closed and Aqaba became a lifeline to the Baghdad regime, especially after Syria shut its border with Iraq in 1982 to help its Iranian ally. Transit cargoes increased from 7 per cent to 63 per cent of Aqaba's total imports between 1979 and 1985. In the same period, the number of vessels using the port rose from 1238 to 2671 and total imports rose from 2.3 million tons to 6.3 million tons. Most of the growth was attributable to Iraqi transit trade. Indeed, by 1982 Aqaba handled more cargo for Iraq than for Jordan. Exports and imports in that year totalled over 12 million tons, some fifteen times the cargo handled by neighbouring Eilat. The gap has continued to widen, as Eilat's trade declines and Aqaba's grows. Parenthetically, Eilat and Aqaba handled roughly the same level of cargo as recently as 1970.

In a decade or so, Aqaba was transformed from a small town into a major growth pole in the Jordanian space economy. Since the mid-1970s, the population has grown at an annual rate of 17 per cent, equivalent to a doubling every four years. By 2000, Aqaba is projected to have between 140,000 and 180,000 inhabitants, completely dwarfing Eilat and all other settlements in the Gulf of Aqaba region. The landscape has also been transformed by the considerable industrial development that has occurred, particularly in a planned industrial zone near the Saudi Arabian border, which has chemical fertiliser, potash, wood processing, and other plants. Because of the shortness of Jordan's coastline, careful attention has been paid to land-use planning. However, the combination of rapid port development and industrialisation has not been compatible with the tourist industry that Jordan has tried to encourage along its coastline. Aqaba's six modern hotels, with almost 2000 beds, have, unlike Eilat, not attracted large numbers of tourists. Moreover, the tourist potential of the coastline is being diminished by marine pollution from phosphate dust, sedimentation and oil, which has caused extensive and irreversible damage to the 140 types of coral, many of them unique. Aqaba almost became the terminus for a pipeline with a capacity to transport 1 million barrels of oil daily from Iraq. Significantly, the plan was dropped in part because of Iraqi fears about the pipeline's close proximity to Israel.

CONCLUSION

The border landscape of the upper Gulf of Aqaba region has evolved in response to events in the broader political-geographical environment as well as to the particular needs of each of the riparian states. Jordan's sector of the coastline has experienced the greatest development both because it is Jordan's only coastline and because Jordan's alternative outlets to the sea through Israel, Lebanon and Syria have been unusable or unreliable. Despite Aqaba's dramatic growth, it remains very much a vulnerable outpost in a strategically important and sensitive border zone. It is interesting to speculate what its future might be if Jordan and Israel made peace and resumed trade and commerce, or if Lebanon's troubles ended, or if Syria and Iraq agreed to a rapprochement, or if Iraq's ports enjoyed security once again, or if Egypt reneged on its peace agreement with Israel.... •

REFERENCES

Blake, Gerald H. (1989) 'International Boundaries of Arabia: The Peaceful Resolution of Disputes', a paper presented at the conference on 'War, Peace and Geography', Haifa University.
Drysdale, Alasdair (1987) 'Political conflict and Jordanian access to the sea', *Geographical Review*, Vol. 77, pp. 86–102.
Gradus, Yehuda and Stern, Eliahu (1977) 'New perspectives on the Negev continental bridge', *Geoforum*, Vol. 8, pp. 311–18.
Al-Hakim, Ali (1979) *The Middle Eastern States and the Law of the Sea* (Manchester: Manchester University Press).
Hazan, Reuven (1988) 'Peaceful conflict resolution in the Middle East: The Taba negotiations', *Journal of the Middle East Studies Society*, Vol. 2, pp. 39–65.
Khouri, Fred (1976) *The Arab-Israeli Dilemma*, 2nd edition (Syracuse, NY: Syracuse University Press).
Kliot, Nurit (1987) 'The development of the Egyptian–Israeli boundaries, 1906–1986' in Gerald H. Blake and Richard N. Schofield (eds) *Boundaries and State Territory in the Middle East and North Africa* (Wisbech: Menas Press).
Lapidot, Ruth (1986) 'The Taba controversy', *Jerusalem Quarterly*, Vol. 37.
Melamid, Alexander (1957) 'The political geography of the Gulf of Aqaba', *Annals*, Association of American Geographers, Vol. 47, pp. 231–40.
Orni, E. and Efrat, E. (1971) *The Geography of Israel* (Jerusalem: Israel Sc. Translations).
Raafat, Waheed (1983) 'The Taba case', *Revue Égyptienne de Droit International*, Vol. 39.
Schofield, Richard N. and Blake, Gerald H. (eds) (1988) *Arabian Boundaries: Primary Documents, 1853–1957*, Vol 5 (London: Archive Editions).

216 *Alasdair Drysdale*

Stern, Eliahu and Hayuth, Yehuda (1984) 'Developmental effects of politically located Ports', in B. S. Hoyle and D. Hilling (eds) *Seaport Systems and Spatial Change* (New York: John Wiley & Sons).

Stern, Eliahu, Hayuth, Yehuda, and Gradus, Yehuda (1983) 'The Negev continental bridge: a chain in an intermodal transport system', *Geoforum*, Vol. 14, pp. 461–69.

Warburg, R. (1979) 'The Sinai peninsula borders, 1906–47', *Journal of Contemporary History*, Vol. 14, pp. 677–92.

12 The evolution and contemporary significance of the Bophuthatswana–Botswana border landscape

James Drummond and Andrew H. Manson

'The question of boundaries is the first to be encountered, from it all others flow. To draw a border around anything is to define, analyse and reconstruct it.'
F. Braudel, *The Mediterranean World in the Age of Phillip II*

'In spite of his intense dislike of apartheid, Seretse Khama of Botswana must get along with South Africa. Botswana has no choice – a common problem for land-locked countries – or as Seretse Khama himself explained in 1970, "We cannot obliterate the harsh facts of history and geography."'
Legum, 1973, 179, cited in Reitsma, 1980, 134.

INTRODUCTION

The fact that artificial boundaries were imposed upon Africa, particularly by the articles laid down and later acted upon at the Berlin Conference of 1884–5, has long been recognised by geographers and historians. An established tradition in the field of African political geography and international relations has been the analysis of the evolution, characteristics and consequences of the boundaries themselves (Barbour, 1961; Brownlie, 1979; Prescott, 1979; Best and Zinyama, 1985). Further, the demarcation of the boundaries has created fourteen land-locked countries; the study of whose dependency relations with transit and coastal states has been outlined by Reitsma (1980). The issue of Africa's inherited borders has also been central to secession wars and to political conflict between African states seeking to achieve a greater degree of economic and political independence (Griffiths, 1986). Discussing the subject, Asiwaju (1985) has suggested that the historian's interest in Africa's political geography has tended to focus on the politics of partition and the intrigues of European diplomacy in Africa. He has drawn attention to

218   *James Drummond and Andrew H. Mason*

Figure 12.1   Southern Africa: Political map 1988

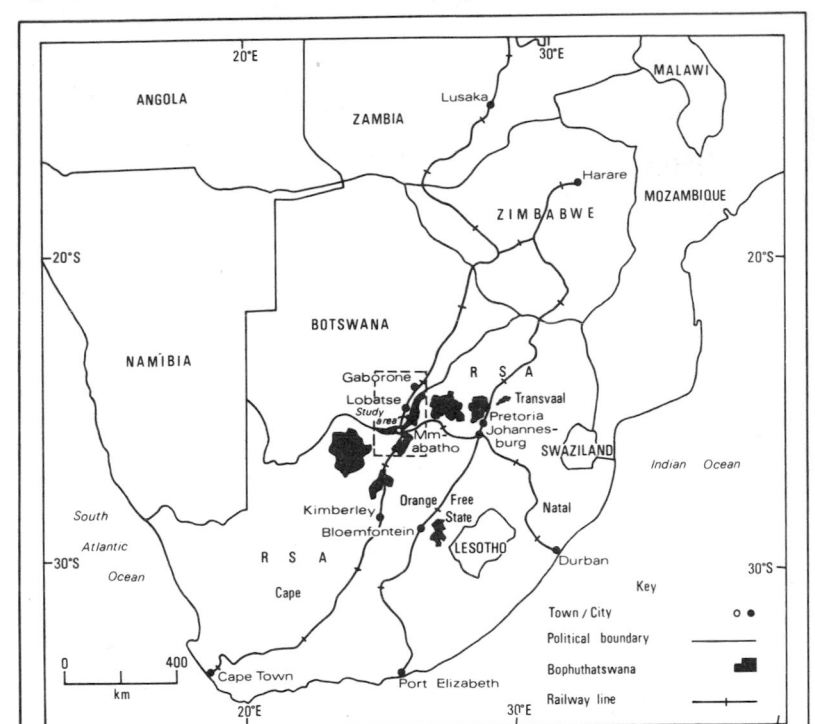

the need for studies which analyse the impact of Africa's evolving
boundaries on its border populations. Reviewing the literature, he
has pointed out that 'it remains a fact ... that Africans in strictly
partitioned situations have continued to be neglected' (Asiwaju,
1985: 7).

This chapter combines both geographical and historical approaches
in that it examines the causes underlying the creation and evolution
of international boundaries and analyses the effects of boundaries on
the people of a changing border landscape. Specifically, this chapter
examines the origins of the boundary between Bophuthatswana and
Botswana; traces the problems arising from the location of the
border and examines its contemporary geopolitical significance
(Figure 12.1). Our focus is on two particular regions, the extreme
western area of the Transvaal (now incorporated into Bophuthatswana
and historically occupied by the Hurutshe people) and the extreme
northern district of the Cape Province (similarly incorporated into

Figure 12.2   Study area showing Bophuthatswana–Botswana border

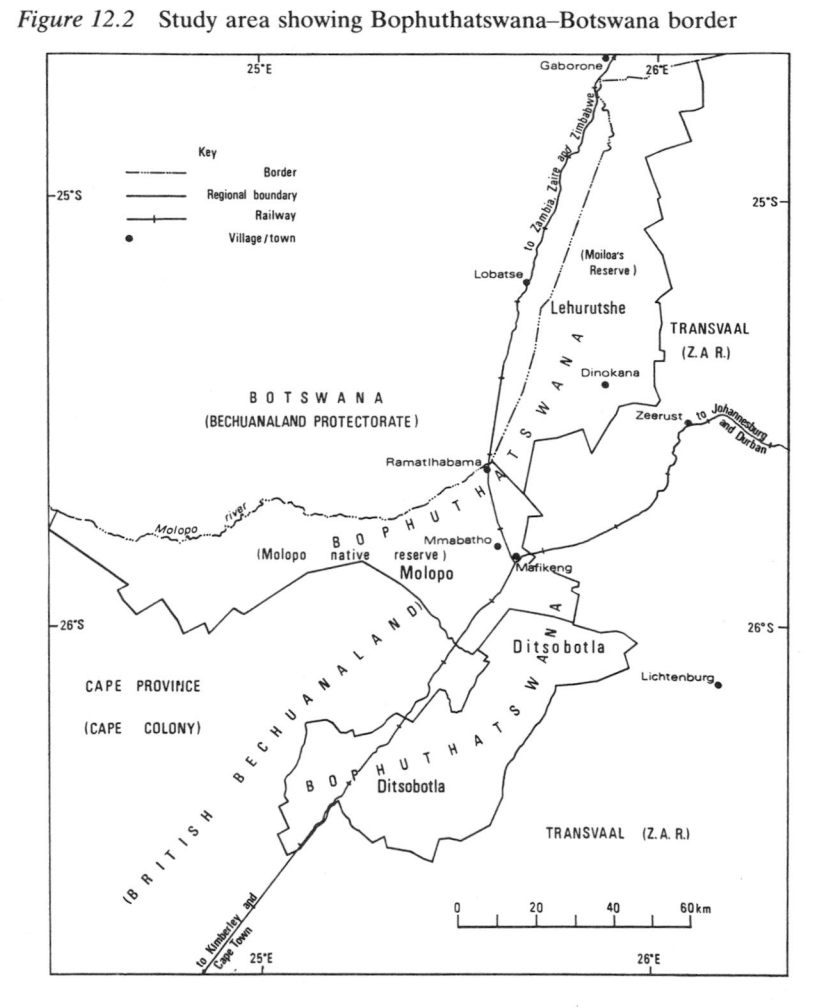

Bophuthatswana and historically the home of the Rolong). These areas were formerly 'native reserves' known as Moiloa's Reserve and the Molopo Native Reserve, presently referred to respectively as the Lehurutshe and Molopo districts of Bophuthatswana (Figure 12.2).

It should be noted that this region has undergone significant political change since the mid-nineteenth century, giving rise to a series of states with differing names. In the early nineteenth century the western highveld of southern Africa was inhabited by the Tswana, a group of Bantu-speaking peoples. In the mid-nineteenth century the migration of Dutch-speaking people from the Cape into

the interior of South Africa gave rise to the Zuid Afrikaansche Republiek (ZAR) or the Transvaal, which included tracts of Tswana-held lands. After the extension of British control into the territory of the Tswana in the latter half of the century the Tswana were divided again. Those living north of the Molopo River were placed under British protection in 1885 (in the Bechuanaland Protectorate) whilst those living south of the river fell under Crown Colony rule (in British Bechuanaland). In 1895 British Bechuanaland was annexed by the Cape Colony. The Tswana chiefdoms in the Protectorate, however, remained directly under the British crown. In 1902, after the South African War, the Transvaal became a Crown Colony. Eight years later the Transvaal in association with the Cape Colony, Natal and the Orange Free State, became a province in the new Union of South Africa. In 1966 the Bechuanaland Protectorate was given its independence by Britain and became Botswana, whilst in 1977 Bophuthatswana came into being in accordance with South Africa's 'grand apartheid policy' of creating separate 'independent ethnic homelands' for its African population. Bophuthatswana's 'independence' has not been recognised by any country other than South Africa.

The preceding overview, brief and simplified as it is, is necessary to guide the reader through the complex chain of historical events which have helped to delineate the political map of southern Africa. Such an appreciation of the past is essential to aid our contemporary understanding of the region. As it is our contention that the border between Bophuthatswana and Botswana has emerged from a fundamental remodelling of the relations of production and power in southern Africa, it will be necessary, however, to elaborate in more detail on this evolving process.

PRE-COLONIAL PERIOD

In the early nineteenth century, the western highveld of South Africa, the area under review, was inhabited by the Tswana. They were a people who spoke a similar language and shared common cultural features but who lived in separate and politically autonomous chiefdoms. The ethnic borders that now characterise much of the southern African geopolitical landscape did not exist before the nineteenth century. It has been noted that in this context 'ethnicity is very much a colonial and post-colonial phenomenon; the product of the process of socio-political modernisation that has accompanied economic development' (Harries, 1986: 1). Although the Tswana

chiefdoms recognised informal 'borders' designating their separate spheres of influence, there was, in periods of stability, a degree of interaction and migration across them. There was also a sharing of scarce resources of land and water between chiefdoms which was vital to these cattle-keeping people. During times of stress, due to environmental decline, competition for trade or the rise of autocratic rulers, Tswana communities often split apart either to form separate entities or to join with stronger or more benevolent rulers, depending on the circumstances of the time (Schapera, 1984). It is clear that during the pre-colonial period there were no fixed borders to restrict human and livestock migrations within the area occupied by the Tswana people.

THE ZUID AFRIKAANSCHE REPUBLIEK (ZAR)

The ZAR was officially declared by the Afrikaner Trekkers in 1851 although groups of them had informally taken possession of land in the central and western highveld in the 1840s. This was by virtue of their displacement of the previously dominant Ndebele people, a group of intruders from south-east Africa who had carved out a militaristic state in the western highveld shortly after the Tswana had been displaced by the Difaqane.[1] In the mid-nineteenth century it was actually the Dwarsberg that marked the point at which Trekker occupation of the north-west highveld ended. The Afrikaners were unsuccessful in their attempts to settle in the Limpopo Valley due to the prevalence of malaria and the resistance of local African communities. However 'contemporary maps customarily marked the Limpopo as the boundary and South African historians have accepted this fiction as if before the 1900's the ZAR had indeed "filled out" as far north-west as the Limpopo' (Parsons, 1973: 73). The ZAR failed to accurately define its borders. Indeed, it was unable to publish official maps illustrating its frontiers. The Hurutshe chiefdom, which was able to keep its lands on the Republic's western border by agreement with Andries Pretorius, a Trekker leader, had their boundary explained to them verbally. Later attempts to establish a boundary along the western edge of the Hurutshe reserve by the placing of beacons met with little success because the Hurutshe's Tswana neighbours to the west, the Ngwaketse, simply removed them (Ngcongco, 1979).

In 1868, when gold was thought to have been found at Tati (near present day Francistown, Botswana), the ZAR attempted to put forward claims to ownership of the goldfields (which were well to the

west of recognised Afrikaner occupation). This claim was easily repelled by the local Tswana chiefdom, the Ngwato. It becomes apparent that in the middle decades of the nineteenth century the underpopulated and administratively inefficient ZAR was at times unable to successfully demarcate its borders. Further, it did not have the power to enforce observance of its boundaries even where these had been claimed and beaconed off (Manson, 1990).

MINERAL DISCOVERIES AND BRITISH IMPERIAL EXPANSION

The next stage in the evolution of the boundaries was set in motion by the discovery of diamonds near Kimberley in 1867 and the subsequent discovery of gold deposits on the Witwatersrand twenty years later. The opening of the diamond fields raised the crucial issue of their ownership. Competing claims were advanced by the Tlhaping (Tswana), the Griquas, the Afrikaner republics of the Orange Free State and the Transvaal (ZAR) and by the British-ruled Cape Colony. Even British commercial interests in Kimberley were aware that 'without imperial intervention the British were in serious danger of being turned out by the "rightful owners . . . the local (Tswana) chiefs"' (Shillington, 1985: 43).

The disputed territory was subjected to British arbitration in 1870 and in 1871 Britain effectively annexed control of the fields through granting ownership to the Griqua people, who, indebted to Britain and unable to effectively govern the growing new colony of Griqualand West, soon handed control over to Britain. The British realised that in order to effectively exploit the full potential of the diamond discoveries it was necessary to procure a free flow of labour. The independent African chiefdoms and the Afrikaner republics of the Transvaal and Orange Free State were considered to be encapsulating labour which might otherwise have been employed in Griqualand West. Britain accordingly attempted to bring them under suzerainty as a prelude to modernising their state apparatus to allow for the release of labour (Marks and Atmore, 1980).

Central to this process was the need to define boundaries. In 1871, the contentious Keate Award, based on evidence submitted to the Bloemhof Commission by all parties interested in the diamond fields dispute (the Tswana, the Griquas and the Afrikaners) formalised the borders of the Transvaal. The Keate Award had a dual role, firstly to ensure British control over the fields by rejecting the Tlhaping (a southern Tswana chiefdom) claims; and secondly to keep the

Figure 12.3 The study area in the nineteenth century

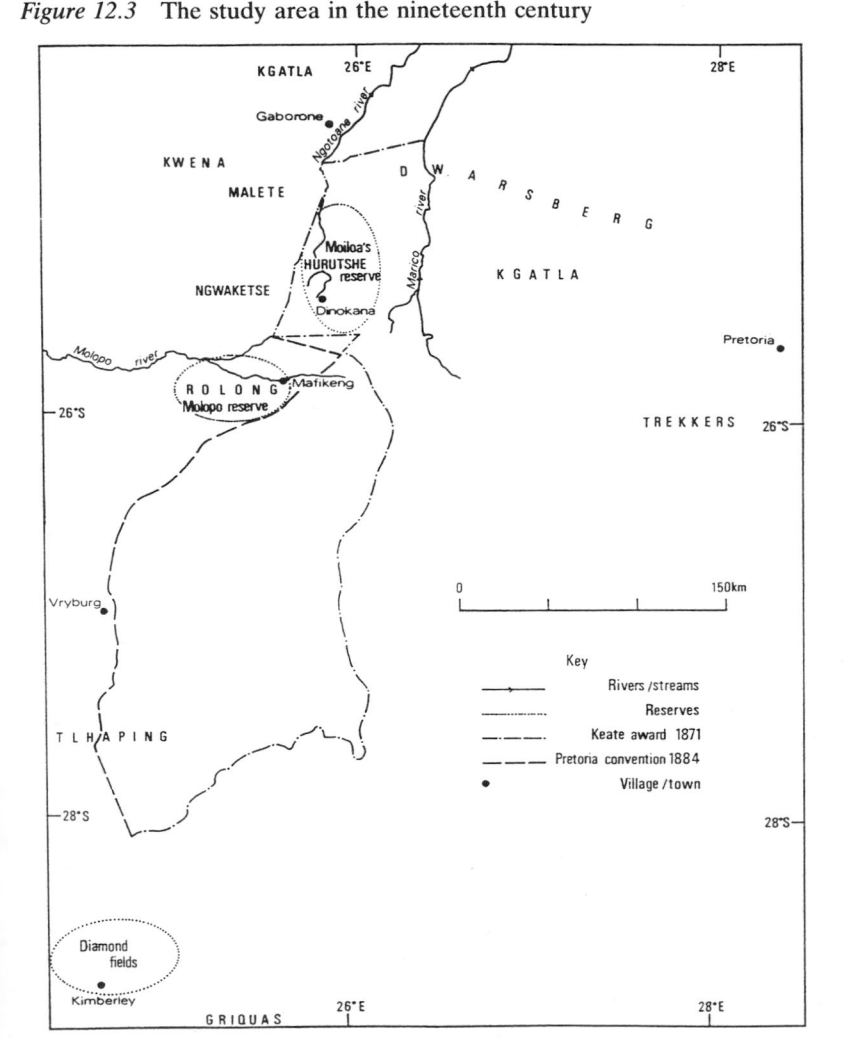

so-called 'road to the north' open for the expansion of British trade and influence further into the interior of southern Africa. It was necessary therefore to lay down a firm western border for the Transvaal in order to prevent Afrikaner encroachment into the territory of the still independent Tswana chiefdoms. Interestingly, the Transvaal's western border was based on evidence given by the Hurutshe chief Moiloa and the Rolong chiefs Montshiwa and Moswete,

as to where the boundary was considered to be. Although Keate delineated this border as a straight line following a number of beacons (Figure 12.3) (the Keate Award corresponds to the western boundary of Lehurutshe), it is an example of the kind discussed by Griffiths (1986) where the establishment of African colonial borders was substantially influenced by Africans themselves. In this case, however, we must remember that the primary motivation behind the delineation of the border was to serve British interests, which were to resist the westward expansion of the Transvaal. Moiloa stated at the Commission that his 'boundary' had been fixed by common agreement with the Ngwaketse, their western neighbours.[2]

It should be noted that Keate's boundary closely followed the line of landmarks pointed out by the Hurutshe themselves, because to have followed the natural physical boundary, the Ngotoane River, would have split Moiloa's Reserve in two. This would indicate that the territorial integrity of the reserve had been accepted by both the Trekkers and the British. However, it was only in the northern end of the reserve where the Hurutshe themselves recognised the Ngotoane as their boundary that Keate made the unfortunate decision to draw the boundary in a continuous straight line, for reasons which remain buried in the colonial past, and so laid the foundation for later conflict.

Almost immediately after Keate's decision, the ZAR intrigued with a faction of the Rolong under chief Moswete who were well disposed to the Transvaalers, to acquire access to land outside the Republic borders. In 1875 Moswete ceded territory to the Transvaal and the ZAR's president formally extended the jurisdiction of the Transvaal beyond the Keate Award line. Britain was not prepared at this stage to intervene and could only protest at this move (Cloete, 1975: 39–40). The Rolong faction opposed to Boer transgressions then took refuge with the Ngwaketse to the north, a good example of the independence of political action during a period before the concepts of borders or nations had taken hold in the area.

In 1877, with imperial interests dominating British policy making, Britain annexed the Transvaal and this act put paid to any thoughts of Afrikaner expansion westward for the time being. In 1881 however, the Boers defeated the British (the first Anglo-Boer War) and the Transvaal retroceded to the Afrikaners. As a consequence of this shift in the balance of power the Transvaal's western border was redrawn in terms of the Pretoria Convention of 1881 to give the ZAR considerably more land than before. The Convention appointed a Royal Commission which attempted to survey accurately the disputed

boundaries of the Transvaal. While this commission was fulfilling its task, groups of Boer mercenaries, clearly unrestrained by the clauses in the Pretoria Convention which was intended to restrict white encroachment onto Tswana occupied territory, allied with Moswete's faction of the Rolong and tried once again to displace Montshiwa's people from the water sources along the Molopo River. The Afrikaners were then able to establish two new republics, Goshen and Stellaland, in the greater Molopo region.

These events resulted in a more determined thrust of imperial intervention. In 1884 imperial and humanitarian interests in South Africa acted in tandem to reduce the republics of Stellaland and Goshen into a colonial settlement with the Cape (Schreuder, 1980; Shillington, 1985). In 1885, the Reverend J. Mackenzie of the London Missionary Society (LMS) and General Sir Charles Warren travelled north of the Molopo River to gain cessions of submission from Tswana chiefs. Warren then established British jurisdiction over the area south of 22 degrees south latitude and between the Transvaal and 20 degrees east. Originally Warren planned to have the whole area declared a Crown Colony but finally, due to fears of incurring expensive administrative costs, the area was divided at the Molopo River; the territory south becoming the Crown Colony of British Bechuanaland, the north being declared a protectorate. At the time probably neither the British authorities nor the missionaries nor the Tswana leaders realised the implications this division was to have.

The Rolong chiefdom was partitioned because of the need to find a physical feature to demarcate the border. The lands of the formerly free Tswana were therefore given boundaries entirely on the basis of British proclamations.[3] The Protectorate was administered from the Imperial Reserve in Mafeking, a colonial town in the Crown Colony, which in 1895 was incorporated into the Cape Colony and thus in 1910 became part of the Union of South Africa. This situation persisted until 1966. The chiefs in the Protectorate successfully resisted the proposed transference of the territory to the Cape Colony, principally by a personal visit to Britain to explain their case. The concomitant discrediting of Rhodes's British South Africa Company (BSAC), which was also contending for control of the Protectorate, ensured that the territory remained under direct imperial rule rather than sub-imperial rule. The Tswana in the Crown Colony were given little opportunity to resist their incorporation into the Cape, an event which was to have fateful consequences for them later. However, the 'issue of the ultimate fate of the Protectorate, which was promised both to South Africa and the BSAC's Rhodesia

at various times until 1910, remained uncertain until well into the 1950's' (Picard, 1985: 10).

The conferment of colonial statehood upon the Tswana in the Bechuanaland Protectorate (BP) necessitated stricter observance of the border now dividing two separate states. Colonial officials came to define and safeguard the territorial integrity of the BP, especially after the appointment of the Gould–Adams Commission to fix the internal borders (between the Protectorate's chiefdoms) which by extension defined the outer limits of each chief's jurisdiction. Furthermore the colonial presence ensured a stricter demarcation of the border. For example in 1896 a British–Transvaal Joint Boundary Commission under the Presidency of F. W. Panzera recommended the erection of a fence along the 104 kilometres separating the Hurutshe Reserve from Bechuanaland, partly to prevent continual illegal entry into both states and to prevent the movement of cattle as part of a wider attempt to stem the spread of the deadly Rinderpest epidemic of 1896.

The above discussion has focused on the emergence of boundaries and states in southern Africa to 1910. We turn now to an examination of how these events affected the people 'on the ground'. Our focus will be mainly upon the Hurutshe people whose reserve lay along the margins of the ZAR and whose western boundary was also the Transvaal–BP border.

THE BOUNDARY AND LOCAL COMMUNITIES TO 1871

It is apparent that during the ZAR period there was little to prevent the Tswana on either side of the border from conducting normal economic, social or political intercourse. As Morton (1985) has shown, the nominal partition of the Kgatla people by the border did little to affect the unity of the pre-partition period. The Kgatla regent in the Transvaal crossed with impunity out of the territory in 1869 to avoid the exactions of Afrikaner overrule. His was by no means an isolated case. A major Hurutshe chief, Mangope, led his followers across the Molopo River to seek sanctuary with the Kwena outside the ZAR in 1858. Another Hurutshe chief, Moiloa, crossed the line twice between 1852 and 1853 to escape the consequences of conflict between the Afrikaners and their Tswana neighbours (Manson, 1990). Such movements accord with the frequently observed 'protest migration' of African communities from areas of oppression and insecurity to areas of greater freedom (Asiwaju, 1976; Musambachime, 1988). The Hurutshe (inside the ZAR) and the

Ngwaketse (outside) grazed their cattle across the line and kept cattle posts in each other's territory.[4] From their side, the Transvaalers were unrestrained, following up stolen cattle and attacking incompliant Tswana chiefdoms outside the Transvaal – in one well-documented raid destroying the mission station of David Livingstone, the LMS missionary with the Kwena. The accounts of hunters and traders, who traded extensively through the ZAR to Lake Ngami or to the hunting fields, bear little indication of their knowledge that a 'border' existed at all.

THE POST-KEATE PERIOD TO THE SOUTH AFRICAN WAR (1871–99)

This period, coinciding as it did with the phase of post-mercantile expansion, saw the emergence of greater acceptance in theory of a border. Except for the brief period after the British retreat from the Transvaal (1882), the Afrikaners showed signs of accepting a western boundary. In 1875 for example, the Ngwato chief Kgama was able to enforce some acknowledgement of the limits of the Boer domain, by appealing for British assistance in preventing Afrikaner passage through Ngwato territory. For the Hurutshe situated along the margins of the border, the more formal establishment of the boundary by the London Convention of 1884, and the subsequent arrival of missionaries and administrators in the Protectorate, began to cut them off from cattle posts, lands and water sources to which they had had almost unlimited access for the past sixty years. For example, in 1889 the followers of chief Gopane's Hurutshe were forcibly ejected from land inside the Protectorate on orders from W. Surmon, the Assistant Commissioner for Southern Bechuanaland. Hurutshe claims to this territory were dismissed by Surmon on the grounds that 'it is very late to make such a report now if it has not been made before', a wholly unreasonable assertion in the light of the fact that these Hurutshe had ploughed such land for five years after the formalisation of the border without suffering any consequences. A small Hurutshe village at Peleng just inside the Protectorate's border transferred allegiance to the Ngwaketse rather than lose those lands (Manson, 1990).

In addition, a stretch of the boundary which ran straight instead of following the Ngotoane River cut off people on either side of the river from access to water (Figure 12.4). The Joint Boundary Commission of 1896, in investigating transgressions of the boundary, recognised the limitations of such a border but felt incompetent to

Figure 12.4   Boundary intersection of Ngotoane River

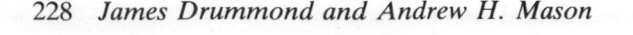

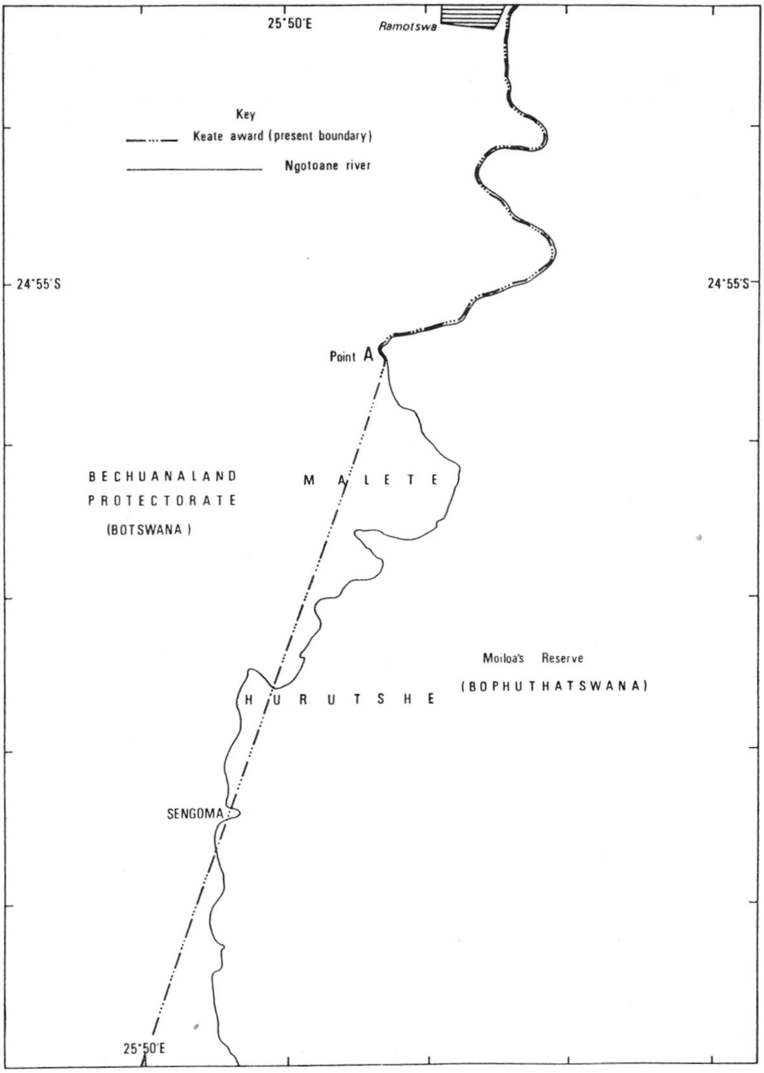

overturn the precedents of the more binding Keate Award and
London Convention. Panzera, the chairman, noted prophetically at
the time that 'I consider nothing is more calculated to cause end-
less trouble between the Bahurutshe and Bamalete people' (cited
Manson, 1990: ch. V, 29). Both the instances cited above provide

palpable evidence for the way in which Europeans imposed boundaries in Africa with little regard, in Asiwaju's words, to 'the essentially fluid socio-political situation prevailing in (those) localities' (Asiwaju, 1985: 8). An interesting point to note is that the stricter enforcement of the border in the last two decades was related to the fact that land within the Protectorate was being privatised. It was the Reverend Good, missionary to the Ngwaketse, who first complained to the authorities about the Hurutshe ploughing on land ceded to him by the Ngwaketse regent Bathoen (Chirenje, 1976). Similarly it was the manager of the Kanya Exploration Company whose complaints triggered off the removal of Hurutshe who were cutting trees on company land in 1894.

Nevertheless the border by no means fully 'closed off' the populations living along it from each other. Indeed it is the gradual way in which the boundaries really came to be effective that is the dominant theme of this period, up to contemporary times. Morton's study of the Kgatla indicates that in Linchwe's period of rule (1874–1921) 'the international boundary was less a barrier and more a line distinguishing economic and political regions within the area of Kgatla occupation . . . More often than not, the border was used or ignored to suit their own convenience' (Morton, 1985: 136). The Kgatla and the Hurutshe for example, used the international boundary as a refuge, claiming immunity from prosecution after appropriating cattle from the Transvaal and Protectorate respectively. In addition, despite the rebuffs of the early 1890s, Gopane's Hurutshe still crossed into the Bechuanaland Protectorate to water their cattle. Along the southern BP border Tlhaping families from the southern end of the Crown Colony migrated to join welcoming chiefs in the Protectorate. The colonial administrators in the Colony recognised that 'in consequence of the length of open boundary between Bechuanaland and the Colony . . . it would be impossible to strictly enforce Section 50 (requiring permission to cross the boundary) without a large force of police to constantly patrol the border'.[5] In 1894 the Inspector of Native Reserves in the Colony reported that Rolong in the Molopo region and Thlaro from as far south as Kuruman were moving their stock into the BP knowing that 'by doing this they get unlimited grazing ground for their cattle and escape paying both the Hut Tax and Wheel Tax'.[6]

THE BORDER AS A VETERINARY CORDON: 1900–60

This period in the evolution of the border landscape was one of comparative stability. The border had been demarcated in 1897 by the Joint Border Commission, which effectively laid down the border as we know it today (Figure 12.2). This act, taken in conjunction with the decision of the British authorities in the previous year to impose a hut tax on natives residing in the Bechuanaland Protectorate, closed it off as a tax refuge for the Tswana south of the Molopo and helped to reduce the incidence of border related disputes. However, the most notable feature of this period was the emergence of a mutually accepted fencing agreement to prevent the spread of stock diseases across the border.[7]

The elements of a common policy towards the border were set down in the first decade of this century, when the British victory in the South African War led to the establishment of British colonial administrators in the Cape, the Transvaal and the BP. Administrators agreed to consult with each other to smooth out border issues where these affected local populations. This attitude of cooperation generally prevailed in the three decades after the creation of the Union of South Africa (1910), when administrators dealing with the border followed many of the precedents laid down in the first decade of the century.

The emergence of 'give and take' arrangements regarding the establishment of veterinary fences, which did not always correspond to the defined border, illustrates a degree of flexibility and lack of concern for the rigid observance of the boundary. In addition, the 1897 Joint Border Commission recommendation that the boundary line should follow the Ngotoane River from Sengoma to Point A (Figure 12.4) seems to have been mutually adhered to until the 1960s when political circumstances were to change. Thus the Malete people in the BP and the Hurutshe in the Union had continued access to the Ngotoane River from Sengoma northwards.

The only circumstances in which the boundary was invoked were during periods of stock diseases. There was a 'give and take' agreement which allowed people to graze animals on either side of the fence but during animal epidemics the inhabitants along the border had to bring their cattle back inside their respective boundaries which were then 'closed'. In 1904 for example twenty-four Hurutshe cattle in the BP were shot dead because their owners had not timeously moved them back into Moiloa's Reserve.[8] Again in 1932 and during subsequent periods up to the mid-1940s the border was

enforced to prevent the spread of 'foot and mouth' disease within the Protectorate and South Africa. The periodic restrictions on cross-border movement presumably confused the local populations, who for long periods had enjoyed unfettered freedom of movement across the border.

During this period when the border served veterinary rather then political ends none of the usual requirements or formalities of international travel applied. Travellers on the main routes in and out of both countries merely opened gates to cross the border – no passports were necessary nor were there any border officials present at the gates (Interview, Minchin, 4 August 1988).

THE IMPACT OF BOTSWANA'S INDEPENDENCE UPON THE BORDER LANDSCAPE

In the early 1960s when Botswana's independence was imminent the Bechuanaland and South African authorities felt it necessary to re-examine the boundary to ensure that future disputes would not arise. Consequently on 16 January 1963, a meeting was held in Pretoria between representatives of the British High Commissioner's office, and the Bechuanaland Protectorate and South African governments concerning the precise definition of the boundary between South Africa and the Bechuanaland Protectorate. Both authorities noted that certain parts of the border were likely to be contended and recommended that a commission be established to effect a precise demarcation. Even at this stage, the authorities were concerned not to upset local arrangements regarding access to water and grazing land. For example, both parties agreed that 'The well in the river bed opposite the farm "Welkom" which had the only sweet water in the area, should provide a supply for human consumption to people on both sides of the boundary, whether it was found to be in the Bechuanaland Protectorate or South Africa'.[9] Unfortunately, there seems to be no trace of this commission's report, but it appears that the recommendations were acted upon.

However, this sympathetic attitude to the needs of the local border populations diminished with the coming to power of Seretse Khama's government at Botswana's independence in 1966. Two factors contributed to the need for Botswana to enforce the territorial limits of its jurisdiction. The first of these was the continuing existence of the illegal Smith regime in Rhodesia and the subsequent imposition of sanctions on that country, which necessitated closer control over economic interaction on the northern border. It should

Figure 12.5   Contemporary border landscape

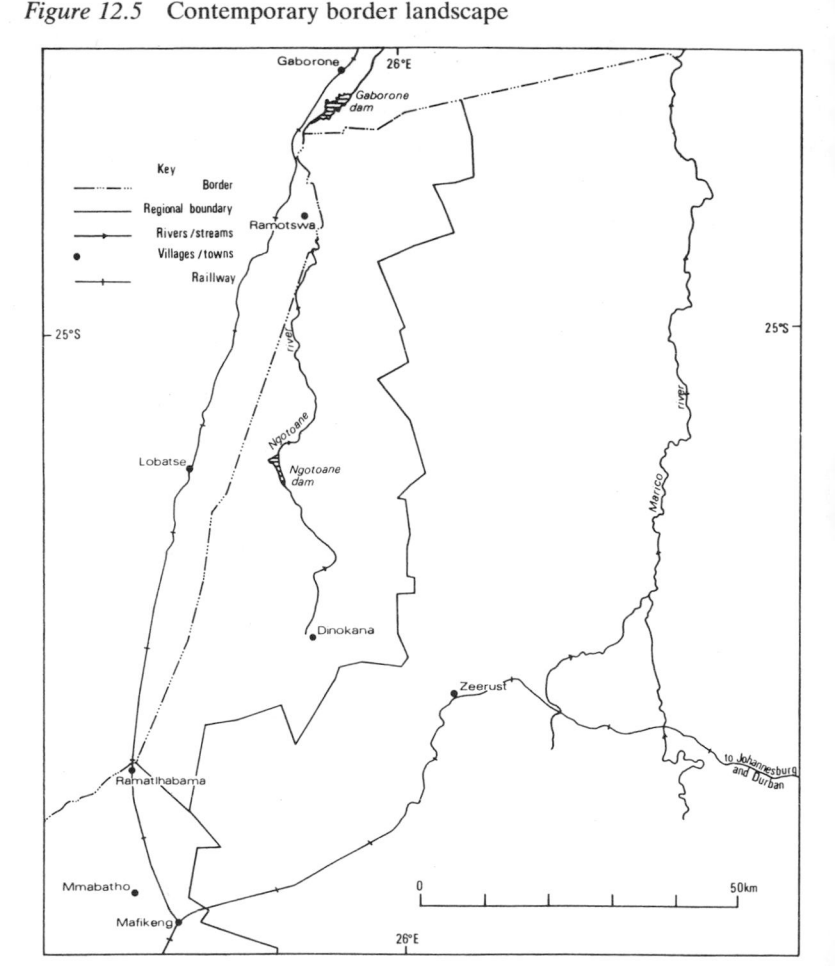

be stressed that the fact that Botswana lay astride the railway line from Rhodesia to South Africa's ports conferred upon the Botswana government a key role in the continuance or collapse of white rule in Rhodesia. The Smith regime, realising this, considered building a direct rail link with South Africa (*Mafeking Mail*, 18 February 1966), a plan which came to fruition in the mid-1970s (Figure 12.5), but which did little to forestall the collapse of Smith's government later. The second development was Botswana's firmer commitment to the removal of white rule in South Africa as well, symbolised by its joining the Organisation of African Unity (OAU) in 1969.

For the residents of Botswana and South Africa the most visible and keenly felt effects of independence were the need to carry passports and the sealing off of the cross-border communities from each other. In Morton's words independence led to 'an international boundary reconstituted as a line across which moved national passport holders, not pass-carrying tribesmen' (Morton, 1985: 145). The four communities most affected were the Kgatla, whose survival as a 'single' people came to an end (Morton, 1985), the Malete and Hurutshe, whose long accepted rights to grazing in South Africa and Botswana respectively were taken away, and the Rolong who lost farms inside Botswana in 1970 (Comaroff, 1982). Even those Rolong who attempted to settle on the 'Barolong farms' inside Botswana prior to independence were prosecuted for not having passports (*Mafeking Mail*, 1 July 1966). The economic dislocation caused by this was considerable. These developments marked the beginning of the process of estrangement of the Tswana of Botswana from those in the Republic of South Africa, a fact which the Botswana government was quite prepared to accept.

A final feature of the changing border landscape attendant upon Botswana's independence was the decline in the importance of Mafeking. The capital was moved to Gaborone and Mafeking lost its status as an administrative capital (Best, 1970). The population of the town declined and it went into a phase of economic stagnation (*Mafeking Mail*, 30 December 1966; Interview, Minchin, 4 August 1988).

THE IMPACT OF BOPHUTHATSWANA'S INDEPENDENCE UPON THE BORDER LANDSCAPE

With the rise of grand apartheid in the 1950s and 1960s, orchestrated by H. F. Verwoerd, the former native reserves came to be viewed by the South African government as the 'traditional homelands' of the African people. Hattingh (1988: 10) has pointed out that 'in response to the Tomlinson Commission's report ... the government's white paper *shifted from spatial separation to demarcation of Black areas on ethnic grounds*' (emphasis added). The Promotion of Bantu Self-Government Act, No. 46 of 1959, recognised eight ethnic groups which led to the eventual demarcation of ten 'homelands' or 'national states', of which Transkei, Bophuthatswana, Venda and Ciskei have become 'independent'. Bophuthatswana was actually granted 'independence' by South Africa on 6 December 1977.

An enduring feature of Bophuthatswana's political programme has

been its drive to secure international recognition. Despite some success in luring parties of businessmen and politicians from West European countries such as Britain, West Germany and Denmark, little headway has been achieved. Botswana has consistently refused to recognise Bophuthatswana and ironically has distanced itself even further from Bophuthatswana after that country gained independence from Pretoria. In 1977, President Seretse Khama of Botswana in denouncing Bophuthatswana as a 'child of apartheid' prophetically remarked that 'Botswana was likely to face difficulties . . . if these countries (Bophuthatswana, Rhodesia and South Africa) became hotbeds of violent conflict' (*Mafeking Mail*, 1 July 1977).

Bophuthatswana's attitude to Botswana has, by contrast, been more ambivalent. On the one hand, Bophuthatswana's leaders have appealed to a sense of common Tswana identity to gain acceptance by Botswana, and by extension, to the rest of the international community. This line of argument appears to have little chance of success for it assumes the historical reality of an earlier common Tswana nationhood, whereas nationhood was conferred separately on Botswana by Britain, and on Bophuthatswana by South Africa. An officially sponsored study on Bophuthatswana has claimed that 'of major significance for the future is the fact that while the Tswana lost their independence as tribes, they regained it as a nation, encompassed within a Tswana state' (Anon., 1977: 205). On the other hand, while this policy of seeking international recognition has never been abandoned, Bophuthatswana from 1981 has attempted to exert pressure on Botswana, as part of an attempt to force that country into negotiations and low-level diplomatic contacts which would implicitly recognise and lend credibility to Bophuthatswana's existence as a state. This has backfired and stiffened Botswana's resolve not to recognise Bophuthatswana. This policy has created a climate of suspicion which has damaged possibilities of solving border-related disputes.

Two examples of border-related disputes will serve to illustrate how this policy of coercion has manifested itself. The first of these is the case of water rights. The problem of interstate cooperation elsewhere in southern Africa, where river systems cross political boundaries, has been examined by Funnell (1988). In the case under consideration here, two rivers, the Ngotoane and the Molopo, which have their headwaters in Bophuthatswana, flow into Botswana where the water is used for domestic and agricultural purposes. The Ngotoane is also the major water source for the Gaborone Dam, which supplies the capital city with its water (Figure 12.5). In 1979

construction of the Ngotoane Dam was undertaken in the Lehurutshe district of Bophuthatswana with the purpose of using the water to establish an irrigation-based agricultural project (*Mafeking Mail*, 26 February 1982). At the same time the Molopo River was dammed for the purposes of irrigation-based agricultural development and also for recreation. These dams seriously diminished the flow of water into Botswana during a period of particularly bad drought. The Bophuthatswana government offered Botswana the opportunity to participate in the decision-making process which led to the construction of the dams. Botswana rejected these overtures but chose to negotiate with South Africa on the basis that the construction of the Ngotoane Dam would violate a previous agreement between South Africa, Botswana, Zimbabwe and Mozambique not to build dams on the Limpopo River or its headwaters without prior negotiation. Bophuthatswana took the view that this 'was an exercise in futility' as the dams were constructed on 'our territory, and the sovereignty over it is ours, and ours alone' (*Mafeking Mail*, 30 April 1982). Sources in Bophuthatswana called openly for a 'round table conference between the two countries with the establishment of diplomatic relations' offering as a *quid pro quo* the wilingness of Bophuthatswana to 'allow some water from the two rivers to flow into Botswana to alleviate the position' (*Mafeking Mail*, 20 May 1983). While Botswana's stand could be construed as laudable in terms of its support for the OAU and the United Nations' calls for the non-recognition of Bophuthatswana, it could also be argued that Botswana failed to acknowledge the realities of its own geographical location and the *de facto* existence of Bophuthatswana on its south-eastern border.

The second and most recent border-related dispute emerged in December 1986 and continued until August 1987. Bophuthatswana, still maintaining its campaign for diplomatic links with Botswana, took advantage of its geopolitical location in southern Africa, lying astride Botswana's vital rail link to South Africa's ports (Figure 12.1), to exert pressure on Botswana. Effectively Bophuthatswana acts as a transit state through which Botswana's imports and exports must pass. Botswana therefore falls into that category of African states described by Reitsma (1980) as being 'double land-locked', and which are especially vulnerable to action by the transit state (Bophuthatswana) as well as the coastal state (South Africa).

On 31 December 1986, Bophuthatswana informed Botswana that it required that Botswana citizens wishing to visit Bophuthatswana should acquire visas thirty days before making such visits. Previously no visas were necessary. By this action, Bophuthatswana was

demanding some form of recognition and was effectively closing the border to Botswana citizens. This severely disrupted Botswana's rail and road traffic with Bophuthatswana and also its transit trade to South Africa (*Mafeking Mail*, 13 March 1987). In addition, Zimbabwe, Zambia and Zaire were affected, as those countries also rely on the rail link for their trade with South Africa. The rationale behind Bophuthatswana's actions can be illustrated by the words of President L. M. Mangope, who, during the ninth anniversary celebrations of Bophuthatswana on 6 December 1986, warned that 'if Botswana cannot change its foreign policy on Bophuthatswana and continues with its mud-slinging, then Bophuthatswana will be left with no option but to retaliate . . . and . . . in quite a few areas of our coexistence we could be difficult to the extreme discomfort of Botswana' (*Mafeking Mail*, 12 December 1986).

The visa requirement had severe repercussions on cross-border trade and also caused great hardship to those people from Botswana who were prevented from entering Bophuthatswana. For example the *Mafeking Mail* of 16 January 1987 reported that at the Ramatlhabama border people were prevented entry into Bophuthatswana to attend funerals, visit sick relatives, seek medical treatment or shop, whilst even Botswana miners returning to South Africa were told they needed visas and were turned back. By mid-February the introduction of the visa requirement had affected most of the shops in Mafeking with several reporting a drop in business. Furthermore, the Bophuthatswana authorities increased their pressure on Botswana (and Zimbabwe) by insisting on 11 February 1987 that train crews of the National Railways of Zimbabwe bringing trains into Mafeking from the Ramatlhabama border would need valid visas to enter Bophuthatswana. The crews did not apply for visas and the impasse was only resolved by South African crews taking over at the border (Figure 12.5). This changeover, however, created difficulties and led to 'much concern in both Botswana and Zimbabwe as trains entering Bophuthatswana were delayed and traffic was disrupted, becoming erratic' (*Mafeking Mail*, 13 March 1987).[10]

The dispute dragged on throughout the first half of the year. Botswana clearly saw Bophuthatswana's stand as an attempt to get some recognition from the Frontline States and was not prepared to negotiate directly with Bophuthatswana. Botswana approached South Africa on the issue and clearly put pressure on South Africa to persuade Bophuthatswana to drop the visa requirement. In mid-March these tactics paid off when South Africa's Ministers of Foreign Affairs and Transport held talks in Mmabatho with the Bophuthatswana

government at which they pressurised Bophuthatswana to settle the matter. The economic factor of the continuing loss of trade to Mafeking's shops (particularly a nearly completed major shopping complex) whose trade depended on the Botswana market, must also have weighed heavily in the considerations of the Bophuthatswana government. Eventually the Bophuthatswana government quietly lifted the visa requirement on 1 August 1987. The position of the Bophuthatswana Government over the railway dispute was summarised succintly by the *Mafeking Mail* (16 January 1987) in an editorial when it stated that the visa requirement 'it can be argued . . . is a ploy by Bophuthatswana to force diplomatic recognition by Botswana. Be that as it may, Botswana depends not only economically, but also for transit facilities to South Africa, Lesotho and Swaziland, on Bophuthatswana. For this reason it needed to ratify its relations with this country. This is obvious or should have been obvious to Botswana in the first place.'

It is interesting that Bophuthatswana used the tactic of closing the border to try to force Botswana to establish diplomatic relations. Although unsuccessful on this occasion, Bophuthatswana clearly possesses a powerful political lever in its relations with Botswana, and that is its geographical location. This presents a problem to Botswana and one that is not easy to solve while Botswana continues to refuse recognition. There are voices in Botswana which have called for closer ties with Bophuthatswana. For example Chief Bathoeng of Kanye, an opposition politician, said that it was 'imperative that the two countries come together. If rail links between the two countries were cut both would suffer but Botswana would suffer more' (*Mafeking Mail*, 9 January 1987). Although this is probably true, the majority opinion in Botswana, and certainly that of the government, is that Botswana will not recognise Bophuthatswana although it will allow trade, family ties and legal access to continue. This is reinforced by the fact that the border landscape is atypical, in that it has become a region of comparatively high population density on either side, and is characterised also by a relatively high level of economic development. Indeed both capital cities (Mmabatho and Gaborone) are within 20 kilometres of the border. This siting of the 'core economy' of both territories near the border obviously leads to extensive economic contact.

NEW DRIVES FOR BOPHUTHATSWANA'S RECOGNITION

The ultimately ineffective and contradictory outcome of Bophuthatswana's policy of coercion upon Botswana has given way, in the last year, to a renewal of demands for recognition based on Tswana ethnic unity, and a denunciation of the colonial borders which, it is argued, separate culturally and linguistically homogeneous peoples.

The implication of this argument – that Bophuthatswana be incorporated into Botswana – has not been put forward; rather Bophuthatswana has demanded that it be recognised as an independent nation in its own right on the basis of its 'unique' historical background. Specifically, the incorporation of British Bechuanaland into the Cape in 1895 is cited as a negation of a prior agreement to honour the independence of the Tswana chiefdoms resident in the Crown Colony. This argument rests on the rather shaky belief that history can be rolled back in an uncomplicated manner. Indeed most African countries have followed a policy of absolute boundary maintenance since the last century, to the extent of fighting to defend colonial borders. It is the stated policy of the OAU that the boundaries should be maintained as they were at the independence of member states (Asiwaju, 1985). Furthermore, the largest and most populous areas of Bophuthatswana do not correspond at all to the territory of the former Crown Colony, being largely situated in the Western Transvaal. Nevertheless arguments have been advanced that the colonial borders of Africa are not sacrosanct and should be subject to review by the OAU (Griffiths, 1986). Some headway has been made in gaining the support of prominent British and West German members of parliament and visitors, many of whom have accepted state-sponsored visits to Bophuthatswana (*Bophuthatswana Pioneer*, May/June 1988). In 1987 President Mangope, through representations made by his supporters, was able to address the British House of Commons Foreign Affairs Committee to state his point of view (*Mafeking Mail*, 4 September 1987).

In the final analysis Bophuthatswana stands little chance of recognition as a separate independent state, in its present form. Firstly, it is unlikely to shed the stigma of its indebtedness and dependence upon South Africa; highlighted by the intervention of the South African Defence Force which aborted the attempted coup of February 1988. Secondly, Bophuthatswana as a territory remains fragmented, at present consisting of seven regions separated by South African land (Figure 12.1), a fact hardly consonant with the concept of territorial integrity.

One final development which puts paid to any idea of future boundary adjustments is the militarisation of the border landscape. This feature arises out of the intensification of guerrilla activity in South Africa, principally by the outlawed African National Congres (ANC). Attacks apparently originate in Botswana and have incurred the wrath of the South African state which has launched frequent cross-border raids on presumed ANC bases and supporters in Botswana (Laurence, 1985). These activities have led to patrols on either side of the border, the erection of security fences, and an intensified military presence at border gates. The Bophuthatswana Defence Force, which has supported South African forces in their anti-insurgency activities, has its major bases within 15 kilometres of the Botswana border, a symbolic testimony to the current state of relations.

CONCLUSION

The evolution of the border landscape between the countries discussed in this chapter can be seen in separate phases, which relate directly to the relations of political power and economic dominance in the region over the past century or more. The northward expansion of British interests into south-central Africa carved out loosely defined spheres of influence. The extension of formal British control required a more distinct definition of borders, to enable administrators to resolve the affairs of the people they governed and to protect them from incursions by 'outsiders'. Once the colonial pattern of control was established, border relations were characterised by 'give and take' agreements which were neglected only in periods of stock disease. This was probably a rational response to the problem of a boundary which divided culturally similar people, and accords with Griffiths' (1986: 215) suggestion that 'the use of administrative boundaries avoiding transfer of sovereignty would go some way towards easing Africa's problem of divided culture groups'. However, from the time of Botswana's independence in 1966, political realities steadily transcended cultural and language considerations. The border was legally enforced and then, from the birth of Bophuthatswana, was manipulated to achieve political ends. Militarisation, the final stage of the evolution of the border landscape, suggests that no new demarcations are possible. For local populations, the vision of the border similarly has changed from a loosely conceived line of differentiation, to a legal barrier to exit or entry, and finally to a cordon separating politically opposed states.

240 *James Drummond and Andrew H. Mason*

Remarkably, the developing form of a legal and enforced boundary continued to be negated by events 'on the ground'. However, we would agree with Merrett (1984: 91) that 'in the long term the international boundaries set up within South Africa may prove more resilient than anticipated: they may be perpetuated more successfully by the local elites whose position is dependent upon them, than by the national political economy'. There is still considerable human interaction between Bophuthatswana and Botswana, whose residents considered the visa requirement to enter Bophuthatswana an affront to their personal rights. Nor, at the time of writing, does there appear to be any decrease of economic contact between the two territories. There is clearly a marked contrast between the political form of this particular border landscape and the substance of events at a social and economic level.

NOTES

1 The process of population displacement caused by the rise of the powerful and expansionist Zulu state in south-east Africa. For an alternative view however, see Cobbing (1988).
2 See evidence given by Chief Gatsietsoe of the Bangoaketse to the Bloemhof Commission of 1871 to investigate competing land claims to the diamond diggings, pp. 188–9.
3 British Parliamentary Papers, C-4889, Report of the Commissioners to Determine Land Claims . . . in British Bechuanaland, Annexure E, p. 66.
4 See evidence given to the Bloemhof Commission of 1871 to investigate competing land claims to the diamond diggings, p. 189.
5 Botswana National Archives (BNA), Major Lowe, R.M. Taung to Colonial Secretary, Vryburg, 20 May 1893. Enclosure in Despatch No.142 G30/5/93.
6 BNA C. St Quinton to Colonial Secretary, 3 July 1894. Enclosure in Despatch No.110 G11/7/94.
7 Transvaal Archives (TA), NTS Vol. 1644, 534/272, Grensheining Moiloa Reserwe en Betshuanaland Protektoraat, 17 August 1956.
8 TA, LTG Box 58, 70/27. Native Commissioner Western Transvaal to Secretary for Native Affairs, 10 June 1904.
9 BNA, S194/3/2. Note for information of Executive Council re. Bechuanaland Protectorate/South African boundary, 19 January 1963, p. 1.
10 It should be noted that by mutual agreement Rhodesian Railways operated the railway line from Mafeking through the Protectorate to Rhodesia. This was a legacy from the colonial past when Mafeking had been the capital of Bechuanaland Protectorate.

REFERENCES

Anon. (1977) *The Republic of Bophuthatswana* (Johannesburg: Chris van Rensburg Publications).

Asiwaju, A. I. (1976) 'Migration as revolt: the examples of Ivory Coast and Upper Volta before 1945', *Journal of African History*, Vol. 17, pp. 577–94.

Asiwaju, A. I., (ed.) (1985) *Partitioned Africans: Ethnic Relations Across Africa's International Boundaries, 1884–1984* (London: Hurst).

Barbour, K. M. (1961) 'A geographical analysis of boundaries in tropical Africa', in K. M. Barbour and R. M. Prothero (eds.) *Essays on African Population* (London: Routledge and Kegan Paul).

Best, A. C. G. (1970) 'Gaberone: problems and prospects of a new capital', *Geographical Review*, Vol. 60, pp. 1–14.

Best, J. and Zinyama, L.M. (1985) 'The evolution of the national boundary of Zimbabwe', *Journal of Historical Geography*, Vol. 11, pp. 419–32.

Bophuthatswana Pioneer, newspaper, Vol. 10, No. 3, May/June 1988, Mmabatho, Bophuthatswana.

Brownlie, I. (1979) *African Boundaries: a Legal and Diplomatic Encyclopaedia* (London: Hurst).

Chirenje, J. M. (1976) *A History of Northern Botswana, 1850–1910* (New York: Fairleigh Dickinson).

Cloete, R. (1975) 'The conflict on the western border of the Transvaal, 1846–1877', Unpublished BA (Hons) dissertation, University of the Witwatersrand, Johannesburg.

Cobbing, J. (1988) 'The Mfecane as alibi: thoughts on Dithakong and Mbolompo', *Journal of African History*, Vol. 29, pp. 487–519.

Comaroff, J. L. (1982) 'Dialectical systems, history and anthropology: units of study and questions of theory', *Journal of Southern African Studies*, Vol. 8, pp. 143–72.

Funnell, D. C. (1988) 'Water resources and the political geography of development in Southern Africa: the case of Swaziland', *Geoforum*, Vol. 19, pp. 497–505.

Griffiths, I. Ll. (1986) 'The scramble for Africa: inherited political boundaries', *Geographical Journal*, Vol. 152, pp. 204–16.

Harries, P. (1986) 'The Politics of language construction and the roots of ethnicity : the Tsonga of south-east Africa', Unpublished paper presented to the Conference on Pre-colonial History, University of Cape Town.

Hattingh, P. S. (1988) 'Geographers and the political system or "there are those who make things happen"', *South African Geographical Journal*, Vol. 70, pp. 3–19.

Laurence, P. (1985) 'Out on the border: Botswana, Bophuthatswana and the ANC', *Indicator South Africa*, Vol. 3, pp. 10–12.

Legum, C. (1973) 'The problems of land-locked countries of Southern Africa', in Z. Cervenka (ed.) *Land-locked Countries of Africa* (Uppsala: Scandanavian Institute of African affairs), pp. 165–81.

Mafeking Mail, weekly newspaper, Mafeking, Bophuthatswana.

Manson, A. H. (1990) 'The Hurutshe in the Marico District of the Transvaal, 1848–1913', Unpublished D.Phil. thesis, University of Cape Town, Cape Town.

Marks S., and Atmore, A. (eds) (1980) *Economy and Society in Pre-Industrial South Africa* (London: Longman).

242   *James Drummond and Andrew H. Mason*

Minchin, Mr S., interview with this lifelong resident of Mafeking and Attorney in both Mafeking and Gaborone, Mafeking, 4 August 1988.

Merrett, C. (1984) 'The significance of the political boundary in the apartheid state, with particular reference to Transkei', *South African Geographical Journal*, Vol. 66, pp. 79–93.

Morton, R. F. (1985) 'Chiefs and ethnic unity in two colonial worlds: the Bakgatla Baga Kgafela of the Bechuanaland Protectorate and the Transvaal, 1872–1966', in A. I. Asiwaju (ed.) *Partitioned Africans: Ethnic Relations Across Africa's International Boundaries, 1884–1984* (London: Hurst) pp. 127–53.

Musambachime, M. C (1988) 'Protest Migrations in Mweru-Luapula 1900–40', *African Studies*, Vol. 47, pp. 19–34.

Ngcongco, L. (1979) 'Aspects of the history of the Bangwaketse up to 1910', Unpublished Ph.D. thesis, Dalhousie University.

Parsons, Q. N. (1973) 'Khama III, the Bamangwato and the British, with special reference to 1895–1923', Unpublished Ph.D thesis, University of Edinburgh.

Picard, L. A. (ed.) (1985) *The Evolution of Modern Botswana* (London: Rex Collings).

Prescott, J. R. V. (1979) 'Africa's boundary problems', *Optima*, Vol. 28, pp. 2–21.

Reitsma, H. J. A. (1980) 'Africa's land-locked countries: a study of dependency relations', *Tijdschrift voor Economische en Sociale Geografie*, Vol. 71, pp. 130–41.

Schapera, I. (1984) *The Tswana* (London: KPI).

Schreuder, D. M. (1980) *The Scramble for Southern Africa, 1877–95* (Cambridge: Cambridge University Press).

Shillington, K. (1985) *The Colonisation of the Southern Tswana* (Johannesburg: Ravan Press).

13 Where the Colorado flows into Mexico

John E. Chappell Jr

INTRODUCTION

Nowhere else on earth do the developed world and the Third World meet face to face across such a lengthy border, as along the one between the United States of America and Mexico. This chapter deals mainly with one small but relatively densely populated portion of that starkly differentiated borderland between affluence and relative poverty: the delta of the Colorado River, including parts of the states of California and Arizona to the north, and of Baja California Norte and Sonora to the south (Figure 13.1). It results from a lengthy if intermittent period of fieldwork, extending from 1964 through 1988, and most heavily concentrated in 1973 and 1988.

The chapter will especially aim to cast light on the situation in the Colorado Delta by relating it to other and wider areas. Such references to broader context provide important clues to interpreting the empirical situation in terms of environmental causation theory – an unjustly disdained realm of thought which I have studied separately for many years (Chappell, 1981) before realising how it might properly be applied to this border region. Yet with or without such theory, of course, the story of the Colorado Delta clearly involves the triumph of human labour and ingenuity in turning an utterly barren desert into productive farmland.

I shall also introduce other sorts of theory that are closer to the traditional concepts of political geography – some related to Kristof's classic analysis of frontiers, and some representing newer ideas about borderland cultural dynamics.

RESPONDING TO THE CHALLENGE OF NATURE

The basin of the Lower Colorado River, including its delta, presents a severe challenge to human settlement because of its aridity and

Figure 13.1   The Colorado River Delta

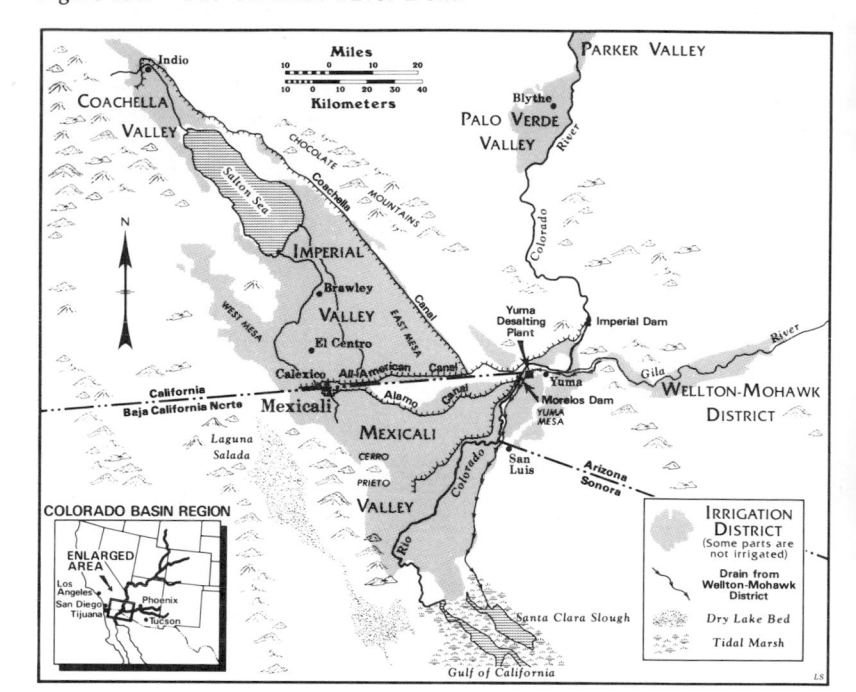

extreme heat. Where orographic enhancement does not occur,
precipitation is limited to about 8 or 10 centimetres per year; and at
the lower elevations, temperatures exceed 38°C (100°F) almost every
day for about four months, from May to September.

The major prehistoric response to this challenge began around 250
BC, when the Hohokam people started to build a system of irrigation
canals, much elaborated after 700 AD, about 300 kilometres east of
the Colorado along the Salt River (which flows into the Gila, a
tributary of the Colorado). The rapid collapse of this culture after
1400 AD may have resulted from increasing aridity, together with
resulting accelerated soil salinisation. (The name 'Phoenix' was
advisedly given to the modern city rising from the ruins left by the
Hohokam.) Along the Colorado River itself, Yuman Indians practised much simpler floodwater irrigation methods.

Settlers of European origin along the river were very few until the
completion of a transcontinental railroad through Yuma in 1885.
Significant irrigation in the delta region began only in 1901, when a
canal designed by Canadian engineer George Chaffey first brought

water westward along the Alamo Canal, leading into Imperial Valley by way of Mexico (Kahrl, 1979: 39). This route followed the natural slope of the delta, which had been deposited across what once was the northern end of the Gulf of California (the Sea of Cortez) and over against the coastal ranges of the Californias, leaving on its northern flank a below-sea-level valley. Although the Colorado had intermittently flowed into this valley, it was essentially dry in the late 1800s. Then in 1905 an engineering error (made after Chaffey had departed) allowed the entire river to break through into the canal system and flow toward the lowest part of the valley, the Salton Sink. By the time it was dammed off in 1907, the river had created here a sizeable new lake, the Salton Sea. Much used for boating and fishing, this lake is – despite now being more saline than the ocean – even more important to agriculture in a very unusual way.

After a few years' delay until the problem of salt build-up in soils – universal in desert irrigation projects – became serious, irrigators began in 1929 to construct a large drainage network, carrying their saline runoff downhill along natural slopes into the fortuitously convenient collector formed by the Salton Sea, which thereby has had its level kept nearly constant over the years. This network is composed partly of surface drains and streams, but more importantly, of nearly 50,000 kilometres of underground tubular drains (on an irrigated area of slightly under 200,000 hectares). Earlier made of clay pipe, these 'tiles' now consist primarily of flexible black plastic tubing, perforated with slits to accept the drainage water.

The tiling business continues to prosper, as not only do older drains need to be cleaned periodically, but new ones continue to be laid, both to increase the density of the existing network, and to provide new systems for the less than 10 per cent of the valley's irrigated area still remaining untiled (and thus usually experiencing declining yields). A complex trenching machine unrolls the plastic 'tile' into ditches about 2 metres deep, and then a smaller machine covers the tile with a layer of highly permeable gravel, before the original soil is packed back on top. The gravel, of course, facilitates the drainage process (illustrated in Chappell, 1974).

Accordingly, where nature provides comparatively permeable, lighter and sandier soils, underground tiles are seldom needed to achieve adequate drainage, as long as there is enough slope to carry the water away from the fields. This is the case in the near vicinity of most streams: on both sides of the Colorado near Yuma; in the smaller irrigation districts along the river north of Yuma (the largest of which are the Palo Verde and Parker Valleys); and in the

Coachella Valley north of the Salton Sea, which has soils derived mainly from coarse alluvium washed from nearby mountains. In contrast, Imperial Valley soils are made relatively impermeable by many clay barriers among its complex profiles.

The Mexican portion of the delta, or the Mexicali Valley (the part east of the river is at times called the San Luis Valley), has mainly sandy soils in the east; and where heavier soils prevail, in the north-central and especially north-western areas, virtually no attempt has been made to lay tiles. Instead, recent efforts to improve the efficiency of irrigation in the Mexican fields have consisted primarily of the concrete lining of canals, eliminating substantial water loss through seepage. This lining programme was vigorously pursued in the 1970s, and was nearly complete by 1976 – well before declining worldwide demand for petroleum hit Mexico in 1982 with a still-continuing economic crisis, severely reducing funding for public works.[1]

In contrast, more than one-third of Imperial Valley canals lose water into unlined beds and banks. So also does the huge All-American Canal, which since 1942 has delivered all irrigation water to the Imperial Valley along a new route entirely within the US, crossing a belt of thirsty sand dunes just east of the valley.

Advanced farming technology recently adopted in the delta, most extensively on the US side, includes levelling of land more precisely with the help of laser beams, and measuring soil moisture more sensitively by 'neutron probes'. Both procedures help make water use more efficient.[2]

THE DOWNSTREAM HANDICAP

Mexicans in the Colorado Delta have no choice but to pay careful attention to water conservation. The Colorado does not offer much water in the first place: although it drains a huge area ranging from the states of Wyoming and Colorado south-westward, its usual flow equals only about 8–10 per cent as much as that of the Columbia in the much better-watered Pacific North-west. Evaporation in the hot desert air helps to keep this flow low, and to further concentrate the materials dissolved and suspended in it. Add to this the fact that Mexico lies downstream from all US diversions from the river, and it becomes quite obvious that its share of Colorado River water will be saltier, siltier, and much smaller than that of the US.

In 1944, however, a treaty was signed guaranteeing Mexico a fixed quantity of river water: 1.5 million acre-feet (maf; one acre-foot

Plate 13.1   Morelos Dam, outlet and bypass drains.

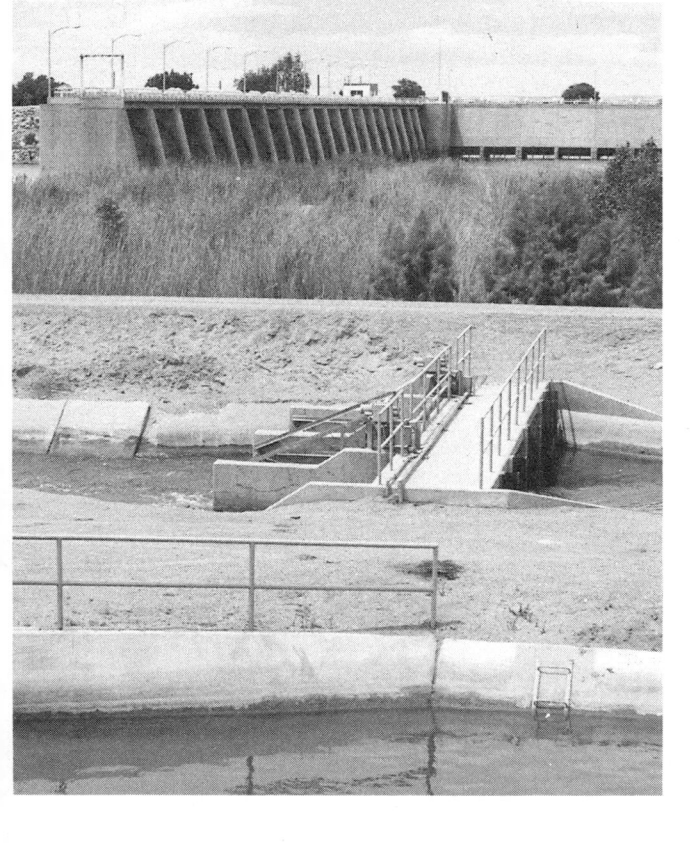

Note: Looking west from a point almost 10 kilometres west of Yuma. In the distance is Morelos Dam straddling the Colorado River and the international border. To its right are the gates through which water is diverted into canals that reach most of the irrigated land in the Mexicali Valley. In the foreground, on the US side, at the top is the outlet drain which in 1965 began to carry saline drainage from the Wellton-Mohawk District to an outlet just downstream from the Morelos Dam; at the bottom, is the new bypass drain which since 1977 has carried this drainage to Santa Clara Slough.

equals about 1.23 million litres) per year. This figure is only slightly more than half the amount used by the Imperial Valley, which is almost the same size as the Mexicali Valley and only about a tenth as populous. It was determined on the basis of river flow during approximately the first quarter of the twentieth century, as was the 15 maf per year divided among the seven US states in the Colorado basin, worked out in difficult, highly competitive negotiations between

1922 and 1963, and largely fixed by 1944 (see Hundley, 1986, and Brown, 1988). It was first assumed that the severe, wide-ranging droughts of the 1930s – the driest decade in at least 300 years, according to tree-ring studies – had been only unusual aberrations from a much wetter norm.

As time went on, evidence of various types, including more tree-ring studies, began to suggest that it was the very moist first quarter-century that had departed most widely from the norm, and that there would often be insufficient water in the river to fulfil the allocations made in 1944. Whereas during the twenty-five years from 1906 through 1930 the estimated natural flow of the Colorado River in mid-course had fallen below 14 maf per year only three times, it did so *twenty-seven* times in the next fifty years. In many years, the various diversions for both agricultural and municipal use left the riverbed nearly empty just below Morelos Dam, the principal Mexican canal intake, not far west of Yuma (Plate 13.1). At the least, Mexicans could take some encouragement from the fact that the 1944 agreement guaranteed to them their 1.5 maf per year, regardless of the total flow in the Colorado; shortfalls would have to be borne by the various US states.

Unfortunately, only the *quantity* and not the *quality*, of the river water had been guaranteed to Mexico. Quality became a serious issue after 1952, when the US opened a new irrigation district, the Wellton-Mohawk, straddling the Gila River east of Yuma. Substantial flow in the Gila had largely ceased after the completion in 1911 of Theodore Roosevelt Dam upstream on the Salt River, to provide irrigation water and flood control for the Phoenix area; thus the Wellton-Mohawk District had to draw its water from the Colorado. The soils and bedrock of the lower Gila Valley dissolve large amounts of sodium into downward-percolating irrigation water, which because of confining stratigraphy, not offering any convenient collecting basin like the Salton Sink, cannot escape easily in any direction. To prevent it from rising to root level and ruining crops, in 1961 this sodium-laden wastewater began to be pumped up and sent through a drain into the Colorado River, which it entered not far upstream from Morelos Dam (Hundley, 1986: 38).

Most crops grown in the delta, not to mention its human inhabitants, have difficulty tolerating salinities above the 1000 parts per million (ppm or mg/litre). The salinity of Mexican irrigation water had usually remained comfortably below that level; but starting in 1961 it soared far above it – at times, even above 3000 ppm. Much of the Mexican cropland – more than one-third, by most estimates –

began to deteriorate, in some cases even displaying a whitish layer of salt on the surface.

In response to this crisis, the Mexican water was slightly freshened by extra releases from US dams; but, in general, from the early 1960s to the late 1970s, whenever nature provided surplus water, nearly all of it was either sent by aqueduct to the booming coastal cities of southern California, or used to fill Lake Powell, the newly created reservoir behind Glen Canyon Dam near the Arizona-Utah border. This filling, extended in time by unusually porous sandstones along much of the shoreline, lasted from 1962 to 1980. (Glen Canyon dam was built to supplement the flood control, irrigation, hydropower, and recreational functions of the gigantic Hoover Dam, much further downstream near the southern end of the canyonlands.)

Angry rallies were held on the Mexican side, and some argued that hundreds of thousands of Mexicans were having their livelihood and health severely threatened for the benefit of only a few hundred farmers in the Wellton-Mohawk District. Farmers and officials in the US typically countered by accusing the Mexicans of hurting themselves by 'poor farming methods'. This minor but locally intense international crisis was somewhat alleviated in 1965, when a new extension of the main outlet drain from the Wellton-Mohawk District began to convey the saline drain water to a point on the river just below Morelos Dam (Plate 13.1).

But Mexican complaints continued, because the highly saline drainage still found its way from the bed of the Colorado into the groundwater, which provides more than one-third of all irrigation water in the Mexicali Valley, most of it pumped near the river. Further negotiations led to a comprehensive 1974 treaty, which provides that Mexican water should not be more than 145 ppm saltier than that at Imperial Dam, where water for all US irrigation districts downstream from Palo Verde Valley is now diverted. To this purpose, a new 'bypass drain' was built; completed in 1977, it now carries the Wellton-Mohawk effluent to Santa Clara Slough near the ocean (Plate 13.1).

The same treaty provided for the construction, just west of Yuma, of the world's largest reverse-osmosis desalinisation plant to be operated by the US Bureau of Reclamation. Because of the new bypass drain, this plant will not be needed to lower salinity in Mexican fields. But after completion in 1991, it will be able to create from the Wellton-Mohawk drainage an amount of fresh water equal to 5 – 6 per cent of the Mexican water entitlement. Even such a small amount would have been important during many of the predominantly dry years of the recent past.

Yet in the late 1970s and early 1980s, the flow of the Colorado increased substantially. The huge runoff of 1983, given added impact by a policy of high storage behind Hoover and Glen Canyon Dams, produced considerable flood damage in both the US and Mexico. In that year, Mexico received over six times its legal entitlement of water; floods destroyed homes, bridges and fields, and killed five people (Gottlieb, 1988: 225–6). Yet the excess water also provided benefits, by leaching salts from soils and replenishing groundwater. In 1988, my first thorough exploration of the Mexican portion of the delta in fifteen years revealed newly expanded acreage, more abundant crop growth, and generally healthier soils.

This run of very wet years increased already existing scepticism about the cost-effectiveness of the 'desalting' facility (Miller *et al*,. 1986: 38–9 and 60–62). One expert estimates that it will not be needed at all in as many as 40 per cent of future years. At the least, however, most of its new technology is already on display for the benefit of frequent visitors from many parts of the world.

Originally, heavy *silt* content in Colorado waters seriously troubled irrigators. But the trapping effect of the various dams, including Davis and Parker Dams between Hoover and Imperial, and also three large 'desilting basins' at the head of the All-American Canal, have greatly reduced this problem on both sides of the border.

MIGRATION FOR AMENITIES

The scarcity and marginal quality of Colorado River water depend not only on natural factors, but also on the number of people who use it. This rapidly increasing figure involves both population growth within the basin, and the utilisation of the water both directly and indirectly by many who live elsewhere.

The high rate of migration into the general area is determined by two very different processes on either side of the border. Domestic migration into the south-west United States since the late nineteenth century has resulted largely from what Edward Ullman (1954) termed a search for amenities, or pleasant living conditions – most notably for a warm, dry climate and for the easy-going life style that it makes possible, as opposed to the moist, variable and stimulating climate of the North-east valued by Huntington and others. Migration for such motives has been very rare in human history. It would be difficult to carry out without a surplus of resources somewhere in the nation, enabling part of its population to achieve partial freedom from the usual urgent economic concerns.

Since Ullman wrote, little change has occurred in the general trend of internal migration towards the South-west and, to a lesser degree, the South-east. California has passed New York as the most populous state in the union. San Diego and Phoenix have joined Los Angeles among the nation's ten most populous cities, drawing ever more heavily on the entitlements of California River water assigned to California (4.4 maf per year) and Arizona (2.8 maf per year).

At first Arizona could not use most of its share, since its population was heavily concentrated around Phoenix and Tucson, far to the east and uphill from the Colorado. Most of this surplus was regularly used by California, being sent out of the basin to Los Angeles and San Diego through an aqueduct built in 1938–40. However, after long legal battles and over a decade of construction (Reisner, 1987: 264–316), in 1985 the new Central Arizona Project began pumping Colorado River water uphill from behind Parker Dam all the way to Phoenix; by about 1991, this water will supply even more water-scarce Tucson. In anticipation of this diversion, in the 1960s the third and longest aqueduct to southern California was built, bringing water from the Feather River basin in the northern Sierra Nevada. (The first aqueduct, opened in 1913, still delivers considerable water from the Owens River Valley, east of the southern Sierra Nevada, where it aroused bitter opposition.)[3]

In Phoenix and Tucson, even extremely hot summer temperatures have not prevented rapid metropolitan growth. In the Colorado Delta – only very slightly hotter – growth is also rapid, but population remains relatively small, oriented mainly to providing services for the agricultural sector, military personnel, and cross-country travellers. In both areas, vast numbers of winter 'snowbirds' from colder states and from Canada move in, often in mobile homes, to enjoy several months of mild winter weather. Yuma, the largest population centre in the US portion of the delta with a permanent population of around 75,000 (including adjacent unincorporated areas), not only has doubled this total in about fifteen years, but also temporarily increases it by 50–60 per cent with each yearly influx of snowbirds. These winter visitors, largely made up of retirees, are still more numerous around Phoenix and Tucson, although comprising a smaller proportion there.

Combining Ullman's concept with traditional borderland terminology as delineated by Ladis Kristof (1959), the south-western United States can perhaps be described as a sort of 'amenities frontier'. Like other frontiers, the amenities frontier is not a political concept, so much as an expression of an outer-oriented drive towards a certain

way of life – in this case, one promising more comfortable and enjoyable living.

In continuation of the spirit of the earlier Mid-western frontier, the frontier of the Southwest was, even long after the gold rushes of the nineteenth century, also seen as a means to greater freedom and economic opportunity. Certainly my own grandfathers viewed it that way when they both moved to California in the early 1920s. But in terms of traditional skills and economic structure, before the contemporary era of high-tech and service industries, such goals proved unexpectedly elusive to many new migrants. Most kinds of manufacturing, many minerals, and some food resources remained concentrated in the Midwest or East, limiting potential employment and also requiring massive imports from those areas.

Above all, the amenity represented by warm and sunny skies means limited rainfall – hence the aforementioned need to import water for urban uses from other drainage basins several hundreds of kilometres away. But such uses require less than 20 per cent of the total water use in the South-west. Over 80 per cent of this water goes to irrigated agriculture; and since much of the resulting fruit and vegetable produce is shipped far to the north and east, it can truly be said that the entire nation, as well as Canada, shares in the use and depletion of Colorado River water.

In general, the 'Anglo' (non-Spanish-speaking Caucasian) frontier does not extend beyond the former northern half of Mexico taken by the US in 1848 after the Mexican War. With few exceptions, any impulse to relocate permanently to the south has been discouraged by the language barrier, by the wide belt of desert just across the border, and by a general perception of poverty and peril in that direction. Many US citizens do, however, travel to Mexico for vacations, or for brief trips into what are widely perceived as sordidly enticing border cities. (Such an image may fit Tijuana, situated near cool ocean breezes and heavily visited from populous and nearby San Diego, and it may fit other cities to the east; but not Mexicali and San Luis, which because of searing summer heat and the small populations just across the border, are not much involved in entertaining visitors.)

In another sense, however, the frontier *has* pushed into Mexico, not through human movement but in the form of commercialised agriculture and certain types of industry. This type of influence, which represents a newer type of imperialism of an economic nature, will be discussed further in the following sections.

A FRONTIER OF ECONOMIC OPPORTUNITY

The northern frontier of Mexico, also a frontier for all of Latin America, has a much different character. Shaped by the traditional search for economic advantage, it extends well north of the rather porous international border, into and beyond what long ago was part of Mexico. Those who speak Spanish at home constitute about 8 per cent of the population of the United States, and nearly two-thirds of these are of Mexican origin. In the South-west, of course, an even higher proportion is Mexican. Spanish speakers constitute 13 per cent of the population of California, 12 per cent in Arizona, 31 per cent in New Mexico (the area first settled by Mexicans), and 19 per cent in Texas. Close to the border, the percentage is still higher: for example, about 36 per cent in Yuma.

Both Mexicali and San Luis, which have doubled to their present sizes of about 750,000 and 100,000 in approximately the past fifteen years, seem to represent a human tide pushing up against the tall chain-link fences marking the international border at their northern city limits. As if to stem this tide somewhat, as well as to watch for the illegal drugs often sent northwards from Latin America, wary US immigration and customs officials at the official border crossings often slow traffic to a crawl, creating huge lines, as they ask questions and occasionally pull vehicles to the side. Driving across in the other direction, however, is seldom met with more than a perfunctory wave of the hand from a uniformed Mexican.

Most characteristically, Mexicans moving to these border locations, often from far to the south, are looking for work as agricultural labourers. Such work is most abundant in the huge Central Valley of California, but can also be found in many other locales as far north as the states of Washington and North Dakota. Many find it as illegal entrants, but many other workers, probably a majority, carry the official 'green card' which identifies them as resident aliens, allowed to cross at will back and forth between the US and Mexico. These migrant field workers typically will stay in the US for 6–8 months during the warmer seasons, sending money back to their families throughout Mexico, and return home when work is slack (Johnson, 1984: 217–225). 'For certain groups', writes Belasso, 'this migration is a part of culture; it is a way of life' (1981: 155).

The motivation behind this pattern of movement is obvious: wages of all kinds – in agriculture, industry, and services – have for many years been about 6–10 times higher in the US, than in Mexico. Accordingly, in the US you can earn in one hour about the same as,

or even more than, you can earn in a full day in Mexico: roughly four or five US dollars (Sanderson, 1986: 79). But the basic cost of living is also appreciably lower in Mexico, especially for the many who live simply, eating mainly beans and grain products. Appliance and utility expenses also tend to be minimal; clothes are often washed by hand on scrub boards, and food may be prepared over an open fire in the yard. (In a small city east of Mexicali, I once saw a meal being cooked over a fire for fifteen people, all of whom lived in what in the US would be considered a very small single-family home.) Not only such lower expenses, but also the more congenial social atmosphere for Spanish speakers, lacking the frequent discrimination and suspicion they experience in the US, result in over 90 per cent of Mexicans who work on farms in the US portion of the delta choosing to maintain a permanent home just inside Mexico. In the midst of the peak harvest season (here, the winter), roughly 10,000 of them leave Mexicali before dawn each work day, boarding trucks or buses for fields in the nearby valleys.

An alternative to field labour for Mexicans in the northern borderlands became necessary when in 1964 the US ended its '*bracero*' programme, an often-abused system utilising temporary field labourers who lacked resident alien status. Thus in 1965 in Mexico the '*maquiladora*' or 'twin plant' system was initiated (Johnson, 1985: 211-213). This allowed foreign-owned firms to ship parts manufactured in plants located elsewhere to assembly plants (maquiladors) just inside Mexico. There, Mexican workers assemble products as diverse as metal chairs, cassette tapes and sophisticated medical apparatus, on which duty is paid only for the value added during assembly, when they are shipped abroad. Well over 300,000 Mexicans, primarily younger women, now work in maquiladoras in Mexicali, San Luis, and several other border cities (and recently, also in a few places further south). Their combined earnings and benefits, although often double the usual amount for Mexico, still fall far short of what comparable work brings in the US, and tend to lose value quickly during the rapid inflation since 1982. However, many consider the maquiladoras to be beneficial to Mexico; they have risen to second rank, behind tourism, as an earner of foreign exchange.

Nevertheless, vast numbers of Mexicans still surge northward; and those without legal documents the US tries to stop. Besides the high fences bordering cities (which I have seen small Mexican children climb and cross just for sport), heavy cables are strung out to discourage automobile crossings, and many hundreds of border patrol employees work to find and return 'illegals'. Apprehended

illegals, including repeaters and those caught far from the border, increased from 110,000 yearly in 1965 to over a million regularly since 1982; and the proportion from Mexico went up from about a half to over 80 per cent in the same period. These efforts have still not prevented millions from living in the US illegally; widely varying estimates of their number average about 6–8 million, slightly more than half of them Mexican (Simcox, 1988: 24-29).

Late in 1986, the US initiated an amnesty programme, offering for a limited time green cards and immunity from punishment to illegals who had been in the US since before 1982. (No such mercy has been shown to the many thousands of more recent refugees from military and death-squad terror in US-backed El Salvador and Guatemala, whom the Reagan administration callously classified as 'economic' migrants, and usually sent back if caught.) When this programme ended in May 1988, slightly more than two million had applied for amnesty. However, the old pattern of constant illegal crossing still continues, despite the risks of being sent back, and of being maltreated by the 'coyotes' who often charge hundreds of dollars for sneaking people across the border, despite new regulations penalising US employers for hiring illegal aliens.

Illegal field workers naturally compete with legalised Mexican-Americans, who often view them as threats to the higher wage scales and other benefits achieved through the US farm labour movement. The charismatic, soft-spoken Cesar Chavez, leader of this movement since he formed his United Farm Workers (UFW) in 1962, was born in Somerton, a small Arizona town south of Yuma. Chavez's organising efforts, which extend over much of the lower Colorado basin and into several other areas where migrant labour is concentrated, have been vigorously opposed by growers and others. This conflict occasionally turns violent; in 1973 I saw the charred remains of a torched UFW office in Calexico, and shortly after I had interviewed UFW grape strikers in the Coachella Valley, I read about two of their number being killed up north in the Central Valley. Counter-violence by the UFW also occurs at times, despite the Ghandi-like teachings of Chavez. However, the level of violence seems to have declined in recent years, perhaps because the perceived threat represented by the UFW has also waned. Things finally seemed to be looking up for the UFW when in 1977 the competing, grower-backed Teamsters Union withdrew from organising field workers; but since then, unsympathetic state governments in both California and Arizona have increasingly sided with growers to thwart UFW efforts.

Many observers believe that the heavy influx of Mexicans is harmful to US society, lowering the standard of living. However, I tend to agree with arguments like those of ecologist Paul Ehrlich who argues that Mexicans in the US do primarily the difficult, humble labour that longer-established Anglos try to avoid; and that they probably add more to the economy than they take from it (Ehrlich *et al.*, 1979).

BORDERLAND CONTRASTS AND CULTURAL AVERAGING

Where can we look for explanations of the very different customs and conditions found in these highly contrasting frontiers? Possible realms of causation include the genetic composition of the population, its culture, and its natural environment. As is widely acknowledged in the current era, relative poverty cannot reasonably be blamed on racial or other genetic differences. To one degree or another, any culture involves adaptations to the natural environment; and this is most obvious in harsh environments such as deserts. Of course, human will and ingenuity are also important variables; but at any level, desert culture is constrained within narrow limits as to which choices it can make that offer any possible advantage. The question remains, of course, why two such very different cultures exist side by side; and to answer this we need to look beyond the local environment.

Let us first consider how cultural determinists often presume to refute environmental causation theory by means of the 'same environment/different culture' argument. This approach takes three different forms. First, the different cultures may be separated in time, as in the French possibilist claim that since cultures change through the course of history while their natural environments remain the same, environment cannot determine culture. However, the claim of environmental stability has been decisively refuted by much recent work proving the reality and importance of historical climatic change (Lamb, 1982), which may well induce cultural change. Furthermore, it does not eliminate the possibility of environmental causes, to show how culture depends on human ingenuity or its own internal dynamics; multicausal explanations are to be expected for any complex phenomenon.

Second, the cultures may be contemporary but far apart in *space*, in essentially similar environments. For instance, the lower Colorado Basin has been invoked in support of the claim that culture is not shaped by environment, by considering it to offer conditions virtually

the same as those in the Lower Nile Valley, which for millennia had a much more 'advanced', or at least more complex, culture than any achieved along the Colorado. Yet even if the two environments were exactly the same – which they are not – relative sparsity of population, earlier stage of societal evolution and greater distance from most centres of creativity would have kept the Yumans of the lower Colorado from equalling Egyptian culture; ecological influences in a particular environment may be real and yet be outweighed by other factors.

In the third form of the argument, the natural environments *are* virtually the same, because they are *adjacent*, and yet contain two very different cultures, typically separated by a political boundary. Same environment, different culture. But this in no way proves culture to be independent of natural environment. Human beings do not react to environmental influences like grass sprouting up after a rain; to deny that they do is to battle with a straw person. Culture manifests active, evolving responses to natural constraints and suggestions, as perceived with varying and hopefully increasing degrees of acuteness and wisdom. Cultural landscapes, along borders as elsewhere, are changing, open systems; they take time to develop, and respond to influences from over a broad area.

For example, grapes and soft fruits are grown just north of the US border near Oliver in interior British Columbia, but are virtually absent from the predominantly apple-growing Okanogan Valley of Washington, immediately to the south. Yet such situations do not mean, as some observers have claimed, that human decision alone shapes cultural patterns. In this example, it means that cultural features have evolved in an attempt to respond intelligently and profitably to climatic conditions established by nature, not only locally but over broad regions and even entire nations: nowhere else in Canada west of the Great Lakes is there such a suitably warm and lengthy growing season for grapes, cherries, peaches, and the like, whereas warmer and more nearly ideal conditions are common in the US.

Similarly, it takes only common sense and simple logic to realise that we should examine the entire areas of the United States and Mexico, not just the zone around their common border, to explain the contrasts found along that border. Most crucially, the US has a far richer agricultural base, providing wealth that allows other sectors of society to flourish as well. If we combine figures for population, land area, and percentage of land-producing crops, we find that the US has about *four times as much* harvested land per person as does

Plate 13.2   Irrigation canal, fields and adobe hut not far southeast of Mexicali

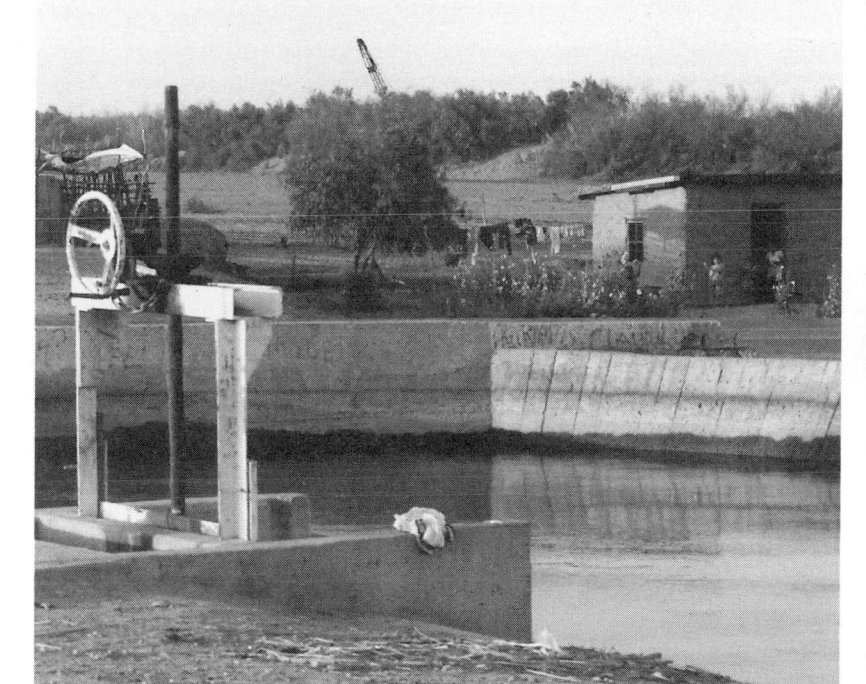

Note: The sloping land in the background is unusual for the Mexicali Valley.

Mexico. The US endowment excels in quality as well as quantity; no other large area on earth approaches the Corn Belt in terms of suitability of soils and climate for non-irrigated grain farming. Combined with such other factors as more abundant capital, this advantage allows US farmland to yield about *twice as much* per hectare as Mexican farmland. Multiplying, we obtain a ratio of *eight times as much* agricultural production per person in the US, as in Mexico. It seems no mere coincidence that this is about the same ratio as that applying to wages in the two countries.[4]

The comparison looks even worse for Mexico in light of the rapid increase in recent decades of commercial export farming, partly

financed from the US and concentrated in the north-western oases – most of which are south of the Mexicali Valley, mainly in Sonora and Sinaloa. Mexico thereby has become a major supplier of winter and spring produce (tomatoes, melons, green onions, and so on) to many parts of the US and Canada. However, land devoted to this purpose reduces the amount available for subsistence farming of crops like dry beans and maize (Plate 13.2). This situation, combined with rapidly increasing population – now about 88 million which has quadrupled in less than fifty years – led during the 1970s to the disturbing result of making Mexico a *net importer* of food (Barkin and Suarez, 1985; Sanderson, 1986).

As Kristof points out, political boundaries define the limits of forces which tend to *integrate* a nation, 'not only administratively and economically but also by means of a state idea or "crede"' (1959: 271). In other words, within national borders *cultural averaging* tends to occur; the standard of living as well as language and other cultural features are to some extent – rarely completely – spatially averaged out and homogenised. And so the higher standard of living on the US side of the delta is not due primarily to possible minor advantages in its natural environment, or to its upstream location, or to having fewer residents to support; and surely not because of superior genes or to an objectively superior culture. The basic reason is that *other* parts of the US are more productive than *other* parts of Mexico, and the resulting average levels of affluence have been spread widely within each political unit.

Among the most obvious indications of such averaging out or homogenisation of national wealth is the fact that the largest and third largest employers in and near Yuma are an army weapons testing range and a Marine Corps Air Station, clearly not maintained by local resources alone. (The second largest is a regional medical centre.) There is no such substantial military presence in the Mexicali Valley.

CLIMATIC ADAPTATIONS AND CULTURAL CONVERGENCE

North of the border, the homogenised culture of the US is manifested in some ways which are notably unadaptive to the hot desert climate. Both private homes and public buildings are usually surrounded by lush green lawns, reflecting cultural habits derived from the moister climates of the north-eastern states and of north-western Europe. And the usual '9-to-5' workday, overlapping the hottest afternoon hours, is common in most US offices and businesses.

But as time goes on, we can identify an increasing degree of modification or abandonment of such unsuitable habits, in favour of practices already common across the border in Mexico that are better attuned to heat and aridity – a kind of *borderland cultural convergence*. Presumably this process will continue, unless forces aimed at an unreasonable degree of nationwide conformity discourage it. One well-known but far from universal adaptation is to employ thick adobe walls for temperature insulation (Plate 13.2). Increasingly found, although still unusual, is landscaping utilising not water-demanding grass but the desert vegetation and rocks typical of Mexico. Perhaps because they enjoy more air-conditioning, office workers in the US still rarely copy the prevailing Mexican habit of taking a 'siesta' break of two or more hours during the afternoon heat, and then later working on into the early evening. But outdoor workers such as telephone linemen have adjusted, frequently starting at 5 or 6 a.m. and finishing by early afternoon, just as farm labourers do. On the other hand, with a cultural tradition derived largely from semi-arid Spain, northern Mexico can learn little from the US in the way of better climatic adaptations. What cultural convergence of this type occurs on the Mexican side, such as the occasional lawn around a Mexicali home, amounts to defying the climate, perhaps to display individual affluence.

It is in culture apart from climatic considerations, such as in the matter of standard of living, that the Mexican side of the delta is coming more to resemble the United States. In Mexicali, although rarely in the small cities amidst the farmland, street paving was being much increased before 1982. Throughout the Mexican north-west, as Angel Bassols Batalla (1972) points out, greater affluence than is found in most of the rest of Mexico shows up in such simple ways as greater consumption of meat and more frequent use of shoes. Such abundance obviously depends largely on proximity to US job opportunities and markets.

Agriculture has no choice but to adjust quickly to climatic conditions. The delta area enjoys a particular climatic advantage in terms of its relative warmth in winter and early spring, when, along with southern Florida and other parts of north-west Mexico, it becomes a prime source of vegetables – most notably lettuce, carrots, cauliflower, broccoli, onions, tomatoes and asparagus – for all of Anglo-America.

Asparagus exemplifies here a type of adjustment to climate now widespread in US agriculture, but of questionable value: moving crops southward in order to obtain earlier harvests and higher

early-season prices, sacrificing the higher *quality* that tends to prevail near the northern limit of a crop's range (Huntington, 1940: 233–240). Asparagus was once more highly concentrated in California's Sacramento-San Joaquin Delta, where soft, peaty soils and generally cooler temperatures yield a superior crop. Conversely, California and Arizona – both in the Colorado Delta area and well beyond it – produce the best quality of citrus fruit, because they offer the coldest conditions, with only mild winter frosts, in which citrus can grow.

Although the summer heat is harmful to most crops, it is ideal for the ripening stages of melons, sugar beets and table grapes, all major products of the delta area. Dates, produced mainly in the Coachella Valley and near Yuma, will not grow in any other region of the US. The heat and aridity also suit cotton, which once totally dominated the Mexicali Valley and is still common throughout the delta.

In many parts of the delta, and especially in the US, far more land goes to a hay crop, alfalfa (lucerne), than to any other crop, because this is now a major cattle-feeding area, illustrating the tendency for the cattle-feeding industry to shift to the South-west along with population (Chappell, 1976). In the Imperial Valley, cattle regularly earn more money than any other product. By using awnings for shade, cattle death loss can be kept below that in cold Midwestern winters. The Mexicali Valley also has several feedlots. On both sides of the border, hump-backed East Indian cattle are becoming common. In contrast, a dairy industry developed in the Imperial Valley by Swiss immigrants gradually declined because cows inevitably give less milk as the weather turns hot.

LAND TENURE, POLITICS AND CULTURAL REVERSAL

The size and nature of the farms that produce these products may be more significant than any other cultural factor in defining the essentials of life in the Colorado Delta. On the US side, farms of many hundreds or even thousands of hectares, often managed by corporations, dominate the landscape. Yet a few farmers growing high-value crops make a good living here on as little as 20 hectares. The Reclamation Act of 1902 aimed to promote in the irrigated lands of the Far West the same kind of modestly-scaled, efficient family farms typical of the Midwest, by limiting the amount of land that could receive water from federal (nationally financed) irrigation projects to 65 hectares per person. Many legal and safely illegal ways were found to evade the purpose of this law, but none were more decisive than the special ruling, made just before Franklin Roosevelt

became President in 1933, to exempt the entire Imperial Valley from any of its provisions.

A new general law in 1982 raised the limit of land on which one farmer could receive federal water by *six times*, from 65 to 390 hectares. It also eliminated the rarely-enforced provision that he must live on his land. As before, all such water is heavily subsidised (often to over 90 per cent of its value), by such means as exemptions from interest, and the use of revenue from hydroelectric power sales (Getches and Meyers, 1986: 54). Farming on federally irrigated lands has clearly become an occupation for a fortunate few, offering the chance of great wealth.[5]

Below the border, the situation differs. As few in the US realise, contemporary Mexico was shaped by a revolution (1910–17). Its egalitarian objectives have often (but less so recently) been promoted as standard policy by the Institutional Revolutionary Party (PRI), which has ruled with broad popular support for over 70 years. 'Mexico showed that revolution can produce stability', as Martin Needler puts it (1987: 75; as many tend to forget, so also did the United States). This has been done by meeting the needs of several groups at once. In rural areas, many large estates have been broken up into small parcels for landless peasants, while at the same time, for the sake of high productivity, many of the more efficient medium and large farms were not split up, but instead given support (Needler, 1971: 57–61).

The most decisive steps in land redistribution occurred from 1934 to 1940 under the strongly nationalist and populist President Lázaro Cárdenas (Burns, 1982: 176–79; Ruiz, 1980). This reform heavily impacted the Mexicali Valley, originally almost fully controlled by a single US-owned firm. Most land in the valley was divided into plots of 20 hectares or less, grouped into *ejidos*, communities in which the farmer has only use rights but not ownership, or *colonias*, where he does own the land. One may complain that too many of these parcels are now being leased out to US commerical farmers (Yates, 1981: 175; Weisman, 1986: 162), or that the pace of redistribution has greatly slowed since the 1960s, leaving too many landless 'peons', but one cannot deny that the long-term trend has been towards smaller and more numerous holdings rather than larger and fewer ones.

If 'democracy' implies benefits for large numbers of people rather than for a privileged elite, then it seems very much as if, in these differing patterns and trends in land tenure, we find more democracy in the southern portion of the Colorado Delta, than in the northern portion. Of course, democracy involves other factors as well. The

very low and often disdained status of the agricultural labourer north of the border can be contrasted with the more widespread sympathy for poverty and humble status that prevails south of it; in other words, there may be a greater degree of social democracy, as well as of economic equality, on the Mexican side of the border.

Furthermore, independent political sentiments are nowhere in Mexico stronger than in the north, long used to receiving minimal attention from the distant national capital and fending for itself. The conservative, business-oriented National Action Party (PAN) has been strong over much of northern Mexico; and in July 1989, in Baja California Norte, it won the first gubernatorial election in sixty years not won by the PRI. (Also, evidently in response to the economic crisis, a left-wing party led by Cuauhtemoc Cárdenas, the son of Lázaro, won over 30 per cent of the vote in the 1988 presidential election – the strongest challenge to the PRI since the revolution.[6]) Yet, in contrast, in the southerly states of the US, one tends to find more political and social conformism than in states further north. Often, as in the Imperial Valley, this is linked to economic inequality and reactionary, imperialist politics.[7]

This does not fit the usual pattern, wherein democracies flourish best in more affluent lands and in more poleward climates. Nor does it fit with the respective overall political situations; Mexico does, after all, still have single-party rule. There appears to be in operation a process both in the south-western US and north-west Mexico, not easy to define or explain, which might be called *borderland cultural reversal*. On each side of the border, the tendency towards cultural convergence may have reached so far, as if straining to emulate the averaged-out national culture beyond it, as to become closer to that average, than to the oppositely directed segment of that culture just across the border. (The trend in farming areas of the south-western US seems to illustrate the empirical tendency for societies in hot climates to display considerable social and political inequality; but most such cases appear to involve more serious limitations in per capita resources than prevail here.)

This is not to say that we may expect democratic pluralism some day to be more characteristic of Mexico, than of the United States. But possibly the contrast between levels of affluence could be much reduced. This might depend on a drastic decline in the fortunes of the US, resulting from environmental degradation such as massive erosion of topsoil (already well advanced); from energy shortages putting at risk the continuation of energy-deficit mechanised farming (which contrasts shockingly with the net energy gain realised by a

Mexican peasant using a hoe); or perhaps from declines in yields resulting from climatic change. But it must be borne in mind that erosion and other environmental damage is becoming serious in Mexico also.

ACKNOWLEDGEMENTS

Of the many who have generously shared with me their knowledge of the Colorado Delta, I wish to express special thanks to Hector Gracia Galván, John Colvin, Ben Yellen, John Newton, Bill Blackledge, Wayne Flanagan, Jay Murley, Edmundo Agramont Mendoza, John Armstrong, John Steppling, Eugenio Guerrero Guemez, Robert Moody, Bob Hardebeck, Santiago Guzman Monforte, Reynaldo Ayala and the late Steve Zdravecky.

Valuable feedback on related papers as well as useful comparative data were received at the Adelaide pre-IGU meeting on 'Resource Management in the Drylands' in 1988.

I am also truly grateful to political scientist Martin Needler of the University of New Mexico, for his knowledgeable and incisive writings on Mexico as well as for constructive comments on an early draft of this chapter.

NOTES

1 Technological progess is strikingly evident in the first geothermal power plant to be built in the delta, at Cerro Prieto, near a hill of the same name south-east of Mexicali. In April 1973 I attended the ceremonies formally opening this plant, and noticed a degree of surprise and puzzlement among some US visitors in the audience who had evidently accepted a myth claiming that Mexicans have a lot of trouble learning advanced technology. Of course, their real problem is finding enough capital for such tasks; in the early 1970s it was available. The notorious San Andreas fault system runs right through the Colorado Delta and down the middle of the Gulf of California, which it created as it split Baja California away from the mainland within the past several million years. Naturally escaping geothermal steam is generated in some fissures along the fault system, most abundantly near Cerro Prieto. This steam has been augmented by drilling numerous wells, to produce about half of the power used in all of Baja California. Since 1973, a few smaller geothermal plants have been built in the Imperial Valley.

2 Even greater efficiency is possible, as I learned in 1988 in Renmark, along the Murray River in South Australia. Here in 1887, the same George Chaffey who later helped to irrigate the Imperial Valley initiated (with the help of his brother William) Australia's first substantial irrigation project. The irrigated area around Renmark, about only one-fortieth the size of the Imperial Valley, receives its water by pipe, eliminating not only seepage but also evaporation in transit. The higher cost involved is borne by growing only high-value crops such as grapes, citrus and vegetables, avoiding the less profitable hay and small grain plantings that occupy major

portions of the cropland in the Colorado Delta. Chaffey had become well known after he developed an irrigation colony around Ontario (named after his home in Canada), about 60 kilometres east of Los Angeles; it was superior not only in technology but also in organisation, being a mutual company in which landowners controlled their own water (Kahrl, 1979: 24).

3 While the Phoenix area can utilise water from reservoirs upstream on the Salt River and its tributaries, Tucson has no comparable advantage and must depend mainly on groundwater, which has been drastically depleted, requiring very low per capita water use. Such problems led Arizona to promulgate in 1980 an unusually enlightened, conservation-oriented groundwater law.

The Metropolitan Water District (which includes both Los Angeles and San Diego), aiming to replace part of the Colorado river excess soon to be claimed by Arizona, agreed in late 1988 to pay for various conservation measures (including canal lining) in the Imperial Valley, in return for water equal to the amount thereby conserved; but the deal is being held up in the courts. A similar exchange may finance the concrete lining of the All-American Canal. Some critics would prefer that any surplus from the Imperial Irrigation District be saved for eventual application on the West or East Mesas, within the district but so far undeveloped; new land in those areas might then be available to aspiring family farmers. (On water supplies for coastal Southern California, see Vaux, 1988.)

4 Comparison of agricultural yields between the US and Mexico based mainly on the figures for 'total cereals' (maize, wheat, sorghum, and so on) given in the United Nations *FAO Yearbook* for 1987. The average yield for the six years listed is 2163 kilograms per hectare for Mexico and 4444 kg/ha for the United States. Yields of 'total pulses' (beans, peas and so on) run about two-and-a-half times higher in the US than in Mexico.

The US also has a natural advantage in terms of the stimulating effect of its generally cooler and more variable climate, but I lack space here to adequately develop this complex and controversial theme. Energy-inducing climates also involve negative influences, such as unusually high incidence of circulatory and respiratory diseases. (A climatic consideration possibly more directly relevant to the lower Colorado basin is the correlation between emotionally volatile behaviour and hot – especially hot and dry – weather, supported by numerous studies, including those on foehn winds in Europe.)

5 The 1982 law does, however, specify that only one person per household should receive the new larger allotment of water. Water users had previously gotten away with interpreting the 1902 law to mean that every member of the family was entitled to one 65-hectare allotment. Absentee owners using hired managers have long controlled large amounts of federally irrigated land, thereby contradicting the original aim of creating a class of family farmers in the arid west. This new law was passed early in the Reagan presidency; throughout the history of federal water law there has been a strong positive correlation between Republican administrations and decisions on behalf of big farmers, while attempts to enforce the 1902 law occurred almost entirely during Democratic presidencies.

A pamphlet issued by the Salt River Project in Phoenix states that it is a

'long-standing reclamation principle' to use revenues from electricity sales to pay for federal water projects. In some irrigation projects, such sales subsidise by as much as 90 per cent or more the cost of the water.

6 Support for Cardenas is strongest in the poorer central and southern parts of Mexico. Many have charged fraud in the 1988 election, believing that Cardenas actually received more votes than Carlos Salinas de Gortari, the PRI winner (officially, Salinas received 50.4 per cent, Cardenas 31 per cent and the PAN candidate 17 per cent). On 20 August 1989, the *Los Angeles Times* published results of a poll taken throughout Mexico in which only 24 per cent said that they felt sure that Salinas really won, while 35 per cent were sure he did not. Yet 79 per cent gave Salinas a favourable job rating. Most astoundingly, 47 per cent replied that they thought that armed revolution was likely within five years (presidential terms last for six years). A given revolution may indeed lead to stability, but so also may a serious economic crisis undermine that stability.

7 The only US Presidents to be born and raised in states bordering Mexico have been Lyndon Johnson from Texas and Richard Nixon from California, the two major prosecutors of the misconceived and horribly destructive Vietnam War. Ronald Reagan, who has lived for many years in California and served as its Governor before becoming President, believed strongly in the presumed virtue of that war, as did Barry Goldwater of Arizona, who was defeated by Johnson in the 1964 election, and George Bush, who moved to Texas and considers it his adopted state. All of these except Johnson have been primarily social-Darwinist in their domestic policies. San Diego, the largest US city close to the Mexican border, is noted for a political climate distinctly more right wing than that of most of California; it produced Pete Wilson, a Republican Senator who voted for Reagan's position on nearly all issues.

The 'political flavour' of the Imperial Valley is typified by a sign which I saw in an El Centro barber shop window in May 1988 – 'Ollie North haircut, $7.00'. I stepped inside long enough to ask the barber if this meant that I paid *him* the $7.00, or he paid me!

Life has been difficult, however, for the few humanitarians who have tried to stand up for the economically disadvantaged while living right in the Imperial Valley. One of these was Steve Zdravecky, an idealistic but very disillusioned state employee who died prematurely of a heart attack. Another is Dr Ben Yellen, an elderly physician in Brawley, who for many years published newsletters and took legal actions aimed at getting the 1902 Reclamation Act enforced, and occasionally received favourable publicity in the national media (Chappell, 1978). In 1984, his medical license was finally taken away, and with it most of the financial support for his activism.

The high proportion of imperialist and social-Darwinist political attitudes near the Mexican border may be significantly linked to fear and distrust of the Mexican underclass, most of whom speak very limited or no English, have tawny rather than 'white' skins, and often live in what is perceived as a disagreeable degree of poverty. Not entirely dissimilar attitudes help to differentiate classes and accentuate inequalities in several Latin American states south of Mexico, some of which harbour

severe prejudice against darker-skinned segments of the population.
Perhaps it is them, more closely than Mexico with its continuing if
weakened commitment to egalitarianism and its majority of 'mestizo'
(mixed blood) inhabitants, which the US South-west is, in effect, coming
to emulate most closely through a process of borderland cultural
reversal.

REFERENCES

Barkin, D. and Suarez, B. (1985) *El Fin de la Autosuficiencia Alimentaria*
(Mexico D. F.: Centro de Ecodesarrollo (Ediciones Oceano)).
Bassols Batalla, Angel (1972) *El Noroeste de Mexico* (Mexico D. F.:
Universidad Nacional Autónoma de Mexico, Instituto de Investigaciones
Económicas).
Belasso, G. (1981) 'Undocumented Mexican workers in the U.S.: a Mexican
perspective', in R. H. McBride (ed.) *Mexico and the United States*
(Englewood Cliffs: Prentice-Hall).
Brown, B. (1988) 'Climate variability and the Colorado River compact:
Implications for responding to climatic change', in M. H. Glantz (ed.)
Societal Responses to Regional Climatic Change (Boulder: Westview), pp.
279–305.
Burns, E. B. (1982) *Latin America* (Englewood Cliffs: Prentice-Hall).
Chappell, John E., Jr. (1974) 'Salinity problems in the Colorado Delta',
Geog. Mag., Vol. 46, No. 10, pp. 568–74. (See also author's letter in *Geog.
Mag.*, Vol. 47, No. 4 (Jan. 1975), p. 276).
—— (1976) Paper on cattle feeding in the United States, published in
Proceedings of the I. G. C., Moscow.
—— (1978) 'California Survey: Water, Land and Energy', *Transition*, (Dept
of Geography, University of Cincinnati), Vol. 8 (3), pp. 10–18.
—— (1981) 'Environmental Causation,' in M. Harvey and B. Holly (eds)
Themes in Geographic Thought (London: Croom Helm), pp. 163–86.
Ehrlich, Paul, Bilderback, Loy and Ehrlich, Anne H. (1979) *The Golden
Door: International Migration, Mexico, and the United States*. (New York:
Ballantine Books).
Getches, D. H. and Meyers, C. J. (1986) 'The river of controversy: persistent
issues', in G. D. Weatherford and F. L. Brown (eds) *New Courses for
the Colorado River: Major Issues for the Next Century* (Albuquerque:
University of New Mexico Press), pp. 51–86.
Gottlieb, R. (1988) *A Life of its Own: The Politics and Power of Water* (San
Diego: Harcourt Brace Jovanovich).
Hundley, N. Jr (1986) 'The West against itself: the Colorado River – an
institutional history', in Weatherford and Brown, *op. cit.*, pp. 9–49.
Huntington, E. (1940) *Principles of Economic Geography* (New York:
Wiley).
Johnson, K. F. (1984) *Mexican Democracy: A Critical View* (New York:
Praeger).
Kahrl, W. L. (ed.) (1979) *The California Water Atlas* (Sacramento:
California Dept. of Water Resources).
Kristof, Ladis K. D. (1959) 'The nature of frontiers and boundaries', *Annals*,
Assocn. Amer. Geogs., Vol. 49, pp. 269–82.

Lamb, H. H. (1982) *Climate, History and the Modern World* (London: Methuen).

Miller, T. O., Weatherford, G. D. and Thorson, J. E. (1986) *The Salty Colorado* (Washington, DC: The Conservation Foundation).

Needler, M. C. (1971) *Politics and Society in Mexico* (Albuquerque: University of New Mexico).

—— (1987) *The Problem of Democracy in Latin America* (Lexington: Heath).

Reisner, M. (1987) *Cadillac Desert; the American West and its Disappearing Water* (New York: Penguin).

Ruiz, J. U. (1980) *La Crisi Agricola en la reforma agraria de Mexico* (Mexico D. F., Editorial Domes).

Sanderson, Steven (1986) *The Transformation of Mexican Agriculture* (Princeton: Princeton Univ. Press).

Simcox, David E. (1988) *Immigration in the 1980s: Reappraisal and Reform* (Boulder: Westview Press).

Taylor, P. S. (1979) *Essays on Land, Water, and the Law in California* (New York: Arno Press).

Ullman, Edward L (1954) 'Amenities as a Factor in Regional Growth', *Geogr. Rev.*, Vol. 44, pp. 119–32.

Vaux, H. V., Jr (1988) 'Growth and water in the south coastal basin of California', in M. T. El-Ahsry and D. C. Gibbons (eds) *Water and Arid Lands of the Western United States* (Cambridge: Cambridge University Press), pp. 233–79.

Weisman, A. (1986) *La Frontera: the United States Border with Mexico* (San Diego: Harcourt Brace Jovanovich).

Yates, P. L. (1981) *Mexico's Agricultural Dilemma* (Tucson: University of Arizona Press).

14 Peacekeeping missions and landscapes

Stanley D. Brunn

INTRODUCTION

An examination of international boundaries on the current world political map reveals both stability and dynamism. Stable boundaries appear where the states have signed and honoured treaties recognising their sovereignty and agreed on the delimitation and demarcation of common borders. Some of these boundaries, for example, those separating some southern and western European states have been intact for centuries and there is little likelihood of change. Most South and Central American international boundaries have been stable for much of this century. Elsewhere the interstate boundaries represent places of recent conflict. Examples were in Western and Eastern Europe during the First World War and the Second World War and during the 1980s along boundaries separating Nicaragua and Honduras, Thailand and Vietnam, Vietnam and Kampuchea, Chad and Libya, and Namibia and Angola (van der Wusten, 1985). There are also contemporary boundary situations where the potential for protracted aggressive military actions might surface were it not for third parties currently separating military forces of member states. Examples include Lebanon–Israel, the Turkish and Greek populations on Cyprus, Iran–Iraq, and India–Pakistan in the state of Jammu and Kashmir. It is along these boundaries that United Nations peacekeeping forces are stationed. These forces are comprised of infantry, commanders and units from the international community of states who are provided with equipment and supplies from many UN members. The primary purposes of these forces are to prevent conflict and contact between the warring states, to monitor truces, and to promote a political climate where a peaceful and enduring resolution to the conflict may be possible.

This study of peacekeeping missions and landscapes is considered

within the rich tradition of political geography research on international boundaries and borders.

Political geographers have a lengthy record of books, articles and monographs that address the origins of international boundaries, their delimitation, their dynamic character, conflicts and the significance of boundaries and boundary changes on regional, continental, and world and regional political maps (Boggs, 1940; Prescott, 1965, 1987; Minghi, 1963, 1982; Burghardt, 1973; *Regio Basiliensis*, 1982; Douglas, 1985). Two areas of recent research into political boundaries have been in the nature of security landscapes (Soffer and Minghi, 1986) and on the salient features of peace and military landscapes (Brunn, 1987). A neglected topic in both traditional and contemporary research on boundaries and boundary conflict and resolution is an investigation into the roles, missions and operations of regional and international peacekeeping forces. There exist on the present world political map a number of areas where these forces play a major role both in efforts to resolve conflicts and in preventing heightened and sustained conflicts.

There are additional areas of international border tension where these forces and missions might be stationed during the next decade. A political and military world where there is greater effort on the part of adversaries to resolve conflicts without engaging in sustained armed conflict will likely see the rise of regional and international peacekeeping forces (Diehl, 1988).

The purpose of this chapter is to examine and identify the nature of United Nations peacekeeping forces and to describe the distinctive features of peacekeeping landscapes. Following a general discussion of peacekeeping forces and missions, the focus turns to UN missions and operations, the contributions and contributors to these missions by UN member states, and distinctive geographic elements of these landscapes; also I introduce the concept of peacekeeping cartography, as opposed to military cartography. The chapter concludes with reflections on the increased role these forces are likely to play during the next few decades.

PEACEKEEPING FORCES AND MISSIONS

Peacekeeping forces are associated with a number of international bodies; most are regional in nature. Examples include forces associated with the Organisation of American States, the Organisation for African Unity (OAU), Arab League and Association of Southeast Asian States (Glassner, 1989). These forces are assembled when conflict occurs between member states and there is a need for a third

party or force to separate the warring factions and to promote a resolution of the conflict. Member states of regional organisations provide the leadership, troops, material and logistical support. The importance of these regional organisations is significant in resolving or attempting to resolve small-scale border conflicts or international conflict.

In the Organisation of American States, the RIO Pact provides a role for peacekeeping forces in settling disputes among member states. Within the past four decades, there have been sixteen forces sent to member states; ten of these have involved country clashes. Examples include the Costa Rica–Nicaragua conflict in 1948 and the Honduras–El Salvador Soccer War in 1969. The OAU has provisions for peacekeeping, but the organisation has primarily been involved in settling disputes, not in sending forces. The organisation did intervene in the Nigeria–Chad dispute in 1979. The League of Arab States sent a peacekeeping mission to Kuwait in 1961 to resolve a potential conflict (Glassner, 1989). In mid-1989, the same group was striving for a resolution to the Lebanese civil war and especially with efforts to remove Syrian troops. While these regional organisations and peacekeeping missions are an important part of the peacekeeping missions and landscapes and the reconciliation of international border disputes, they are not the primary focus of this chapter.

United Nations peacekeeping forces represent the major international units associated with preserving and maintaining peace or an absence of conflict along highly volatile international borders on the world scale. There have been sixteen UN peacekeeping missions in operation during the past forty years (Table 14.1). These include current and long-standing forces in Lebanon (UNEFL), Cyprus (UNIFICYP), and India–Pakistan (UNMOGIP) to short-term missions in Congo (OUNC), Yemen (UNYOM), and the Dominican Republic (DOMREP). The three most recent missions have been to areas of protracted strife, Afghanistan (UNGOMAP), the Persian Gulf (UNIIMOG), and Namibia (UNTAG).

Rikhye *et al.* (1974: xii) has described the United Nations peacekeeping forces as 'the thin blue line'. The blue refers to the light blue berets, helmets or caps which UN forces wear with the military uniforms of their own countries. Rikhye states this label 'aptly describes the size and capacity of the United Nations peacekeeping forces and observer missions that have exercised truce supervision or been interposed between hostile forces in interstate and domestic disputes since 1946 – a thin thread, more often than not, has by its presence provided a defusing of tensions and a de-escalation of violent conflict.'

Table 14.1 Peacekeeping forces and missions

Mission	Name	Location	Function
UNTSO	Truce Supervisor Organisation	Various locations in the Middle East	Assist in supervising truces in Palestine (1948), cease-fire Suez Canal and Golan Heights (1967), and in Beirut and Sinai
UNEF I	Emergency Force I (Gaza)	Gaza, Sinai peninsula	Secure and supervise cessation of hostilities, including France, Israel and UK from Egyptian territory; later a buffer between Egyptian and Israeli forces
UNEF II	Emergency Force II	Suez Canal and later Sinai	Supervise cease-fire agreements between Egypt and Israel and redeployment of their forces, man and control buffer zone
UNDOF	Disengagement Observer Force	Syrian Golan Heights	Supervise cease-fire between Israel and Syria, redeployment of their forces and establish a buffer zone
UNIFIL	Interim Force in Lebanon	Southern Lebanon	Confirm withdrawal of Israeli forces from southern Lebanon and ensure effective governmental authority
UNMOGIP	Military Observer Force in India and Pakistan	State of Jammu and Kashmir	Supervise cease-fire between India and Pakistan
UIPOM	India–Pakistan Obsevation Mission	Along border from Kashmir to Arabian Sea	Supervise cease-fire along border and withdrawals of armed personnel
UNOGIL	Observation Group in Lebanon	Syria–Lebanon border	Ensure no illegal infiltration of personnel, arms or material

Table 14.1 Continued

Mission	Name	Location	Function
UNYOM	Yemen Observation Mission	Yemen	Observe and certify disengagement agreement Saudia Arabia and UAR
OUNC	UN Operation in the Congo	Congo (now Zaire)	Ensure withdrawal of Belgian forces, assist government in maintaining law and order
DOMREP	Mission of Rep. of Sec-Gen. in Dominican Republic	Dominican Republic	Report on breaches of cease-fire between two *de facto* authorities
UNFICYP	Force in Cyprus	Cyprus	Prevent recurrence of fighthing and contribute to restoration of law and order, mantain buffer zone
UNIMOG	Iran–Iraq Military Observer Group	Iran–Iraq borders	Prevent recurrence of fighting
UNGOMAP	Good Offices Mission in Afghanistan and Pakistan	Afghanistan	Assist settlement of refugees
UNTAG	Transition Assistance Group	Namibia	Supervise removal of outside forces; assist government in restoring law and order and ensuring effective authority
UN Security Force in West New Guinea			Maintain peace and security established by agreement between Indonesia and the Netherlands.

Source: United Nations, 1985: pp. 329–50.

274   *Stanley D. Brunn*

UN MISSIONS AND OPERATIONS

UN peacekeeping forces have been operating since the 1940s in areas
of international conflict. Fabian (1971: 17–18) describes their early
history and role:

> As early as the 1940s, peacekeeping maps were dotted at Greece,
> on the borders of the new state of Israel, in Indonesia, and in
> Kashmir. The next decade added Gaza and Sinai in Egypt, and
> then Lebanon. The 1960s added the Congo, West Irian (West New
> Guinea), Yemen, Cyprus, the India–Pakistan boundaries, and
> again the Middle East.
>
> Cease-fires have been monitored, borders patrolled, troop
> disengagements supervised, truces guaranteed, hostile armies
> insulated at safe distances, internal security maintained, and essen-
> tial governmental functions preserved with the assistance of peace-
> keeping presences. Circumstances and political or operational
> requirements have dictated great diversity in the detailed organisa-
> tion of these missions and in the specific mixture of techniques they
> have used.
>
> Some of the smaller, so-called observer missions have performed
> largely symbolic, sometimes only face-saving services; or they have
> engaged in what, relatively speaking, are functionally simple
> assignments such as investigations, reporting, verification, and
> other information-handling chores. Occasionally, local mediation
> and other third-party assistance is given.

Some 500,000 persons (mostly military, but also some civilians)
from fifty-eight countries have served as UN peacekeepers since 1948
(*UN Chronicle*, 1988). The current yearly cost of these operations is
about US$230 million or more than one-fourth of the UN annual
budget. There are currently slightly more than 10,000 individuals
from thirty-five countries in seven peacekeeping operations. As
mentioned above, three have become operational since mid-1988,
one to monitor the Geneva accords with respect to a settlement of the
Afghanistan conflict, the second to halt the hostilities associated with
the Iran–Iraq war, and the third to assist Namibia in becoming a
stable and independent state. During the tenure of all UN operations, 733 peacekeepers have died.

The sixteen peacekeeping missions have been in six different
regions: Middle East (8), southern Asia (3), Africa (2), South-east
Asia (1), Europe (1), and Latin America (1). The largest number of
individual states affected by the stationing of these forces along parts

of their international borders are Israel, Lebanon, Syria and Egypt. While these UN forces have been primarily associated with resolving interstate conflicts, exceptions exist in the case of the Dominican Republic and the Congo where UN forces were called in to stabilise internal political party dissension (in the case of the Dominican Republic) or reduce conflict among strong national rivalries (in the Congo). In most cases the UN forces were also to prevent further cross-border violations by bordering states, for example, along Israel's boundaries with Egypt, Lebanon and Syria and along Iran–Iraq borders in the Persian Gulf. The situation in Cyprus exists because the Greek and Turkish populations were unable to co-exist as a single island state following independence in 1960; the peace-keeping forces arrived in 1964 to maintain stability. The UN military observer group in the Jammu–Kashmir state polices a cease-fire line.

The cost of peacekeeping operations varies depending on the length of the mission and the size of the force. Of eight missions completed, the most expensive missions were to Lebanon ($666 million for UNEF I and UNEF II) and the Congo ($400 million) (Table 14.2). It is these same missions that have commanded the largest military support and had the largest number of casualties. The least costly missions were those to Yemen (UNYOM), the India–Pakistan Observation Mission (UNIPOM), and the Dominican Republic.

Table 14.2 Previous peacekeeping operations: Costs, deaths and strengths

	Year	Cost (US$)	Deaths	Maximum Strength
UNEF I	1956–7	220 million	90	6,000
UNOGIL	1956	3.6 million	–	591
ONUC	1960–4	400 million	234	19,828
West Irian	1962–3	*	–	1,500
UNYOM	1963–4	1.8 million	–	189
DOMREP	1965–6	0.275 million	–	3
UNIPOM	1965–6	1.7 million	–	96
UNEF II	1973–9	446 million	52	6,973

* Cost financed in equal amounts by Indonesia and the Netherlands. Specific figures not provided.
Source: UN Chronicle, 1988: 19.

Of the current UN missions, the most costly to date have been those in Lebanon (UNIFIL) (Table 14.3). The UNIFIL mission exceeds the combined costs of the next three largest missions to Iran–Iraq (UNIIMOG), the Syrian Golan Heights (UNDOF), and Cyprus

(UNFICYP). The costs of observation missions to Afghanistan, India–Pakistan, and various Middle East locations (UNTSO) are much less.

The April 1989 independence of Namibia did not occur without previous decades of internal regional conflicts among strong nationalities and border clashes with troops from South Africa and Angola (Cuban troops). Obtaining and maintaining political and military stability in Namibia will not occur without UN assistance. The newest UN peacekeeping effort, UNTAG, is designed to assist this state in its efforts to ensure stability and preclude cross-border conflict. It is estimated the cost of this mission will be $416 million for a 4650-person force. That force will include three infantry battalions of about 850 soldiers each, 350 mobile military observers, 1700 logistic troops and some 100 headquarters staff. In addition, a 2500-strong reserve group in additional home countries can be airlifted if required. Another 7500 could be mobilised if necessary (*UN Chronicle*, 1989).

Table 14.3 Current peacekeeping missions: Costs and participants

	Year Created	Cost (US$)	Participants
UNIIMOG	1988	37.6 million (first 3 months)	350 unarmed observers
UNGOMAP	1988	3.7 million	50 observers
UNIFIL	1978	139.9 million	5,800 troops
UNDOF	1974	34.7 million	1,300 troops and observers
UNFICYP	1964	25.2 million	2,150 troops, 35 police
UNMOGIP	1949	not available	38 observers
UNTSO	1948	not available	300 troops

Source: UN Chronicle, 1988: 9.

CONTRIBUTIONS

UN members are responsible for supporting UN peacekeeping missions, yet not all do. The amount of support depends on the state and the conflict in question. Fabian (1971: 25) provided the following insights into the countries of origin of peacekeeping forces:

> Few states are natural, automatic choices as peacekeepers, and each circumstance tends to add a few of its own criteria for acceptability. Yet time after time, the bargaining has narrowed the range of candidates predictably. Regularly during its peacekeeping career, the UN has drawn on the same small reservoir of volunteers.

By almost every yardstick the prominent national suppliers of military personnel have always been Canada and the small states of northern Europe. The rank ordering of participating frequencies in all twelve peacekeeping missions is Sweden (ten), Canada (nine), Denmark (eight), seven apiece for Norway, Ireland, and Finland, and six apiece for the Netherlands, New Zealand, Italy and India. That so much responsibility for peacekeeping has been absorbed by this tiny fraction of the UN membership says something about how strong the commitment to the peacekeeping idea is in most of these countries. But perhaps it says even more about how stable the ingredients of impartiality are and how constant a reputation for political aloofness can be. As in the Orwellian barnyard, some states are more impartial than others. In spite of the subjective, contingent judgments required each time candidates are selected, northern Europeans and Canadians have repeatedly exhibited enough of the trademarks of impartiality-absence of significant political or economic interests in Third World areas of conflict, lack of prejudicial colonial or imperial histories, identification in and outside the UN with active, independent internationalism. Along with this nonpartisanship, these states regularly give their firm political support to UN peacekeeping and possess the requisite military expertise to qualify as participants.

A tabular account of the states providing contributions and the general nature of their contributions to all except the most recent peacekeeping missions is provided in a UN publication *The Blue Helmets* (1985). While similar data are not available post-1985 and for current operations in the Persian Gulf or Namibia, the above source is useful in illustrating the extent of membership participation in UN peacekeeping missions and operations.

The contributions are varied and run the gamut from infantry, staff personnel, and military observers to medical aid, air units, to food and munitions, and the salaries (Table 14.4). A wide range of goods and support systems are necessary in order to fulfil the specific objectives of the mission or operation. For example, in UNDOF (in the Syrian Golan Heights), Austria, Finland, Iran and Peru provided infantry, logistics (signals, supply and transport units) from Canada, and engineers and some transport service from Poland. Commanders in the mission have come from Peru, Austria, Finland, and Sweden. In Cyprus (UNFICYP) civilian police came from Australia, Austria, New Zealand and Sweden; field hospital and medical centres from Austria, Canada and the United Kingdom; infantry from Austria,

Canada, Finland, Ireland, Denmark, Sweden and the UK; and logistics and air units from the UK. Commanders since 1964 have come from India, the UK, Finland, Ireland and Austria.

In addition to contributing directly to UN missions, members may contribute various other forms of assistance without cost to the UN. In the Cyprus mission, airlift was provided by Italy, Sweden, the UK, and United States; salaries and pay of service and professional personnel were contributed by Austria (for medical and police contingents), Denmark, Finland, Ireland, New Zealand and Sweden. In the lengthy Congo operation, Canada, Switzerland, the USSR, the UK and the US provided the airlift of goods, equipment, and other supplies. The United States paid for the airlift of Ghanian, Guinean, Moroccan, Swedish and Tunisian troops and the sealift of Malaysian troops.

The *Blue Helmets* provides the official contributions and other contributions of member states for all but the three most recent UN operations listed in Table 14.1. This source does not provide the specific dollar amount by each state. Some of these data and documents are listed in Wainhouse (1973) and Higgins (1969) where detailed accounts are provided of individual missions. Fifty-two members contributed to one or more of these peacekeeping missions/ operations, listed in Table 14.1. The largest number of states contributing were from Europe (13), Africa and Asia (11 each) and Latin America (10). Both the United States and Canada have participated as have Australia, New Zealand, Fiji, the USSR, Poland and Yugoslavia.

Table 14.4 Examples of military contributions

Infantry
Medical units
Signal, engineer, air transport maintenance
Transport and signal units
Airlift of food, supplies, troops
Air units
Logistics: signals, air and service units
Cash contributions for airlifting troops
Arms and ammunition for contingents
Aircraft
Military observers
Staff personnel
Parachute companies
Salaries of personnel

Source: United Nations, 1985.

The most frequent states contributing were in Europe (Table 14.5). This observation is not surprising considering the historic role a number of states have played in conflict reduction and resolution in former colonial and territorial holdings in Africa and Asia. The northern countries and Canada, as mentioned above, have been in the forefront of international peacekeeping missions. Canada has contributed to every peacekeeping force assembled by the UN, a distinction no other country can make (Anon., 1988).

Table 14.5 Most frequent contributors to UN missions

Canada	11	Nepal	4
Sweden	9	Sri Lanka	4
Denmark	8	United States	4
Finland	8	Argentina	3
Italy	8	Belgium	3
Norway	8	Brazil	3
Ireland	7	Iran	3
Netherlands	6	Nigeria	3
Australia	5	Pakistan	3
Austria	5	Peru	3
New Zealand	5	Yugoslavia	3
Burma	4	Ecuador	2
Chile	4	Ethiopia	2
Ghana	4	Fiji	2
India	4	France	2
Indonesia	4		

Source: United Nations, 1985: 329–50.

There has been a significant Third World element in these missions as well. Seven states have provided contributions to four missions and another six to three. Four Latin American states have contributed to more than three missions; the same is true for seven Asian states. African contributions have been the fewest of any region. Among the UN members that have contributed to only one mission are not only some African states, most of whom are experiencing financial difficulties themselves, but the USSR, Mexico, Venezuela, Uruguay, the UK and Portugal. West Germany, Japan and China have provided no contributions. The members providing other contributions is somewhat similar to those listed in Table 14.5. Few states (only twenty) provided assistance. The most frequent contributors were Canada and the United States (6 missions each), Australia (4), and the UK, Italy and Switzerland (3 each).

The commanders and chiefs of staff represent another contribution

to peacekeeping operations. Many states have provided more than one and most missions rotate their commanders and chiefs of staff on a somewhat regular basis. The twenty-five countries that have provided the sixty leaders reflect the international political community: Europe (9), Latin America (6), Asia (4), Africa (3), North America (2), and Australia (1). In terms of individual member states, the largest number (31) came from six states; Sweden (7), India (6), Ireland and Canada (5 each), Finland and Norway (4 each). Brazil and Ghana have provided three each. Three examples illustrate the variation in the leadership of these UN missions. The officers-in-charge of OUNC (Congo) came from Sweden, Ghana, Haiti and Mexico and the commanders came from Sweden, Ireland, Ethiopia, Norway and Nigeria. Special representatives came from the United States, India and Sudan. In Cyprus (the UNFICYP missions) the commanders came from India, the UK, Finland, India, Ireland and Austria. Special representatives came from Ecuador, Brazil, Italy, Mexico, Peru, El Salvador, Argentina and Chile. Most special representatives and commanders came from countries outside the region. Mediators in Cyprus, who were needed during the first eighteen months of the operation, came from Finland and Ecuador. UNTSO, which operates in various Middle East locations, has had chiefs of staff from Sweden (six individuals), the United States (three individuals), Finland, Ireland and Ghana (two), and one each from Denmark, Canada, Norway and Australia. Contributors to military observers have come from Argentina, Australia, Austria, Belgium, Burma, Canada, Chile, Denmark, Finland, France, Ireland, Italy, Netherlands, New Zealand, Norway, Sweden, the USSR, and the United States. Four members, Belgium, France, Sweden, and the United States have contributed observers since 1948. Canada, Denmark and New Zealand have since 1954 and Argentina, Austria, Chile and Finland since 1967.

Two patterns of support are apparent in peacekeeping operations. One is regional support for the peacekeeping mission. African states contributed the most to OUNC (Congo) and European states to UNFICYP (Cyprus). The African states contributed to the Congo operation and many only to this mission. Examples of support included infantry, two medical units, staff personnel, and police companies from Ghana; infantry, movement control, and staff personnel from Liberia; infantry from Guinea, Sierra Leone, Sudan, and Tunisia; and infantry and parachute battalions from Morocco and Egypt. Rikhye *et al.* (1974: 85) noted that:

Of the 93,000 men from 35 states who served in ONUC during the four years of the operation, the majority (82.4%) came from 19 Afro-Asian states, with most of the technical units and specialists being provided by the Western countries. Yugoslavia contributed a small contingent during the first few months, while the Congo itself made available an ANC battalion, which served in the force for a period of 18 months.

Six European members have provided various contributions to the Cyprus mission. Civilian police have come from Austria, Denmark, Sweden and the United Kingdom; field hospital personnel and medical centres from Austria and the UK; military police from Finland, and infantry from Denmark, Finland, Sweden and the UK. In the other contributions category (without cost to the UN) assistance came from Austria, Denmark, Finland, Sweden and Ireland to pay for professional personnel and salaries to medical and police contingents. Airlifts were paid for by Italy, Sweden and the UK. Wainhouse (1973: 3–5) states the following about the Cyprus mission:

> while we can look at UNFICYUP as the model of an 'ideal peacekeeping operation' from the national support viewpoint, UNFICYP can serve as a yardstick against which to measure and compare support aspects of more typical peacekeeping operations. Military forces, even UN peacekeeping forces, are prodigious consumers of material, supplies, and services. Problems arise when they deploy in the field and must provide for their own needs. In Cyprus, where we see the peacekeeping force operating on the 'supermarket parking lot'; the logistical tasks boil down to providing for special needs and developing the highest order of efficiency and economy in what is essentially an 'off-the-shelf' support system.

The second pattern is international support for the peacekeeping missions. Three examples are in the Lebanon (UNEF I and UNEF II), in the Jammu–Kashmir state and in Yemen. In UNEF I infantry units were provided by Brazil, Colombia, Denmark, Finland, India, Indonesia, Norway, Sweden and Yugoslavia; medical units from Canada and Norway, transport and signal units from India, and signal, engineer and air transport maintenance from Canada. Other contributions (the airlift of troops and supplies) were provided by Canada, Italy, Switzerland and the United States. Similar international participation was associated with UNEF II, which was along

the Suez Canal in 1973 and later in the Sinai peninsula. Infantry came from Austria, Finland, Ghana, Indonesia, Ireland, Nepal, Panama, Peru, Senegal, and Sweden. Logistics (signal, air and service units) were provided by Canada, medical and transport units from Poland, and air unit (helicopters and personnel from Australia). Other contributions (without cost to the UN) included Australia providing the airflift of Nepalese troops from Calcutta to Cairo, West Germany providing the airlift of Ghanian and Senegalese troops, the USSR providing the airlift of Austrian and Finnish troops and heavy equipment from Finland, and Japan providing a cash contribution for the airlift of Nepalese troops from Kathmandu–Calcutta and the transport of its UNEF equipment. Norway, Sweden and Poland also airlifted troops. The United Kingdom airlifted Austrian, Finnish, Irish and Swedish troops and vehicles. The United States assistance included the airlift of troops from Ireland, Finland, Peru, Austria, Indonesia and Panama. UNIPOM (the India–Pakistan mission) has been provided with contributions from Australia, Belgium, Canada, Chile, Denmark, Finland, Ireland, Italy, the Netherlands, New Zealand, Norway and Sweden in its initial stage (from UNTSO and UNMOGIP) and later from Brazil, Burma, Canada, Ethiopia, Ireland, Nepal, the Netherlands, Nigeria, Sri Lanka and Venezuela. Most of the contributions to the Yemen missions (UNYOM) were military observers; these were provided by Australia, Denmark, Ghana, India, Italy, the Netherlands, Norway, Sweden and Yugoslavia. Canada provided an air unit and Yugoslavia also a reconnaissance unit.

LANDSCAPES AND PEACEKEEPING CARTOGRAPHY

Peacekeeping landscapes are similar in many appearances to military landscapes of parties at war or conflict (Brunn, 1987). There are specific locations for military barracks, for infantry and staff personnel, maintenance and repair shops, field hospitals and medical units, warehouses for munitions, designated areas for tanks, jeeps and smaller vehicles, trucks, boats, and aircraft, training area for manoeuvres, communications and telecommunications facilities, and observation posts. Major differences will be in the marking of vehicles (jeeps, cars, buses, and so on) with UN lettering, the blue and white UN flag flying at bases, on vehicles, and on observation posts, and the international composition of the forces and commanders, and integrated headquarters camp commands, and an atmosphere where diplomacy and negotiating skills prevail. Not only

the infantry, but also the medical, police, transportation and communication units will be comprised of citizens from Africa, Asia, European, and Latin American states.

A major responsibility of the UN peacekeeping forces in preventing conflict is to patrol roads, beaches, passes and other areas where infiltration might occur and to staff permanent observation posts in strategic locations. Enforcing the truce means that international borders and/or zones have to be constantly and carefully monitored. The forces are not only to ensure that the buffer zones or areas are maintained, but to prevent those neutral zones and international borders from being encroached on by aircraft, naval vessels, armed vehicles, or individual commandos or guerrilla units. When and if incursions occur, it is the responsibility of the peacekeeping force to halt them and prevent the intensity of conflict from spreading.

Life along highly tense border areas continues in spite of the presence of international troops, armed vehicles and checkpoints. Farmers work in fields in the buffer zone in Cyprus and farmers and herders in southern Lebanon till their fields and tend to their sheep. Residents in villages in northern Israel carry on their day's business, even though there may be surprise attacks from southern Lebanon or earlier from Syria; the same applies for residents living in southern Lebanon who are in villages strafed and bombed by Israeli aircraft. Pelcovitz (1984: 23) wrote the following about UNIFIL's role in southern Lebanon:

the military observers from UNTSO assigned to UNIFIL as the Observer Group Lebanon (OGL) have stressed that their primary mission is to reassure the local population and to help preserve Lebanese sovereignty and integrity for the future. Some sixty-five unarmed military observers (UNMOs) were assigned to OGL under UNIFILs operational control. The UNMOs five man observation posts (OPs) along the armistice line, report and document any 'violations' across the line, and patrol the roads in southern Lebanon. Their main purpose has been to show the international presence and the UN flag, to keep in contact with village leaders and notables, and to help pacify local disputes. Just as the OPs report and document only Israeli violations-overflights, vehicle traffic, and 'permanent violations', that is, Israeli military facilities on the Lebanese side of the fence – so the protective function of the road patrols is intended mainly to show concern about the IDF presence and actions.

Pelcovitz also wrote the following (p. 27) about the problems of

protecting northern Israeli settlements from terrorist attacks, for example, Kiryat Shemona and Misgav Am:

> No government could afford to admit that the northern settlements could not be fully protected, nor could it accept without paying a high political price the fact of the hemorrhaging of the population from these settlements which followed terrorist attacks and shelling. Since UNIFIL could not prevent the shelling nor completely staunch infiltration through its area, it came to be viewed as more hindrance than help in the struggle against the PLO.

During the withdrawal of Israeli forces from the Sinai there were occasional problems dealing with treaty violations. Pelcovitz (1984: 75, 76) noted:

> One (problem) has to do with infiltration through the demilitarized Zone C and across the border, involving hostile acts (mine-laying) and the smuggling of arms and infiltration of terrorists. ... Most unauthorized movement through Zone C and across the border consists of Bedouins, who have ignored frontiers since time immemorial and who sometimes smuggle wristwatches, tape-recorders, and similar goods. The MFO's position has been that routine border control is a matter between Egypt and Israel. What remains uncertain is the amount of such traffic, how much of it is habitual Bedouin visiting and 'commerce' across the border, and how much has hostile intent. If border-crossers are carrying hand-grenades or rifles with intent to take hostile action, the question of the MFO's responsibility arises.

UN peacekeeping landscapes have distinctive geographical features in that the national forces operate in certain areas and are responsible for specific roles or areas. The landscapes can be depicted in what is termed peacekeeping cartography, that is, the depiction of various elements of operations and missions. Several examples illustrate the international character of these landscapes and are depicted on UN maps. The UNDOF (Syrian Golan Heights) as of October 1985 was staffed by units from Austria, Poland, Finland and Canada (Figure 14.1). Observation posts exist along the boundaries of the buffer zone from the northern Golan Heights to the Jordan border. UNIFIL in southern Lebanon had areas designed with forces from Norway, Finland, France, Fiji, Ghana, Nepal and Ireland (Figure 14.2). In most of these districts, there was both a battalion headquarters and a Lebanese unit. Five UTSO observation posts existed near the Israel – Lebanon boundary. The deployment of

Figure 14.1 UN disengagement observer force (UNDOT) in Syrian Golan
Heights, October 1985

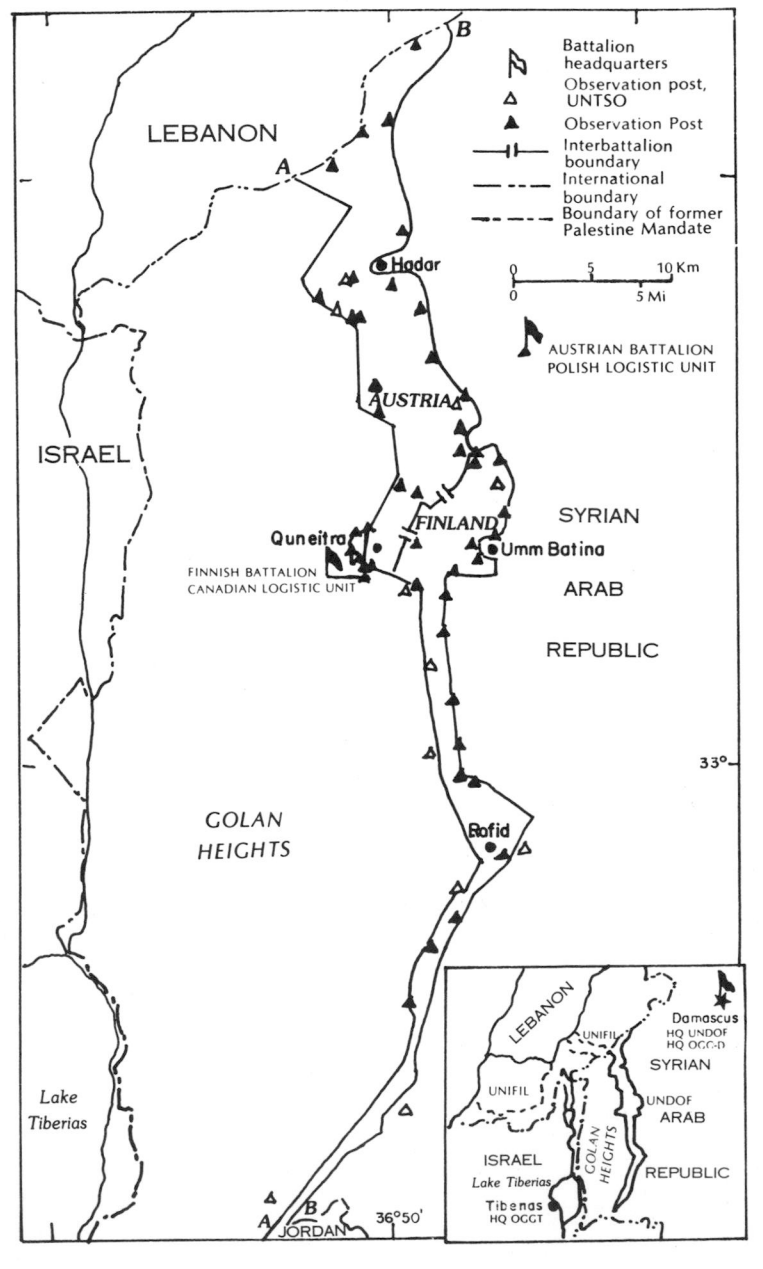

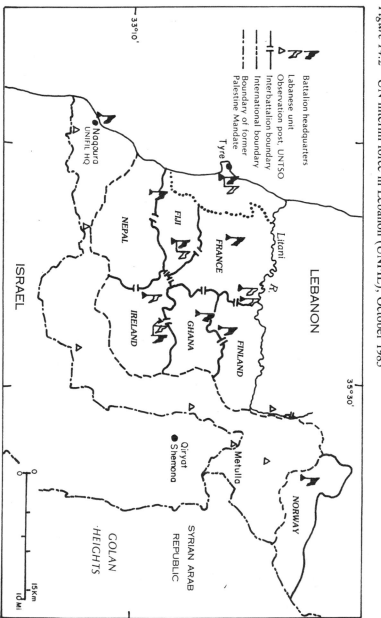

Figure 14.2 UN interim force in Lebanon (UNFIL), October 1985

Figure 14.3   UN emergency force (UNEF I) in Gaza Strip, August 1957

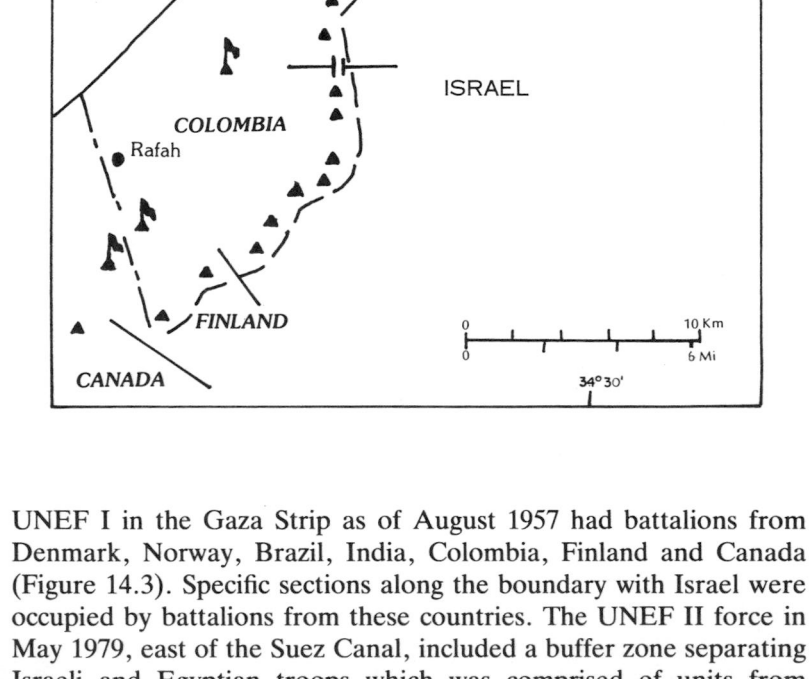

UNEF I in the Gaza Strip as of August 1957 had battalions from
Denmark, Norway, Brazil, India, Colombia, Finland and Canada
(Figure 14.3). Specific sections along the boundary with Israel were
occupied by battalions from these countries. The UNEF II force in
May 1979, east of the Suez Canal, included a buffer zone separating
Israeli and Egyptian troops which was comprised of units from
Sweden, Ghana and Indonesia. Finnish units were near the Gulf of
Suez in various posts and zones (Figure 14.4). The deployment of

Figure 14.4   Second UN emergency force (UNEF II) near Gulf of Suez, May 1979

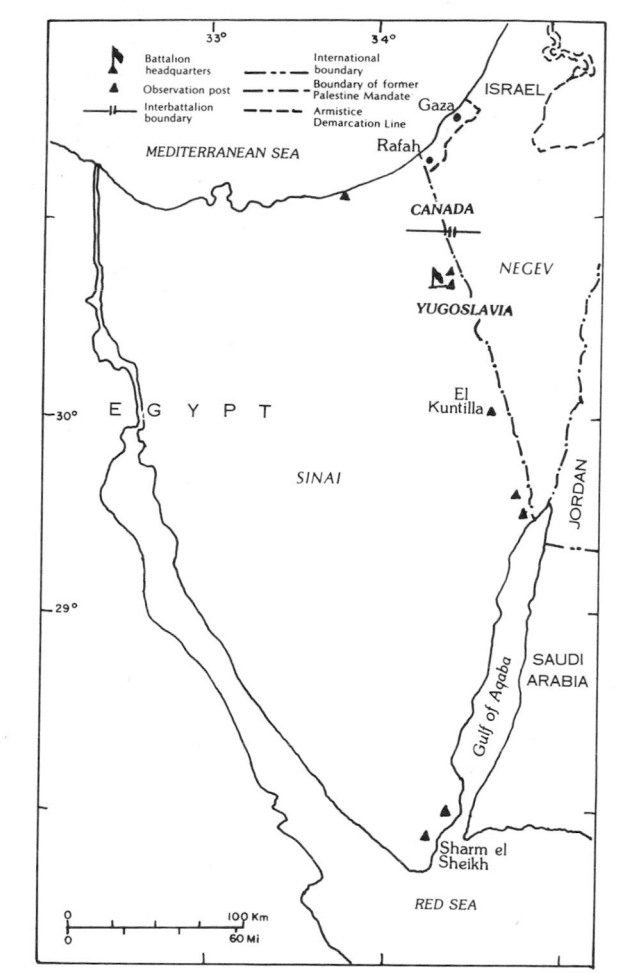

forces in Cyprus (UNFICYP) in December 1965 was evident by the island being divided into six districts (Figure 14.5a). Within each battalion districts, there was a contingent from one country and the civilian policy from another. Twenty years later the island had a cease-fire line separating the Cyprus National Guard and the Turkish Forces. This line was enforced by infantry from Denmark, the UK, Canada, Sweden, and Australia (Figure 14.5b). Detachments were

Figure 14.5 UN peacekeeping operation in Cyprus (UNFICYP)

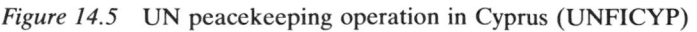

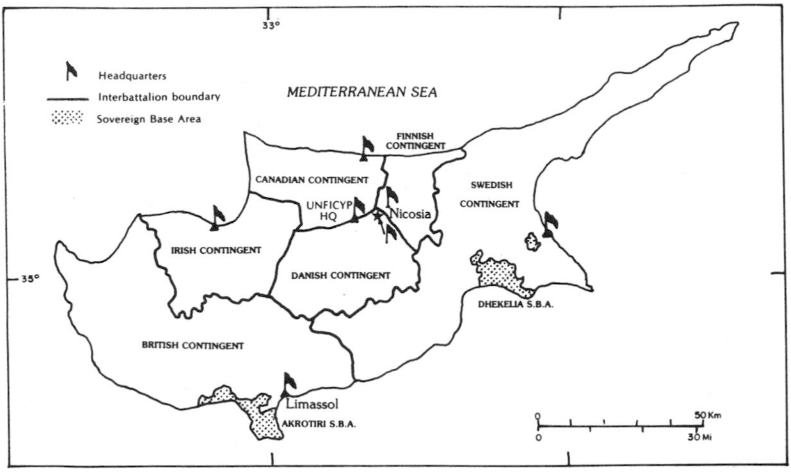

(a)

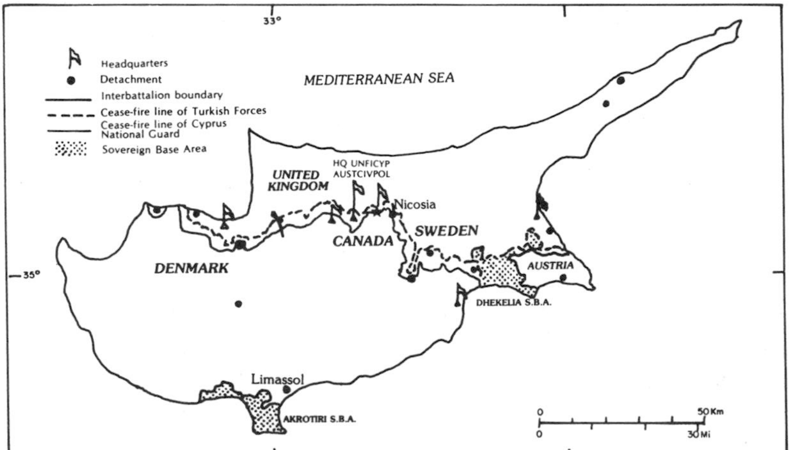

(b)

stationed in ten locations in or near the cease-fire lines. The head-quarters were located at sites outside and inside the buffer zone.

In the Congo operation (OUNC) in 1961, there were nine countries contributing to the peacekeeping force (Figure 14.6). In some provinces, there were UN forces from only one country. Some cities which faced intense fighting had forces from two states. The

Figure 14.6 UN operation in the Congo (ONUC), June 1961

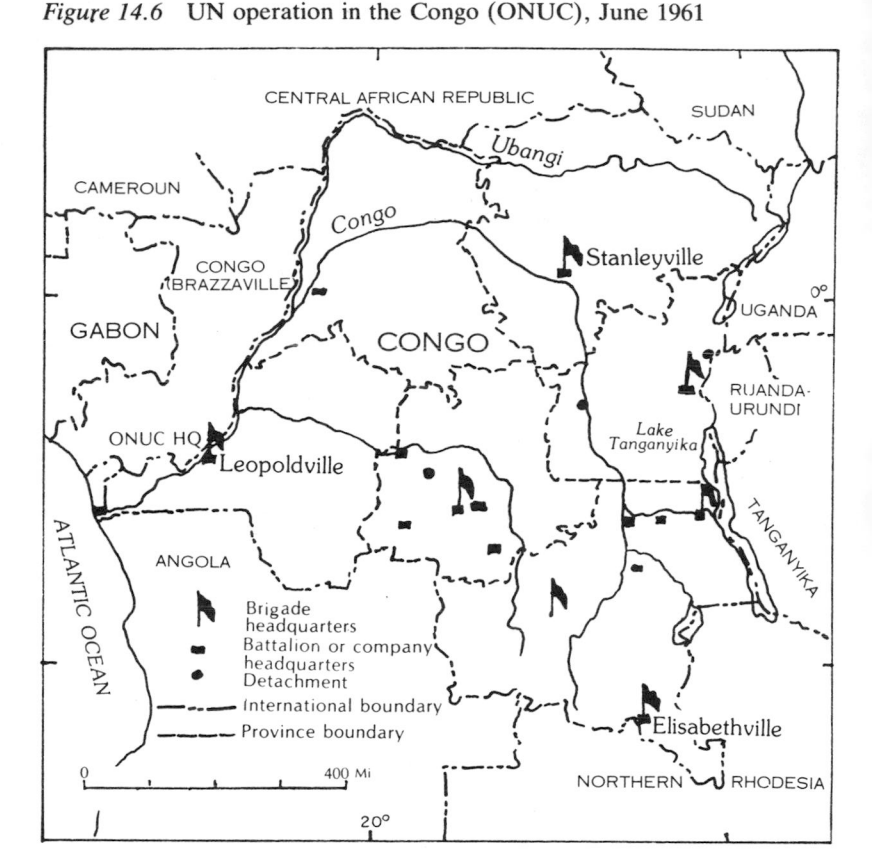

battalions and detachments were concentrated especially in southern and eastern Congo. African states were major contributors to this UN operation. The deployment of UNEF in the Gaza Strip as of 19 May 1967 (prior to the Six Day War) had changed somewhat since 1957. Scandinavian battalions were in the north, Indian forces in the centre of the strip, and Brazilian forces nearest the Egyptian border. The UNEF along the Egyptian–Israeli border in 1973 operated in an area separating the two armies (Figure 14.7). The Egypt–Israel peace treaty in March 1979 called for a multinational force and corps of civilian observers to monitor the arrangements. Once the Israelis relinquished their last hold in the Sinai in April 1982 a ten-nation 2,500-man force was deployed. Pelcovitz (1984: 7–8) wrote the following about the force and arrangements:

Figure 14.7 UNEF in 1973

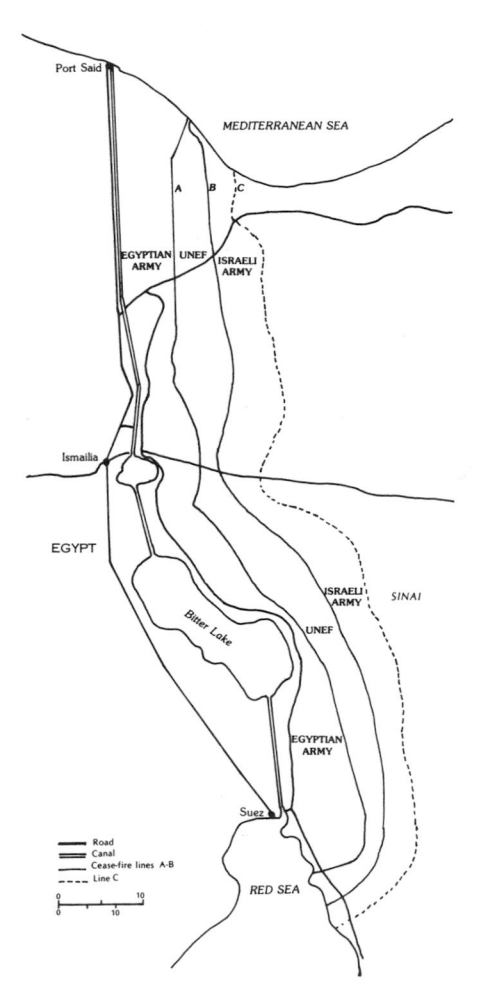

Colombia, Fiji, and the United States provided infantry battalions; Australia, France, Italy, the Netherlands, New Zealand, the United Kingdom, and Uruguay contributed specialized units; and the United States also provided a logistical support unit and approximately forty personnel for the civilian observer unit. Expenses,

which come to about $100 million a year, were split three ways by the United States, Egypt, and Israel.

The mission of the MFO was to monitor and verify the security arrangements in Annex I of the peace treaty, which established limitations on men and arms permitted within the four zones – three in the Sinai and one in Israel along the international border. These were the duties that the UN force and observers had originally been expected to perform. In Zone A, nearest the canal (see map), Egypt was permitted one mechanical infantry division of up to a total of 22,000 personnel; in Zone B, four border battalions comprising up to 4,000 soldiers; and in the demilitarized Zone C, the treaty as amended by the protocol allowed only MFO military components, although Egypt may maintain civilian police units armed with light weapons. In Zone D, Israel was allowed up to four infantry battalions totalling not more than 4,000 personnel. Limits were also placed on the number and types of military equipment and arms allowed in each zone. Operationally, the peacekeepers were assigned four essential tasks: (1) operating checkpoints, reconnaissance patrols, and observation posts within Zone C, and along the international boundary in line B; (2) periodic verification, not less than twice a month of limitations on men and arms in the other three zones; (3) additional verification within forty-eight hours after receiving a request from either party; and (4) ensuring freedom of navigation through the Strait of Tiran in accordance with Article V of the treaty.

Similar arrangements of national and international forces exist in other locations where UN peacekeeping forces operate. Along lengthy borders a number of nations frequently share the tasks of staffing observation posts, field hospitals, and communications units.

CONCLUSION

As political geographers continue to pursue their studies on international boundaries and their impact on nations and states, it would be desirable to expand our efforts by conducting research on elements of peace and peacekeeping landscapes. The importance of these landscapes and forces increases, especially in a global political climate where negotiated settlements rather than protracted conflict are in favour. The awarding of the Nobel Peace Prize in October 1988 to UN peacekeeping forces recognizes the role and importance of these missions in reducing conflict and in promoting resolution to interstate conflict.

UN forces are likely to be dispatched to Western Sahara and possibly to Kampuchea in the near future. Regional forces might be utilized in Central America and southern Africa and in individual states with multinational populations facing internal divisions, such as Lebanon, Pakistan and Sri Lanka. Future studies might examine the evolution and devolution of peacekeeping landscapes over time. Questions worth investigating include: how have the contributions and contributors been evident in the landscapes? How have they been reflected in the political cartography of peacekeeping? How have the landscapes changed with formal treaties being signed by member states and the peacekeeping forces being withdrawn? While this study has focused on UN missions and operations, it would be important to examine the peacekeeping missions, contributors, and landscapes of other regional organizations that have temporary or permanent peacekeeping forces. With these and similar efforts we will augment our contributions to studies on international relations and especially on the dynamics of international boundaries and conflict resolution (van der Wusten, 1984; O'Loughlin and van der Wusten, 1986; O'Loughlin, 1986; van der Wusten and O'Loughlin, 1986).

REFERENCES

Anon. (1988). 'Warriors for peace', *McLean's*, Vol. 101 (36), pp. 10–17.
Boggs, S. W. (1940) *International Boundaries: A Study of Boundary Functions and Problems* (New York: Columbia University Press).
Brunn, S. D. (1987) 'A World of Peace and Military Landscapes', *Journal of Geography*, Vol. 86, pp. 253–62.
Burghardt, A. F. (1973) 'The bases of territorial claims', *Geographical Review*, Vol. 63, pp. 225–45.
Diehl, P. (1988) 'Peacekeeping operations and the quest for peace', *Political Science Quarterly*, Vol. 103, pp. 485–507.
Douglas, J. N. H. (1985) 'Conflicts between states', in M. Pacione (ed.) *Progress in Political Geography* (London: Croom Helm), pp. 77–110.
Fabian, L. (1971) *Soldiers without Enemies: Preparing the United Nations for Peacekeeping* (Washington D.C.: Brookings Institution).
Glassner, M. (1989) 'A Comparison of U.N. and non-U.N. Peacekeeping Forces', Paper presented at the International Seminar on War, Peace, and Geography, University of Haifa, Israel.
Higgins, M. (1969) *United Nations Peacekeeping, 1946–1967. Documents and Commentary* (London: Oxford University Press).
Jenkins, A. (1985) 'Geographers in search of peace', in D. Pepper and A. Jenkins, (eds.) *The Geography of Peace and War* (Oxford: Basil Blackwell), pp. 1–10.
Minghi J. V. (1963) 'Boundary studies in political geography', *Annals*, Association of American Geographers, Vol. 53, pp. 407–28.

294   *Stanley D. Brunn*

—— (1982) 'Border disputes: from Argentina to Somalia', in D. Gordon Bennett, (ed.) *Tension Areas of the World* (Delray Beach, FL: Park Press), pp. 89–108.

O'Loughlin, J. (1986) 'Spatial Models of International Conflict: Extending current theories of war behaviour', *Annals*, Association of American Geographers, Vol. 76, pp. 63–80.

O'Loughlin, J. and van der Wusten, H. (1986) 'Geography, war and peace: Notes for a revived political geography', *Progress in Human Geography*, Vol. 10, pp. 484–510.

Pelcovitz, N. A. (1984) *Peacekeeping on Arab–Israeli Fronts: Lessons from the Sinai and Lebanon* (Boulder, CO: Westview Press).

Prescott, J. R. V. (1965) *The Geography of Frontiers and Boundaries* (Chicago: Aldine).

—— (1987) 'Border Landscapes', in *Political Frontiers and Boundaries* (Boston: Allen and Unwin), pp. 159–72.

Regio Basiliensis (1982) 'International symposium: Grenze and Kulturlandschaft' (Boundaries and the Cultural Landscape), Vol. 22, pp. 49–290.

Rikhye, U. J. *et al.* (1974) *The Thin Blue Line. International Peacekeeping and Its Future* (New Haven: Yale University Press).

Soffer, A. and Minghi, J. V. (1986) 'Israel's security landscapes: The impact of military considerations on land use', *Professional Geographer*, Vol. 38, pp. 24–41.

United Nations (1985) *The Blue Helmets. A Review of United Nations Peacekeeping* (New York: Department of Public Information).

UN Chronicle (1988) 'The quest for Peace', Vol. 25, pp. 4–19.

UN Chronicle (1989) 'Namibia: The making of new nation', Vol. 26, p. 34.

Wainhouse, D.W. (1973) *International Peacekeeping at the Crossroads. National Support-Experience and Prospects* (Baltimore: John Hopkins University Press).

van der Wusten, H. (1984) 'Geography and war/peace studies', in P. Taylor and J. House, (eds.) *Political Geography: Recent Advances and Future Directions* (London: Croom Helm), pp. 191–201.

—— (1985) 'The geography of conflict since 1945', in D. Pepper and A. Jenkins, (eds.) *The Geography of Peace and War* (Oxford: Basil Blackwell), pp. 13–28.

van der Wusten, H. and O'Loughlin, J. (1986) 'Claiming new territories for a stable peace: How geography can contribute', *Professional Geographer*, Vol. 38, pp. 18–27.

Conclusion
Border landscapes: Themes and directions

INTRODUCTION

The aim of this brief conclusion is to distill some of the main themes in present border landscape research which have emerged in this volume. Second, it will attempt to identify some possible future directions for such research. As in all political-geographical research, the underlying purpose is to describe, explain and evaluate the dynamics of the political organisation of space and their environmental relationships.

BORDER LANDSCAPE THEMES

The description, classification and explanation of the evolution and change of border landscapes has been approached from a number of methodological perspectives in this volume. However, each perspective has been concerned in some way with the impress of a complex and changing set of interrelationships among society, economy, political system and space. Clearly, these relationships are 'set' within a broader political, economic and social context. For example, it is possible, even likely, that the international environment will be a significant explanatory component in the evolution and change of border landscapes (see Chapters 4 and 11, for example).

The spatial and temporal outcome will be dependent upon the composition and structure of the main components and obviously to a degree will reflect the nature of relationships between the neighbouring states. The most direct indicator of this component clearly will be the nature and strength of interstate interaction. A more indirect indicator is the structure of border landscape symbolism, a study of which could make use of pre-existing concepts in cultural geography.

Each of the main components is likely to be geographically differentiated either side of the political boundary and/or along the

length of the political boundary. In addition, it would be a mistake to portray the boundary simply as a point. Such differentiation would include:

1 social differentiation between and within states – this includes majority – minority relations (Chapter 5);
2 economic differentiation between and within states – this includes level of economic development (Chapters 2 and 13);
3 political differentiation between and within states – this includes level of 'political development' (Chapter 10);
4 nature of interstate interaction – includes the spectrum of full cooperation and even union of some kind to overt hostility. The one results in a border landscape which exhibits harmony, the other is reflected in a well-defined 'security landscape' (Chapters 1 and 14);

The spatial outcome of 1–4 forms the essential basis of description, classification and explanation of the changing structure of border landscapes. In addition, the fundamental role of the dynamic processes associated with the interaction of state policies with social and political ideology in the creation of border landscape differentiation must be considered. The nature of border landscapes cannot be fully comprehended outside of the context of the policies of contiguous states. In addition, an important question centres on the relative importance attached to borderland territory by contiguous states (Chapter 11) What actually *functions* as core and periphery? Can geographical periphery, in fact, be *central*?

The impact of technological change is also crucial. This is especially true for boundary functions, and, hence boundary effects in terms of, first, the 'demise of the territorial state' argument which, in turn, reinforces the nature of interstate interaction. Second, William Bunge reminded us more than twenty years ago that the dimensions of state boundaries have necessarily changed in an era of intercontinental missiles. Boundaries are now two-dimensional – that is, they represent not the edge of a state, but its whole surface (Bunge, 1966: 110). This fundamental change brings with it new challenges for political-geographical research, especially in terms of dealing with multidimensional power relations, the colonisation of outer space and even the implications of the location of a 'penal planet'! In addition, the host of questions posed by the territorial distribution of power *within* states, the spatial structures which they express at different scales and their changes, the conflicts which they generate, the various attempts at compromise and the resultant geographical

outcomes (spatial, environmental as well as landscape) all invite serious study by geographers and others.

It has been stated that border landscape differentiation has been conceptualised in part by John House. Elaboration in this volume has been along three primary spatial dimensions:

1 state–state differentiation – for example, symmetry/asymmetry, laws, uses (Chapters 2 and 6), values, traditions and so on, as well as the economic and political power of contiguous states (Chapters 8 and 9);
2 the intra-state core – periphery dimension – especially the peripherality of border landscapes in contiguous states and the concept of a 'borderland mentality' (Chapters 3 and 7);
3 boundary-length differentiation (Chapter 12).

BORDER LANDSCAPE DIRECTIONS

Clearly, one direction for future research lies in the possibility for developing border landscape theory via comparative analysis of contextually similar categories (see Rumley, 1987). Dimensions might include level of political development (see Lane and Ersson, 1989), ideology, conflict–harmony, and so on. It may then be possible to develop a cross-classification scheme, including possible outcomes.

Second, border landscape research can make a contribution to political development studies. Perhaps there exists a spectrum of landscape outcomes given the local context on a range from conflict to harmony, although the former is inherent in all borderlands. Harmony has to do with the 'reformist' view of the ideals associated with the political organisation of space – that is, the issue of why is space political organised, what functions does this serve and how well are they served? This may result in a new form of classifying states on political-geographical criteria and not from a purely economic perspective.

Third, there is clearly a need to systematise border landscape inquiry and to elaborate borderland processes within a conceptual framework which would include the following:

1 borderland mentality – there is need for a thorough evaluation of use of these concepts in social science and a full exploration of their relevance;
2 perception of the boundary;
3 behaviour along and across the boundary;

4 impact of the boundary on the landscape;
5 government policy regarding the boundary;
6 international economic and political environment;

The nature of global political, social and economic change will obviously impact upon the political organisation of space and the functions of international political boundaries. In particular, the interaction of processes associated with the global dynamics of the geography of political participation, the resurgence of regionally based ethnic identity, increasing economic interconnectedness and the continuing emergence of Pacific economic power will likely lead to a reshaping of the structure and function of the world political map. In 'socialist' Eastern Europe, for example, demands for democratisation and ethnic resurgence will inevitably lead to a change in the functions of international political boundaries and even to the emergence of new boundaries. These processes in turn will be coupled with landscape changes, new interaction patterns and changed perceptions of boundaries on the part of border zone inhabitants. All of these responses should provide fertile ground for future political-geographical inquiry.

Overall, the present volume has emphasised the need to break out of the narrow confines of conceptual definition of the term border landscape. The concept needs to be 'opened up' to other influences and to scrutiny and to criticism. As part of this process, there is a need to connect not only with developments in cultural geography in terms of the landscape concept, but with the other social sciences. In the final analysis, the fundamental question which has to be confronted is, 'does or can border landscape research have any relevance for social science in general and for geography in particular?'. Hopefully, the present volume represents a step in the right direction.

REFERENCES

Bunge, W. (1966) *Theoretical Geography* (Lund: Gleerup).
Lane, J. E. and Ersson, S. (1989) 'Unpacking the political development concept', *Political Geography Quarterly*, Vol. 8, pp. 123–144.
Rumley, D. (1987) 'Structural effects in different contexts', *Political Geography Quarterly*, Vol. 6, pp. 36–41.

Index